A
MICHENER
MISCELLANY:
1950–1970

*Selected and edited
by Ben Hibbs*

 A READER'S DIGEST PRESS BOOK

A Michener Miscellany: 1950-1970

James A. Michener

RANDOM HOUSE : NEW YORK

Copyright © 1973 by Random House, Inc., and The Reader's
Digest Association, Inc.
All rights reserved under International and Pan-American
Copyright Conventions. Published in the United States by
Random House, Inc., New York, and simultaneously in Canada
by Random House of Canada Limited, Toronto.

Library of Congress Cataloging in Publication Data
Michener, James Albert, 1907–
A Michener miscellany: 1950–1970.
"A Reader's Digest Press book."
Essays published in Reader's digest, here largely revised.
I. Title.
PS3525.I19M5   814'.5'4   72–10926
ISBN 0–394–47948–3

Manufactured in the United States of America
First Edition

ACKNOWLEDGMENTS

THIS I BELIEVE: Copyright 1954 by Help, Inc.

THE GIFT OF PHAN TAT THANH: © 1956 by Reader's Digest Association, Inc.

THE CHRISTMAS PRESENT: © 1967 by Reader's Digest Association, Inc.

THE HARDEST-WORKING WOMEN IN THE WORLD: © 1959 by Reader's Digest Association, Inc.

WHEN DOES EDUCATION STOP?: © 1962 by Reader's Digest Association, Inc.

THE WEAPONS WE NEED TO FIGHT PORNOGRAPHY: © 1968 by Reader's Digest Association, Inc.

GMRX: AN ALTERNATIVE TO MOVIE CENSORSHIP: © 1968 by Reader's Digest Association, Inc.

DON'T KNOCK THE ROCK: © 1965 by Marjay Productions, Inc. Reprinted by permission of William Morris Agency on behalf of the author

WHY I LIKE JAPAN: © 1956 by Reader's Digest Association, Inc.

HAWAII: THE CASE FOR OUR FIFTIETH STATE: © 1958 by Reader's Digest Association, Inc.

LEGACY: THE AUSTRALIAN WAY: Copyright © 1956 by Reader's Digest Association, Inc.

814
M

TO DEWITT AND LILA WALLACE

CONTENTS

A
MICHENER
MISCELLANY:
1950–1970

BY WAY OF EXPLANATION

This book is the record of an extraordinary friendship. In 1951 I received a peremptory telephone call from a man whose name I did not catch. He explained that he had been looking at some of my writing and liked it. Only belatedly in the conversation did I suspect that if he liked a writer's work, he was in a position to do something about it.

"What was your name again?" I asked.

"DeWitt Wallace," he said. "I work at the *Reader's Digest.*"

I had recently quit my salaried job to see if I could make my living as a free-lance writer, and I was breaking my back on the lecture circuit, which brought me the funds on which I lived. To have a real editor call was not only news; it was startling. What he had to say was more so. "I've been keeping a file on what you do," Wallace said, "and you seem to have something to say. I'd be most pleased if you'd come up to Pleasantville and have lunch with me."

I shall never forget that first train ride to Pleasantville. After leaving the tunnel that carried me under New York City and riding through the suburbs, we came to those three cemeteries that lie right beside the tracks, and the first four tombstones

I passed had names beginning with the letter M. "There's an omen if I ever saw one," I said.

The meeting was bewildering to me, satisfying to Wallace and his staff. They asked me about two hundred questions, some of which hit with uncanny skill on subjects I had been thinking about for the past couple of years. At the end of the meal Mr. Wallace said goodbye, I got on the train, nodded to the cemeteries and returned to my work in the city. A few days later I received a letter from one of the junior editors, Hobart Lewis, advising me that the luncheon committee had come up with seven likely subjects on which I might want to try my hand. He added those words which were so important at that time, "We can offer you no guarantees that we will purchase what you do, but we will cover any reasonable expenses you may incur."

I was between books, with time to spare, and out of the seven suggestions I found two upon which I did have something to say. I worked diligently and produced articles which were well received. After that the trips to the editorial luncheons became more frequent, the suggestions for articles more enticing, the relationship constantly more pleasant.

This part of my experience was not remarkable. Many writers have worked on assignment for the *Reader's Digest*. Most of them have traveled to Pleasantville to talk over their projects. And all have received their pay checks in due course. Some few have objected to having their original material cut and have broken the relationship after a couple of years. A number have discovered that they couldn't write the kind of concise material the *Digest* was looking for, and they wisely quit trying. But an equal number of tough-minded professionals have found that now and then, between other jobs, they could write on some subject of national or international interest and get for it the kind of hearing they wanted, both in the United States and overseas. So my experience, which fell into the latter category, was not unusual.

What was unusual was the working arrangement I evolved under the supervision of my bright young editor, Hobart Lewis. I had never worked for a magazine and so lacked training in concise writing. Nor had I worked for a newspaper, where I would have learned to write those expert leads which attract the reader and lure him into the body of the story. Therefore my first articles were both too long and lacking in effective openings. They came back. I tried my hand at cutting, and failed; obviously this called for a skill I did not have. Usually my attempts at shortening these opening paragraphs, and at the same time cramming them with alluring tastes of what was to come, resulted in even longer ones than I started with and were of interest to no one.

So I asked for a meeting with Lewis. I said, "I can't seem to write the way you require. And when it comes to writing leads, I'm pitiful. If you want to waste your time with me it will have to be with the understanding that I will write the way I want to, in as many words as I find necessary, and leave to your people the job of cutting. Also, I'm never again going to bother with an opening paragraph, because any of your secretaries can do that job better than I, and for me to waste my time and yours would be fruitless." To my surprise Lewis replied, "Cutters and lead-writers we have."

It proved a most productive arrangement. The first article I submitted under the new rules gave the editors sixty-four pages of copy when they needed eight. I have maintained that proportion, more or less, through the years. I have been well treated by the cutters, for often they have made my inchoate reporting neat and my rambling thoughts concise. In my introductory notes to the articles on Afghanistan and Malaya, I will explain why I write long articles even though I know that short ones are required. I should add that Lewis proved to be understanding in dealing with my weaknesses, although when I placed my first assignment on his desk he cried, "My God!" As late as the autumn of 1971, when I submitted an unusually long piece, he wrote in the margin: "Michener still hasn't figured out whom he's writing for."

As for my leads, so far as I can remember, the editors have written them all. They have never been able to use one that I provided. It is my custom when I see an article of mine in print, to say, "Damn! Why didn't I think of starting it that way?" When I hear writers complaining of the way they are treated by their editors, I can only think how much better off they would be if they could share the amiable relationship I have with Hobart Lewis.

The friendship of which I spoke was not with Lewis, however, but with DeWitt Wallace. After my first articles were submitted, he invited me at least once a year to work at the *Digest*, offering me the kinds of jobs a young writer would ordinarily dream of, at salaries beyond even his fanciful expectation. For some reason I have yet to discover, Mr. Wallace agreed with my approaches to problems; he liked the manner in which I expressed myself; and he found me congenial. He wanted me to work with him in any capacity I cared to define. Each year when I said no, he devised some new offer more tantalizing than the last.

Why did I refuse? I liked DeWitt Wallace immensely; indeed, I felt toward him as a son feels toward an understanding father. I found him easy to talk with and filled with ideas. Nor was I ever afraid to rebut him in argument. I was particularly happy with Hobart Lewis as an editor and developed a friendship with him which has deepened over the decades. It would have been both congenial and reasonable for me to work with these two men, but always I refrained.

It must have been because I am a congenital free lance. I have never been at ease within the confines of any organization, even though I have worked very hard to sustain several. Having taken serious risks in becoming a free agent, I could not see myself retreating from the frontier to the safety of a salaried job. But what it came down to, I suppose, was my intuitive feeling that I prospered spiritually when letters of inquiry began: "Would you be interested in . . ." rather than "Please go to Budapest as soon as possible."

So year by year DeWitt Wallace continued to offer me jobs. This is the more strange in that Mr. Wallace has always been a devout Republican, while I am an equally ardent Democrat, never reticent about defending my party with equal gusto. Several times in the course of our friendship Mr. Wallace has stopped, stared at me and asked, "You aren't really a Democrat, are you?" In 1962, when I ran for Congress in a heavily Republican district, he published an article which helped my candidacy, displaying it prominently at the head of his journal.

What I have to say next is difficult to put into print, but it is such an extraordinary sidelight on writing careers in the middle years of this century that I must do so. When it became apparent that I would probably never work for Mr. Wallace, he invited me to a New York restaurant and told me, "Michener, I'm captivated by your approach to life and by what you're trying to do. I exist because people like you can write. Everything I own comes from the skill that some men and women have with words. Obviously you're not going to take a job with me, so let's have this arrangement. You go anywhere in the world you want to go. You write anything you want to write. I don't care what it covers or if it's something that we couldn't conceivably be interested in. We'll pay all your expenses, no matter where you go or what you do. All that's required is that you let us have first shot at what you've written. If we can't use it, you can sell it elsewhere and you won't owe us a penny."

I wonder if ever a writer received an offer more magnanimous? I was set free to explore the world, to pursue any intellectual interest that might entice me. If I stumbled down blind alleys, as I often did, I no longer had to worry about financial recoupment, for behind me stood this promise of support.

I never availed myself of this offer, for I had reached the stage in my life when my typewriter supported me. However, when my schedule permitted I did undertake specific assignments for the *Digest*, because I felt an obligation to the man who had volunteered to rescue me if my books did not sell.

The significance of Mr. Wallace's offer was this: Whenever I was about to enter into some massive commitment which would require three or four years of research, heavy translation expense, secretarial salary, travel and much else, I was able to take the risk because in the background stood this understanding man who said, "If it turns sour, I'll underwrite the loss and help you start again." That assurance, even

7

though I was not required to draw upon it, was a crucial factor in my being able to try diverse things and to undertake the expensive kind of research which underlies my books.

One of the profoundest things I have read about writing as a career was that passage by George Gissing in which he recalls his demeaning struggles on London's Grub Street. He concluded that whereas starving in an attic was romantic, most writers would produce better books if they were allowed enough income so as to lead rational lives. When I hear of my contemporaries who have tried to be writers with no encouragement, no financial help, and when I watch them abandon the struggle, I wish that they had stumbled upon a friend like DeWitt Wallace.

Because many people are interested in how the *Digest* handles material, I would like to explain briefly my own experience. Five of the articles in this book first appeared in publications other than the *Digest:*

"This I Believe." Condensed from a statement recorded for Edward R. Murrow's memorable series of five-minute broadcasts in which men and women presented their personal philosophies.

"Don't Knock the Rock." Condensed from an essay first published in *The New York Times Magazine.*

"The Milk Run." Condensed from a chapter in the novel *Tales of the South Pacific.*

"The Prison at Recsk." A chapter in the book *The Bridge at Andau.*

"Presidential Lottery." Condensed from a chapter in the book of the same name.

The other twenty articles were written initially for the *Digest*, always at the suggestion of the editors.

Obviously, what I have used in this volume is the original version of each article as submitted; when it was published in the magazine it would be much abbreviated.

I would like to assure the reader that whereas everything has had to be shortened to accommodate it to the space requirements of the magazine, no statement of substance that I wanted retained has ever been dropped. I have experienced no censorship. On only one occasion did an article suffer conspicuously from heavy cutting; more often the brilliant researchers who fine-tooth-comb every sentence helped me to avoid error. In the trade, the *Digest* researchers are known as the best and I have profited from their checking.

Expense accounts have been meticulously inspected, but whenever I have needed to spend money to get a better story, it has been forthcoming. Payment upon purchase of an article has been prompt and occasionally generous. Finally, when I have written in midsummer an article which might conceivably give aid and comfort to the Democrats, it has been accepted and printed without censorship, but somehow its publication has been delayed until the January issue, when the election was safely over.

A BASIC OPTIMISM

The first two articles, brief as they are, illustrate the strengths and weaknesses of my approach. I have been, and continue to be, optimistic about the potential of mankind. I have lived with so many diverse peoples, seeing the best sides of their natures, that I could not be otherwise.

I do not believe that man is infinitely perfectible, and I know that many changes which we call progress are regressions. I do not expect the millennium to arrive in my lifetime, nor do I believe that jails will soon be outmoded.

But I do believe that relative peace can be attained and that the principal ills of society can be diminished. I think life for the average man is somewhat better today than it was when I was a boy. My statement of principles, *This I Believe*, reflects the beliefs I held in 1954. I still subscribe to them.

On the other hand, my word picture of a Vietnamese peasant, written in the hopeful days of 1956, causes me some embarrassment in the confused days of 1972. It is obvious that the optimism we felt in those opening stages of what was to become the Vietnam war was misplaced. It was a series of events, like the sending of this statue to President Eisenhower and the resultant publicity, that launched us on the road to disaster.

During the war I became suspicious of the reckless course on which we had embarked, which explains why I have not written about the Vietnam war even though I was often invited to do so. I had once lived in all four of the countries involved—North Vietnam, South Vietnam, Cambodia, Laos—and was more expert than most in the area. But as the years passed, my knowledge became rusty. The soaring expectations I had once had for a reasonable peace evaporated and my optimism turned sour.

That is the risk we run when we hope for too much, and on insufficient grounds. But that we must continue to hope, I have no doubt. In some of the other essays in this collection I was on surer ground, and the things I hoped for became realities. For example, Afghanistan and Malaya have turned out much better than I predicted. On such a batting average the writer rests his case.

12

This I Believe

I really believe that every man on this earth is my brother. He has a soul like mine, the ability to understand friendship, the capacity to create beauty. In all the continents of this world I have met such men. In the most savage jungles of New Guinea I have met my brother, and in Tokyo I have seen him clearly walking before me.

In my brother's house I have lived without fear. Once in the wildest part of Guadalcanal I had to spend some days with men who still lived and thought in the old Stone Age, but we got along together fine, and I was to see those men in a space of only four weeks ripped from their jungle hideaways and brought down to the airstrips, where some of them learned to drive the ten-ton trucks which carried gasoline to our bombing planes.

Once in India I lived for several days with villagers who didn't know a word of English. But the fact that I couldn't speak their language was no hindrance. Differences in social custom never kept me from getting to know and like savage Melanesians in the New Hebrides. They ate roast dog and I ate Army Spam, and if we had wanted to emphasize differences, I am sure each of us could have concluded the other was nuts. But we stressed similarities, and so long as I could snatch a Navy blanket for them now and then, we had a fine old time with no words spoken.

I believe it was only fortunate experience that enabled me to travel among my brothers and to live with them. Therefore I do not believe it is my duty to preach to other people and insist that they also accept all men as their true and immediate brothers. These things come slow. Sometimes it takes lucky breaks to open our eyes. I had to learn gradually, as I believe the world will one day learn.

To my home in rural Pennsylvania come brown men and yellow men and black men from around the world. In their countries I lived and ate with them. In my country they shall live and eat with me. Until the day I die my home must be free to receive these travelers, and it never seems so big a home or so much a place of love as when some man from India or Japan or Mexico or Tahiti or Fiji shares it with me. For on those happy days it reminds me of the wonderful affection I have known throughout the world.

I believe that all men are my brothers. I know it when I see them sharing my home.

The Gift of
Phan Tat Thanh

Phan Tat Thanh is an extremely thin man with deep-sunk eyes. For many generations his family had been farmers in northern Indochina—about thirty miles north of Hanoi. He himself was a fine farmer, knew rice production, had seven strong young children and was a first-rate photographer. Then the communists seized power in his country. From the communist point of view, there were two things wrong with Thanh: he owned too much land, and he took Buddhism seriously. He even kept a Buddhist god in his home.

The communists solved the first problem by taking away most of his land. As for Buddhism, they said it was ridiculous and that Thanh should get rid of that crazy god. It was then that he decided to flee.

He told no one, not even his immediate family, but quietly he began to sell his possessions, thinking that he could smuggle some money south—to free Vietnam. Quickly the communists caught onto this and froze his assets. So he surrendered the three acres they had left him, his cameras, his brick house, everything.

One night he led his surprised wife and their seven children along a road which skirted Hanoi, and two days later he smuggled them aboard an American ship. When he climbed the gangplank the sailor on guard asked, "What are you carrying there?"

"It's Mr. La Dong Tan," the struggling father replied.

"Who's he?" the guard demanded.

"A god," Thanh replied.

The sailor looked at the figure of a potbellied Chinese god, La Dong Tan. The statue was heavy and cumbersome and difficult to protect, for it was made of porcelain. The god had hair on his chest, needed a shave and was obviously the best-natured deity in the world.

"What are you bringing him for?" the guard asked.

"For six generations of my family, he is good luck," Thanh said.

"Come aboard."

On the long trip south to freedom many refugees and American seamen came to know La Dong Tan, the jovial roly-poly god. "Many, many years ago a man in our family brought this god back from China," Thanh explained. "I am completely unaware of what Mr. La Dong Tan accomplished in life to be made a god, but we have always worshiped him even above Buddha, and he has kept our family together."

Passengers began to rub the god's fat belly for good luck. At the end of the journey, when Thanh and his family landed penniless in Saigon, it was felt that the laughing god would take care of them.

At first he failed. Farmer Thanh could get no land . . . not even part of an acre. Nor could he rent any land near running water so as to grow rice. Day after day he sat in the gloomy refugee camp and wondered what he could do to earn a living for his seven children.

Then, miraculously, through American aid, he was given a set of the implements used by bakers, and although he had never baked a loaf of bread in his life, he announced, "Now I am a baker."

His first bread was pretty bad, but as it improved, his work prospered and he saved enough to rent a house of his own. His family had a home again, and potbellied La Dong Tan presided over Thanh's rising fortunes.

Then one day baker Thanh had a remarkable idea. Carefully he wrapped his fat little god in paper and bundled it off to government headquarters.

"This god has brought me all my good luck," he announced. "I want to send it to the man who made this possible. My god will bring him good luck, too."

At first the idea caused consternation. "You don't send Buddhist gods around like this," an official said. "Anyway, nobody's ever heard of La Dong Tan."

"He brings good luck," the baker insisted.

So the fat little god was shipped overseas, and in due time baker Thanh received a thank-you note which today he cherishes in his bakeshop near Saigon.

> Dear Mr. Thanh:
>
> Your gracious gift, the statuette of La Dong Tan, has been delivered to me.
>
> I know that when one is forced to flee his home in order to remain a free man, the possessions he is able to carry with him are precious and few. For you to send me, as a token of gratitude, one of your cherished treasures touches me deeply. Your gift symbolizes the sincerity and determination of your people in their quest to remain free. . . .
>
> Sincerely,
>
> Dwight D. Eisenhower

17

A PERSONAL NOTE

The lifetime accumulation of a man's writing ought to provide a portrait of what he was like. I believe that this should come by implication from what he has written rather than by formal autobiography. Only the rare person, a Samuel Pepys or a Harold Nicolson, has the gift for writing a lengthy book about himself, and I think the average writer should avoid the attempt.

If he is writing with passion and commitment, a portrait of his inner life will creep into his work. It is this oblique glimpse which is the most revealing and rewarding.

In what I have written I think I stand forth fairly clearly, not delineated by what I say about myself but by what subjects I have dealt with, what characters I have chosen and what incidents I have developed. I prefer it that way.

However, occasionally over a long writing career an opportunity comes to use some specific incident from one's life which better than any other illuminates an inner concern which has not otherwise been expounded. Then, I think, it is permissible to relate the personal. I did so in the story that follows.

All my life I have been perplexed by the problem: Why do

some men and women achieve a reasonable balance in life while others do not?

I am not speaking of success, which I am unable to define. Nor am I speaking of acceptance by one's peers, which is desirable but sometimes not attainable. Nor do I speak of public acclaim, which comes and goes capriciously. I am speaking of reasonable competence, the ability to achieve the reasonable goals that one has set himself, without regard to the judgments of others.

Some people attain this balance easily and early and hold to it throughout their lives. They are fortunate. Others stumble and fumble till they approach their thirties or forties and then discover a satisfactory solution. They are normal. Too many fail ever to find the answer and lead lives of frustration and waste. They deserve commiseration.

I have felt that the difference between these three groups is most often to be explained by differential experience. To the lucky child certain formative experiences occur, such as contact with an especially good teacher, coming under the supervision of a fine athletic coach, finding some older person in the community who says the right word or gives the guiding hint; without this modifying experience the child may never come to focus. In older days this particular differentiation most often came from parents or pastors; now it frequently comes from one's own peer group, but it had better come from somewhere, for without it a growing child can founder.

Far too often young people miss the differential experience which might have launched them on creative courses. The good teacher either isn't available or isn't understood. The clergyman has no message for this particular child. Recreation is not imaginative but merely time-wasting. The crucial book is not read, and a life is wasted.

In the brief account which follows, I recall a differential experience which became a major factor in my development. It seems so trival in the telling. It involved so little. It had no preparation and no follow-up; indeed, it occupied only a few minutes, and even those were of no apparent consequence. Yet it made all the difference.

The Christmas Present

When I was a boy of nine in the little town of Doylestown, Pennsylvania, one of the best things I did was to help
Mrs. Long, and elderly lady who lived across from the Presbyterian church, mow her lawn. She paid me very little for the
chore, which was not surprising, for she didn't have much
money. But she did promise me, "When Christmas comes I
shall have a present for you." And she said this with such
enthusiasm that I felt assured the present would be magnificent.

I spent much time wondering what it would be. The boys
I played with had baseball gloves and bicycles and toy trains
and ice skates, and I was so eager to acquire any one of them,
I convinced myself that my benefactor intended choosing
from that group.

"It would hardly be a baseball glove," I reasoned with myself. "A woman like Mrs. Long wouldn't know much about
baseball." Since she was a frail little person I also ruled out the
bicycle, for how could she manipulate such a contraption?

"What I'd like most would be the train," I told myself. Only
one of the boys in our group owned a train, and his mother
had to make us go home at dusk, so enchanting was the mys-

terious object as it chugged its way along slim, silvery tracks.

On my last Saturday at work—the grass-mowing season was ending—Mrs. Long said, "Now remember, you've been a good boy all summer, and at Christmas I'll have a present waiting. You come to the door and collect it."

These words clinched it. Since she was going to have the present in her house, and since she herself would be handling it, unquestionably she was giving me a pair of ice skates. So convinced of this I became that I could see the skates and imagine myself upon them. As the cold days of November approached and ice began to form on the ponds which were then a feature of rural Doylestown—for they had provided the community with ice during the past hundred years—I began to frequent the ponds to try my luck on the ice that would be sustaining me and my skates through the rest of the winter.

"Get away from that ice!" a man shouted. "It's not strong enough yet." But soon it would be.

As Christmas approached, it was with difficulty that I restrained myself from reporting to Mrs. Long and demanding my present. Our family agreed that the first of December was too early for me to do this. "She may not have your present wrapped yet," someone argued, and this made sense. But the fifteenth was also too early, and the twentieth, too. I argued back on the twentieth, reasoning that if I was going to get a present I might as well get it now, but my mother pointed out that in our family we never opened our presents till Christmas morning and that to have them about the house too early would merely be an added temptation.

Her logic was deadened, somewhat, by the fact that with the first day of winter, which came on the twenty-first of December, a serious cold snap thickened the ice on all the ponds, so that boys who already had ice skates were able to use them with great flourishes, and my longing to get mine within my possession, even though I could not open them for a few days, became overpowering.

On December twenty-second I could restrain myself no longer, and without consulting my cabinet at home I marched down the street, presented myself at the door of the house whose lawn I had tended all summer and said, "I've come for my present, Mrs. Long."

"I've been waiting for you," she said, leading me into her parlor, its windows heavy with purple velvet. She sat me in a chair, disappeared to another room, and in a moment stood before me holding a package which under no conceivable circumstances could hold a train, or a baseball glove, or a bicycle, or even a pair of skates. I was tragically disappointed, but so far as I can recall, did not show it, because during the past week my advisors at home had warned repeatedly, "Whatever she has for you, take it graciously and say thank you."

What she had was an ordinary parcel about nine inches wide, a foot long and no more than a quarter of an inch thick. Looking at it as Mrs. Long held it in her frail hands, my curiosity as to its contents replaced my initial disappointment, and when I lifted it from her hands to mine the extreme lightness of the gift quite captivated me. It weighed almost nothing.

"What is it?" I asked.

"You'll see on Christmas morning."

I shook it. Nothing rattled, but I thought I did catch a sound of some sort—a quiet, muffled sound that was somehow familiar but unidentifiable. "What is it?" I asked again.

"A kind of magic," Mrs. Long said, and that was all.

Her words were enough to set my mind dancing with new possibilities, so that by the time I reached home I had convinced myself of some great wonder. "She gave me a magician's set. I'll turn pitchers of milk into rabbits."

How long the passage to Christmas was! There were other presents of normal dimension and weight: boxes of candy, new shirts, a penknife. But Mrs. Long's box dominated all, for it had to do with magic.

On Christmas morning, before the sun was up, I had this box on my knees, tearing at the reused colored string which bound it. Soon the wrapping paper was off and in my lap lay an oblong box extremely flat, with its top hinged about halfway down. In iridescent letters appeared the words CARBON PAPER REGAL PREMIUM. Of the four words I knew only the second, and what it signified in this context I could not guess.

With great excitement I opened the hinged lid to find inside a shimmering pile of ten flimsy sheets of black paper, each labeled in iridescent letters like those appearing on the box: CARBON PAPER REGAL PREMIUM. Even when I touched my Christmas present, I had no idea what it was. Vaguely I remembered that it had something to do with magic, and with this word on my lips I turned to the elders who had watched me unwrapping my gift.

"What is it?" I asked.

Aunt Laura, who taught school, had the presence of mind to say, "It really is magic!" And she took two pieces of white paper, placed between them one of the black sheets from the box and, with a hard pencil, wrote my name on the upper sheet. Then, removing it and the carbon paper, she handed me the second sheet, which her pencil had in no way touched.

There was my name! It was clean, and very dark, and well formed and as beautiful as Christmas Day itself.

I was enthralled! This was inded magic—of the greatest dimension. That a pencil could write on one piece of paper and mysteriously appear on another was a miracle which was so gratifying to my childish mind, I can honestly say that in that one moment, in the dark of Christmas morning, I understood as much about printing, and the duplication of words, and the fundamental mystery of disseminating ideas as I have learned in the remaining half century of my life.

On a white piece of paper you wrote a word and somehow it was reproduced, and you could send the copy to a friend while retaining the original for yourself, should you wish to consult it again. I wrote and wrote, using up whole tablets, until I had ground off the last shred of blackness from the ten sheets of carbon paper. It was the most enchanting Christmas present a boy like me could have had, infinitely more significant than a baseball glove or a pair of skates. It opened portals of imagination so vast that I have not yet exhausted them. It was exactly the present I needed, and it reached me at precisely that Christmas when I was best able to comprehend it.

In the succeeding years of my life I have received some pretty thundering Christmas presents, but none that ever came close to the magnificence of this one, because the average present merely gratifies a temporary yearning, as the ice skates would have done; the good present illuminates all the years of life that remain.

It was not until some years later that I realized that the ten sheets of CARBON PAPER REGAL PREMIUM which Mrs. Long gave me had cost her nothing. She had used them for her purposes and would normally have thrown them away, except that she had had the ingenuity to guess that a boy like me might profit from a present totally outside the realm of his ordinary experience. Although she had spent no money on me, she had spent something infinitely more valuable: imagination.

I hope that this year some boys and girls will receive from thoughtful adults who really love them gifts which will jolt them out of all they have known up to now, for it is such gifts and such experiences that explode a life and lend it an impetus that may continue for decades. The curious thing is that often such gifts cost little or nothing.

Having failed to get the ice skates when I needed them, I am still unable to skate, a lack which has often distressed me; but because of the carbon paper I have learned something about the reproduction of words, a skill which has given me much pleasure.

WRITING GONE WRONG

S ooner or later, every writer has the frustrating experience of writing something which is quite clear
to him but which his readers interpret in some negative manner that he could not possibly have anticipated. This has happened several times to me, but by far the most astonishing case
involved the following article.

Because several of my novels had spoken well of foreign
women, and because in one of my books an American woman
had been portrayed unsympathetically, I was sometimes ac-
cused of having a bias against American women. This was
intensified when I married a Japanese girl, even though she
had been born in the United States and was really more
American than I.

At any rate, one day when I was sitting in the American
Club in Tokyo, reading a letter from Hobart Lewis asking me
to think about doing an article on Japan, a lady member of the
club asked me petulantly why I didn't make amends for my
past sins by writing a Valentine "to the hardest-working
women in the world . . . us." I asked her what she meant, and
in a few choice sentences, which had obviously been germinat-

ing in her mind for some time, she explained how much harder American women work than the average non-American.

She pointed with some irritation at a group of European and Oriental women who were visiting the club for a luncheon, and said, "Not one of those women has ever worked as hard as my sister in Denver."

I asked what her sister did, half expecting her to say, "She's a truck driver." Instead she said, "She's the mother of three American children, that's what she is. And if you want to see someone work, follow her for one day."

As she spoke I visualized the article I had long wanted to write, a kind of love letter to the young American housewife, one of the most beautiful, well-groomed, socially conscious, hard-working women the world has so far produced. I would make amends for any inadvertent criticism I had voiced in the past, because I loved these long-legged gals who performed their roles so expeditiously.

I therefore conducted a series of interviews with groups of American housewives, with Oriental women, with European women whose husbands were working in Asia, and with a lot of people like cabdrivers, hatcheck girls and secretaries. The more I heard, the more satisfied I was that I was onto a good thing. Furthermore, it was a story that ought to be told, because there were some American husbands who did not appreciate how hard their wives worked, and I judged that my article might redress that balance, too.

If I ever wrote with love in my heart it was when I composed this article. It was skillfully edited by Hobart Lewis and made, I thought, a fine impression in print. And then the roof fell in.

The *Digest* received so many letters of anger and protest that it had, in self-defense, to run two pages of apology in a subsequent edition. At my home, so much mail poured in, most of it abusive, that I had to compose a form letter to send to my outraged correspondents. And when I studied their letters against the article, I still couldn't see what had gone wrong. When the fire was over, and when I had concluded that no man could ever understand women, a group of experts, most of them female, explained the typhoon that had passed over me. I appreciated their guidance, because I certainly hadn't been able to figure it out by myself.

They said: "As American family life becomes more dependent on machines, like dishwashers and clothes dryers, the mother of the family finds that she is less and less needed, in the historic sense of that word. Therefore she finds actual solace in work, and then your article came along and said, 'Women are foolish to work so hard.' Look at the number of letters which say, 'If you take away our work, what would we have left?' "

Indeed, most of the letters made this point, but two others were also made: That the American housewife actually enjoyed the work; that American grandmothers wanted no part of my recommendation that they baby-sit—they preferred to play golf, or drive to Massachusetts, or run boutiques. Obviously I had underestimated the American woman.

One clever woman took me aside and explained, "My husband's company makes a cake mix. It's really the finest mix ever invented, much better than mother used to make, because it ensures absolute success every time. Each ingredient is proportioned and there can be no mistake. It was a flop. Housewives bought one sample, then bought no more. We couldn't understand it until a psychologist explained it to us. The mix was too good, too complete. Baking a cake has always been a warm, family affair, centering on the mother in her kitchen with the kids around. There ought to be a mess, and noise, and the tense anticipation of whether or not the cake will rise. Our mix killed the whole mystique. You poured the powder into a bowl, added water, and nobody could miss. But we fixed it, and now our mix is one of the most popular in America. How? We left out the eggs and the milk. Now the mother can go through the whole ancient routine, simplified. She pours the milk, beats the batter and folds in the eggs. She feels as if she was baking a cake . . . the way her mother used to."

You learn a great deal when you're a writer, but one thing you never learn is how your readers will interpret what you have written.

29

From the perspective of 1973, the storm over this article seems irrelevant. The impact of the Women's Liberation Movement has changed the thinking of both men and women. Today an article like this would occasion little comment.

The Hardest-Working Women in the World

MARCH, 1959 ✖

In the past ten years I have had to spend a good deal of time overseas, and I have made a surprising discovery. The hardest-working women in the world are young American housewives.

In actual physical labor, of course, they are surpassed by the amazing women hod-carriers of Singapore. These sturdy-limbed Chinese, dressed in bright-blue pants and flaming-red nun's headgear, load big square boards with wet plaster and scramble up scaffolding five stories high, lugging these astonishing burdens. In fact, much of the heavy construction in Asia is done by women.

But when these hod-carriers are through work, they don't have complex family or community jobs awaiting them at home. Some other female member of the household has taken care of the children. Older women relatives, serving as maids, have done the marketing, cooking, dish washing, laundry and mending. At home, the Chinese woman has every advantage over the American.

Here are a few of the special American jobs that Asian and European women can ignore: driving husbands to the train, serving as den mothers for Cub Scouts, attending school committees, collecting money for the local hospital, advancing the political life of the community, maintaining an above-average standard of personal attractiveness and mental alertness, and taking an important role in the husband's business life. In such public and cultural spheres, the women of Asia don't know the meaning of work.

It is for this reason that I conclude that the American housewife, particularly one with children, works much harder at a much more complex job than do any of her sisters around the world.

Of course, if one counts only the hours spent on the job as an indication of work, and not the pressures, I suppose that the peasant woman of India takes the championship. She is usually up at dawn trailing cattle to pick up manure which, when dried, will provide the family fire. She hauls the family wash to the river and lugs back water for cooking. But the complexity of her life doesn't begin to equal the American woman's. To take only one example: the standard of cleanliness to be maintained in both home and children's appearance is far simpler in India than in America. Yet the Indian woman almost always has help from several additional females, some of them older relatives, some of them poorly paid servants or daughters who do not go to school.

I would admit that the women of Asia sometimes pay a heavy price for their relaxed way of life. In Afghanistan, for example, women enjoy about the simplest existence on earth. They have no social responsibilities of any kind; the family marketing is usually done by men; most homes have extra women to share what work there is; while all public jobs like serving food in restaurants or working as servants for foreigners are invariably filled by men. Women do nothing. But from the age of thirteen on, they are required by severe custom to live inside sacklike bags that enshroud them from head to toe. I once spent eleven weeks in Afghanistan, and never saw an Afghan woman. I saw silken shrouds, moving ghostlike through the streets, but never a woman.

Then, too, there are certain social customs which an American wife would consider too high a price to pay for leisure. I recall one trip I made along a war-torn country road in Korea. Down a footpath known to be mined proceeded a cautious Korean husband and his wife. Naturally, she went first, gingerly pressing the ground to see if it was safe for her man to cross. Prudently he stayed sufficiently far behind so that if his wife did unfortunately step on a mine, its fragments would not damage him. To complete the picture, he carried nothing while his probing wife lugged on her back the entire family belongings.

My partner, who could speak Korean, stopped our jeep and together we made the man assume the burden and walk in front. He grumbled like a child, and his wife obviously was sorry for him as he tried to adjust his shoulders to the unaccustomed burden. We were not surprised, therefore, on our return trip to find that once more she was out front, bearing the heavy load.

We jammed on the brakes, jumped out and demanded to know what was going on. The woman looked up gently and asked, "What good is it to get your husband home at night if he's all tired out from too much work?"

Other foreign customs would be equally difficult for American women to accept. For example, few self-respecting Japanese husbands take their wives to Tokyo's expensive restaurants, where really fine food is served. They're for men. In Australia, too, men frequently prefer to dine in the masculine grandeur of their clubs, where women are not admitted. And throughout much of Asia men are permitted by custom or religion to take more than one wife.

In Pakistan there has recently been much agitation against this practice, and during the debate one Pakistani wife observed, "It's true that in my household we have three women to do half the work that an average American wife does. But that's small comfort, because in America when the day's work is over, the wife knows that her husband belongs to her. I have to share mine with the two other women who help me with the housework."

But no matter what indignities the women of Asia have to suffer, they have one tremendous advantage over their American counterparts. They can get household help. American women can't, and the pressure on them is becoming terrific.

Take the case of Betsy Anne. She was the prettiest girl in our part of the country. She came from an upper-middle-class family, had a good education and a bright future. Because she was congenial and liked outdoor sports, she was the most popular date in the area, and at the age of twenty-two selected Bill from among her many suitors. They had a bang-up wedding.

Bill was a hard-working, crew-cut kid from Princeton, and their future seemed bright, especially when four years of marriage produced three winsome daughters. Then the merciless drag of American life began to tell.

Betsy Anne was a fine mother and kept her daughters trim in neat dresses . . . at first. Bill earned a good salary, so she began sending her laundry out, but she had to deliver it eight miles away. Naturally, she did the driving. She loved to entertain and was a fine cook, but she quickly limited herself to casseroles and buffets, because she had to do everything before the party, and then wash up after it was over. In school she had acquired many friends, and she liked to visit with them, but before she could do so she had to find a baby-sitter, and since that was impossible where we live, she gradually eliminated contact with many of her acquaintances.

She and Bill loved the theater—musicals, dramas, ballet . . . anything—but without baby-sitters they couldn't drive to New York together. Worst of all, three little girls can wreck a house just about as quickly as three little boys, and Betsy Anne's drudgery was also hard on Bill. He worked hard in the city and commuted long hours. When he reached home he found a noisier world than the one he had just left, a house that was never really clean, and a wife so exhausted that she wanted to go right to bed. On Saturdays there was a lawn full of crab grass. If he asked friends in for an evening of batting the breeze, he felt he ought to prepare the snacks and wash up afterwards. It was obvious that Bill's marriage was headed for trouble.

So a surprising number of people pitched in with help.

Betsy Anne's parents offered financial aid. So did Bill's. But money wasn't the problem. Bill growled, "We don't need charity. We can pay for a maid or a baby-sitter, if we could find one."

His wife confessed, "I've combed the neighborhood. No maids, no cleaning women."

Friends got on the phone and tried to locate help, but in our part of the country there is none. So Betsy Anne had to quit more of the things she longed to do and work harder on those she had to do. Soon she collapsed with a nervous breakdown, and the full burden fell on Bill, who proved as unequal to the task as his wife had been.

So the marriage ended in divorce. A fine young woman had been positively snowed under by the endless work the American housewife has to perform.

When I am in America, my wife and I live in beautiful Bucks County, Pennsylvania, long known as one of the choicest rural areas in the nation. Our back roads are peppered with famous names—writers, artists, actors, politicians—and our standard of living is good. We aren't wealthy, like Connecticut, or really posh, like Southern California, but most of the husbands in our area could afford to pay a little extra each week to ease the work our wives have to do.

Yet in all the families we visit, only two have servants. All the rest of us do all of our own work. For example, my wife and I love to have five or six couples in for a regular sit-down dinner. But if we do, she has to take care of the pre-cleaning, the cooking, the baking, the table arrangement and the serving. When the party is over, she and I stay up till three washing the dishes. She cleans the house, does the marketing, drives me to the train, collects money for the local charities, and accomplishes all the other jobs that in Asia would be handled by a corps of servants. There is no use asking, "Why don't you get her some help?" There is none.

The contrast between American and Asian patterns was vividly brought home to me recently in Tokyo, where I conducted a group interview with fifteen Japanese housewives in the thirty-five to forty-five age group. By Bucks County standards these women were poor. Their combined family income did not equal the pay of the topflight Pan American pilot who lives down the road from me.

I wasn't interested in servants when I started. "How many of you women selected your own husbands?" was my first question. Of the fifteen, only one had made her own choice.

"If you were a typical group of Japanese housewives, how many of your husbands would keep second or third wives on the side? Don't tell me about your own marriages, just imagine the women you know." They thought that about eight to ten husbands would be supporting extra wives, in one way or another.

It was then that I stumbled upon my most revealing question. "By the way, how many of you women have servants?" All fifteen had.

"How many?" The total for fifteen families was thirty-seven, or more than two per family.

"Do all families like yours have servants?" Of course.

"Can you think of any family in your relative social level that lacks servants?" They couldn't think of one.

I was so surprised at this news that I stopped the pretty red-cheeked waitress who was serving us, and asked, "Does your family have a servant at home?" She replied, "Of course!" So did the telephone girl's family, and the hatcheck girl's.

Subsequent investigation showed that many of these so-called servants were family members who were in Tokyo to study and were working for their board. But most of the servants were the old-time working girls who took jobs until they married.

Obviously, the Japanese housewife does not begin to do as much work as an American girl. In Singapore recently I had an opportunity to see how middle-class Chinese wives lived. Mrs. Chan Eng's husband enjoyed an income markedly less than the average in Bucks County, but her day ran something like this: rise at ten; dress in clothes laid out by a personal maid; inspect the children, who were being cared for by an amah; check the day's meals, which would be prepared by a cook and served by a maid; drive to the daily mah-jongg game in a car handled only by the chauffeur; and in the late afternoon return home to rest and dress for her own dinner party, where she will be hostess but for which she has done not a single bit of preparatory work.

In India my good friend Mrs. Mehta is known as one of New Delhi's crack bridge players. She is also a delightful hostess who loves jokes and who likes to entertain politicians and diplomats. To know Mrs. Mehta is to know one of those universal women—the same in all nations—in whose homes people enjoy meeting. That her four children are unusually attractive adds to her charm.

After one big party at which she had entertained sixty people, she nodded appreciatively when I complimented her on the smooth manner in which she had kept so many talkative people fed and happy.

"Don't compliment me," she protested. "It's all Lal's doing."

"Who's Lal?"

"Our cook. He takes care of everything."

"But you tell him what to serve."

"Me! Tell Lal! Mr. Michener, I haven't been inside our kitchen for the past twenty-four years."

It was true. Nor had she laundered, or driven a car, or dusted a room, or tended babies, or washed dishes late at night after a party for her husband's business friends.

I know few Asian women like Mrs. Chan and Mrs. Mehta who could stand up to the normal routine forced upon the American wife. Some younger Asian women, particularly those married to GI's, are trying to learn, but they are appalled by the amount of actual hard work they must do. Their most common complaint: "At home we would have help, especially when the babies come."

Asia's superior system of caring for children is a major reason why so many young American couples who have tasted life abroad want to get back overseas. It isn't that they're spoiled. It's just that a time comes when a young housewife ought to have help, and in America she can't get it.

I remember in Malaya being told by an American mother,

"I was shocked when I first heard an English mother say in Singapore, 'Well, our boy Eric's getting on toward seven. We'll send him back to England for his schooling next month.' It seemed barbarous. But you find that in some ways it's a good system. Getting the children off to school, seven thousand miles away, is one reason why English husbands and wives seem to grow closer together than American couples do."

My friends the Tom McVeighs typify the problem. He's a sharp certified accountant from Philadelphia who married a beautiful airline hostess named Maggie. She was a Missouri girl, a graduate of the state university, and Tom points out, "As an airline hostess she learned what work was, so when we set up housekeeping in Omaha she was prepared for marriage American style."

Of her first two years of married life, Maggie says, "Omaha was an awakening. Tom had dozens of fascinating business friends, but I never met them. Couldn't get baby-sitters. So I stayed home and watched TV. But that was worse, because TV reminded me of all the other worlds I was missing. I was completely tied down at home."

Then something unexpected happened. "We were sent here to Formosa," Maggie says jubilantly. "When word flashed around Omaha, my friends commiserated, 'Oh, Maggie, you're so brave to go way out there!' But I was just beginning to live."

The McVeighs didn't discover luxury on Formosa, by any means. But they were able to employ a staff of helpers such as most Chinese middle-class families would have: three indoor servants, a gardener, a driver. "But what I can't explain," says Maggie, "is the joy of having a built-in baby-sitter."

Tom says, "I think that if I told Maggie tomorrow that we are going back home permanently, she'd leave me. Life out here is so much more sensible for a woman."

Energetic Maggie explains, "Tom's joking. Actually, I work harder here than I do at home—entertaining Tom's friends, organizing charities, studying language, helping our son at school. The big difference is that in Formosa I have time to enjoy my husband and my boy."

Tom adds, "When we go home on leave we visit one couple in Philadelphia who haven't had a vacation away from family pressures for over ten years. He makes more money than I do, but is that living?"

Maggie, reviewing her life in Asia, says, "If Tom had to resume work in the States, of course I'd be proud to tag along. I'd pitch in and do what I had to. I can work harder than any of my friends. But I'd always remember, sometimes with anguish, the happy days in Formosa when I had time to be a human being."

All over Asia and in much of Europe I have met young American couples who don't want to come home. They're patriotic, pay taxes, love America and defended it in war, but they realize that American life has one grave fault: it places much too heavy a burden upon young wives. And this fault is frustrating, because as a nation we aren't taking the steps that would eliminate it.

Consider the Bill Jessups. When I first met them in Japan, Bill was a hot-shot foreign correspondent who wisecracked, "You know what a foreign correspondent really is? A police-court reporter in a trench coat." But he was famous for tracking down stories.

Anne, his wife, was a Philadelphia girl from the suburban Main Line, and with Bill and her two lively children she kept one of the most interesting homes in Tokyo. You could always pick up the latest international gossip there, the children were well trained and the snacks were tasty.

The Jessups budgeted a fair share of their income for servants, and Anne recalled, "It was the best money we spent. Oh, the relaxed joy of being able to say, 'This one time I'll just sleep late!' Because you know the maid will get the children off to school."

Bill was so skilled at his job that his home office called him back to New York, gave him an important promotion and a hefty raise. So the Jessups moved into a swanky suburban town, and like millions of other good American wives, Anne capably took charge of everything.

Of this experience she says, "It's very restful to live in an

39

American house with no servants. There's a secrecy and a joy about it. Especially if you have good modern conveniences to help you.

"But in time it wears you down. Because with children to care for you need an extra pair of hands, two more strong feet and an automatic baby-sitter. Lacking these, the pressures can be very heavy indeed.

"In Tokyo I could read, or go to plays occasionally, or entertain our friends, or help Bill, or take the children on country picnics. I could live creatively. And two special things I remember with longing: our buttons were always sewed on, and if I had to go out in a hurry, my dress was pressed. In America I was chained to the kitchen."

At the end of two years Bill Jessup weighed the values in his life, surrendered his big promotion in New York and lugged his family back to Tokyo. "My wife can breathe again," he says.

Anne Jessup makes an important point: "Of course, the young American mother *can* be the ideal wife . . . so long as she has good health. But if her health even falters, then there's grave trouble. And in our system no safeguards are provided to help her in that crisis."

In recent years a good many critics have proposed one solution to this problem: "Let the American woman stop messing around in community affairs and she won't need cleaning women or baby-sitters." These critics argue that what tires the young wife is not children but her preoccupation with charity drives, her husband's career and socializing. "If she quits this nonsense, she'll be happy."

If I had never lived overseas, I might agree. But I have had a chance to compare average American towns where women take an interest in libraries, hospitals, schools and youth groups with towns in Asia where no one cares. And I appreciate the tremendous contribution made by American women.

American women may find that they will have to slough off some of the jobs they are now attempting, but concern for one's community and a desire to maintain one's intellectual capabilities ought not to be surrendered. In fact, it seems apparent that the American pattern of utilizing women's capacities to the full, plus the development of a system whereby husbands help in the home, will become the world-wide standard. In a recent speech Dag Hammarskjöld jokingly referred to the gradual Americanization of family patterns throughout the world. England, Finland and Ireland seem to be following our lead. "But in France and Austria," Hammarskjöld found, "husbands still flatly refuse to lift a hand."

In the meantime, America ought to pioneer new ways to provide housewives, especially those with children, with needed help. Two steps in the right direction have been frozen foods and mechanical aids. Sometimes we forget how wonderful some of our gadgets are. Sometimes it takes an outsider to remind us.

Reiko Tuttle is a hummingbird little Japanese girl who is admirably qualified to compare Asian and American living patterns, for her husband operates a unique publishing company. Half the year the Tuttles live in Tokyo publishing rare books. The other half they live in Vermont, selling the books from an old farmhouse office that has been used since the first Tuttle went to Harvard generations ago.

Reiko says, "In Tokyo we naturally have the usual quota of servants, and I couldn't live without them. But do you know the part of the year I like best? When we get to Vermont, and I can move into my own kitchen, and cook my own meals, and take care of my husband, and live in privacy with him. American women don't appreciate the wonderful conveniences they have. I love the American pattern of life. And believe me, most of the women in the world would prefer it too, if they ever tasted it."

Of course, she quickly admits, "In Vermont I have no children to care for and I'm not part of the community life, so I don't know about those pressures. But if you think only of housework, life in America is a holiday."

It is frequently proposed that to provide more help for young families, America ought to admit each year up to 100,000 immigrant couples who would be willing to do housework. Certainly they would be employed almost at once by servant-hungry American families.

The weakness of this proposal is obvious. The immigrant families, if they followed the good examples of their predecessors, would not remain servants long. America grew to greatness because it encouraged people who started out as servants to grow into other kinds of work, and surely the process should not be stopped now.

I recall that during the Hungarian Revolution in 1956 several of my friends cabled me: "Will sponsor Hungarian family providing guarantee work for us five years." Obviously no one should be allowed to demand such an assurance, and American laws are severe if anyone attempts to enforce one, even if it is entered into voluntarily. Furthermore, if the 100,000 couples were admitted, they would be snapped up by older and wealthier families, often with no children, and help would not be provided where it is most needed.

Therefore immigration cannot solve this problem. Is there some simpler solution within our own society? Our family doctor evolved a fine scheme. He wanted regular help but felt that he couldn't swing it all by himself, so he hired a young man who turned out to be something of a paragon: fine cook, butler, all-around good guy. Then the doctor let it be known that Morris would be free to work for anyone, four afternoons a week and some nights.

Consequently our social life is different from any that I have ever known elsewhere, because no matter where we go out to dine, chances are we'll meet Morris. He knows what everyone in our gang drinks, our tastes in food, who's trying to reduce and who can't sleep if he has coffee. Next night, if we visit other friends, Morris picks up where he left off the night before. Wives have formed a curious habit: when they plan a dinner they never start with the guests. "We always find out first if Morris is available, because guests we can always get."

Another group of mothers with children adopted an equally bold scheme. Unable to find either baby-sitters or cleaning women, eight families banded together and went to a local cigar factory, where a fine young woman was working for a good salary. They reasoned with her: "Sure your work is pleasant here, and the pay is good. But we think we can offer you a better deal. Work for us. We'll guarantee you a steady wage. We'll give you hot lunch and transportation. You can come and go as you wish, and you'll get three full days off a week."

The girl was interested, so the wives worked out a schedule whereby she spent either a morning or an afternoon in each of the eight homes. Wednesday, Saturday and Sunday were kept clear, but if she wanted extra work on those days or in the evenings, some household in the group could always use her. She now finds that she enjoys such a schedule much more than she did factory work.

Anne Jessup has thought a good deal about the problem and has come up with a logical suggestion: "The American way of life is the best I've seen, but it must work out some way of relieving the burden on young mothers. Why don't we launch a propaganda campaign to convince young grandmothers and able widows that they ought to volunteer—for good wages— to help younger women? The stigma of being a servant could be removed, and in every respect our society would be strengthened."

This makes sense. As our population gradually grows older, due to improved health services, there ought to be an increasing number of senior citizens available to help young wives launch the families upon which our nation will depend in the future. A new occupation—household helper—ought to be developed, with a certain glamour attached to it.

Certainly we are too smart to go on beating down one of the country's greatest assets: its young mothers.

THE PURITAN ETHIC

Many of the articles I have written could serve as monuments marking the passing of an age. Every person and every social organization that surrounded me as I grew up was dedicated to the preservation of the puritan ethic. I can never recall facing any problem as a child or young man in which the answer was not clearly spelled out.

Laziness, radicalism, sex, atheism, failure to do well in school and skipping church were deplorable and there was no question of a wishy-washy neutral position. Things were black or white and grayness was not known.

I remember one athletic coach to whom every aspect of a young man's growing up was clear. He knew what was right and what was wrong and he had no hesitation in telling us. Sex was wrong. Fried foods were wrong. Cigarettes were wrong. So were girls, alcohol, fast automobiles and staying out late on Saturday nights. He was one of the most rigid men I have ever known, and he came along at the precise time in my life when I required a little rigidity. Now he seems rather silly, an opinionated man who apparently never once questioned his standards and who built championship teams from them. However, four of his top six players had no fathers and intuitively we knew that we needed some kind of structure for our lives.

In retrospect, the puritan ethic which dominated my childhood did me a good deal of damage. As an adult I have worked too hard. I have been too afraid of the financial disaster which overtook so many of my contemporaries. The old ideas about sex were far too restrictive. Many of the precepts dear to the conservative leaders of my youth were outmoded then and are in discard now. The human organism seems to flourish if it enjoys somewhat more freedom than I was allowed. There are viable alternatives to puritanism, and people can work out fairly satisfactory life patterns while adhering to them. I have many scars from the puritan ethic which I wish I had missed.

And yet a man must exist within the society he inherits and he cannot escape being molded by it. If the puritan ethic damaged me in part, it also gave my life a central structure. It led me to get an education and to strive, within that education, for excellence. It has helped me to organize my work habits and to keep my eye focused on significant problems. It forced me to develop a character which has kept me plowing ahead during adversity. And it instilled in me a social conscience which has never flagged.

Above all, it has made me confident of certain central truths. I believe more strongly in education today than when I started; I simply cannot comprehend the contemporary reasoning which argues that a young man can make a substantial contribution to society even though he has not trained himself to do something. True, he need not acquire this competence from books; if he can overhaul a gasoline engine he can make himself indispensable to our society. But he must know something; he must have certain skills; and he must have a tough core of resolution.

It seems obvious to me that what is happening to Forty-second Street in New York, with its proliferation of sex shops, sex-exploitation movies and massage parlors, is an abomination which, if long endured, must damage this nation.

When the motion picture industry, aware that censorship was about to descend on it from all sides, contrived a system for rating motion pictures which would indicate to parents what forthcoming movies contained, I was in favor of it, because it seemed to me to be a logical safeguard in a difficult situation. Recently I have been reading attacks on the system; perhaps it needs overhauling. But if someone argues that motion pictures can exist for long in this country without some kind of reasonable self-policing, he makes no sense to me. The form of self-discipline may vary from decade to decade, and contradictions may surface requiring correction, but some kind of restraint is not only necessary but desirable.

Some of my friends have been surprised that a novelist, and one who has dealt with some fairly strong themes, should be willing to speak out against pornography or in favor of a rating system for motion pictures. They felt that in doing so I was strengthening the hand of censorship.

I feel just the opposite. I am against censorship. As a writer I would have to be. I have seen in certain foreign countries in which I have lived the evil effects that follow when the state censors ideas, and I would spend all my energies fighting against such a system.

But I am in favor of self-restraint, primarily because it forestalls censorship. I hold in contempt those artists who feel they can capture an audience only by serving up large helpings of near-pornography. I suppose it's the puritan ethic of my childhood reasserting itself. At any rate, the three following essays stem from that inheritance.

When Does Education Stop?

During the summer vacation a fine-looking young man, who was majoring in literature at a top university, asked for an interview, and before we had talked for five minutes, he launched into his complaint.

"Can you imagine?" he lamented. "During vacation I have to write a three-thousand-word term paper about your books." He felt very sorry for himself.

His whimpering irritated me, and on the spur of the moment I shoved at him a card which had become famous in World War II. It was once used on me while I was "bitching" to a chaplain on Guadalcanal. It read:

> Young man, your sad story
> is truly heartbreaking.
> Excuse me while I fetch a
> crying towel.

My complaining visitor reacted as I had done twenty years earlier. He burst into laughter and asked, "Did I sound that bad?"

"Worse!" I snapped. Then I pointed to a novel of mine

which he was using as the basis for his term paper. "You're bellyaching about a three-thousand-word paper which at most will occupy you for a month. When I started work on *Hawaii*, I faced the prospect of a three-million-word term paper. And five years of work. Frankly, you sound silly."

This strong language encouraged an excellent discussion of the preparation it takes to write a major novel. Five years of research, months of character development, extensive work on plot and setting, endless speculation on psychology and concentrated work on historical backgrounds.

"When I was finally ready to write," I replied under questioning, "I holed up in a bare-wall, no-telephone Waikiki room and stuck at my typewriter every morning for eighteen months. Seven days a week I wrestled with the words that would not come, with ideas that refused to jell. When I broke a tooth, I told the dentist I'd have to see him at night. When DeWitt Wallace, the editor of the *Reader's Digest* and a man to whom I am much indebted, came to Hawaii on vacation, I wanted to hike with him but had to say, 'In the late afternoon. In the morning I work.' "

I explained to my caller that I write all my books slowly, with two fingers on an old typewriter, and the actual task of getting the words on paper is difficult. Nothing I write is good enough to be used in first draft, not even important personal letters, so I am required to rewrite everything at least twice. Important work, like a novel, must be written over and over again, up to six or seven times. For example, *Hawaii* went very slowly and needed constant revision. Since the final version contained about 500,000 words, and since I wrote it all many times, I had to type in my painstaking fashion about 3,000,000 words.

At this news, my visitor whistled and asked, "How many research books did you have to consult?"

"Several thousand. When I started the actual writing, there were about five hundred that I kept in my office."

"How many personal interviews?"

"About two hundred. Each two or three hours long."

"Did you write much that you weren't able to use?"

49

"I had to throw away about half a million words."

The young scholar looked again at the chaplain's card and returned it reverently to my desk. "Would you have the energy to undertake such a task again?" he asked.

"I would always like to be engaged in such tasks," I replied, and he turned to other questions.

Young people, especially those in college who should know better, frequently fail to realize that men and women who wish to accomplish anything must apply themselves to tasks of tremendous magnitude. A new vaccine may take years to perfect. A Broadway play is never written, cast and produced in a week. A foreign policy is never evolved in a brief time by diplomats relaxing in Washington, London or Geneva.

The good work of the world is accomplished principally by people who dedicate themselves unstintingly to the big job at hand. Weeks, months, years pass, but the good workman knows that he is gambling on an ultimate achievement which cannot be measured in time spent. Responsible men and women leap to the challenge of jobs that require enormous dedication and years to fulfill, and are happiest when they are so involved.

This means that men and women who hope to make a real contribution to American life must prepare themselves to tackle big jobs, and the interesting fact is that no college or university in the world can give anyone the specific education he will ultimately need. Adults who are unwilling to reeducate themselves periodically are doomed to mediocrity.

For in American life, the average man—let's leave out doctors and highly specialized scientists—can expect to work in three radically different fields before he retires. The trained lawyer is dragged into a business reorganization and winds up a college president. The engineer uses his slide rule for a short time, finds himself a sales expert and ends his career in labor relations. The schoolteacher becomes a principal and later on heads the town's Buick agency.

Obviously no college education could prepare a young man for all that he will have to do in his years of employment. The best a college can do is to inspire him with the urge to reeducate himself constantly.

I first discovered this fact on Guadalcanal in 1945, when the war had passed us by and we could see certain victory ahead. Relieved of pressure, our top admirals and generals could have been excused if they loafed, but the ones I knew well in those days took free time and gave themselves orderly courses in new fields. One carrier admiral studied everything he could get on tank warfare. The head of our outfit, William Lowndes Calhoun, spent six hours a day learning French.

I asked him about this. "Admiral, what's this big deal with French?"

"How do I know where I'll be sent when the war's over?" he countered.

But what impressed me most was the next tier of officers, the young Army colonels and the Navy commanders. They divided sharply into two groups: those who spent their spare time learning something and those who didn't. In the years that followed, I noticed in the newspapers that whenever President Truman or President Eisenhower chose men for military positions of great power, they always picked from the officers who had reeducated themselves.

More significant to me personally was my stay with the brilliant doctors of an Army hospital in the jungles of Espiritu Santo. The entire staff of a general hospital in Denver, Colorado, had been picked up and flown out to care for our wounded, and they experienced days of overwork followed by weeks of tedium. In the latter periods the doctors organized voluntary study groups by which to further their professional competence.

By good luck, I was allowed to participate in a group that was analyzing alcoholism, and one night the leader asked me, as we were breaking up, "What are you studying, Michener?" The question stunned me, for I had been studying exactly nothing.

I drove back through the jungle and that very night started working on something that I had been toying with for some months. In a lantern-lit, mosquito-filled tin shack, I started writing *Tales of the South Pacific.*

I have been the typical American in that I have had widely scattered jobs: teacher, businessman, soldier, traveler, writer.

51

And my college education gave me no specific preparation for any of these jobs.

But it gave me something much better. I attended Swarthmore College, outside Philadelphia, and by fantastic luck, I got there just as the college was launching an experiment which was to transform the institution and those of us who participated. At the end of my sophomore year the faculty assembled a group of us and said, "Life does not consist of taking courses in small segments. A productive life consists of finding huge tasks and mastering them with whatever tools of intelligence and energy we have. We are going to turn you loose on some huge tasks. Let's see what you can do with them."

Accordingly, we were excused from all future class attendance and were told, "Pick out three fields that interest you." I chose logic, English history and the novel. The faculty said, "For the next two years go to the library and learn what you can about your fields. At the end of two years we'll bring in some outside experts from Harvard and Yale, whom you've never seen, and they will determine whether or not you have educated yourselves."

What followed was an experience in intellectual grandeur. The Swarthmore professors, realizing that when I was tested they would be tested too, helped me to gain as thorough an education as a young man could absorb. For it was in their interest to see that I understood the fine points of the fields I had chosen.

When the two years ended, the visiting experts arrived and for a week they probed and tested and heckled. At the end of this exciting time one of the examiners told me, "You have the beginning of a real education."

He was right. Nothing that I studied in college has been of use to me in my various jobs. But what I did learn was how to learn, how to organize, how to write term papers. If my education had ended the week I stood before those strange examiners, I would have proved a fairly useless citizen.

While I was reflecting on these matters, my young scholar asked, "If you were a young man today and wanted to be a writer, what kind of education would you seek?"

52

I replied, "I'd choose some very difficult field and try to master it. I'd seek out professors who really poured it on. Long term papers and many of them, tough laboratory work."

"Why?" he pressed.

"Because we learn only those things at which we have to work very hard. It's ridiculous to give a bright fellow like you a three-thousand-word term paper. It ought to be fifteen thousand words—or thirty. Tackle a real job. Then, when you're through, you're on the way to facing big jobs in adult life."

My visitor made a few marks in his notebook, then asked, "When you were in college, the scientific revolution hadn't occurred yet. Today, would you stick with liberal arts—things like logic and history—or would you switch to science, where the good jobs are?"

I didn't hesitate a minute on this one. "Unless I had extraordinary aptitude in the sciences, I'd stick with liberal arts every time. The pay isn't as good. The jobs aren't waiting when you graduate. And when you want to get married, it's tough to tell your girl's father, 'I'm studying philosophy.' But forty years from now the scientists in your class will be scientists. And the liberal arts men will be governing the world."

The idea was so startling that my young visitor wished to discuss it further. "You mean there's a chance for fellows like me?"

"Every year your prospects grow brighter," I insisted. "The more complex the world becomes, the more desperately it needs men trained in liberal arts. For the government of the world must always rely upon the man with broad human knowledge. And the government of a business or a university or a newspaper requires the same kind of man."

"Why?" he asked, forgetting his notebook.

"Because governing anything requires knowledge of men, a balanced judgment, a gift for conciliation and, above all, a constant weighing of good versus bad. Only men with broad educations can perform such tasks."

"Can't scientists do this?" he asked.

"They surely can. If, after they graduate, they give themselves courses in the humanities."

I finished our interview by telling a story. "In 1942 the United States Navy was hungry for talent, and four of us were taken into a small room where we sat around shivering in our shorts. A grim-faced selection committee asked the first would-be officer, 'What can you do?' and the man replied, 'I'm a buyer for Macy's, and I can judge very quickly between markets and prices and trends.' The selection board replied, 'But you can't do anything practical?' The man said no, and he was shunted off to one side.

"The next man was a lawyer, and when the board asked him if he could do anything practical, he had to confess, 'I can weigh evidence and organize information,' and he was rejected.

"I was the third in line, and when I answered, 'I know language and a good deal of history,' the board groaned and I was sent shivering away.

"But when the fourth man said boldly, 'I'm from Georgia Tech and I can overhaul diesel engines,' the committee jumped up, practically embraced him and made him an officer on the spot."

"That's what I mean," my young scholar pointed out.

"At the end of the war," I continued, "the buyer from Macy's was assistant to the Secretary of the Navy, in charge of many complex responsibilities requiring instant good judgment. He gave himself courses in naval management and government procedures until he became one of the nation's real experts.

"The lawyer wound up as assistant to Admiral Halsey, and in a crucial battle, deduced where the Japanese fleet had to be. He came out covered with medals.

"I was given the job of naval secretary to several Congressional committees who were determining the future of America in the South Pacific. And what was the engineer doing at the end of the war? He was still overhauling diesel engines."

"You're sure there's hope for the liberal-arts man?" the young scholar repeated.

"If he learns to tackle the big jobs—the big ones historically or morally or culturally or politically."

We parted on that note, but when he had gone, I realized that I had not made my statement nearly strong enough. I should have said, "The world is positively hungry for young men who have dedicated themselves to big jobs. If your present professors aren't training you for such work, quit them and find others who will drive you. If your present college isn't making you work to the limit of your ability, drop out and go to another that will. Because if you don't discipline your brain now, you'll never be prepared for the years when it's a question of work or perish."

Parents or professors who do not encourage their young to tackle big jobs commit a moral crime against those young people. For we know that when the young are properly challenged, they will rise to the occasion and they will prepare themselves for the great work that remains to be done.

The Weapons We Need to Fight Pornography

DECEMBER, 1968

Recently a friend of mine found his thirteen-year-old son secretly reading a sex book. The father assumed that it was the typical erotic nonsense that teen-agers have surreptitiously read for the last two hundred years with awe, and usually with no bad aftermath.

But he was wrong. When he inspected the book he found to his horror that it was not primarily a sex yarn. It was a savage blend of sadism, masochism and violence made attractive and exciting by an intermixture of sex. Even the sex was perverted and hideously brutal.

Let's be specific. This is a problem that many American families are facing right now, and we all need some kind of guidance.

The book was sadistic in that the men tortured the women. It was masochistic in that the men asked the women to beat them with whips. It was violent in that the men killed one of the women. And it was perverted in that normal sexual relations between men and women were never referred to, whereas various abnormal practices were paraded as natural.

In disgust, and in defense of his children, my friend began to ask why the sale of such books was permitted in his city. He discovered that in April, 1968, the Supreme Court upheld a state statute banning the dissemination of indecent material to juveniles. But he also found, to his astonishment, that recent Supreme Court decisions have made it difficult, if not impossible, for local communities or states to know what standards to apply in obscenity cases, especially in dealing with books.

"In any case, such material will continue to get into the hands of teen-agers as long as it is printed," my friend complained to me. And he asked me what I thought ought to be done. Here is what I think.

Establishing the Guidelines. I am enthusiastically in favor of sex. It is one of the finest of all human experiences, the somewhat mystical means whereby our race perpetuates itself. And it is also the source of enormous human pleasure. I have found sex to be ennobling, hilarious, tender, ribald and creative, and I would never agree to anything which diminished its free exercise.

As a writer I am professionally interested in sex, since it provides the artist with a large portion of his best material. In my novels dealing with the great conflicts that engulf men and women in love, I have written about some fairly robust situations and have never held back from using four-letter words to describe the actions of my characters when such words were germane to the situation. The older I grow, the more impressed I am with the marvelous force of sex in art, from Shakespeare's stunning tragedy of *Romeo and Juliet* through Verdi's *Aïda* and on to the powerful novels and plays being offered today. I would deplore any act of my society which deprived artists of this greatest of subject matters. I am constitutionally opposed to censorship.

Nevertheless, today's traffic among our teen-agers in books of perverted sex and violence should be stopped. If present laws are unable to handle this problem, new ones should be passed. And if present constitutional or judicial interpretations make more difficult the enforcement of such laws, then changes must be made in either the Constitution or the judicial interpretation, or both.

If you ask, "Are you then recommending censorship?" I will

have to reply, "Yes." But I want to make one point very clear.

I am against this flood of sex-sadism for one specific reason, a reason so solid that I cannot imagine opposition to it.

It is wrong, and terribly dangerous, to put into the hands of young people—who are in the process of establishing the guidelines for their sexual behavior—books and pictures which would pervert or prevent the development of satisfactory habits. I do not want young boys seduced into homosexual relations before they have even had a chance to discover for themselves how satisfactory heterosexual relations can be. I do not want girls to be taught that whips and chains are normal concomitants of sex before they find out for themselves that they are not.

I realize, of course, that chances are small that permanent damage will result from just a passing exposure to pornography. That's not my point. My point is that such material has absolutely no place in the lives of children.

Unfettered Squalor. Children under certain ages cannot buy cigarettes or whiskey. They are forbidden to drive cars, can't have guns, contract bills or get married. Yet in this most difficult of areas, our nation has failed to set clear and enforceable standards to prevent the sale of sexually destructive material to minors.

Take three startling cases.

In Fresno, California, Sanford E. Aday conducted a flourishing business publishing lurid paperback books; in one five-month period he distributed 826,840 volumes. One well-known book was *Sex Life of a Cop*, in which two policemen in a prowl car engage in sadism and in a series of rapid and bizarre conquests featuring virgins, prostitutes, the wife of the mayor, a policewoman and waitresses, not to mention each other's wives. How *Sex Life of a Cop* could circulate under the protection of the First Amendment, which guarantees freedom of the press, is impossible for an average citizen to explain, but the book is still available in hot-item newsstands across the country.

In New York City's Times Square, Sidney Friedman ran a bookstore featuring "bondage" books and magazines. Two of the books' titles will indicate their emphasis on flagellation and other sexual deviations: *Bondage Boarding School* and *Travelling Saleslady Gets Spanked.* I cannot see how the average reader could find any literary merit whatever in them, nor how young children could fail to get from them a perverted attitude toward sex.

In Los Angeles, California, Harry Schackman and associates operated a nudie film arcade in which they exhibited 16-millimeter films which are known by such curious titles as 0-7, 0-12, and D–15. 0-12 showed a buxom model almost fully exposed above the waist and wearing transparent panties through which the viewer could see her complete anatomy, which she twitched and twisted through a series of provocative poses. The camera kept returning to the model's pelvic area, and wandered to her face so that the viewer could see her lips move as she clearly spoke inviting vulgarisims.

Many even worse books and films are being distributed freely in our nation today. Has there been no public attempt to halt this wretched flow?

Supreme Court vs. the Lower Courts. As a matter of fact, society has made a rather strong effort to stamp out the worst of this material. Citizens' committees, watchful district attorneys, police forces and ordinary mothers and fathers have vigorously advocated enforcement of obscenity laws or have brought suit in local, state and federal courts. And they have won some striking successes.

Let's follow the three cases described previously.

Aday and his associate were brought to trial in Grand Rapids, Michigan, where a federal jury found *Sex Life of a Cop* to be unredeemed pornography. When this verdict was appealed by the publisher and his associate, the Court of Appeals Sixth Circuit confirmed the judgment.

In the case of the Times Square "bondage" books and magazines, a three-judge lower court ruled the books to be hardcore pornography. Then a three-judge intermediate court approved the findings.

And a Los Angeles jury found Schackman's nudie films to be obscene, a judgment which the Appellate Department of

59

the Los Angeles Superior Court affirmed. A federal district judge held the films to be obscene.

Similar cases were being similarly decided in other states, and it looked as if at last our country had found a proper balance between permitting true freedom of the press, even on sexual material, and protecting itself against hard-core pornography wedded to violence.

Then something went wrong! Something went badly wrong, and America found that *Sex Life of a Cop* and a flood of things infinitely worse were again free to circulate openly.

In the October, 1966 term, appeals were considered by the Supreme Court against convictions in the three cases we have been talking about, plus twenty-three others. The nine Justices conducted extended private debates among themselves, trying to decide what pornography was. In May and June, 1967, the Supreme Court handed down a series of startling decisions on the twenty-six cases: Schackman's nudie films, Friedman's "bondage" books and magazines and *Sex Life of a Cop*, among others, must be allowed to circulate freely.

With these decisions the Supreme Court destroyed the attempts of thirteen separate states to control the dissemination of salacious material, and reversed eight juries which had held that insofar as their communities were concerned, the books and films in question were offensive to public taste.

A Landmark Decision. Observe that the Court did not pass on the legal correctness of the cases, but rather upon the question of whether a book like *Sex Life of a Cop* is protected by the First Amendment to the Constitution. That is, was it indeed pornography? By this switch the nine Justices passed over from being conservators of legal tradition to being censors of individual books and films. This is a most unfortunate conversion, and if the Justices persist, they will outrage their society, waste their time and tarnish their effectiveness as judges of legal matters.

How did our Supreme Court stumble into this mess?

When I was a boy, American communities made damned fools of themselves by censoring everything. Boston banned perfectly good books. Police sergeants in small cities decided what movies could be screened. Postal inspectors decided on their own as to what printed matter one could receive through the mails.

Then famous trials were held on acknowledged works of art like D.H. Lawrence's *Lady Chatterley's Lover* and James Joyce's *Ulysses*, and the courts, striking down narrow-mindedness, decided that such books ought to be allowed to circulate.

So things progressed in what I would consider normal patterns through June, 1957, when the Court handed down its extremely wise decision in the Roth Case: "Implicit in the history of the First Amendment is the rejection of obscenity as utterly without redeeming social importance. We hold that obscenity is not within the area of constitutionally protected speech or press." The test was to be "whether to the average person, applying contemporary community standards, the dominant theme of the material taken as a whole appeals to prurient interest."

Thus, if anyone wanted to censor my novels, or anyone else's, he must judge "the dominant theme of the material taken as a whole." He could not pick out a sentence here and a sentence there to prove that I had used a couple of dirty words. I thought this a sterling decision and one that I could live under.

What went wrong?

From Jurists to Censors. In subsequent cases the Supreme Court began to entrap itself by handing down judgments on individual works. Justice Hugo Black had warned against this very pitfall: "My belief is that this Court is about the most inappropriate supreme board of censors that could be found. So far as I know, judges possess no special expertise providing exceptional competency to set standards and to supervise the private morals of the nation. In addition, the Justices of this Court seem especially unsuited to make the kind of value judgments . . . as to what movies are good or bad for local communities."

The trouble with recent decisions is that any sane man can look at the filth thus protected and say, "No matter what anyone says, this stuff has got to be pornographic, and I don't

61

want my kids reading it." When an average citizen finds a governmental decision ridiculous on the face of it, government is in trouble.

I believe that a three-point program will provide the way out of this mess.

1. The Supreme Court should refuse to review individual works to determine whether or not they are pornographic.

2. Congress should pass a law empowering the highest courts of the fifty states, or subsidiary courts nominated by the states, to serve as courts of last appeal as to whether a work is pornographic. The U.S. Supreme Court would continue, of course, to review the legal proceedings of such courts to ensure protection under the law, but it would no longer be allowed to go behind the lower court's findings of fact.

3. Each state would thus return to the principle enunciated in Roth of "applying contemporary community standards" in judging pornography. Trials would be by a jury of citizens, who would be presumed to know what the standards of their community were. If they ran hogwild and turned in arbitrary or illegal verdicts, a higher state court would redress the balance.

Judge Samuel Hofstadter, of New York's Supreme Court, has spoken wisely on the problem: "Essentially, the problem of obscenity is one of municipal order. It is not intrinsically a constitutional question. Hence it cannot be decided properly at the summit but must be disposed of at the base."

One final word. Although most recent Supreme Court decisions have made it easier for smut peddlers to hawk their wares, local communities must not give up in this field. An arrest based on a proper warrant, a trial which observes the fine points of law, a district attorney well prepared to present his case, a fair judge and an intelligent jury can combine to convict such people. Says Arlen Specter, the hard-working district attorney in Philadelphia, "I intend to keep fighting these cases. While adults may decide for themselves what to read, the Supreme Court says that juveniles require protection during their tender years. We have followed up on that new ruling by bringing prosecutions."

We must remember what we are fighting against. Not sexy or bawdy stories. But works in which perversion, sadism and brutality are paraded. The other day, to check on what is now being peddled publicly, I picked up a magazine which showed two nude young men committing multiple perversions upon each other. The picture revolted me, but so far as I know it didn't harm me. But to a twelve-year-old boy trying to find out what sex is all about, it might be tragically harmful.

GMRX: An Alternative to Movie Censorship

JANUARY, 1969 ✂

Strange things have been happening in our movie houses. Patrons have been startled by the sex and violence they are seeing.

The Detective. A group of college girls in central Pennsylvania went to see this show and were aghast when Frank Sinatra, in the opening minutes, reported matter-of-factly to his Negro assistant as they stood over the body of a murdered homosexual, "Penis cut off." One of the coeds was so startled she nearly fainted.

The Graduate. A sophisticated neighbor of mine—an artist who works in New York—took his wife to see this film and reported, "We were really shocked at the seduction scene when Ann Bancroft appears totally nude before the young fellow and tells him he can call her any time he feels the need."

The Fox. Other neighbors who know the world fairly well were disgusted by this one. "When you have two lesbians making love together in bed, that's bad enough. But when one of them is shown completely nude in the bathroom masturbating . . . finish."

Sound of Music. Believe it or not, the most vocal protest I have so far heard came in connection with this family-style movie.

An editor friend of mine reports, "Of course it wasn't the main film I'm complaining about. I took my five daughters to see it, thinking that nothing could go wrong with such a picture, and they loved it. But when the trailers came on for next week's show, what did we get? The six most lurid scenes from Antonioni's *Blow-Up*. Two nude teeny-boppers chasing the photographer around his studio. My daughters, all of them under fourteen, wanted to know, 'What's going on, Daddy?' "

Sex Is the Game People Play. Wanting to refresh myself as to just what was going on in our movies, I went to one of the sexploitation theaters on Forty-second Street in New York and sat in steamy silence along with about two hundred other unattached males to watch this film about four suburban couples playing strip poker, and before I lost count I saw eleven separate acts of sexual intercourse photographed in one tricky way after another.

Three distinct developments in the motion picture industry accounted for the radical changes I have been describing. First, serious films like *The Detective* and *The Graduate* have grown much bolder in treating adult themes like homosexuality and adultery and in using rough language. This stems, I think, from the necessity Hollywood faced of competing economically with foreign films like Fellini's *La Dolce Vita* and Antonioni's *Blow-Up*, which coined money in the United States because they dealt vividly with subject matter denied American film makers. In other words, Hollywood had to catch up with Europe, or go out of business.

What had held Hollywood back? In the late 1920's American movies underwent a great crisis. Scandals like the Fatty Arbuckle case had rocked the industry. Church groups were demanding a clean-up. Government agencies were threatening some system of national censorship.

To avoid repression, the film industry compiled its "Code to Govern the Making of Motion Pictures, 1930" and turned it over to Will Hays for administration. By this device the movies saved themselves from outside censorship, but at a heavy cost in creativity. How simple and secure were the rules governing movie sex in those tranquil days!

In the case of impure love, the love which society has always regarded as wrong and which has been banned by divine law, the following are important:

Impure love must not be presented as attractive and beautiful.

It must not be the subject of comedy or farce, or treated as material for laughter.

It must not be presented in such a way as to arouse passion.

Says James R. Webb, top-ranking screenwriter with an Academy Award to his credit, "I can recall when you couldn't put a man and a woman into a bedroom even to fix the curtains."

Under this code, Hollywood prospered; that is, until foreign blockbusters started cleaning up the money. Says Robert Ferguson, vice-president of Columbia Pictures, "The imports were attracting growing audiences, and so the American picture makers said that in order for us to compete, there must be a change in the attitude of the Code."

So in 1966 the Code was sharply revised. Not only were the teeth of the earlier Code drawn, but also its fingernails and even the toenails until almost anything could be presented on screen. Where the earlier Code had forbidden even the mention of homosexuality, the new Code said simply, "Restraint and care shall be exercised in presentations dealing with sex aberrations."

It was this revision, necessitated by pressure from Europe, that brought the wave of so-called "adult" motion pictures to the screens of our first-run and neighborhood houses.

Nudity became so commonplace that when film critic Judith Crist wanted to remind her readers where they had seen Essy Persson, the Swedish actress, she wrote, "Aficionados will recognize her from *I, A Woman* by the spinal dimples in her derrière." Things got so bad that in October, 1967, when a gathering of film people was shown a long sampling from the movies scheduled for the next year, Martin Quigley, Jr., spokesman for much of the industry, wrote: "The cumulative effect was deeply disturbing. Never in the long history of the screen had so much raw sex and excessive violence been inflicted on an audience at one time. Even veteran showmen were stunned. After the screening, this writer was urged to speak out even more sharply than in the past about the dangers of the current cycles of raw sex and excessive violence."

But many theater owners reported that the public liked the new pictures. In Washington, D.C., theater operator Don King said, "Nobody goes to Doris Day movies any more. And Disney films are dying in the houses. Sex is where the action is. Audiences are more sophisticated and want films about life."

Meanwhile a second development was under way, the proliferation of sexploitation films. For many years theaters had picked up a little extra money from inoffensive films with exciting titles like *Dracula Meets Frankenstein*. If properly exploited, with lurid advertising, such films would entice paying customers and were referred to in the trade as exploitation movies. Now this principle was applied to sex films: *Housewives on Call* and *The Orgy at Lil's Place*. They were nothing new. Throughout this century a constant supply of nasty little pictures, promising more in the way of sex than they delivered, had proved profitable. They first appeared in peepshows, where the customer dropped his nickel into a slot machine and hand-cranked a jerky film showing a French model undressing. They progressed to florid features playing in one or two recognized movie houses in each of our major cities, spurred on to new levels of boldness by what has been happening in standard theaters.

Today they have developed into a lucrative business. California alone has thirty companies making sex movies, and the rest of the country has seventy more. In place of the two or three dozen theaters which used to grind them out, today there are 312 across the nation, plus another 300 planning to enter the field. One expert on the subject thinks there may ultimately be as many as 800.

Nor are the new sexploitation theaters restricted to the

cheaper mid-city areas where they used to grub out a meager existence. Now they flourish in all parts of a city, even residential suburbs. New York, which used to have ten theaters in the Times Square area, now has twenty-five scattered throughout the city. In rural areas many drive-ins have gone over to a policy of showing two standard films plus one shock job.

One secret in making a sexploitation theater a success is to run lengthy explicit trailers for next week's attraction. These are often the best part of the show, for they consist of anthologies of the sex and violence coming up. At one show I attended, the trailers ran for about twenty minutes, and at a theater in Washington one patron demanded his money back when, because of a time bind, the trailer had to be eliminated. The trailer for *The Female* repeated the few juicy scenes in this otherwise somber film five times each, trusting that the audience would not catch on that what they were seeing was the same sex scene.

Today there is money in the business. Mrs. Chelly Wilson, a charming, matronly-looking woman, runs a company in New York that spends about $20,000 a film to produce quickies like *Johnny Whip's Women*, which can earn back as much as $100,000.

On the West Coast, Russ Meyer, one of the kings of the sex film, made one sex epic for only $24,000 and has earned $1,-200,000 from it so far. Another, *Good Morning . . . and Goodbye*, described by one reviewer as "a drama of marital infidelity and lust down on the farm," apparently was so bad that another critic wrote of it as "moving rapidly down the sewer as it swirls from one sextitillation to another." Yet when it played in one southern college town, it outgrossed *Hawaii* and has become a minor sensation on other college campuses.

Meyer defends his type of film by pointing out, "It's hard today to stay one step ahead of the majors. Why should the man on the street shell out to see a Russ Meyer movie when he can see nudity in *Blow-Up*, lesbianism and masturbation in *The Fox*, and blood and guts in *Bonnie and Clyde?*"

Observe what has happened. First, European films pressure Hollywood, forcing our producers to issue more violent subject matter. Second, Hollywood pressures the sex-and-sadism producers, so they turn to subjects that are increasingly raw. Third, the circle completes itself! A writer for a major Hollywood company is speaking: "You can be sure that what Russ Meyer is doing today will be done by the majors tomorrow."

If this prediction is true, moviegoers are in for a rough time, because in the dozen sexploitation films I reviewed I found that for a movie to be a success it had to include the following ingredients: at least six scenes of complete sexual intercourse; one long-drawn-out scene of a nearly nude man beating a nude woman with a whip; lesbianism; an older man seducing a very young girl; and always at least one scene of two nude girls making love to one man. Dick Adler, feature writer for the *Los Angeles Times*, recently spent two weeks reviewing the flood of such pictures hitting his town, and concluded that they were so miserable "they were giving sex a bad name."

The third development was less spectacular than the first two and less commented upon, since it did not involve sex, but when *Bonnie and Clyde* began to break records everywhere, with children identifying with the two stars, our nation became aware that it was engulfed in a wave of violence. Movies, television and paperback books were filled with stabbings, shootings, brutal beatings, rape and murder, made increasingly attractive by the polished form in which they were presented. Few recent movies have been better made than *Bonnie and Clyde*, few more totally immoral.

The original Hollywood Code had been both specific and severe in its prohibitions regarding brutality:

> Details of crime must never be shown.
> Action suggestive of wholesale slaughter of human beings will not be allowed.
> There must be no suggestion of excessive brutality.
> There must be no display of machine guns in the hands of gangsters or other criminals.

The 1966 revision simplified all this to "Detailed and protracted acts of brutality, cruelty, physical violence, torture and abuse shall not be presented," but such acts, if not detailed and protracted, whatever that means, could be presented. And were.

The flood of violence that resulted was not restricted to American films. As before, European movies showed our people how to get away with murder, and the results became so frightening that one day last September, England's chief movie censor, John Trevelyan, conducted what must have been one of history's most remarkable film shows. In London's Festival Hall he assembled an audience of some 2,000 movie people, most of whom objected to censorship, and showed them two hours of the things he had been clipping from recent films offered for exhibition in England.

The *Daily Telegraph* film critic said, "I was nauseated." The *Manchester Guardian* man was "horrified." One observer reported, "Many in the audience buried their heads in their arms when a cut from a French gangster movie showed a man being strangled by a sadist who released his fingers around his victim's neck ten times to permit him faint gasps of air before finally doing him in." Others were repelled by a Japanese film starring a maniac with an obsession about slicing off the ears of naked young virgins, or the French one in which a living girl had her leg sawed off and thrown into a furnace.

This sudden flood of sex and violence in our good films, of obscenity and depravity in our bad ones, comes at an unfortunate time. Because rarely in our history have films been so important to our nation. In order to understand why, you must know what has been happening to film audiences.

If you take the 138,000,000 Americans over the age of sixteen, they divide in this way: eighteen percent attend the movies once a month or more and see an average of thirty-eight films a year; fifty-two percent attend once every three months and see about four films a year; thirty percent never go at all and see no movies throughout the year . . . except on television.

Now if you look to see who makes up that eighteen percent of our population who comprise the moviegoing audience in this nation, you are in for some shocks. They are mostly in the sixteen to twenty-four age group. They are mostly single. And as soon as they marry, they drop the habit of going to movies.

Thus this marvelous art form, one of America's foremost contributions to world culture and our principal ambassador abroad, has become primarily a diversion of the young. The final irony is that the more adult our pictures have become, the more they appeal to our youth. The contrary is also true: adult films do not seem to appeal to adults, who find them too outspoken, too shocking and too brutal.

What happens within that massive fifty-two percent of people who used to go to the movies a great deal and who now go only four times a year— 72,000,000 citizens, who, if they resumed going to the movies, would explode the theaters? Study after study shows that these people want to see films like *The Sound of Music.* "I saw that one five times" is a common response. But there aren't many films like that, nor have there ever been. So these infrequent patrons wait for some well-publicized picture like *Who's Afraid of Virginia Woolf?* or *Bonnie and Clyde* and report later to their friends, "I hated it. Too much bad language. Too violent."

As for the thirty percent who no longer go to the movies at all (some 41,000,000 people), it seems that nothing is going to lure them back into the theaters, so Hollywood says, quite practically, "We are making our pictures for kids between the ages of sixteen and twenty-four."

In a way this is good. Because this is the age group that really respond to the movies. I know three young college girls who have each seen *Blow-Up* four times. "This we dig," they say. Other young friends have seen *The Graduate* repeatedly, and it has had a more profound effect on them than most of their college courses, because it speaks to them in their idiom. A young painter who has exhibited in our top museums has quit his profession to make films. "It's where the action is," he tells me. "It's what young people talk about." In 120 major colleges, 1,500 film courses are offered, attended by 60,000 students.

One perceptive observer has pointed out that college students today lead two lives, their real lives and their reel lives. And for young people who don't go to college, the impact is even greater. Film has become the great educator of our

71

young, and the rest of us should do whatever we can to help the movies perform this task of education.

Wherever I look I see evidence that a new type of young American is evolving. One might describe these people as the nonverbal young. They react to movies and television rather than to books. James Beveridge, formerly of the Canadian Film Board and currently on the film faculty at New York University, says, "This category of young person has a proprietary interest in film. He's impatient with writing. Written communication bores him—and this is reflected in his spelling." Herb Alpert, famous for his Tijuana Brass, is launching a new film company, described by his partner as follows: "Most of Hollywood is just not in tune with what's happening today. We hope to make films of significant contemporary content and in a style that appeals to the visceral, nonverbal nature of today's young people." The other day I was visited by the head of a major chain of drive-in theaters who told me "Michener, if you could only write us a motion picture featuring motorcyclists, you and I would both clean up. Not much dialogue. Lots of action. Because today's kids respond to machines and motion, not to words. No motorcycle picture we've ever run has lost money. Because that swinging, swaying motion through traffic is the kids' world. That they understand."

It is doubtful if old-time standards of what is good for the young can be applied today. Mrs. Ursula Lewis, an attractive widow with two grown sons and a thirteen-year-old daughter, has for a dozen years run the enormously successful Thalia theater in upper New York City. Here each summer she offers a festival of the world's greatest films, with seven different double features each week. Here you can see, each summer, such classics as *Children of Paradise*, *Rashomon* and *Stagecoach*. Mrs. Lewis says, "I want my children to see these films. How better can you educate children to our world? My daughter Debby and her friends asked permission to see *Rosemary's Baby*. I wondered about letting them go, but when they came back they said, 'Isn't it wonderful? The baby you have when you're married can grow up to be almost anything. Rosemary's baby grew up to be the next savior of the world.' Children learn such things from good films. All the girls in her class have seen *The Graduate* . . . and they understood it, too."

I have followed this sweeping change in our movies with unusual interest, for there cannot have been many people in this country as faithful to the movies as I have been. I love them, attend them constantly in all parts of the world and make it my business to go back and catch any good ones, American or foreign, that I have missed.

I remember the joy I experienced as a young man when I first saw the great films reaching our country from Europe. They opened my eyes to a whole new world of adult attitudes, and I would have been only half educated had I missed them. Marlene Dietrich thrilled me in *The Blue Angel* with her naughty sexiness; Raimu in *The Baker's Wife* showed me a sophisticated attitude toward repressive rural love. *Carnival in Flanders* opened up a whole new aspect of art, one which influenced me deeply. *The Grand Illusion,* with its noble French and German cast, was better than a college course in history.

I also profited intellectually from good American films like *The Informer, Gone with the Wind* and *All Quiet on the Western Front.* And because I once lived in the west, I have always been a sucker for a good western like *Stagecoach* or *The Oxbow Incident.* In fact, I might be described as a member of the first generation in America to have been raised on the movies, just as today there are people entering their twenties who will in the future be classified as the first television generation. The impact of the movies was pervasive.

I remember with intense clarity that first afternoon when I learned what the art of storytelling was. A bunch of us kids under the age of ten were attending the opening episode of what was to be a fifteen-part serial. In order to hook us, this first installment had to have a strong story line. So there was a beautiful girl in trouble, a dauntless hero and about as ugly a villain as I had ever seen. To make us hate the villain so that we would remember him through fifteen episodes, the screenwriter had shown him doing three vile things. He kicked a dog. He punched his mother. (We thought the former the worse of his two crimes.) And in order to find a piece of paper

73

on which to write a ransom note, he tore a page out of the Bible, whereupon a bolt of lightning descended and struck the mutilated book.

When the movie ended I found that whereas some of my friends had already forgotten the girl and the hero, all remembered the villain and could hardly wait for next Saturday to see him get his. I think it was then that I decided that a book or a movie was good if it showed heroes being heroic and villains being villainous, rather than talking about it.

With this background of devotion to movies and respect for them, I was happy to see the Hollywood Code of 1930 revised in 1966, because I agreed with John Cardinal Krol of Philadelphia, who said of the movies, "Mature audiences must not be bound to a level of entertainment fit, from a moral point of view, solely for children."

I liked the new movies. I saw nothing wrong for adults in *The Graduate, The Detective* and *Who's Afraid of Virginia Woolf?* I commended the new maturity of films like *In the Heat of the Night* and *The Pawnbroker.*

But then I saw a film of extraordinary technical beauty but questionable content. *The Trip* starred Peter Fonda as a young experimenter with LSD and featured a hallucinatory dream in which he imagined himself in bed with an attractive girl he had recently met, and their sexual adventures were photographed in detail. It was hardly a film for children, yet there were very young people in the audience when I saw it. Clearly, something was wrong.

When I studied the matter I began to hear the rumblings that were rising across this nation. Adults who were clearly not bluenoses or eager to impose censorship voiced real concerns about the profanity in *Who's Afraid of Virginia Woolf?* Or the lesbianism in *The Fox.* Or the brutality in *Bonnie and Clyde.* Or the wisecracking immorality of *Prudence and the Pill.* Or the miserable situation in *The Graduate,* in which a young college man sleeps with an older woman, then marries her daughter.

In Congress, Senator Margaret Chase Smith of Maine proposed a federal classification system which would permit such movies to be made but which would flag them so as to keep children from seeing them.

In California, Bishop Gerald Kennedy said, "All of us have some responsibility to prevent conscienceless adults from exploiting the young. Youngsters ought not to get their first impressions of life from the neurotic, the twisted and the warped. People who are either obsessed by sex or have forgotten, if indeed they ever knew, that it is healthy and good, cannot be set loose to make pictures without rules. Let me be even more corny and say that young people have a right to see sex as mysterious, miraculous and beautiful."

Even in Hollywood the clamor rose. Gregory Peck stated, "The present level of permissiveness is, in my opinion, abdication of responsibility. If parents aren't sure enough of themselves to draw lines for their children, then the citizenry at large must do it."

Otto Preminger said about the same thing. Famed for his production of *The Moon Is Blue*, which failed to get Code approval because it used the word *abortion*, he says, "I've advocated classification for years. I've always insisted that parents be warned in advance regarding movies."

And among thoughtful people everywhere a basic question was being discussed: Suppose we stay away from the theaters now . . . because we don't like the sex and sadism. Next year these same films will be on television . . . in our homes. If America has abandoned the movies to the young, that means one thing so far as theaters are concerned. But if the resulting movies later on dominate television, it means that we have turned our aesthetic and moral judgments over to the young, and I wonder if this is best for our nation?

By January of 1968 it had become pretty obvious that if the movie industry did not discipline itself, government censorship of some kind would. In fact, the Supreme Court had indicated that it was ready to approve certain kinds of censorship, if they could be based on proper legal procedures. The city of Dallas, Texas, had drawn up a code establishing a Motion Picture Classification Board of nine members empowered to identify offensive motion pictures as "not suitable for young persons under the age of sixteen." Dallas movie houses were then forbidden to show such films to anyone under that age, on penalty of losing their licenses.

On April 22, 1968, the Supreme Court declared the Dallas Classification Board unconstitutional, but only on the grounds that the enabling legislation was too vague. The supposition was that if the law had been more carefully written, the Board would have been approved.

On the same day the Supreme Court handed down a decision in the case of Sam Ginsberg, a Long Island lunch-counter operator who had sold two girlie magazines to a sixteen-year-old boy. The Court said, in a historic decision, that a state had a right to prevent children from buying erotic material which adults would be allowed to buy.

The way was now clear for the motion picture industry to make a crucial decision. On the one hand, it wanted to avoid censorship. It had fought many years to place its films under the protection of the First Amendment, and it did not propose to surrender its rights now, simply because producers were making adult films which were improper for children. Louis Nizer, legal counsel to the Motion Picture Association of America, said bluntly, "We have fought censorship and will continue to fight it. We will have no truck with official censorship of any kind, because it is bad for the nation. And it's bad for motion pictures." But he added, "However, we stand ready to police ourselves."

Under the strong leadership of Jack Valenti, president of the M.P.A.A., the industry proceeded to do just that. Valenti, who saw clearly that it was going to be either private restraint or public censorship, worked endlessly with producers, theater owners, importers who brought films in from Europe, and artistic guilds of writers, workers and actors, religious groups and newspapers and television, preaching only one message: "We must help parents protect their children from films which they do not want their children to see."

Valenti and Nizer together then worked out a system which

would accomplish these good ends. After November 1, 1968, films produced in the United States or imported from abroad would be classified under one of four headings:

G: Suggested for general audiences.

M: Suggested for mature audiences, but children may attend if they wish.

R: Restricted. Persons under the age of sixteen not admitted unless accompanied by parent or adult guardian.

X: Persons under sixteen not admitted under any circumstances.

Concerning the last category, Nizer adds, "I don't think any of our big companies will be making X films."

The entire industry is excited about the possibilities of this system. Those who make films can now plan for an adult motion picture like *The Fox* and know from the start that when it is finished, children will not be allowed to see it unless their parents specifically want them to do so. Or they can shoot for the entire family trade with a picture like *The Sound of Music* and know that their product will benefit from being so labeled across the nation.

Nizer says, "The day is past when the average motion picture can be considered as having been made for a universal audience. With our new system of classification the various audiences will be able to identify the precise type of picture they want to see . . . or not see."

Valenti says, "The new system is a cooperative venture between the motion picture industry and the public. We have the responsibility to make good pictures and classify them honestly, and this we will do. The public has the responsibility of checking the classification and familiarizing itself with what the symbols mean. It can be a fruitful cooperation."

The *Motion Picture Herald* is more blunt in its analysis: "The new rating system is born out of fear: fear that unless the industry does something about classification, governments at all levels will pass laws." But this same journal was hopeful

77

that the system would solve the problem: "If it works as contemplated, it will be beneficial to the entire industry. If it fails, the consequences may be dire."

Since this system will ultimately affect all of us, whether we see our movies in theaters or on television, details are important, and various questions that naturally come to mind should be answered.

Who determines the classifications? A board of seven people, working in Hollywood. The chairman will be Geoffrey Shurlock, who for many years has administered the Code. Four of his assistants will be former members of his staff, who have worked on the Code for from three to twenty years. The two new members are Jacqueline Bouhoutsos, a psychologist specializing in child behavior, and James C. Bouras, a twenty-seven-year-old lawyer.

When did the system start? Films released after November 1, 1968, will be classified and will be given a clear designation of G, M, R or X. This classification must appear in all advertising.

Will all films be submitted to the classification board? Not quite. The major producing firms have agreed to submit all of their films, so that the typical film you or I shall be seeing in the future will have been classified. But if some independent wants to produce a dirty little quickie titled *The Sadists Meet the Lesbians,* fully aware that it will be classified X, he may save his $150—producers pay from $25 to $3,000 a film for having it classified—and self-apply an X. Or he may release his film without any classification, in which case the theater can advertise it as an X.

Will foreign films be classified, too? Yes. The powerful International Film Importers and Distributors of America, who account for the vast majority of imports from abroad, have agreed that each film they bring in will be submitted for classification. From now on you will know what to expect from a French, Swedish or Japanese film.

Who will operate the system? The National Association of Theater Owners have agreed to abide by the new classifications.

Its president, Julian S. Rifkin, a theater owner from Boston who pilots his own airplane to meetings around the country, was very instrumental in lining up his fellow theater owners in support of the system. He says, "American films have run a cycle in one direction. Toward franker sex. Toward a more adult handling of major themes. And this was desirable. But theater owners were getting complaints. About profanity. About sex that was all right for adults but not all right for kids. So we saw that it was better to self-regulate than to be regulated by outside forces. I like the Mature and Restricted differentiation. There are some films which children ought to see, because the camera is the intellectual instrument of this generation. But there are other films which they ought to see only if their parents take them." Rifkin makes the additional point, "So if you want your daughter to see a Restricted picture, you better bring her to my box office, because if she comes alone I'm not going to let her in. No matter what she says you said. And if the picture is classified X, don't bother to bring her, because under no circumstances will we admit her."

Does the law have any responsibility for policing the system? No. This is a voluntary system of self-control. But of course any law currently on the books covering obscene films still applies. One of the reasons why sexploitation theaters need not pay attention to the classification system is that criminal law already prevents them from admitting minors. Policemen will not keep your children out of an R film, but the theater owner will . . . unless you come along.

Is the cut-off age sixteen or seventeen? Literature explaining the new system uses the cut-off age of sixteen for Restricted and X films, but adds, "Exhibitors may apply a higher age limit if in their judgment it is required by local circumstances." In Pennsylvania and New York, for example, the law already states that minors under the age of seventeen may not purchase obscene materials. In Rhode Island and Reno, Nevada, the law uses the age of eighteen. So the age will vary from place to place.

Are all theaters going to observe the classifications? No. Sexploitation theaters would have no reason to do so, because all their films are automatically X and the law already keeps minors out. Of the rest, all the major chains except one have said they would observe the system. Valenti estimates, "I judge that eighty to eighty-five percent of all theaters will abide by the classifications, and since these comprise most of the big houses, I judge that ninety to ninety-five percent of all admissions sold will be to theaters which are observing our new rules."

Do the churches approve of the plan? Yes. Father Patrick J. Sullivan of the National Catholic Office for Motion Pictures (formerly The Legion of Decency, a severe critic of films in the past) has announced his group's "full and genuine support" of the new system. The Reverend William F. Fore, Protestant director of the Broadcasting and Film Commission of the National Council of Churches, has called for a conscientious effort to make the new plan work. It is highly significant that these two groups made their statements at a joint session, indicating their united support of the plan.

What about the trailer problem? This major source of irritation has been licked. If you take your family to a G film, you can be assured that any trailer you see will also be in the G classification. It might advertise a pretty rough sex film, like *The Fox*, but the scenes shown on screen will be inoffensive. Similarly, if you attend a Mature film, you will see only Mature or General trailers, no matter what type of film they are advertising.

What about printed advertising? Any advertisement for a classified film, whether in a newspaper or on the marquee, must state what category that film falls into. If you go to a Restricted film thinking it was General, the fault is yours.

Has the Hollywood Code been abandoned? No. All movies submitted for classification will still have to be passed by the Code.

Will the classification committee give advice on scripts? Yes. If as a producer you have an important film on which you want a Mature rating, so as to attract children as well as adults, and if your script contains material which might throw that film

80

into a Restricted category, the classification office will advise you on how to eliminate offensive materials so as to escape a Restricted rating. "Of course," Valenti warns, "we'd still reserve judgment till the finished film was in, because they can do a lot of funny things in the shooting. But we'll help out wherever we can."

Is classification a new idea? No. As a matter of fact, the United States was the only major western nation without such a system. Great Britain has prospered under one which started in 1911. One of the reasons why European countries were able to make those great films which had such a profound effect on me years ago was that at home such films were reserved for mature audiences only. In other words, we Americans saw films that the children of Europe were properly not allowed to see.

Is the system foolproof? Of course not. Valenti is quick to point out several difficult problems. "How can the theater owner tell whether a rugged-looking young fellow is sixteen or seventeen? Well, how can a bartender tell whether the same boy is old enough to buy a beer? They learn. Also, suppose a kid twelve years old wants to attend a Restricted movie. His parents won't take him, so he hangs around the box office and begs some chance adult to take him in. As soon as he gets inside he leaves the adult. This will be difficult to police. Also, what do you do when a sixteen-year-old boy brings a fifteen-year-old girl to a Restricted show? He's allowed in, but is he an adult? Is he qualified to bring in an underage person? We think not." Walter Brecher sees a more basic problem: "I have this friend who runs a theater uptown. His problem is this. When he runs a picture for adults only, how does he keep the neighborhood kids from sneaking in through the exit doors which they break down with crowbars?" Nizer says, "It will work if the citizens of this country make it work."

Has there been opposition to the plan? Yes. Saul David, a young and argumentative producer, observes, "It is pathetically funny to hear a generation which cannot prevent or persuade its progeny from embracing drugs, dirt or wholesale bad manners, proposing to stem the tide by classifying motion pictures

81

which even now only dimly reflect the realities known to every high school kid."

Anne Childress, the young movie editor for the *Baltimore News-American*, argues, "Isn't it a little silly, as well as unfair to the theater owner, to impose film censorship when movies like *Divorce Italian Style* and *Never on Sunday* are shown on network television?"

What percentage of films will fall into the various classifications? Neither Valenti nor Nizer has wanted to anticipate what their judges will do. But a Catholic rating agency recently judged thirty-two new films and found only six of which it could give a classification equal to General, and none which it would condemn as X. This meant that four out of five films in that group would have received either a Mature or a Restricted. If this ratio holds, parents are going to have to make decisions on most films as to whether or not they will want their children to see them.

From the evidence I have been able to assemble, I judge that if you consider all films distributed in 1967—247 domestic, 172 imported, 130 low-budget sexploitation quickies—the distribution among the categories might run something like this: General, nineteen percent; Mature, twenty-nine percent; Restricted, twenty-five percent; X, twenty-seven percent.

I would suppose that in the future I will attend mostly Mature and Restricted, plus an occasional General. I doubt that I shall ever again bother with an X. Having been forced to sit through a dozen in preparation for this study, I must say that I found the sex so antiseptic and fairy-tale formalized that I longed for the simpler days when Rhett Butler grabbed Scarlet O'Hara in his arms and carried her upstairs. That was real sex!

The new classification system solves far more problems than it creates. It is a fine alternative to censorship, which I loathe. I agree with Valenti when he says, "Our plan deserves a full year of testing." It is in the interest of all that it be given a fair chance to succeed, for it is much better than any of the alternatives I've heard so far.

The major value of the plan may not be realized until some

years have passed. Then, when the current crop of movies reaches television, the ratings will go with them. Perhaps some plan will be worked out whereby no Restricted film will be shown before eleven o'clock at night. Some networks may prefer not to play them at all for home audiences.

WORK HABITS

How does a writer get his ideas?

In 1963 I became aware of the revolution that was taking place in the field of popular music, but I relegated this fugitive knowledge to the back of my mind as something scarcely worth attention. My tastes in music were classical, although I did enjoy certain popular songs such as "Jack of Diamonds," "Blues in the Night," "Begin the Beguine" and "Night and Day." I also appreciated the great swing numbers like "Chattanooga Choo Choo," "String of Pearls," "Muskrat Ramble," "Bugle Call Rag" and especially "Two O'clock Jump."

In 1965 I began listening to the new music seriously, and much of what I heard I liked. I began filing away, in odd corners of my mind, bits and pieces that had impressed me, and although I was by no means informed on the subject, I was at least conversant with what was happening.

Several times during the course of that year I mentioned my interest in popular music and was distressed that parents who should have been concerned with what their children were listening to showed no concern in the matter. To them the new music was noise, and repellent noise at that. In this cavalier manner an art form that was modifying the lives of their children was dismissed. Looking back on it now, from the vantage point of Woodstock and the mania for music, it seems obvious that the sounds I was listening to were playing a more formative role in American history than books, movies or the moral teaching in schools. Music was the great new language of youth, and people who should have known better were ignoring it.

As a result of my comments, I was invited to judge a rock-and-roll contest, with results as reported. What the article does not cover, for this happened subsequently, was that several of the groups maintained correspondence with me for some years, keeping me informed as to their successes, their new songs, their attitudes toward society. Some of the players I came to know rather well, and I was allowed to assess the new music through their evaluation of it. (Incidentally, every member of every group that I took an interest in went on to college, paying for his education with music.)

For the next three years, whenever I got a chance, I studied rock and soul and protest and country. I was constantly surprised at how good some of the songs were, and I recall one evening in the country when I played my choicest selection of wild songs for André Kostelanetz. The concert lasted four hours and he agreed that some of the music I had chosen stood with the best popular music of this century. He also agreed that much of it was clanging noise.

In late 1968 I began to work seriously on a long novel I had been brooding about for some time. *The Drifters* I called it, a study of six young people knocking around Europe and Africa, and whenever I stared at my typewriter, trying to visualize my characters and to imagine what they would honestly be doing on such and such an occasion, I found them always in the company of music. They were listening to it on some juke box, or playing it on guitars, or singing it on rural hillsides, or simply humming it to themselves when they were alone, savoring its message and its new rhythms.

All the blind preparatory work I had done in the years from

1963 through 1968 began to bear fruit, for although I could not respond to this new music as my young people did, and although it was ten or twenty times more significant to them than it was to me, I could at least hear what they were hearing, and I did not dismiss it as inconsequential. What I thought about it I have reported in the novel.

The point I would like to make here is that when a writer in 1965 engages in a project which may at that time seem completely out of character and of no possible permanent artistic significance to him, he may be doing the precise kind of homework that will be necessary if some project, years ahead and not at that moment dreamed of, is to materialize. A writer is a man condemned to work his way through an enormous mass of experience: organizing it, rejecting it, filing portions of it away. He cannot possibly know at any given moment what will be of crucial value a decade hence.

Quite a few of my *Digest* articles have been filed and permanently forgotten. The experiences they reported will never be of use to me again. They were interesting at the time, and worthy of my attention, but for me their vitality perished on publication. Others, like this curious and out-of-character essay on rock-and-roll, persist in memory, germinate, grow more and more significant and explode at last as full-fledged segments of a novel.

Of the twenty-five essays in this anthology, ten provided basic research on which, sometimes years later, I built books. These essays and their dates of composition are listed here, followed by the related books and their dates of publication:

"Islam: The Misunderstood Religion," 1954——*The Source*, 1965.

"Afghanistan: Meeting Place of Nations," 1955——*Caravans*, 1963.

"Why I Like Japan," 1954——*Sayonara*, 1954.

"The Prison at Recsk," 1956——*The Bridge at Andau*, 1957.

"Malaya: Crossroads of the World," 1957——*The Source*, 1965.

"Hawaii: The Case for Our Fiftieth State," 1958——*Hawaii*, 1959.

"The Magic Hand of Hokusai," 1958——*Hokusai's Sketch Books*, 1958.

"The Prado: Madrid," 1964——*Iberia*, 1968.

"Don't Knock the Rock," 1965——*The Drifters*, 1971.

"Presidential Lottery," 1968——*Presidential Lottery*, 1969.

Don't Knock the Rock

When my neighbor, St. John Terrell, proprietor of the Music Circus, a theater in a tent in Lambertville, N. J., advised me that he had picked me to be one of the judges in the finals of his nationwide rock 'n' roll world championship, I thought he must be out of his cotton-pickin' mind.

"Imagine!" he cried persuasively. "You'll be sitting there with Cousin Brucey on one side and Phil Spector on the other and you'll be deciding the fate of American music."

"Who is Cousin Brucey?" I asked.

Terrell gasped. "You mean you're not with it? You mean you don't listen to one of the most significant forces in the power structure today? You mean . . ."

"Okay. So who's Phil Spector?"

The look this time was compassionate, and from his pocket Terrell produced a newspaper article which showed an extraordinary young man in his early twenties, with very long hair, dressed in exquisite clothes and possessed of one of the sharpest physiognomies I have seen in many years. The article informed teen-agers that their purchase of the records he produces had made him a millionaire three times over.

The fourth judge was to be Harry Haenigsen, the cartoonist, a dignified square who would wear normal clothes and with whom I would be at least able to talk while Cousin Brucey and Phil Spector were communicating with the teenagers. I agreed, and in doing so propelled myself into a fascinating world.

To my astonishment, more than four hundred bands from all parts of America had applied for entry blanks and eightyeight had been chosen to report to the big tent in Lambertville for the initial weeding-out. (The finals would be held on Labor Day.) The winning band would receive $1,000 in cash, a television appearance, a chance to cut a record and a hopeful start on the road to a professional career. When I awakened to the excitement this contest had generated, I decided to take some time off to talk with the contestants and to discover what was happening in their world.

I began with the average adult's sketchy information about rock 'n' roll. I had spent an apprenticeship at the Dom, the Greenwich Village headquarters of the cult, watching with envy as youngsters did the watusi and the frug. I had checked in at Arthur, which had one of the best groups of musicians on hand I'd heard in a long time. And throughout most of the countries of Europe, I had found rock the prevailing choice of teen-agers.

I had also watched on television such shows as *Hullabaloo* and *Shindig*. I knew the Beatles and Elvis and the Dave Clark Five. I thought "Downtown" one of the most compelling songs of this decade and had even spent my own money to buy a copy of the record because I felt it to be a next step in the classic tradition of "One O'Clock Jump" and "The Saints Go Marching In."

I wasn't entirely a square, but I wasn't hip, either. When the new sound was well played, I liked it. And as a novelist I was fascinated by the sociology that accompanied the mania: the long hair, the Edwardian elegance among boys who would normally be repelled by such fashion, the "in" jargon, the tempting experiment with marijuana and LSD, the phenomenon of teen-age screaming and, most important of all, the presence of great protest.

I began my job of judging by reading the stack of applications, and quickly learned that to these young men music was certainly more important than spelling: The Vandles of Northumberland, Pennsylvania; The Infinits of Brooklyn; The Tormenters of Virginia. The Limitations, also from Brooklyn, announced that they were going to play "Hi Heal Sneakers."

But along with the near-illiteracy came the voice of great aspiration, and no one could read these letters without feeling a sense of identification with the writers. Said the Telestars of Trenton: "We are all eager to get ahead and make something of ourselves." One letter exemplified almost ideally the basic attitudes of these bands: "The accordion player is studying music he looks forward to a brake in show business he can play any thing. Our sax man is tops with great showman ship his playing has made many a young fellow envy him. This is a fine good all american team I as there manager enjoy helping them when ever I can."

It was a blazing hot summer afternoon when I reported for the first of the elimination contests, and as the bands arrived and began to unpack their gear I received my first shock. I had expected groups of four or five musicians, carrying guitars, perhaps a double bass and a set of drums. Little Caesar and His Romans from Lewiston, Maine, disabused me. The five young men arrived in a private car, followed by a truck from which they took a dozen large electronic speakers, five amplifiers, four additional microphones, an organ requiring four men to carry it and literally hundreds of feet of special electric cord.

I asked Ronald Poulin, the sixteen-year-old leader of the group, how much money his boys had invested in their equipment and he suggested the following, although he didn't have accurate figures at hand:

One organ	$1,500
Complete set of drums	750
Two saxophones	400
Two guitars	1,600

91

Amplifiers, mikes, etc.	525
Music for 120 songs	100
Trailer	800

All this equipment had been paid for by the money these five boys, the oldest eighteen, had earned playing in night-clubs, at birthday parties and at the Friday night Pal Hops held by the city of Lewiston, at which 1,500 kids regularly appear.

All members of Poulin's team spoke French, took music lessons and could play four or five different instruments. At the end of my questions, Poulin volunteered, "One of the best things about our group is that not one boy has ever been in trouble." (I thought, "Earning the money you have tied up in your gear would keep you too busy.") Poulin added, "We all expect to graduate from high school."

The cost figure for the Little Caesars was by no means the highest, because these boys had no reverberator chambers, no echo boxes, no pillow speakers and no special amplifiers for their organ. In questioning other groups I found that $2,000 was about the minimum and $6,000 not unusual. I also learned that in many cases parents, enticed by the money earned by the Beatles, had supplied both the initial cash and the impetus. It was not unusual to read on an application blank: "Leader Mike Provenzio, age 17. Manager Lila Provenzio, age 37." During the entire world's championships, the judges ran into only one bit of unpleasantness, when a distracted mother threatened to tear the tent apart if her son's band was not given a higher rating. "I could tell they were the best by just listening," she said.

From helping the bands unpack I gained two distinct impressions which never left me. First, the young men engaged in this wild and passionate art form are above average in looks, cleanliness, charm and good manners. Even those who featured outlandish garb—The Prophets of Fredericksburg, Virginia, appeared in togas and leather shoes whose thongs crisscrossed to their knees, while The Monkey Men of Yard-

92

ville, N. J., played from inside a cage which they carried with them—were orderly and delightful to be with.

Second, the musical instrument of itself seems to be less important than the electronic systems that reproduce it and throw it full volume at the listener. If—and this happened during the finals—the electricity happens to go off, the music of this generation subsides into a meaningless whisper. Five amplifiers and four mikes were about the least a self-respecting band could get away with.

One aspect of the rock 'n' roll world took me by surprise. Each of the bands carried a supply of formal calling cards. (Favored were highly marbleized ones in pastel 1890 colors with rounded corners and florid printing styles.) These cards are presented to new groups when introductions are made, and if one watches bands assembling, it is like observing a convention of bullfighters or actors or other professionals. A stately formalism prevails.

I was also surprised by the lack of Negro musicians. If the four hundred bands whose histories I studied were typical, rock 'n' roll is largely a white phenomenon. Could it be that the cost of the required electrical gear excludes the Negro? Was it an accident that the two bands with the most complete electronic gear carried off the $1,000 and $500 prizes?

On the first day I attended, forty-three bands were competing. They were arranged side by side in an enormous circle around the outer edge of the circus tent while the judges sat at desks on the stage in the center, turning to face each of the contestants as they began. I wish everyone who wanted an introduction to rock 'n' roll could have been there during the five minutes before the trials started. Some two hundred musicians, each with his amplifier turned on full volume, ran through his private problems for the last time. It was noise such as the world has rarely heard—absolute cacophony, metallic, brash, the sound of our age.

I don't know for how long the human ear could stand such noise as we heard that day, but I must confess I rather liked it. It hurtled at me from all sides, from some four hundred amplifiers, and was as near to total noise as anything I have ever experienced. A music manufacturer had approached Mr. Terrell some days earlier, proposing that he be allowed to supply all contestants with the instruments to be used in the finals. His argument was: "I don't make the best musical instruments in the country, but I do make the loudest. Our engineers have come up with a new electronic circuit which eliminates all the old-style music and produces instead the perfect metallic sound."

He demonstrated the new development with one of his guitars. Today's guitar is solid wood; the old-fashioned vibrating chamber had to be eliminated because it produces music with unwanted overtones rather than an uncontaminated metallic impulse which can be amplified electronically. I recognized the sound coming out of this manufacturer's new-style guitar as the one that I had grown to like in "hard" rock 'n' roll bands, and during the ensuing contests I invariably found myself voting for the band that could produce precisely this sound.

In the songs of rock 'n' roll, if indeed they can be called songs, I noticed the advent of much protest music stemming in a direct line from ballads like Nat King Cole's success of 1951, "They Tried to Tell Us We're Too Young." In one song the leader of the pack is killed in a motorcycle crash, but that is all right because he died living up to the code of his gang. In another, the musicians lament the fate of the world: if they cleaned things up in Vietnam there'd still be Selma, Alabama. One song which gained enthusiastic approval told of how a boy was refused admission to high school because his hair was too long. Terrell explained, "Rock is being married to folk music and the offspring is protest."

On the day of the finals I met for the first time Cousin Brucey, a tall, handsome, well-groomed and literate young man. His radio and television schedules (he is a disk jockey for ABC) had necessitated arriving by helicopter, and he asked if I would excuse him while he slipped into an iridescent blue-and-silver suit that was notably more dignified—even reserved—than it sounds. He had an extraordinary way with the teenagers who crowded the tent and referred constantly to his radio and television shows, which apparently have an enormous impact on younger people along the Eastern Seaboard.

"It may surprise you," he told me, "to know that my most important following is in the colleges. They don't have too much time to listen to music, and they know they can trust me to spot the new trends."

Along the edge of the crowd I noticed an important political leader, a man with an advanced degree in music, whom one would not expect to be interested in rock. "I'm not," he said, "but my kids heard that Cousin Brucey was going to be here and they consider him as more significant than Albert Schweitzer, Adlai Stevenson and John F. Kennedy together."

We had received some evidence of the disk jockey's power sometime earlier. Mr. Terrell had risked his shirt by importing The Righteous Brothers in hopes they would fill his tent at two dollars and three dollars a head, but ticket sales were deplorable and the affair was about to be a bust when an expert on such matters asked, "Have you advertised?"

Terrell said that he always did, and the man asked, "Where?" Terrell rattled off the names of the newspapers, and the man expressed amazement. "Newspapers? The people who come to hear The Righteous Brothers never read. Get on the radio. That's all they listen to."

So Terrell called a disk jockey, who made a brief comment on his show to the effect that all the cousins who were really in the know were trekking on down to the Music Circus to hear the living greatest. And within a few hours all seats were sold.

At one point in Bruce's dialogue with his fans a young man asked, "Cousin Brucey, it says here that points will be awarded for showmanship. What's showmanship?" Cousin Brucey thought for a moment, made two false starts, then pointed to an astonishing young man approaching the stage and cried, "Here's showmanship."

It was Phil Spector, the twenty-four-year-old king of the rocks. He wore a skin-tight Edwardian suit with the narrowest trousers I've yet seen. (Explained one contestant when I asked about trousers, "You might say, Mr. Michener, that any boy in this competition would rather drop dead than put his pants on after he had put his shoes on." Another boy said, "Frankly, if you can pull your trousers on over your shoes, neither the trousers nor the shoes are worth wearing.")

Spector also wore a jazzy white-lace cavalier shirt with the biggest ruffles at the cuffs so far made, plus sharply pointed boots with three-inch heels. His hair was beyond my powers of description: a kind of real wig hanging down to his shoulders and teased into a wonderful bundle. The kids in the audience went wild with approval.

In the judging arena, Spector told me, "You listen for the lead voice. If he can convey, the band can make it."

"What else do you listen for?"

"A total beat. If they have a total beat, they can make it."

It quickly became apparent that the world championship would go either to the long-haired, very clever Rockin' Paramounts of Buffalo, N.Y., or to the controlled, big-tone Galaxies of Trenton, N.J. The Paramounts were handicapped by the fact that two of their band had to be lifted onto the stage before they could play. One was sick with mononucleosis and had covered the distance from Buffalo in an improvised ambulance; another, with long flowing hair, had broken something while playing football. But when they were propped up they played like demons and I shudder to think what they might have accomplished in good health. Cousin Brucey whispered, "These boys are bound to become top professionals."

The Galaxies featured the hardest, most metallic sound heard in the competition, plus a wild rhythm and a screaming vocal. They had perfected a clever way of ending each number with a coda in which tempo, key, frenzy and volume were all accelerated—I shouted to Haenigsen, "At last I know what escalation means"—so they had to be declared the winners.

It was a popular verdict. Each of the last six bands was of professional quality. As soon as the winners had been announced, things started happening. The Merv Griffin television show. An invitation to cut a record. Engagements in areas unexplored before. And that good old $1,000 in cash to pay for some fresh electronic equipment.

My lasting impressions of the world championship are varied. I found that I liked rock 'n' roll in music the way I like pepper in cooking: not as a steady diet but appreciated as a vital accent. I especially like the young people who made the music, my favorite contestant being sixteen-year-old Jon Van Eaton, leader of The Trees from Trenton. Jon has studied music, plays the guitar, clarinet, bass, sax, oboe, bassoon, harmonica, English horn and flute. He says of his group, "We try to be gentlemen and scholars and I suppose I'll go on to college. If I make it, it'll be because music paid the way."

The best thing about the competition was that incredible five minutes when the bands were tuning up (tuning their electronics, that is, not their instruments). But the experience I shall not soon forget was a report on The Impostors of New York, written by their fourteen-year-old drummer. This letter seems to me to summarize what rock 'n' roll means to many teen-agers:

> Our group is one which can make good and go professional. Even though we are only fifteen we have the most natural music talent in Peter Cooper Village or Stuyvesant Town either. Our leader, Barry Flast, is a very outstanding person. He writes music like there is no tomorrow. Already he has written 50 songs. He like myself feels a strange new power when we play. All of us love our music to us it is the second most important thing except school. When I get up on that stage to practice I feel as if I could cry because nobody is around to hear us. Our parents say give up: stop dreaming. But I listen to the radio and say to myself: Oh, if only Cousin Brucey could hear the songs played by we Imposters. Would they sound professional to him? I say they would if we touched them up a bit.
>
> Very truly yours,
>
> Mark Litt.

P.S. Barry Flast has said my feel for the drums is re-markable. He says I am an empressionist as well as a great drummer that is one of the reasons this group is on the ball.

The reason why The Impostors couldn't get to the world championship was a crisis common to such groups: their families had taken them to five different locales for their vacations and they couldn't get together for practice.

THE SPIRIT OF THE AGE

I was lucky in that I came along at a time when the reading public of the United States was eager to inspect the world beyond its boundaries. Our traditional insularity had been exploded by World War II, the growth of the airplane and the number of American companies who were sending their men to work at installations overseas. It was a rare family which did not have some member or some close neighbor who had spent time out of the country.

Fortuitously, I corresponded to this awakening. I wanted to write about the very areas that Americans in general wanted to read about. It was a happy symbiosis, in that the more I traveled and wrote, the more the reading public supported me in my exploration.

But this did not come about by accident. As a boy I had prepared myself by the most extensive reading in geography and history; as a young man I traveled widely both in this country and abroad; and as a working man I had continued my study of foreign cultures. If the American family was about to expand outward, I had the background to write about its experiences.

At no time during my long years of preparation did I even

vaguely perceive what was about to happen, or that I was working toward an objective. I understood less than most the vast change that was under way. I would suppose it was people like the editors of *The New York Times* and *Time* magazine, who were already sending their men abroad, who first appreciated what was happening. It was men like David Rockefeller of the Chase Manhattan Bank and Juan Trippe of Pan American Airways who understood the outward explosion. And certainly it was people like the managers of the *Reader's Digest* who were establishing overseas editions which would be printed in twenty foreign countries, in thirteen different languages, and in an edition of twenty-nine million copies.

They understood. I was a foot-loose young man who stumbled happily, and largely unconsciously, onto the scene. That my time coincided with their time was a lucky break for me, but in some subtle way that is reserved for the semi-autonomic artist, I came close to representing the spirit of my age, insofar as this one characteristic was concerned.

Thus I saw very early that the Muslim world was bound to be important not only to the world at large but especially to the United States; I consciously spent time in Muslim countries like Indonesia, Malaya, Turkey and Tunis. I knew unconsciously that the Pacific Ocean area was going to play a significant role in American life. I saw that Japan would become our principal trade ally, our constant point of contact in Asia. And long before Hawaii became a state, or had assumed its central role in the Pacific, I perceived that this would happen, and that Americans of all persuasions would be concerned about Hawaii and would want to know more about it. The same was true of Israel.

But I did not guess that Spain, about which I had long wanted to write a highly personal book, would shortly become one of the principal tourist countries of Europe, with 24,-000,000 visitors in 1967, whereas a few years before, it had had only 500,000. I had thought, when writing a group of articles on Spain for the *Digest*, that this country was a private thing, savored by odd types like me but not appreciated by the general public. How wrong I was.

Why I Like Japan

AUGUST, 1956

One of the strangest aspects of my adult life has been the fact that each week I receive two or three letters from Americans who are desperately eager to get back to Japan. I can almost predict the letter that will arrive next week:

> I am a GI who fought against Japan in World War II. After the surrender I was stationed in Tokyo and signed up for an additional tour of duty there. Then I was sent home and for three years I've been trying to get back. Mr. Michener, I'll do anything at all if you can only help me. What I had in mind was, would you write to the Army or maybe President Eisenhower.

And the letter will be signed by some young man I have never seen.

Why do sensible young Americans dream of returning to a country where it is impossible to earn a living, where the ways of life are alien to our own and where the future is uncertain? I don't know the answers, but I have been able to make a few generalizations.

First, of course, is love. Many of our young soldiers had never dated American girls before going to war, and Japanese girls can be utterly delectable. But while our boys were in Japan they wisely concluded that it would be difficult to take a Japanese bride home with them. So thousands of them said tearful goodbyes at Yokohama, but when they reached the United States—and I have hundreds of letters to prove this— these young lovers found that they could not forget Keiko or Kimiko or Kazuko, and in frenzy they were willing to try anything to get back to Japan and "marry the girl who I was afraid wouldn't fit in."

There was nothing especially Japanese about such situations. I know other young soldiers who served in Iceland and went back to marry Icelandic girls. Certainly this explosion of youthful love occurred many times in Germany and England. What was special in Japan was the agonizing debates our men went through while contemplating marriage to a Japanese girl: another race, another color and belonging to a land that had so recently been our mortal enemy.

Some of the most poignant love stories I know took place in Japan. Three years ago as Christmas approached in Tokyo a young Yale graduate who worked for a famous American journal was tragically bewildered over the question of whether to marry his Japanese girl. She was a lovely person, but his good friends pointed out that she might imperil his promotion. The fact that she could speak no English would, they argued, damage his chances of moving into new lines of work. I was afraid he might crack up.

Then, happily, everything was settled for him. His big boss in New York cabled him to come home at once, to a big new job. So he packed hurriedly and we were glad that his months of indecision were over. He did not marry the girl.

But at the end of his 10,000-mile flight home he stepped on to the gray, wintry asphalt of New York and gasped, "I left behind the best part of my life." And that very day he hopped another plane, flew another 10,000 miles, burst into Tokyo on Christmas Eve and married the girl. Immediately thereafter he plumped her into a third plane and flew all the way back to his boss and said, "Meet the wife." She is the darling of her community and he has prospered in his work.

So most of the letters I receive lament some lost love, and to these I invariably reply: "You had really better try to forget this girl and marry some attractive girl in your home town. Believe me, things usually work out better that way."

But invariably there is in the batch of mail one letter which haunts me and sets my mind to wandering through paths of beauty. "What I miss," these letters say, "is the Japanese way of life. I want to enjoy that peaceful, simple life again."

Then I do whatever I can to help my correspondent return, hoping that when he has again tasted the rare wine of Japanese living he will knock the nostalgia out of his system and return to America better able to bring into our life some of the precious things he found in an Asian culture.

I say these letters haunt me, because they remind me of the loveliness I found in Japan. Here is what I remember.

The single fact which best explains Japan is the crowdedness. Into an area little larger than California, Japan squeezes in nearly 90,000,000 people. This means that ways of life which apply to other parts of the world cannot exist in Japan, and I have grown to respect the ways in which the Japanese evolve new patterns of living.

Take the matter of gardens, for example. The average house cannot afford a spacious lawn, so the Japanese gardener has become incredibly expert in transforming tiny bits of land into an illusion of space. So in Japan a handsome rock, which might look like a mountain if set down in a tiny garden, fetches a higher price than a tree might in London or Chicago.

The trick of making a little land suggest a huge park becomes almost a game, and the skilled gardener will know where to place a stone lantern so that it creates an illusion of space.

When I first saw these tiny gardens I yearned for the open spaces of land-rich Colorado and the big lawns of Pennsylvania, but later I discovered one of the profound truths of Japan: a minute portion, exquisitely contrived, may yield more of the essence of life than a great glob thrown haphazardly into one's face.

103

If it is the very essence of life you seek, visit Japan. The wine is served piping hot in the tiniest thimble bowls, and it is better than gulping beakers of cold sauterne. Some of the finest Japanese sculptures are no larger than a walnut and can be worn as the tassel to one's belt. In the Japanese dance, one tightly controlled gesture stands for an entire routine, and in the theater the merest corner of a handkerchief pressed to the eye symbolizes unbearable grief.

This concentration of human expression into small forms arose partly because Japan was so impossibly crowded, for not only are the four islands of Japan quite small; they are composed mostly of mountains where food cannot be grown or villages established. Of the world's major nations, Japan provides the lowest percentage of arable land. Of every hundred acres, eighty-six are useless except for timber. All the people must crowd onto the remaining fourteen acres.

The crowding is inconceivable to an American. Once I rode at dusk through miles of Japanese countryside and saw not a single field, for the houses of the farmers clung hungrily to the highway, until I realized with a shock that I had entered a new city. There had been no countryside.

I recall long walks through the fields themselves where for miles there would not be a single tree, for the land was too precious to waste on trees. I saw farms where there was no flower garden, temples with no lawn, farms with no edging of wild shrubbery.

Why does such a country captivate so many Americans? I think it is because here one sees with absolute clarity the fact that all men live upon the land and what it can produce. Here, wherever you look, you see humble people wrestling with their tiny fragment of soil and you catch some glimmer of the grandeur of man.

Japan also pleases me mightily because it is so lovely to look at. Its panorama of beauty is so varied, and the movement from one amazing scene to another so quickly taken that my eye is constantly charmed.

Rise early and see the mists of morning tenderly creeping

away from the rice fields that stretch out from every sleepy village. Stand on some hillside at midday and see the thousand rural workers fanning out over the fields, toiling endlessly in the shadow of some magnificent mountain. Walk along some curving beach of glistening sand at nightfall and see the moon coming up against pine trees of immemorial age. Truly, a man would have to be blind not to see beauty in Japan.

Nowhere is the beauty of the sea so inescapable as here. Sometimes the mountains rush down and plunge their precipices into the pounding surf. Elsewhere the sea creeps silently into some glorious bay fringed by lamplit fishing villages. No matter where you travel in Japan, the cold gray sea of winter and the pastel oceans of summer are near at hand, for without the sea crowded Japan could not live. It supplies the abundant fish that combine with rice to yield a nourishing diet.

As for the mountains, they are the dominant beauty of Japan. On them tall pines grow and deer flourish. Down their sides torrential streams plummet bearing silt, and as soon as the merest fragment of land begins to collect along their banks, hundreds of human beings cluster and chop out fields so small you cannot even see them from a hundred yards away. Here is where the rice fields begin, and as the mountain bases flatten out into substantial fields, millions of men quickly accumulate, taking strength as it were from the mountains which throw down each year a little soil and much water for the rice.

Of Mount Fuji, the queen of all mountains, little new can be said. Some artists have spent their lives contemplating its serene majesty, but none has completely captured the wonder of this perfect volcano that dominates central Japan. Its gently sloping sides and irregular snowy cap are exactly as they would be if one set out to draw the world's ideal mountain, and the varied aspects in which Fuji can be seen contribute to this unearthly quality. Once I saw Fuji when it was truly a heavenly mountain.

A winter's rain had been falling upon dead snow at the base of the mountain, and mists had risen so that the earth around me had been blotted out. I was riding down from a lake and had to hurry before night overtook me on the obscured road, when suddenly I looked back over my shoulder and saw an overpowering sight. Directly above the low mists and suspended free of them hung mighty Fuji, its lower rocks washed free of snow. Its heavy nightcap of snow rose far into the pale blue sky, and there the majestic volcano hovered, a magnificent cone of brown and white, with a thin wisp of snow blowing free from its summit.

Then, as I continued my way downward through the mists, I came upon the inevitable little village which in America would house perhaps sixty people. But this was Japan, and there were nearly six thousand. They were the crowded, patient, hard-working children of Fuji, grubbing along the foot of the mountain for a few grains of rice.

But I would not delight in Japan if it were only a place of fine scenery. It is the unpredictable, friendly, hard-working and sometimes stubborn people who provide the permanent attraction.

Like many Americans who have grown to love Japan, I first met the Japanese in war, where in the steaming South Pacific they were terrible enemies. Then, like many of my friends in uniform, I next saw the Japanese in their homeland, and they seemed at first aloof and almost morbidly serious. In those cold days of little food, the people of Tokyo hurried along crowded streets with never a smile, their minds apparently absorbed in problems of unbearable gravity. Even today, strangers on a hurried trip through Japan rarely attain even a clue as to what the people of Japan are like, for in no other nation of the world does a frigid and formal exterior so completely mask a warm and even hilarious interior life.

Oh, the boisterous fun of knowing a Japanese family well! Take the letter I received last month from a former GI:

> I flew back from the front in Korea with an introduction from my buddy to a family in Kamakura. When I first met them, they stood like statues and I thought, let's get out of here. Ten days later, at the end of my leave, I

wanted to stay with them forever. Looking back, I think it was the constant laughter.

In recent years several million Americans have discovered this hidden laughter. It dominates their most poignant memories of Japan. Let me explain how gently this laughter arises.

The Kato family lives on the outskirts of Tokyo, in a small house with practically no furniture. The floors are immaculately clean and when you arrive some evening with Kato-san, he shows you where to kick off your shoes. Then, ceremonially, he seats you beside a brazier, glowing with charcoal which will warm the tips of your fingers and little more.

Mrs. Kato appears with hot green tea, and the four children file in. The talk is extremely stilted, but as the evening wears on and as the food passes around, everyone starts to unbend and you suddenly realize that most of the night has been spent laughing.

What about? Well, the Katos tell ridiculous stories about themselves. They relate amusing incidents involving Americans. They burlesque the police, the Russians, pompous officials and Americans in jeeps. When it is time to leave, you hope you will be invited back to such delightful surroundings, and as you meet with the Katos during the ensuing months, you find that you have rarely before laughed so much or enjoyed so deeply the pleasures of simply talking with new friends.

It is the crowdedness of Japan that has produced these enviable virtues. The house cannot be large, therefore it must be compact and people must sit together. There is no loneliness for the stranger to get lost in. The pressure of life is so great that you work especially hard to make the inner home a place of relaxation and contentment.

But if the Japanese are so much fun when you know them off guard, why are they so rigidly formal the rest of the time? If they laugh so much in a circle of friendship, why do so many lonely Japanese commit suicide each year? If, as individuals, they are the gentlest and tenderest people I have ever known, why do they, as a nation, present such a formidable appearance?

Four powerful traditions of Japanese life determine behavior, and to transgress these in public would be unthinkable. The first requirement is that Japanese must always exhibit a stoical ability to endure hardship or pain. In English one might say, "They can take it." In the Japanese army, which was founded upon this principle, the constant admonition to soldiers who showed signs of cracking up was, "Put strength in your stomach."

Under pressure from this requirement of stoical fortitude, Japanese can perform extraordinary feats. Men will hike miles in a blazing sun. Women will toil in the fields up to the day their baby is born and resume work soon thereafter. Some often display unbelievable stoicism in sublimating their own desires if their parents object to them.

The second requirement is that one's duty must be performed with no public display of emotion. I saw a girl of nineteen who had hoped to marry a Frenchman say goodbye to him at the airport. Even after the plane had been aloft for fifteen minutes her supremely controlled face showed not a quiver of pain, although she was to commit suicide three days later. Most Americans who know Japan can recite cases in which a family has sat stoically through the long evening of a day which had brought great tragedy. To weep over the loss of a fortune, or the death of child, would be unseemly.

The third controlling tradition is loyalty . . . to Japan, to the Emperor and to one's immediate superior. The history of Japan is practically the history of this profound tradition.

The final characteristic, of course, is politeness. I have often watched two Japanese meet, click their heels, press their hands against their sides and engage in a series of at least six formal bows. You become adept in detecting which of the men has the more important job, for the other man bows a little lower, stays down a wee bit longer.

This extreme politeness marks most aspects of Japanese life. In the old days, two professional wrestlers, each weighing at least four hundred pounds, would bow, kneel and pursue an involved ritual for ninety minutes before finally trying to tear each other to bits. Today, because of life's increased tempo, the bowing is restricted to about eight minutes.

The finest exhibition of the required Japanese characteristics is in the classical theater, where time-honored plays are built around the stoical behavior of feudal life. For example, a loyal underling will sacrifice his own son in order to save the heir of his lord; but even as he kills his child he will suppress all emotion and will then exhibit an exaggerated politeness to the enemy who has commanded such a hideous act.

One of the things I enjoyed most about Japan was the fact that whenever I thought I understood the country, some utterly zany event would prove that I knew very little.

Once I inspected a southern prefecture with a team of efficiency experts sent down by General MacArthur to eliminate the fearful duplication of work that hamstrings Japanese administration. We found 1,100 employees who sat around doing nothing. For example, in one office a man would copy in longhand all papers handed to him. Then he would pass them along to two other men, who would also copy them. Finally, all three copies would be filed in the same drawer, and no one could recall why the system had grown up.

"Eliminate those eleven hundred unnecessary jobs at once," our team ordered.

"At once," the governor agreed.

Eight months later an investigator found that not a single man had been fired. "Didn't General MacArthur order you to eliminate eleven hundred jobs?" the investigator demanded.

"Of course he did," agreed the governor, bowing low. "But he didn't say to fire the men."

"But why did you keep them around, doing nothing?"

The governor looked up in great surprise, "In Japan," he said, "we never break another man's rice bowl."

"But what work are you going to give them?" the American pleaded.

"This time," the governor explained softly, "they will copy a different group of papers, in a different department."

Many of the apparent contradictions make sense. Consider the case of a friend of mine who encountered serious trouble because he fired at a burglar who was wrecking his home. "It was lucky for you," the police growled, "that you didn't hit him."

"He was robbing me!" my friend protested.

"But when you fired he was clearly running away from your house."

In court the officials minced no words: "If you shoot a burglar who seems about to enter your house, you are in serious trouble, because then you must prove that the burglar was going to injure you personally and not your goods. If you fire at him while he is actually in your room, it isn't so bad, because you can argue that you were really afraid he might assault you. But if you fire at a defenseless burglar who is already running away, you are in great trouble, for he has already demonstrated that he had no intention of harming you personally."

"But what about the stuff he stole?" my friend cried.

"Who would shoot a poor burglar just for a few trinkets?" the court asked.

Later my friend showed me a newspaper clipping and admitted that he hadn't appreciated how lucky he was that his shot had missed. For a burglar had successfully sued a victim who had left a ladder lying carelessly around. The robber had stumbled over it as he was *leaving* the house, and the owner was fined for negligence.

Similarly, an American woman whose house burned down complained to the fire department that it had been delinquent in providing protection, only to find that the fire chief was having *her* arrested, on the grounds that anyone who permitted his house to catch fire was obviously a public menace.

I have said that Japan is probably the politest nation on earth, but this does not apply to trains or subways. I have frequently been about to board a coach when some 105-pound woman with a baby strapped to her back would hit me from the rear, elbow me aside as I caromed off a doorjamb, and dive for a seat without ever causing her baby one bad bounce. Once I took an American football player on a subway trip, and after having been blocked and tackled by a handful of tiny Japanese women, he grunted, "Boy, if Southern Methodist could grab eleven of these girls, goodbye Notre Dame!"

And occasionally something happens in Japan that makes you stop in wonder. Not long ago an ineffectual art teacher in southern Japan decided to rob a bank, but he was such a mild-mannered little man that he was unable to scare the tellers into giving him any money. A few weeks later he tried again with no success. So late one afternoon he marched officially into the bank dressed like a doctor. Announcing that the government was concerned about health in the area, he lined up the fifteen employees.

"You look awful," he said, whereupon he popped pills into the fifteen mouths, and when the employees fell to the floor in writhing death struggles that killed thirteen of them, he calmly proceeded to rob the bank. He had given everyone strychnine.

Less gruesome was the case of a handsome young clerk who worked for a business acquaintance of mine. This clerk handled his job so well that when my friend had to go to New York on a short trip, he left everything in the clerk's hands.

As soon as the airplane was aloft this quiet young man hired eight of the longest, blackest limousines in Tokyo, reserved an entire summer resort, invited all his business associates to a week-long celebration, carted two dozen of the most famous geisha girls up to the resort for entertainment, and gave everyone several handsome presents.

The bill was over $26,000 and nearly broke the company. When the boss got back from New York to pick up the pieces, the young clerk explained it all quite simply. "When you left me in charge of this important business, I wanted to act like a real American."

The incident that I most frequently recall took place when some Japanese engineers called on the American expert who handed out permits for new buildings. "I can't give you a permit for such a crazy operation," the American snorted. "Who ever heard of building the entire basement of a skyscraper on top of the ground?"

111

Patiently, the Japanese explained a new scheme they had dreamed up. "When the basement is completed, we rock it back and forth until it sinks into the ground level with the pavement. Then we build the skyscraper on top of it."

"Impossible!" cried the American. "It can't be done."

"Esteemed sir," the Japanese asked quietly, "how do you suppose we built the building you're sitting in?"

I have known many nations with attractive landscapes and appealing people, and if that was all that Japan contained, it would still be a lovely land, but it would not be unique. The essential element of the nation is its extraordinary love of beauty.

Japan is a nation of artists, where even the most inconspicuous kitchen utensil may be an object of purest beauty. Whenever I revisit the crowded islands, I feel that I have come back to the place where art lives in the streets.

I have always suspected that the Japanese acquire their exquisite taste in the tedious years they must spend learning to write. Their language is so complicated and the ideographs so complex, that students spend about six years memorizing and drawing characters. In the process, each student becomes a minor artist, for he must draw exquisitely, shade well and place his characters with perfection. In other words, while he learns writing he also learns art.

I think the most perfect expression of this nationwide art comes in pottery, which enjoys a special place in Japanese life. Consider the Kagogawa family. Their total income is less than $3,000 a year, but I was present one night when Kagogawa-san arrived home with a simple clay bowl which looked to me as if it had been slapped into some country kiln after having been decorated by some amateur with a dripping brush.

But the Kagogawa family studied it with rapture while their father said, "I bought it at the exhibition for only a hundred and thirty-five dollars."

As I tried to discover what was special about the bowl, I reflected that in America I would pay about six dollars for such a piece of kitchen crockery. But over the months, as I lived with the $135 bowl and studied it, I had to admit that it had been created by a profound artist, whereas my six-dollar American bowl would have been machine-made. The rough exterior and the slapdash design grew constantly more lovely on Kagogawa-san's bowl, and I finally agreed that he had bought a bargain.

Here are the simple things I have seen recently in Japan that were so beautiful they should have been in museums: a handle to a garden gate, a soup bowl, fabric for a girl's dress, a doorway into a kitchen, a tobacco pouch and its lock, a pine tree bending over a stone lantern, a sliding door, a charcoal drawing of a horse, a spray of flowers in a shallow dish. In Japan art invades all life.

I must quickly point out, however, that the casual visitor may never see this hoard of beauty, for the average Japanese community is not externally attractive. Small houses of weather-beaten boards line muddy streets, while public areas are apt to be littered because so many people must use them.

Many Americans who visit Japan depart with a sense of keen disappointment. "Where was the beauty you speak about?" they ask.

It lies within the home, within the heart. Here is a grimy, mud-spattered house that resembles a million others in Japan, but step inside and it becomes a chaste, inspiring temple of beauty. Floors and walls blend together in subtle straw colors. Raw wood, unvarnished and made smooth by years of patient care, gives the room character, while set into the wall stands the tokonoma, a combination religious shrine and art gallery, where some exquisite piece of pottery holds a flower against a hanging picture.

When a meal is served in this home, each plate and cup is a work of art, while the food is arranged more carefully than the ordinary western flower garden. And when you go to bed at night, the comforters that cover you as you sleep on the floor are delicately brocaded. In the morning, of course, you peer out upon the careless, perfect garden that invites you to enjoy all nature.

In such an unpretentious house an elderly woman once

113

served me tea in a fragile brown-and-green cup with an uneven lip and a splashed design. It was obviously the most precious treasure of the household, and as custom required she offered me the cup so that its most handsome aspect should face me. Equal to the occasion, I declined that portion of the cup and turned it slowly away from my lips, drinking from a rougher section.

After the ceremony I inquired as to why this particular cup was so precious. "It's from Korea," she said. "It's more than a thousand years old."

"Why do you treasure a Korean cup? Why not Japanese?"

"A Korean piece reminds us of how fortunate we have been in Japan to acquire things of beauty from all nations."

Later, when I found that the cup was historically famous and worth at least $20,000, I asked why such a valuable object should be used so regularly.

"Because it was made to drink from," the woman explained.

So in Japan you find few first-rate public museums, but a minor museum in almost every home. If a picture is delightful, hang it where it can be enjoyed daily. In Japan you will find no imposing mansions crammed with loot from Europe or China. A family needs only a few fine things.

"In the home," says the Japanese, "is where you really need beauty."

And to the home the heart returns.

Hawaii: The Case for Our Fiftieth State

AUGUST, 1953

Every American who can possibly do so ought to visit Hawaii. It is a rare experience: physical beauty, exotic flowers, a new way of life and a social experiment of world importance. No American could visit these fortunate islands without feeling proud that they are part of his country. When you have been in Hawaii for weeks or even months, you will still fail to believe that one small portion of the world could be so crammed with wonder.

There are the mountains! They rise from behind the harbor in great purple heights, clothed forever in forest, with waterfalls drifting down, with clouds hanging above them. They are among the loveliest in the world, for they are accessible, they are close to the sea, and they are an intimate part of island life.

There is the Pali! I have been in Hawaii many times and have been shown the Pali by almost everyone I met, yet I have never ceased to enjoy this remarkable cliff. It is my favorite scene in all America. It is one of many cliffs, green clad with deep serrated valleys, as if massive fingers had shredded the jagged mountains. These cliffs stretch for miles along the coast, and from the Pali you catch an unequaled view of the Pacific. To your left, in a wide-sweeping arc, the giant cliffs enclose a coastal valley of dazzling color. The earth is red, the fields are green, the sea beyond is blue, the rain clouds that sweep over the cliff are gray, and at rare spots the cliffs themselves expose enduring rock of sullen black. This play of color, this majesty of panorama form a theater in which the drama is forever changing. Now a sudden fog invades the valleys, and the cliffs move in and out of vision like a ballet. Now the sun shines upon incoming rain clouds and builds enormous rainbows, two or three concentrically. Or again, on rare days, there will be no cloud and the unhampered tropic sun will illuminate the hills and the shore and the sea as it does nowhere else. At night there is the moon. And all of this is within a few miles of downtown Honolulu.

There are the islands! Hawaii is composed of many islands, each with its own peculiar wonders. Some, like Kahoolawe, are barren wastes, for larger islands cut off their rain. Others, like the main island of Hawaii, contain vast cattle ranches. Still others, like Kauai, have deep and jagged canyons splashed with color. And Oahu contains many things: Honolulu, huge airports, Pearl Harbor, agricultural areas and, as we shall see, a dense tropical jungle. I doubt if anyone knows all the islands of Hawaii, but to know even a part of one—say tiny Waikiki, which is about one-millionth of Hawaii—is to enjoy at least something of a rare land.

There are the flowers! There are long roads lined with flowering trees that droop beautiful blossoms where other trees show leaves. I know a hedge nearly a mile long composed of hibiscus flowers in at least twenty different colors. There are many lath greenhouses in which bank clerks raise rare orchids, and there are open fields where professionals raise common orchids and sell the lovely flowers by the half-ton. Wherever you go there are flowers, more flowers than you have ever seen in one spot before.

Within recent years these prolific flowers have become a major industry, for airplanes flying back to the mainland carry cargoes of orchids to shops throughout America. Most spectacular of the flowers sent to the mainland are the anthurium, big heart-shaped glossy red flowers the size of a dinner plate, from the center of which springs a golden stamen. Even the leaves of this flower are gaudy, twenty inches long by ten wide, and a display of anthurium is startling.

Hawaiians prize the gingers, and rightly so, for the torch ginger is a fantastic thing. It grows fifteen feet high on a handsome red stem that could be used as a club, at the end of which appears a whorl of brilliant red petals, a thin rim of orange dust and a massive central cone that resembles a banana flower. It is an unusual flower, brutal, heavy, florid and unforgettable.

Shampoo ginger I hesitate to describe, for it is constructed like the torch but has a head filled with soft liquid. Children love to get a good grip on the thick stem, whirl it about their shoulders and burst the flower upon some playmate's head, whereupon a rich soapy lather runs down the victim's face and he can, if he wishes, shampoo his hair in natural soap.

It is shell ginger which makes up for the grotesqueries of its cousins. On long spikes bending gracefully to the earth, this gentle, exquisite plant produces hundreds of fragile pale pink or white shells. But lovely as this flower is, my favorite is the small pikake, a jasmine-type rarity. Sometimes, on leaving Hawaii, I have been lucky enough to receive a pikake lei, and for days thereafter, though Hawaii lay far behind me, I could smell those magic flowers and imagine myself once more in the fortunate islands.

The most treasured flower flown to the mainland is the flamboyant, spirit-of-the-islands bird of paradise. It is hopeless to try to describe this flower, but to me it resembles an island on fire from which set out gorgeous green-and-purple canoes filled with warriors in gaudy garments. The colors are those of Hawaii, and it seems as if this unique flower had been created to represent these islands.

Finally, in the end as in the beginning, there are the volcanoes. Somewhere around sixty million years ago a 1,500-mile break occurred in the ocean floor, along which the Hawaiian Islands now rest. This break started near Midway and ran southeast in a fairly straight line to the present island of Hawaii at the southeast extremity. As in other volcanic regions

117

(notably New Zealand), the subterranean movement of magma (molten rock originating within the earth and forming the substances thrown out by volcanoes) was from west to east at an indescribably slow rate. Thus the volcanoes which built the northwest islands appeared first, and those islands are much the oldest, whereas the southeast volcanoes—and hence the southeast islands—are relative youngsters. In fact, the volcanoes on the island of Hawaii are even now in process of building that island, so that no one can safely predict what it will look like eventually.

Consider Oahu, the central island. In the middle period of Hawaii's geologic age, two volcanoes erupted from the ocean floor, the larger to the west and the small one some twenty miles away. Soon—within a few million years—the western cone collapsed, as volcanoes must, and left its sides exposed to ocean erosion and to the winds, while the eastern cone continued to vomit lava. More eons passed and oozing lava obscured each of the original volcanoes, and within a few million more years the flow had accumulated to such an extent that the ocean between had filled in and the two islands had become one.

Now rains fell for a million years and eroded deep valleys. Infant volcanoes sprang up and changed the face of the land. The ocean, driving always from the northeast, cut away the northeast cliffs and formed the majestic Pali. Then, dramatically, the newborn island subsided 250 feet into the ocean, so that only a small portion remained above sea level.

Now it was the sea that fell away, all around the earth, and Oahu rose sixty feet higher than it does today. Vast sandy beaches were uncovered, and marshes. As if in celebration the hills erupted dozens of new volcanoes, which finally determined the principal silhouette that we see today.

At last, only a few million years ago, Oahu assumed its present relationship to the ocean and submitted itself to the erosion of wind and ocean, waiting in glory for the coming of men from the eastern shores of Asia.

Each Hawaiian island was built in this manner and nowhere was the process more spectacular nor more clearly recorded than on Maui, where spacious Haleakala crater rises 8,000 feet above the sea and forms one of the most awe-inspiring sights in the islands. This crater was built not by a volcano but by rivers cutting deep into the face of an enormous lava mound left by some ancient volcano. Gradually such deep canyons were made in the lava that the walls collapsed, forming the present gloomy and foreboding depression. Then, because nothing ever happens halfway in Hawaii, within this barren waste dozens of small volcanoes erupted and left a fantastic museum—miles across and overpowering to the eye—of volcanic history. The last of these tertiary volcanoes was active only two hundred years ago, so that Maui, of course, lies near the southeast end of the great fault line.

But if Maui is the dead museum showing how the islands were built, the island of Hawaii, farther east, is the living laboratory in which we can see an island in the process of creation. Before your eyes the magma that has moved deeply within the earth pushes its way to the surface, explodes with violent sound and assumes its role as part of the earth's surface. That is how it was and that is how it now is.

As the earth goes, the Hawaiian Islands are very young land, and Hawaii itself is really a puling child, possibly not more than ten million years old. It was built by five great volcanoes, two of which are still quite active. Mauna Loa, the highest mountain on earth if we consider its sheer rise from ocean bed, is a massive shield containing a formless central crater which spews forth lava at an unequaled rate. In a hundred years it has erupted twenty-nine times, throwing forth more than three billion cubic yards of material, which rushes down to the sea, erasing forests and farms and villages, plunging at last into the ocean with a roaring cry of steam.

An eruption of Mauna Loa is dangerous, for the rounded top of the mountain encourages lava to run off at considerable speed in any unpredictable direction. Occasionally it heads for the important little city of Hilo less than forty miles away. Up to now it has always hardened before reaching Hilo, but in apprehension of catastrophe a procedure has been evolved whereby bombs from airplanes will divert the lava into some

119

less dangerous channel. There seems reasonable hope for this experiment and Hilo rests more easily.

Smaller than Mauna Loa and much more loved by the Hawaiians is Kilauea, remarkable because its present active pit is accessible by a fine macadam road permitting even the laziest traveler to drive right up to the rim and see one of the world's rarest sights. I say the islanders love Kilauea because they believe that the goddess Pele wanders from one volcano to another across the world, setting them afire, but that she always comes back to her permanent residence in Kilauea. When this volcano erupts, it is a sign of good luck.

Pele was good to me. On the day after I arrived in the islands on my last trip, Kilauea burst into spectacular activity, her most violent in thirty-three years. The islands were ablaze with excitement. Airlines ran special excursions. Newspapers carried daily bulletins, and everyone who saw the flaming pit and the twisting spires of white-hot lava leaping high into the air said that Pele had never been more magnificent. One staid businessman said to me, "Where else in the United States can you drive a Cadillac right up to the doors of hell and watch nature building a new island?" (He sold tickets for a cruise to the crater.)

I spent nine hours there and I would not have been bored had it been nine days. I cannot explain the fascination this violent lake of fire exercised on all who saw it. Some men came back six or seven times and stood transfixed by the tremendous spectacle.

The dead crater of Kilauea contains 2,600 grassy acres, toward the edge of which the present fire pit lies at the bottom of a large hole, 750 feet deep. When Kilauea erupts, the big crater of course remains quiet, but the deep fire pit explodes lava fountains right up to the rim of the crater and higher. A cloud of steam forms over the fire pit and is illuminated by the lava, which reaches a temperature of more than two thousand degrees when exposed to air and unknown degrees when still rising to the pit's surface.

Once while I watched Kilauea a mighty pillar of white-hot lava leaped 770 feet into the air. It was about a hundred feet across and fifty feet through and must therefore have contained around four million cubic feet of material.

It is at night that Kilauea is incomparable. Above the great crater hangs the illuminated cloud, while around the outside rim move hundreds of automobile headlights, spiraling down to the floor of the crater and to the edge of the fire pit, where perhaps a thousand people stare down at the writhing lava.

Now everything irrelevant disappears. You cannot see the sheer cliffs, nor the multicolored stone, nor the old deposits of lava, nor the faces of your friends. You see only the fiery lake, down far below you in the bottom of the pit.

The entire surface is a heaving mass of lava which in daylight looked like solid rock but which now shows hundreds of important fissures, each glowing red in the darkness. These cracks resemble the inflamed nerve system of a medical drawing, twisting in and out to form intricate patterns of fire.

From the center of the pit rise two violent fountains of molten lava, fresh from the vast body of crawling magma that moves beneath us at all times, seeking those faults in the earth's surface through which it can erupt into volcanic activity. Tonight the fountains leap sixty feet into the air and spew a tremendous quantity of lava, which spins aloft, screams and scratches like a living thing, and falls with a sigh onto the side walls of the fountains, from which it moves angrily down a hundred different fingers and into the sullen fissures.

From time to time there are explosions within the fountains and jagged streaks of fire fly off at crazy angles, falling like Roman candles in the dark night air. And always there is the surging lava, the hiss of deep explosions, the convulsive journey of the ash, the slow, snakelike distribution of new material over the surface of what has already fallen. Most spectacular are the explosions which send huge fingers of flame out parallel to the pit floor, for then the crawling lake is brightly illuminated for a moment and from the crowd come spontaneous cries of admiration.

All through the night there will be someone at the rim, for the fascination of Kilauea in the jet tropic darkness holds visitors like a magnet.

But the glory of Hawaii is not the volcanoes or the mountains or the dazzling flowers. It is the people. Here a polyglot population has devised a manner of life which is a lesson and a reproof to the world. In Hawaii people of many races live together in reasonable harmony, and for this alone all men are indebted to these islands.

Hawaii has 465,000 people, about as many as Cincinnati. The principal groups are: Japanese, 189,000; part Hawaiian, 77,000; Caucasian, 69,000; Filipino, 63,000; Chinese, 32,000; pure Hawaiian, 13,000; Puerto Rican, 10,000; Korean, 7,000.

These varied groups arrived primarily as sugar-cane workers, since Hawaiians, like all sensible Polynesians, saw no reason to work and refused to do so. Chinese were imported in 1852, but they were a grave disappointment, for they saved their money instead of getting drunk, studied instead of raising hell, and became merchants and doctors instead of remaining peasants. In 1878 Portuguese from the Azores were tried, but they were little better. They too saved their money and went into business for themselves. The Japanese were next (1885), but they saved money faster than anyone else. South Sea Islanders, Puerto Ricans, Koreans and Spaniards were used in turn, but as soon as they reached these islands the air of freedom affected them and they started to act like Americans: they became petty businessmen and educated their sons. Finally, in 1907 and ending as recently as 1946, Filipinos were imported, but they too are beginning to go to college. Said a Chinese, "There is something about American free private enterprise that is very attractive." He owned much land. His father had been a field worker.

But I would be extraordinarily naïve if I implied that in Hawaii all races and all classes are melded together into one big, happy family. Actually, there is more hard stratification of society there than elsewhere in America because there are more distinctive groups to be stratified and because most of these groups brought ancient distinctions with them from their homelands.

For example, in South China there is a group called the Hakkas, who speak a peculiar tongue and who throughout the centuries have been considered wandering outcasts. Many of them came to Hawaii, and in Honolulu today there are Chinese families who would not tolerate the marriage of their daughter to a Hakka. Some of the Japanese who came to the islands were of the untouchable Eta class, and one of the most liberal young Japanese I met in Hawaii assured me, "I can tell an Eta every time. Pitiful people."

But that is not the kind of stratification I refer to. Let's consider an average Saturday night in Honolulu. As the sun sinks behind Pearl Harbor—since Hawaii is in the tropics, days and nights tend to be of equal length—a distinguished group is gathering at La Pietra, the fabulous Italian Renaissance palace high on the side of Diamond Head. Into the stately courtyard come limousines from which step men and women in strictly formal evening wear. They ascend broad steps to a stunning court adorned with statues. Fountains play into grass-lined pools, tropical trees drop their flowers, and excellent food is served. The Walter Dillinghams are entertaining. He's a railroad tycoon turned builder and economic czar. Tonight his guests are bankers, wealthy descendants of the missionaries who converted the islands, United States senators and world-famous generals and admirals. There is not much drinking, some bad bridge, a lot of good talk and one convention that people on the mainland might envy. At ten o'clock one of the generals rises, says he has work to do and leaves abruptly. An exodus develops, and a banker whispers, "That's the best thing about generals. They have the guts to go home early."

Dinner at La Pietra is exactly what it would be in Boston or London. Except for the profusion of gorgeous flowers you would not know you were in Hawaii, and you do wear formal dress rather more frequently in the islands than you would in London. There is the same general conservatism of social custom, the same preoccupation with business and government.

There is one important difference. In Hawaii the kind of people you meet at a house like La Pietra work very hard; not many retired gentlemen living off income, few millionaires, no playboys, not many hard drinkers. The people at La Pietra run the banks and the businesses and the steamship companies and bitch about the next election.

Halfway up beautiful Manoa Valley the Fred Lams are having a quiet evening party. Fred is a remarkable Chinese doctor, president of the Chinese Chamber of Commerce, member of the board of regents for the university and hero of the Chinese both in Hawaii and on the mainland. Many of them could not bring their wives or relatives into America because they had liver fluke, a disease branded as contagious by our health officials. Dr. Lam conducted ingenious experiments to prove that the disease was not contagious and became responsible for uniting many families.

He was one of fifteen children, but by luck and hard work he attended three mainland universities and helped his brothers and sisters to become notable successes like himself. He married one of the most beautiful Chinese girls in Hawaii and sent his four children to the mainland for education. Their colleges include M.I.T., Vassar, Harvard, Wellesley and Columbia Law School.

Dinner tonight is a quiet affair. Joe Farrington, Hawaii's delegate to Congress, stops by and Dr. Fred shows colored films of his most recent trip around the world. (In Hawaii everyone travels.) His oldest son appears with the pleasing Caucasian girl he met in Minnesota, and Mrs. Lam's sister— called the prettiest woman ever to testify before Congress— comes by to talk about her legal practice. She too has a daughter at Wellesley and is also a heroine among the Chinese, for she was instrumental in clarifying immigration laws pertaining to travel back and forth to China.

I have tried to convey the idea of a gracious, relaxed evening at the Lams, but I fear I have not proved the average Americanism of such Hawaiian nights. The Lams, and the thousands of other families entertaining tonight, are precisely as American in custom and form of thought as the descendants of Irish or German or English families whose ancestors arrived at the Atlantic side of America in the 1870's. This is the salient fact about polyglot Hawaii.

It is evident at the Ishii Garden, where a group of young

Japanese have gathered to discuss the vital Buddhist Youth League. They meet in gardens reminiscent of Japan, where one takes off his shoes, dons a blue-and-white kimono and sits upon the floor looking out at a tiny lake, Korean stone lanterns and Japanese flowers.

But the conversation is not in Japanese. These good-looking secretaries, law students, businessmen and orchid growers resemble their Caucasian counterparts in any mainland city. They are proud of the reputation their Hawaiian-Japanese volunteers earned in Italy during World War II, and they whistle and stomp when the movie *Go for Broke* recounts their experiences. They take justifiable pride in the report contained in the official history of Hawaii's war years: "Despite the beliefs to which some people still cling, all the investigative agencies are agreed that espionage in Hawaii before the war was carried on only by the Japanese consular staff and one other person, a German. They also agree that there was no espionage after the start of the war, no sabotage, no fifth column activity of any sort."

Out in the Kuliouou area past Diamond Head, there is a feast of another sort at the home of hilarious Gardie Perkins, a pure Hawaiian. Her living room looks like any in Vermont or Colorado except that there is more laughter. Flora Hayes, the much-loved woman legislator of Hawaiian blood, is in rare form as she recounts her battles with men politicians in her effort to obtain better schools for Hawaiian children. Then she describes the formal opening of the Hawaiian legislature when policemen and legislators perform a solemn hula to get into the mood for consideration of new legislation.

On the other side of Honolulu, Colonel Hayward, a considerable Marine hero from the Pacific, is entertaining his friends in the Navy-owned housing at Makalapa, off Pearl Harbor. No uniforms are visible, nor are any civilians. It is a military affair, principally because these men have known one another for years, they work at the same job, and their wives have been friends since the births of their children. The trim colonel serves fried chicken and fine stories, passes refreshment with a heavy hand and is quite content, like most of his fellow officers, to conduct his life as if Honolulu and its many races did not exist.

At the Caucasian Dillinghams' the guests were all Caucasians. At the Chinese Lams', mostly Chinese; at the Japanese dinner the young people were Japanese, and at the Hawaiian dinner they were Hawaiians. Here the guests are military people, and throughout the island this pattern of intimate social life maintains. It is not governed by strict laws, and any Hawaiian would be welcome at the Dillinghams' just as any Japanese would be at the Lams'. But as on the mainland, people tend to stick together in small groups of common and congenial background. There is much intermarriage and there will be more, so that a hundred years from now there will probably be a new kind of people on these islands; but for the present there are many families who deplore intermarriage and who do all they can to prevent it.

How do the Hawaiians react to this? At Gardie Perkins' the talk turns to the islands, and without exception the Hawaiians admit that they foresee the day when their blood will be lost in the new race being born. They do not lament this, for they enjoy a special reputation. In Hawaii they are the aristocracy —the elite—and people of all other groups are proud when they can claim Hawaiian blood.

"Still," Flora Hayes insists, "we were robbed of our land and we know it. We are a dreamy people who can be taken advantage of. We would rather have a feast than hard work."

It was a Chinese-Hawaiian politician who panicked an audience by shouting, "In my veins there is Chinese blood and Hawaiian blood and some English blood." His audience knew about the first two but challenged him on the third. Cried the speaker, "One of my ancestors ate Captain Cook."

There is of course more to the tour of Honolulu on an average Saturday night. At Woodland kids of all races gather for popular music. In the plush hotels there are big parties with tuxedoes and evening dresses, but few Honolulans attend these. And along the pitiful reaches of Smith Street, the dives do a prosperous business by catering to lonely servicemen, summed up in one sign I saw: "Beautiful girls. Taxi dances. Beer. Tattooing."

Because Hawaii has made such an effort to achieve racial harmony, some advocates have claimed that it has solved all problems in this area. It hasn't. There are shocking cases of flagrant discrimination. When Keo Nakama, Olympic swimmer and national title holder, tried to enter the swank Outrigger Club (in company with a Hawaiian, who was of course welcome) he was bounced back onto the sidewalk. There was a public outcry but the rule stuck: no Orientals. Some of the finest residential areas are strictly zoned, although the city insists they aren't. The topflight Pacific Club is Caucasian, although occasionally an Oriental attends as a guest. Newspaper advertisements often stipulate that only white people need apply.

I asked more than forty islanders, "Suppose I were a young kid from the mainland with real promise. I get a job with one of the big firms or a bank. They spot me at once as a fellow who's going to get ahead . . . vice-president maybe. Then one morning I announce I'm going to marry a Japanese girl . . . or a Portuguese . . . or a Korean. What happens?"

Without exception my friends said, "Brother, you're a dead duck." They explained that I wouldn't be fired. I might even win a fairly responsible job, but the time would come when I would hit that old blank wall. I would be a dead duck. "Of course," they said, "if you were in some job like selling Fords to the public, it might help to have a Japanese wife."

Why then do I praise Hawaii so highly? Because even though individuals are free to exercise whatever private prejudice they desire, the territory as a legal body permits no discrimination. Japanese girls become school principals. A Chinese is chief of police. A Japanese is president of the senate. A Chinese is speaker of the house. In public and in law, Hawaii is the land of the free, and that is what makes the cherishable difference.

Hawaii is much more than a natural wonderland or a laboratory in good human relations. It is also a sophisticated cultural center. Honolulu's art museum, with a stunning collection of Italian primitives, is probably not equaled in any mainland city of comparable size. Most towns have good libraries, the

127

university is first rate, Broadway plays are popular, and the symphony orchestra has been solvent for fifty-two years and now has $10,000 in the bank.

Classical Hawaiian songs date far back in history and were often composed by members of the royal family, as, for example, "Aloha Oe," which was written by a queen as she returned from the Pali, where she watched one of her handmaidens staring dreamily at a young man. Popular Hawaiian music started with the 1916 nifty "Hello, Hawaii, How Are Ya?" and now includes some of the most haunting modern songs, "Sweet Leilani" and my own favorite "Beyond the Reef."

Hawaii is also sports mad. Island fans will go anywhere to see anything. High school football games draw thousands. Service baseball is a major attraction. Any sports figure passing through the islands is certain of a wild reception, and even wrestling is taken seriously. Probably in no other American city of equal size would the following announcement cause a sensation: "If Lou Thesz wins, the Red Scorpion will be forced to unmask in public!"

Hawaii is also extraordinarily hospitable. Partly because the islands are so far from the mainland, any visiting dignitary is apt to get the jillion-dollar treatment. If a traveler fails to have a good time in Hawaii, I would say there was no hope for him.

It is impossible to say what the term *Hawaiian* signifies. Sometimes it means one of the handsome original Polynesians. At other times it may refer to a resident of the main island. Again it means anyone living in the territory. Everyone has strong feelings about this—there are a few finicky white people living in the islands who would resent being called Hawaiians—but in general usage the word means a Polynesian. However, this leaves no general noun like Texan or Californian to denote the people who live in the islands. I use the word *islanders*, but even that is not satisfactory, for the same white people who would object to *Hawaiian* object to this. They insist on the stilted "residents of the islands."

But on one thing everyone agrees. Whether Hawaiians or islanders or Japanese or Chinese . . . they are Americans and their islands are part of America. The very worst insult you

128

can throw at an islander is to say, "Tomorrow I'm flying back to America." No matter who says that or where, some islander will interrupt and ask, "Didn't you know? You're in America now. You must mean you're flying back to the mainland."

Islanders use many Polynesian words and sometimes a conversation becomes unintelligible to the visitor. Absolutely necessary are the three words *haole, kamaiina* and *malihini.* The first originally meant a foreigner but now means a white man. The second is a long-time resident, the third a newcomer.

My favorite words are unusually expressive. "Don't give me any of that old *hoomalimali* (applesauce)." "I don't want any *pilikia* (trouble)." "If you give me any pilikia I'll put a *kahuna* on you (evil eye or spell)." And the delightfully compact *pau:* "The beefsteak is *pau* and I'm *pau* too (finished or washed up)."

If words fail, you roll your eyes and cry "Auwe, auwe!" which means anything at all but surely something doleful. And during the summer of 1952 a strange new war cry rose over the islands, "Ee Leekee Eekee!" which was the Hawaiian pronunciation of "I Like Ike."

There is futile discussion of the correct way to pronounce the territory's name. From learned old-timers I got *Hah-va'-ee,* with the last syllable noticeably clipped. I am content that this is correct, but the more usual pronunciation is *Hah-wa'-ee.* You will be publicly insulted if you call it *How-wa-ya.* It's *Hoe-noe-loo-loo* and *Hah-wai'-yan.* And if you say in either greeting or farewell *Aloa* you will be reminded that "In the islands we say *A-lo-ha.* Please sound the *h.*"

In visiting Hawaii one is tempted to stay put on gracious, comfortable Oahu and forgo the inconvenience of further travel, which is regrettable. Some visitors never leave the boundaries of Honolulu, which is short-sighted; and there are a few rich people who never leave the narrow confines of Waikiki and the plush hotels, which seems downright cowardly.

One weekend I piled into a small boat with Guy Rothwell, the architect, and we set out for the little-known cliffs and fiords of Molokai Island. It was a rare, sun-swept tropical day as we coasted the inaccessible fiords and looked up at the eight-hundred-foot cliffs inhabited only by wild goats and sea birds. We saw the deep indented valleys that once housed thousands of Polynesians and their taro patches, but now each valley was empty and years may pass without a stranger sleeping in them. Again and again I was reminded, on this sea-washed trip, of the Marquesas, where Melville had once seen similar valleys populated densely and where much later I saw the same valleys denuded both of people and of hope. It seemed incredible that here, so close to Honolulu, these magnificent cliffs and their empty fiords could exist almost unknown, and I recalled what a long-time beachcomber in the Solomons once told me: "If you're around islands, get out in a small boat because islands aren't only land. Mostly they're sea."

I used quite a different sort of transportation to see the island of Kauai. Tony Texeira, a fisherman there, had spent thousands of weary and expensive hours trying to guess where the big fish are. "You waste gasoline, you pay the crew, you go broke and still you don't find the fish. Now it's all different!"

He led me to a small two-seated Luscombe plane and we climbed in. "I go out early in the morning," he shouted, "and I can scout the coastline for miles. When you see a school, they can be depended upon to stay in one area for hours or sometimes days. So I radio my crew and they waste no gas or time getting here."

We roared around Kauai, sometimes at very low altitudes where the crested sea seemed to be playing with us. Tony was a fine man to fly with, for he loved his island and delighted to share with me those things he liked about it. "That canyon down there isn't as big as the Grand Canyon, but it has lots more color. That fine place down there on the bay. A rich man owns it who loves the tropics. But he's on the dry side of the island, so he's piped water in and built a sprinkler system. Only place in the world where a jungle has been built over a sprinkler system. That's the spouting horn, greatest blowhole in the world. It has a boiling cauldron, a waterspout that always works and an echo chamber that whistles and sighs. Some blowhole!"

He took his bouncing plane down into Nualolo Valley, completely cut off by towering mountains, a most strange and forbidding place. Then he showed me the cliffs of Kauai, miniature jeweled masterpieces compared to the more rugged ones of Molokai. They call Kauai "The Garden Island," and I suppose that much grows on the island, but a more appropriate name would be "The Beautiful Island," for I have found no other in the Pacific with such compressed loveliness. I remember most the valley of Koolau the Leper.

This Koolau the Leper was a real man, but so much legend has grown up about him that I shall not even try to tell the truth, for it is not now discernible. Instead, I'll repeat the story as it was told me by Eric Knudsen, one of the fine old men of the islands.

"As a boy I hunted with Koolau. He was strong, and we respected him, but in 1893 a new law was passed requiring lepers to remove to another island, and Koolau was a leper. The sheriff was named Louis Stoltz, and he persuaded Koolau to surrender, promising that Piilani, Koolau's beautiful wife, could accompany him to exile, for she refused to be separated from her husband.

"But when the boat arrived to gather the lepers, Stoltz waited until Koolau went aboard, then he held Piilani, for he had an eye for a pretty girl, and he whispered, 'There is no need for you to go into exile.' From the boat Koolau saw that he had been tricked, and shouted, 'Let my wife come aboard!' but Stoltz called back, 'She should not go among the lepers. She will stay here!' At this, Koolau tried to leap into the sea, but he was held back and an old kanaka sitting on the pier warned the sheriff, 'Stoltz, you'd better send the wife. Koolau will escape and you'll go dead.'

"The ship sailed and Koolau escaped. He found Piilani and took her to the valley you saw this morning. He had an old German needle gun, and Sheriff Stoltz borrowed my brother's Winchester .44 to go after him. The two men met in a rocky pass and Koolau killed the sheriff.

"This could not be permitted, so sixty troops and three cannon set forth to capture Koolau the Leper. They marched bravely up the valley, burned Koolau's empty hut and broke up into small searching parties. For eight days they found nothing. Then, on the ninth day, three soldiers started to climb a hogback leading to what looked as if it might be a cave. From the crevice at the top of this ridge Piilani whispered to Koolau, 'Shoot them now or they will shoot us.' But Koolau said, 'How can I shoot those men? I know them all. They're my friends.' So the three soldiers crept closer, and Piilani said, 'Now you must shoot them,' and Koolau replied, 'If they pass that lehua tree with the red blossoms, I'll fire.'

"The soldiers came to the lehua tree and passed it. Koolau fired and a miracle happened. The first soldier was hit and fell backward, discharging his gun and killing the second soldier. This knocked the third man over the precipice and he was dashed to pieces.

"The commander ordered the three cannons to fire into the cave, but the shots could not be deflected into the opening. Soldiers were let down to the cliff on ropes, but they could not fire into the cave. So a watch was set up to starve the leper out, but on the third night a gale blew and while branches of the trees slapped the cliff, Koolau and Piilani escaped. Three days later a Portugee said, 'I think the cave is empty.'

"I saw this cave in 1895. No one knows what happened. Some years back a convict confessed that many years ago the government had secretly put him ashore to kill Koolau. He had found the leper and they had lived together for a year and a half, but in all that time Piilani was so watchful that she never permitted the convict one chance to murder her husband. Eventually, the convict confessed his evil mission and Koolau sent him away, saying, 'I knew it from the beginning. Piilani told me.' "

Later, from a woman who lives near the valley of Koolau the Leper, I learned that Piilani, her name changed, her history a secret, had moved to another island, where she lived with an American trader, who treated her well. Late in life she told this woman that Koolau had died and she had buried him in the valley from which all the armies of Hawaii had been unable to dislodge him, and she had laid across his chest the German needle gun and Stoltz's Winchester .44.

132

Granting that is quite impossible for a visitor to comprehend Hawaii unless he sees the unique outer islands, I must confess that the traveler with little cash can have a whale of a time on Oahu alone. For example, there are four superb trips on this island which, in a way, summarize the wonder of the territory.

For a few dollars there is the unmatched trip around the island, over the Pali, along the windswept beaches and past the great military establishments. It is quite unlike any other trip in America, but I prefer three rather less known journeys.

The first is past the Schofield Barracks and over Kolekole Pass. It takes special permission to make this trip, for west of the pass is an enormous ammunition dump, but the journey is worth any effort, for you move from a lush tropical land into a desolate desert with perpendicular cliffs cutting it off from the rest of Oahu. The mountains are extraordinarily majestic and the swift transition from jungle to desert is quite breathtaking.

The second trip is along a narrow, largely unknown road that winds high into the mountains of Oahu and across handsome plateaus. Wild orchids line the red-dirt road. Jungle trees encroach upon the river bottoms, and from certain high points you can see the noble Pacific and the northern surf riding in from the Aleutians. Clouds hang over the western hills while bright sunlight floods the hidden valleys filled with strange gray trees. It is difficult to realize that these deep-cut valleys, strewn with dense jungle growth, are part of Oahu, for life in the grand hotels of Waikiki reminds one of New York. This high road is difficult to find, difficult to drive and difficult to believe. But it is worth every effort and it is free.

The third trip is something special. The Waiahole Tunnel is cut right through the heart of the Oahu mountains and delivers water from the wet northeastern slope (280 inches of rain a year), where there are no fields, to the dry southwestern slope (26 inches) where sugar fields abound. Since sugar must have 120 inches of water each year to grow, the tunnel is of vital importance. It carries 35,000,000 gallons of water a day—in flood, 120,000,000—and if you want to find out whether or not you have claustrophobia you can ride through this tunnel in a small boat. It is a two-hour trip, and you sit in a cramped boat which is constantly engulfed by gallons of water seeping from the roof. You get soaked, sometimes your solitary lantern is extinguished by the dripping water, and you are under a thousand feet of solid rock. So far everyone attempting the trip has made it, and if you succeed, you can state definitely that you are not afraid of dark, damp, closed-in places.

On one of my trips around Oahu I met a Japanese girl I had known before, and she said, "It is not quite correct to say that every Japanese remained loyal after Pearl Harbor. There was Harada. I remember him as an unhappy, insecure fellow of thirty who had tried various jobs in various places and had never found happiness in Hawaii. I recall him saying that he was a misfit and he would leave us and go to lonely Niihau, where there were no Japanese and where he could escape his problems and tend sheep."

But instead of finding sanctuary he had come unwittingly to the one spot in the islands—or in all of America, for that matter—where a Japanese would be forced to make the agonizing choice between the United States and his homeland. Harada's decision will be talked about as long as there is a Hawaii.

For the only pilot among the Pearl Harbor raiders that landed safely in the islands on that fatal morning did so on Niihau, and he put his plane down almost in Harada's new front yard. On this lonely island there were no radios, no soldiers, no police, and Harada was chosen to serve as interpreter and later as guard. We do not know what the pilot told this uncertain, unhappy young man, but it had to do with Japan's greatness and the important job Harada would have in the new world.

So Harada helped the pilot assemble a machine gun from the plane, recovered a revolver, and the two set out to capture Niihau for the Emperor. The Japanese succeeded, the first time since the War of 1812 that a foreign enemy had held American soil. Then, by a series of incredible heroics, a small group of loyal Hawaiians, with no arms of any kind, launched a campaign to recapture their island. The battle lasted, believe it or not, for six days and reached a climax when the Japanese shot Beni, the leader of the Hawaiians, three times through the body. This so enraged Beni that he brushed aside the guns, caught the pilot in his bare hands, lifted him high in the air the way he was accustomed to lift sheep, and dashed his brains out on a rock. Harada, the confused Japanese who had fled the crosscurrents of modern life only to have them trail him through the skies, pressed a shotgun to his stomach and blew himself apart. The islanders have forgiven Harada, the strange young man, but of Beni, who survived, they say, "Goes to show you must never shoot a Hawaiian more than twice. After that he gets mad."

It must be obvious by now that I like Hawaii. Therefore, if I point out several things that bewilder visitors, perhaps I may be forgiven. But I won't be. Anyone who says a word against anything Hawaiian gets it in the neck. No citizens of the United States are more savagely protective than those who live in the islands. In Maryland you might hint that you don't cotton to fried chicken and survive, but when I say—as I shall in a moment—that Hawaiian cooking is pretty bad, I'd better stay under cover for some years.

For example, no man is more hated in Hawaii than Harry Truman, not because he is a Democrat but because when he stopped in Hawaii on his way to the historic meeting with General MacArthur on Wake, he refused to wear the welcome leis provided at the airport. Stormed one otherwise placid woman, "The only time in my life I really missed not having a vote was last November. I certainly wanted to vote against that man."

As to cooking, it is one of the curiosities of history that the Tahitians, by all odds the finest cooks in the Pacific, should have become attached to France, whose cooks are the finest in Europe, whereas Hawaii, with the worst Pacific cooks, should have aligned herself with America. Hawaiian cooking is inferior to the rest of Polynesia's because less use is made of seafood, coconut in its various forms and breadfruit. And there is no one dish to compare to the superb raw fish of Tahiti or to the shellfish of the Cook Islands.

135

I do admit that Hawaiian roast pig, served with baked yams and red salt, is excellent, but so costly that it can be served only rarely. But as for poi—"paperhanger's paste served without a brush"—I can say little. I am assured that it is the world's most digestible starch for babies and that a surprising demand has grown up for poi on the part of mainland pediatricians, but I feel sure that this situation has developed only because babies are unable to organize an effective protest. Once on Maui I asked an islander what breed of dog he had, and he said, "Pure poi." Then he explained: "In the old days we kept a certain kind of dog that tasted especially good when served baked with poi." Grudgingly I admitted that under such circumstances poi might be a relief, but otherwise you can keep it on your side of the table, Sweet Leilani.

The second puzzlement is the muumuu, a missionary nightgown transformed into a billowy and shapeless dress. At evening parties women often wear the muumuu as a kind of tribute to old Hawaii, but I have seen some two thousand women in muumuus and I have never seen one at which you would look twice. In fact, looking at those tents even once was trying. I was told that the muumuu had been devised by missionaries to kill all sense of sex in the onlooker. In the history of mankind no moral experiment was ever more completely successful.

The third disappointment is the Hawaiian hula. It's lovely if you've never been farther south than Hawaii, and I grant that its use of hands is exquisitely poetic. One night I went to see Miss Hawaii perform one of the great hulas and I was almost persuaded to admit that it was as good as those in Tahiti; but as bad luck would have it, the very next night James Norman Hall's widow arrived in town with some movies of Germaine of Bora Bora doing the real hula; and to compare the sickly, sentimental Hawaiian dance with that cyclonic explosion of the southern islands would be like comparing Joe's Chevrolet Nine with the New York Yankees.

I should also warn any traveler to Hawaii that there are five subjects on which he had better keep his mouth shut: missionaries, the Big Five, labor unions, statehood and Waikiki Beach.

A brief outline of each will indicate why silence is advisable.

Missionaries played a larger role in Hawaii than in any other Pacific islands, for here they gained the ear of the kings, made phenomenal conversions and established a benevolent rule. But as they worked the spiritual vineyard they also toiled in the sugar fields, the shipping companies and the banks. They married into noble families, acquired much land and came to control the islands' economy. It was said of them that they came into the Pacific to do good and they did right well. Documents exist showing that they advocated withholding communion until chiefs agreed to let their people work for twelve cents a day, and one intemperate man cried that he was tired of collecting church dues in dried fish: "What we want to hear is the ringing sound of hard, cold cash."

But I incline toward the missionaries. In 1778 there were about 300,000 Hawaiians living well in these islands. By 1838, before the missionaries took hold, more than 200,000 of these had perished through the white man's abuse, and I do not doubt that a few more years of exploitation would have erased them pretty much as the Marquesans to the south were erased. Such disaster was avoided largely because missionaries interceded, stopped general debauchery and did their best—as they saw it and to their own profit—to reestablish the native population.

I have been privileged to see most of the Polynesian people living in the world today, and in most respects the Hawaiian is incomparably better off than his brothers. He has a better position in society, more material possessions, more self-respect, a brighter future. These are not just my opinions. I have spoken with some dozen Hawaiians, many of whom know New Zealand, Tahiti, Samoa and other centers, and they report that in Hawaii things are better.

Today the descendants of the missionaries meet each year in April in the old mission home on King Street (officially the Hawaiian Mission Children's Society but popularly the Cousin Society, since missionaries called one another brother and sister). The exciting moment comes when the clerk reads off the names of those ancient ships which brought the missionaries. As each famous family name is called, all descendants of that patriarch rise. "First Company," intones the clerk. "Brig *Thaddeus* 1820. Hiram Bingham." One of his descendants would become senator from Connecticut. "Third Company. Brig *Parthian* 1828. Gerrit Parmelee Judd." So many now rise that William Lyons Phelps cracked that Hawaii is where the rain falls alike on the Judds and un-Judds. "Eighth Company. Barque *Mary Frazier* 1836. Amos Starr Cooke." We shall hear of him in a moment.

Sometimes a single child will rise four times, giving a picture of Hawaiian society: Cooke, Rice, Lyman, Wilcox. At the centennial session there was great rivalry between the Cookes and the Judds to see who was represented by the greater number. Says a Judd, "Disgraceful! The damned Cookes lugged in a three-week-old baby and won by one vote!"

The Big Five have played a major role in Hawaiian history. They are the corporations which served as factors managing the great sugar plantations. Inevitably they branched out into merchandising, shipping, construction, banking, trust operations and airlines. Their derivation explains much Hawaiian history. C. Brewer and Co. was started by Boston shipping men engaged in the sandalwood trade to China. Theo. H. Davies and Co. Ltd. (always spelled with all the periods) was English, and the man who put the outfit on its feet and gave it his name returned to England when the job was done. The American Factors was exclusively German (changed their name, sensibly, in 1918) and ran an important shipping line to Bremen. Castle and Cooke started as business agents for the missionaries and branched out into highly successful businesses of their own. Alexander and Baldwin were the sons of missionaries.

Since the Big Five operated most plantations, they established the character of rural life in Hawaii. Because most of their laborers were illiterate Asians, the Big Five had to take care of everything: housing, roads, schools, hospitals, playgrounds, wages and hours. A visitor, surveying their paternalistic and placid operations in the 1920's, observed, "Here is the only society in world history which justifies feudalism . . . almost."

When the labor movement hit Hawaii belatedly in the mid-1940's the Big Five were emotionally unprepared to make those reasonable concessions that had become commonplace on the mainland through several generations of intense discussion. The inevitable clash with organized labor almost wrecked Hawaii. I have the feeling, studying this wretched period, that all the trouble could have been avoided had the Big Five had one good public relations man who could have banged the corporation table and made himself heard. Certainly the basic working conditions in Hawaii were not intolerable; they were not even bad. Certainly the basic pay was decent, if not lavish. But what was no longer tolerable was a continuation of dictated paternalism.

Today most islanders concede that it was high time labor did organize. Even the most conservative members of the Big Five now admit that the old order had to change. But at the same time almost everyone contends that labor has now gone too far.

It is difficult to explain how completely a strike paralyzes Hawaii. No ships run to the mainland, therefore no food comes in except under emergency rules. Small businesses close down. Big hotels stand half empty. Restaurants grimly try to hold on. (Most of what Hawaii eats comes from the mainland.) Factories cut operations and stores kill orders for goods. A ghastly pall of economic ruin and fear settles over Hawaii, an insidious death that no mainland community can comprehend. I know one man who lost three businesses in succession during recent strikes.

I have experienced three Hawaii strikes and they are the most senseless way of settling an argument that could be devised. Strangely, two of these crippling blows did not concern Hawaii but dealt with shipping conditions on the West Coast. Islanders protest that it is unfair for them to be crucified by disputes which they are powerless to settle.

Statehood presents a most baffling problem. Publicly everybody is for it. A recent study concludes that support of statehood is almost part of the moves which no one would dare to transgress. But privately hundreds of people assure the visitor, "I wouldn't dare say this in public, but statehood would be a disaster!" The customary reason: too many Japanese. The fundamental reason: lots of people make more money in a territorial status than they would under statehood.

I must report three other proposed solutions. A few die-hard romanticists seek to restore the Hawaiian monarchy and establish a kingdom, but since every one of them expects to be prime minister, the plan lags. Some thoughtful men would prefer a kind of dominion status resembling Puerto Rico's. And one night in a bar I met a vociferous group who were going to solve it all: "Complete freedom from the United States so we can get Marshall Aid and Point Four and live like kings."

As for Waikiki Beach, it has suffered both from unfair criticism and unwarranted publicity. True, it is disappointing in size, and buses do run along one edge, but it is still one of the rare beaches in the Pacific. It has two virtues which endear it to nearly everyone. First is a unique underwater coral structure which produces long, tumbling breakers on which surfboards will ride at dizzying speed. It is no trick to stand on a surfboard, since the kinetic energy of the board keeps it stable. Nor is there really much trouble in hoisting a pretty girl onto your shoulders. What does take skill is judging when to get your board moving so as to catch the breaker. Most novices, including me, never master this.

Waikiki's second excellent feature is that it is free. There is no beach in Hawaii which is private. The land leading up to it may be, but not the beach. And if too many buildings encroach, narrow lanes are built between them down which anyone may go to enjoy the surf. I don't know how this freedom was protected but it is one of the islands' most enviable aspects.

Actually, this accessibility has worked to everyone's advantage. A famed hotel expert, imported from the mainland to survey Hawaii's hotels, sat under the spreading hau tree of the Halekulani Hotel and sighed enviously, "You people have the greatest single asset any hotel could have." Asked the Honolulu men, "You mean Waikiki Beach?" "No," the expert from a cold climate replied, "I mean the floor show." And he pointed six feet away to where a dazzling parade of almost nude girls went by: Chinese, Californian, Texan, Korean and Hawaiian. "I couldn't find the money to reproduce a floor show like that in Minneapolis or Chicago." His neck snapped as a bikini went by to the beach, and he added, "Even if I could find the money and the girls, the police would close my place down. Here it's all free."

The fine hotels of Hawaii are something special. The Royal Hawaiian, one of the lushest hotels in America, is the only place I know where up to five in the afternoon you attend the swank bar in the skimpiest bathing suit available, whereas after six, tuxedos are required.

The great Hawaiian hotels have one unique advantage: they have no bad rooms. Either you get a seaside room overlooking the beach or you have a mountain room with a cool breeze blowing in across flower gardens. There are other features. The social director of one of the palaces assured me, "We are probably the only hotel in America which absolutely guarantees to every mother who registers with a marriageable daughter that her girl will have dates. We keep a fleet of station wagons, and if we get more girls than men, we dispatch the station wagons to Pearl Harbor and come back with a load of young naval officers. The hotel picks up the dinner check and each young man gets three free drinks at the bar. If he gets involved with his date, he has to find his own transportation back to the base. Otherwise we send the station wagons back at one-thirty. In this hotel we think highly of the Navy."

A common misconception about Hawaii is that it is an outrider of California, a colorful extension of Los Angeles. Nothing could be more wrong. Apart from the fact that men in each place wear colorful shirts with the tails not tucked in, there is practically no resemblance between the two.

Hawaii is an extension of New England. The first American sea captains to visit the islands were from New England. Hawaii was developed commercially by New Englanders and Christianized by them. Island children were educated in New England schools and still are. Even the factor system developed by the Big Five sprang from New England precedents whereby Boston bankers ran Nashua textile mills. While California was still Spanish, Hawaii had already become a New England suburb and has remained so.

Three aspects of island life are emphatically New England. First is the Boston accent, which is jealously retained and cultivated by many families. ("They have lessons at night after the rest of us have gone to bed.") You hear the broad *a* much more in Honolulu than you do in Philadelphia or Cleveland. Second is business dress, which is even stuffier in Honolulu than it is in Boston. It's all very well for flashy ads in mainland magazines to show handsome men at Waikiki wearing colorful aloha shirts, but let those same men go to a job in any major company in such clothes and they'd be bounced out on their ear. Proper garb, year round, is a dark suit, white shirt, modest tie and dark shoes. As head of an important business you would probably wear a vest too. I shall never forget the look of horror that swept a carful of businessmen when they saw that I intended to accompany them to a business lunch while wearing an aloha shirt. I had the presence of mind to pretend I was out of breath and gasp, "You'll have to wait for me. Got to change this shirt. Been on the beach." I know they didn't believe me, but they could have embraced me for my good sense. We arrived late but proper.

The third reminder of New England is the architecture, which is absolutely as far removed from the low, lovely architecture of California as possible. I have rarely been stumped for words to describe places I love, but I find no words to convey my reaction to Hawaii's ugly, inappropriate architecture. The best I can do is report that one of the massive stone federal buildings with tiny windows and infinite gloom is said to have been built from plans drawn for a similar building in Alaska. This I believe. Most of the old buildings of Honolulu would suit Alaska perfectly.

Today, however, Hawaiian architecture is waking up. The new art academy building is a splendid marriage of classical and Polynesian. The new Waikiki branch of the Bishop National Bank is perfect for Hawaii, a beautiful and appropriate building using coconut-palm motif. I liked particularly the new Ford display room: a tiny central core of masonry surrounded by huge polished concrete floors, low roof and no walls at all. Since Hawaiian temperatures are gentle, the walls of masonry needed in Alaska are entirely unnecessary. Hawaii's new residential architecture is also excellent, but not remotely related to Californian style. The blending is one of Boston-and-Tokyo, with Japan supplying the simplicity, the outdoorness and the sliding doors.

It will come as a surprise to most Americans to discover that one of the very choice times to visit Hawaii is in midsummer. The average temperature then is only seven degrees above the January mean (seventy-seven in August, seventy in January). In fact, the very highest temperature ever recorded in Hawaii is eighty-eight degrees, and the islands never approach the heat of Baltimore, St. Louis or Omaha. I had to interrupt my last visit to fly suddenly to Tokyo, nearly twenty degrees farther north, and that city was so unbearably hot in July and August that some American business firms were sending their men south to Honolulu to cool off and cure their heat itch.

This surprising state of affairs is caused by the trade winds which blow almost incessantly across the islands from the northeast to southwest. When the trades stop, as they do a couple of times a year, Honolulu heat can be intolerable because of the humidity.

But the trades are more than an attraction to the people who live in the islands. They are the life blood of Hawaii, for they drive in the rain clouds that make the islands habitable. The low clouds come rushing in from the ocean, strike the northeast mountains and deposit their burdens on those slopes, which resemble jungle, passing on empty to the southwest slopes, which are rainless deserts. There is one famous mountain on Kauai that receives 618 inches of rain a year—the world record—whereas a smaller mountain only eighteen miles to the southwest receives eighteen inches a year. The second is said to be in the rain shadow of the first, and there are entire islands in Hawaii which lie in the rain shadow of larger islands and thus become barren wastes.

Obviously the welfare of Hawaii depends upon moving

large amounts of water from steep hillsides, where it is not needed, to dry fields, where it is. We have seen that tunnels through mountains do part of the job, but since it takes a ton of water to grow a pound of sugar, extra water has to be found. How this was accomplished is one of the most exciting adventures in island history.

The specific gravity of fresh water is 1.000 while that of salt water is 1.025, or one-fortieth heavier. This means that if fresh water rides on top of salt in a container, a lens of fresh water is formed, one-fortieth of which will rest in an arc above the level of the salt water (the Ghyben-Herzberg principle).

On Oahu the volcanic structure of the island rock permits and encourages rain water to seep into the earth. Thus Oahu itself becomes a container suspended in salt water which forms a base for the fresh water lens to rest upon. This happens all over the world, but on Oahu another condition is present. Along the shore around Honolulu and west a hard, impermeable rock sits down on the lens of clear water and holds it under pressure. About 1890 some smart well-drillers from the mainland figured this out and reasoned that if they could puncture that hard upper crust of waterproof rock, the fresh water underneath would spurt out in vast quantities. Working on a real gamble and sinking all their money into the holes their primitive machines drilled, the enterprisers struck two dry runs. Then they punctured the rock cap, and Hawaii ever since has had unbelievably productive artesian wells, some of which throw the water high enough to service entire fields by gravity.

Agriculture in Hawaii negates every principle I learned in school. Instead of rotating crops to replenish soil, sugar alone —a notoriously destructive crop—is grown on the same land year after year without ever giving the land a single day's rest! I have seen a field of ripe cane burned at dawn (the fire consumes pesky undergrowth and chars the cane so that precious juice is held secure until processing), harvested by dusk, plowed the next day and planted that afternoon.

The secret: scientists carefully compute exactly what minerals are taken from the soil by each crop and in what tonnage.

Then precisely those minerals are returned to the soil while the new crop grows. Minerals soluble in water are dumped into the irrigation ditches. Some are broadcast by airplane. Others are dug into the soil. In this way the famous red land of Hawaii acts as a kind of chemical bank which pays out minerals as needed and which accepts deposits when its funds run low. It is never idle.

But Hawaiian agriculture has its problems. Pineapple, the second crop, has been hard hit by something over which it had no control: frozen orange juice. Some of the big companies have taken terrific lacings ($3,000,000 loss in one year) but it is unlikely that an industry which has faced the problems pineapple has met will allow frozen orange juice to knock it out.

Pineapples were introduced into Hawaii from South America, and the going has always been rough. By 1916 the plants had used up all the free iron in the soil and were starting to die. A chemist found that feeding iron sulphate into the soil would permit the pineapple to come back stronger than before.

By 1922 it was costing too much to weed pineapples by hand and the crop seemed doomed as uneconomical, but a plant expert invented a system of planting young shoots in the center of wide paper strips which would kill weeds but permit the plants to grow, and conserve moisture and heat at the same time. When manufacturers of this paper jacked the price up too high, another chemist discovered that an even better paper could be made from pineapple refuse.

In 1931 it seemed that Hawaiian pineapples were at last faced with extermination. A mealy bug, many-legged and resembling a white powder puff, had started to feed upon pineapple plants. Into the leaf it injected a powerful poison which took effect long after the bug itself had disappeared. An entymologist figured it out. The mealy bug was really a cow that was herded from plant to plant by ants who relished the sticky milk it produced. The ants tended the mealy bugs carefully until such time as the bugs became plump. Then they were butchered and consumed as meat. The solution was simple: a spray which exterminated the cows. By 1934 nematodes (de-

145

structive worms) had established themselves in the red soil and were killing the pineapple roots, but a deep-soil fumigant cured this.

And in 1943 another smart chemist discovered that hormones in the form of napthalene acetic acids could control the flowering and fruiting of the pineapple plant, thus encouraging an increase in size and a ripening of the crop just when it was needed at the factory.

Said a president of one of the big companies, "If we can lick such problems as the mealy bug and the nematode, we can handle frozen orange juice." While I was in the islands the first batch of frozen pineapple juice was shipped to the mainland. It tasted good.

Biologically Hawaii is the end of the road. From Asia came the living things which inhabit the islands: shellfish, marine life, birds and, ultimately, people, so that Hawaii is markedly similar to lands bordering the Indian Ocean. But when they reached Hawaii these organisms could go no farther, for between Hawaii and America lies one of the two or three emptiest reaches of ocean in the world, and only a few fish could make that enormous journey. Thus in natural life, too, Hawaii and California are quite dissimilar.

Hawaii's extraordinary isolation extended into modern history, and as the islands were among the latest born, so were they the latest important feature on the earth's surface to be discovered. (In the late 1500's, for example, there was a brisk trade between Mexico and Manila, but the westward caravels kept well south, seeking favorable ocean currents, and far to the north while returning to Mexico on another current. Literally thousands of ships must have passed Hawaii before Cook discovered the islands.)

Understandably, then, when Hawaii was discovered, much of its wildlife was unique, but those things which have made it famous have all come from the outside in recent years. The Polynesians brought with them coconut, taro, banana and breadfruit from Tahiti. From the Marquesas came the important papaya, and from other remote parts of the world came the rest: lemons and limes (Asia); figs (California); avocados

(Guatemala); guavas (Brazil); passion fruit (Australia); water-melons (Africa).

Two fruits grow in Hawaii better than in their original homes and are the joy of the islands. The mango from Manila is a superb honey-dripping golden fruit encased in a leathery green-and-red skin. Mangoes in some parts of the world are stringy and jam your teeth, but the Hawaiian variety has been cultivated to perfection and is delectable.

The poha, from Cape of Good Hope, is a cherry-like fruit with tiny seeds. Were Hawaii able to grow sufficient quantities of this fruit, I am sure that poha jam would become a rage on the mainland, for it tastes like oranges and rare nuts mixed . . . and poha ice cream is the best.

This migration of fish and shells and fruit from Asia estab-lished a pattern for humans to follow, and by every law of nature Hawaii belongs to Asia; but by every man-made law of good government, education, philosophy, language and air-plane, Hawaii belongs to North America, and it is one of the appropriate breaks of history that this focal group of islands should be available to serve as America's western gateway to Asia. We could have no better.

It is quite likely that future intercourse between Hawaii and Asia will increase rather than diminish, and the University of Hawaii has publicly proposed "a policy which would greatly increase the number of appointments of United States citizens of Chinese, Filipino, Japanese, Negro and other non-Cauca-sian ancestries as representatives of this nation in Asia."

The idea is a good one, for although today it is fashionable to think of Hawaii as an exhibition case to show mainland Americans how people of various races can live together har-moniously, I am sure her major destiny is to serve as a bridge between Asia and America. The day will come when all Americans will congratulate themselves on having in Hawaii a group of people devoutly American yet able to understand Asia, to speak its languages and to go forth as our ambassadors.

The Hawaiian economy today seems not only secure but on the threshold of expansion. One major block, however, is the shortage of land and housing. The problem is so acute that islanders sometimes warn intending permanent visitors to stay out. It is aggravated by a unique and curious system of land ownership.

Suppose you want to build a house. Finding land that you can buy outright is almost impossible, and even if you should stumble upon some, the price is prohibitive, for it is sold by the square foot, and in a desirable suburb a choice lot may run as high as $6 a foot. (That adds up to $261,360 an acre for land which on the mainland might bring $2,000.) In Honolulu proper, land has recently sold for $60 a square foot, or $2,500,000 an acre.

But you won't be able to find land to buy, even if you have the money, for land is leased not sold. The Bishop Estate, for example, holds vast areas willed to it by one of the last princesses of the royal line, Bernice Pauahi Bishop, who directed that its income go to the Kamehameha School for the education of Hawaiian children. The Estate sells no land but will give a lease for fifty-five years.

In many ways the system is not bad, for you can get a fine lot for $265 a year, which is about what you would pay on the mainland for interest on a $5,000 lot. This means that you can put more of your money into the house and little into the land. Of course, if you live fifty-five years your home reverts to the Estate, but they have been good about extending their leases in hardship cases. However, some mainland suckers have been taken hard by local sharpies who sell excellent houses for a few thousand dollars, hiding the fact that in four years the house will legally revert to the Estate.

Some Hawaiians protest this system and insist the courts should force a public sale of all lease lands, but this the courts have refused to do, and there are many in the islands who favor continuation of the present plan. "It does permit building better homes, and besides, the way builders work these days, you can be sure no house will stand up for fifty-five years."

In spite of all difficulties, bright young men from the mainland have invaded Hawaii in recent years and have gained amazing success. Their stories have an enviable monotony and I shall report only three.

Spence Weaver was a Yale man on a trip around the world. He saw Hawaii and said, "This is it." Within a few years he had built a string of crisp restaurants doing a huge business.

Millard Blair says with disarming frankness, "I tried to drink Salt Lake City dry and woke up one morning broke. I said, 'Blair, you're getting to be an old man.' I was thirty and recalled how good Hawaii had looked to me when I worked there for the Navy." Now, at thirty-eight, this stocky redhead with excellent artistic taste turns out superb wood carvings and will do well over a quarter of a million dollars' worth of business this year.

Nat Norfleet, from Los Angeles, did as well with his big idea: the aloha shirt. Today he sells 250,000 of them a year to one store alone and has profitable customers around the world. His cloth, mainland-made, reproduces authentic South Seas designs borrowed from tapas and batiks. (Few self-respecting islanders wear flashy pineapple or hula-girl patterns any more. Many island men, essentially conservative, wear the shirttail tucked in.) Today the aloha shirt has become so much a part of Hawaii that it boasts its own poet laureate, Harriet Gallet, who has been fighting for twenty-two years to get businessmen to doff their hot coats, at least in July and August:

> Common sense, comfort, climatic conditions,
> These should decide a man's garments, it seems.
> Warm coats, tight collars, long sleeves if discarded,
> Might at long last fulfill man's fondest dreams.
> Dreams of replacing hot garments for cool ones,
> Dreams of the freedom such changes might give,
> Leading, of course, to a plan not too drastic,
> All in the spirit of live and let live.

I must not end this rambling discourse on a too-serious note. Hawaii is one terrific place to visit. I like the joyous life, the beautiful girls, the trade winds, the sky overflowing with dark gray clouds, the poha jam, the dripping mangoes, the myriad fish down in the dark caves, the steady conservative heartbeat,

149

the exciting surf and the fat women with armfuls of leis and crazy banana hats. I like a place where a man, proud of his ancestry, can call himself Killarney Opiopio.

As a bleary-eyed friend told me one night when he thought with horror of returning to a cold climate the next day, "When Hawaii calls, Bub, more better you listen."

Legacy: The Australian Way

One day last month a freckled-faced boy of nine stood sullenly before a juvenile court in Sydney, Australia. The magistrate, grim-lipped and handsome Frank Murphy, said sharply, "Let the boy Ritchie come forward."

Tom Ritchie, who seemed obviously on the road to juvenile delinquency, glared at the magistrate.

"Tom," the judge asked. "Did you break into the railway works?"

"Yes."

"Did you find a hammer and do a hundred and twenty pounds' worth of damage?"

"Yes."

"Why?"

Tom stared back defiantly.

The magistrate then addressed the boy's mother and asked, "Mrs. Ritchie, can you explain your son's actions?"

A thin, red-haired woman tried unsuccessfully to control her tears and finally blurted, "Tom's a good boy. He can do fine in school. But since his father's death I can't do nothing with him."

At this point a court official interrupted. "Your honor, this boy's father served gallantly as a soldier in North Africa."

Immediately the magistrate's face brightened and he asked, "Is the boy eligible for Legacy?"

From the back of the court stepped an inconspicuous man of forty. He wore an inexpensive suit that needed pressing and a tie that shied away from the neck. He said awkwardly, "My name's George Norton. Legatee Norton. I request your honor to remand this boy to me. Legacy will take full charge."

Magistrate Murphy called young Ritchie before him and said severely, "Son, you're getting the finest second chance a boy ever had. But if Legacy can't keep you out of trouble, I'll have to send you to an institution."

"He'll never be back in court," Legatee Norton said quietly. Then he took Tom's hand and led him off to one of the most amazing social services in the world.

Within three days George Norton, who runs a small plumbing establishment, persuaded Legacy, a volunteer group of ex-servicemen who care for widows and orphans of Australian fighting men, to take the following steps to protect the Ritchie family:

First, Mrs. Ritchie was given a weekly cash allowance which would bring her family up to the minimum required for decent living in Australia.

Second, a Legacy committee started the paper work necessary for her to get a government pension.

Third, the family was moved from a substandard home into a new flat, with Legacy paying the moving charges and the first month's rent.

Fourth, Mrs. Ritchie was sent to the Legacy dentist, who without charge fixed her teeth, which had been unattended during her husband's long illness.

Fifth, Legatee Norton visited two stores from which Mrs. Ritchie had bought goods on the hire-purchase plan (installment buying) and persuaded them to suspend payments for two months until the family finances were organized.

Sixth, for three successive nights Legatee Norton met with Mrs. Ritchie and went over in the most careful detail every financial, social and general problem faced by the widow.

Only then, after the Ritchie family had been firmly reestablished, did Legatee Norton begin to worry about nine-year-old Tom, who owed the railroad more than $500 for malicious damage.

At this point I visited the president of the Sydney chapter of Legacy, and when I asked him about Tom Ritchie, he said firmly, "Understand first that Legacy is not a charity. Nor is it interested primarily in juvenile delinquency. We're a bunch of soldiers who by the grace of God lived through war. For the rest of our lives we are determined that the families of our mates who did not live shall know some security.

"Take the case of young Ritchie. We didn't know his father had died. But as soon as we heard of the boy's trouble, we assigned Legatee Norton to the case. His first job was to help Mrs. Ritchie. When this was accomplished, he brought young Tom into our Sydney offices and enrolled him in a gymnasium class where he'll meet boys of his own age. Then our doctor gave him a complete physical and sent him to one of the highest-paid specialists in Australia for free treatment. Our dentist filled three cavities without cost, and our psychiatrist studied the boy and found him well adjusted but badly frightened by his father's death.

"What do you suppose the committee recommended as our first action in taking care of Tom Ritchie? They decided Tom should have a new, bigger bed. And they thought a boy his age should have at least about thirty cents in pocket money each week. Next we sent him on vacation to a country home where he could settle down. And sometime next month we'll talk to him and his mother concerning ways in which the money can be repaid to the railway."

When I saw Tom Ritchie again, he looked like an ordinary, well-behaved nine-year-old, freckled and happy. If he behaves himself and does reasonably well in school, he can depend on Legacy for these things:

First, Legacy will pay for his complete education, if money is needed.

Second, Legacy will provide full vocational guidance and will help him get a job at any time.

153

Third, Legacy will provide free of charge the finest medical and dental care available.

Fourth, Legacy will take the boy on vacations, arrange holidays in the homes of Legacy members, provide recreation two nights a week and keep him in contact with healthy boys his own age.

Fifth, no matter where in Australia Tom goes, some Legacy member will be alerted to look after him.

Sixth, if he shows academic promise, Legacy will either try to get him a university scholarship or will pay the tuition.

Seventh, if Tom should show promise in some advanced field like medicine or law, Legacy will provide living quarters, at very low cost, while he studies.

Eighth, if he should have an inclination toward business or a trade, Legacy will provide supervised living quarters at low cost during the period of his apprenticeship.

And finally, if Tom should die and leave his widowed mother with no support, Legacy will take care of her for as long as she lives, providing a home if necessary.

In short, no nation in the world cares for its war widows and orphans with as much generosity, thoughtfulness and love as Australia. The reason is Legacy.

Prior to World War I, Australia was provincial in outlook. Stuck away on a continent of its own across the world from England, it had developed a self-reliant individualism. Only recently had the six enormous and somewhat independent states united in a federal government, and a national spirit had not yet evolved.

But in World War I Australian troops surged across France and the Near East, winning great laurels and a new sensation of brotherhood, so that when the men returned home they were determined not to lose this newly discovered Australian spirit. Specifically, they swore never to ignore the memories of their mates who had died overseas.

Throughout the nation veterans expressed a hope that something tangible could be done to perpetuate the new spirit. Enormous monuments were erected. Parade grounds were built and statues festooned the land. In addition, impromptu groups sprang up, including the Remembrance Club in the island state of Tasmania. Soon members of the Tasmanian group were meeting with like-minded veterans in Melbourne, and by 1926 Legacy, as such, was flourishing.

It is an extraordinary society, for it has no central authority. Each club is its own boss, fully competent to handle its own affairs without domination from any national body.

It is severely anonymous and the names of individual Legatees never appear in the press. It acts only through committees, so that when Legatee George Norton was directed to take charge of the Ritchie family he was allowed to do nothing without previous consultation with one of the permanent committees. Funds are obtained solely from public subscription.

Legacy enjoys an unrivaled reputation throughout Australia. A leading politician told me, "It's about our only institution whose motives have never been questioned." This spotless name is protected by a tradition which prohibits any Legatee from profiting by his connection with Legacy. Recently a Legatee forgot this rule and circularized members with the information that he was opening an insurance agency and would appreciate their patronage. He was ousted.

A veteran can work for Legacy only if he served overseas, but membership is by no means automatic, as George Norton discovered when he applied.

Norton's father was killed at Ypres, in World War I, and some years thereafter his mother deserted him. In 1926 the Sydney Legacy found him knocking about from one family to another and petitioned the court to assign the boy to them.

George Norton's entire education, his apprenticeship to a plumber and his start in adult life were provided by Legacy. In 1939 he volunteered for military service and spent seven years in Africa and Europe.

Upon returning from World War II, he had to work overtime to establish his business and had no time to spare for Legacy, but in 1954 things were going well and he wished to repay the debt he owed the men who had helped him.

155

He applied for membership and was told by the committee, "We will accept you only if you are prepared to give freely of your time, yourself and your love." No mention was made of money, and none has ever been collected from Norton. He did have to promise, however, that he would give at least one lunch period and two nights a week to Legacy.

The committee, satisfied that Norton understood his obligations, then kept him waiting for three months while they investigated his personal life. "We don't want any risks in Legacy," the chairman said. "If you've ever been in jail, or mixed up in a morals case, or charged with dishonest practices, please withdraw your application now."

Norton passed, but while I was in Sydney a petitioner passed the local investigations only to have an unsavory incident that occurred 3,000 miles away turn up. He was allowed to retreat without comment from anyone.

George Norton now entered his internship, which consisted of watching the major committees at work. He saw how family problems are handled, how girls are helped, how truancy is combated and how elderly widows are cared for. He found, to his surprise, that over 60 percent of all appeals to Legacy involve no money, only advice. The most constant refrain he heard during his period of listening to interviews was: "I just couldn't go on. I didn't know what to do." He was amazed at how much good the men of Legacy did simply by talking to families where there was no father.

When he had completed his indoctrination, Norton was given his choice of committees, and replied quietly that he liked to work with boys, since he knew from his own life how important that was. His second job was Tom Ritchie.

Legatee Norton sees young Tom at least twice a week, and on his own he spends some of the money he makes as a plumber giving Tom the little opportunities a boy of nine should have. He is quite severe with the boy where schoolwork is concerned, and Tom is beginning to look like a good student.

From what I have seen of Tom Ritchie's progress since Legatee Norton took over, I would say there wasn't one chance in ten thousand that this little boy will ever develop into a juvenile delinquent. George Norton, in his quiet way, wouldn't allow it.

Sydney, like most Australian communities, is marked by signs of Legacy's compassion. One suburb contains a handsome private residence turned into a home for elderly war widows like Rose Ellen Lush, eighty, whose husband joined the army in 1898, to die in France in 1918. She says of Legacy, "Never heard of it till I was in my seventies. But what a lovely home this is. I wish all my old friends had a place half as nice."

Not far away is a special home for children who need sea air. There are excellent dormitories with sweeping flower gardens for teen-age girls and homes with tennis courts for orphaned boys who are learning trades.

But no work of Legacy is more touching than its efforts to provide growing girls with a sense of having a father who is interested in them. One evening I met Mrs. Phyllis Hall, a most attractive war widow who earns a satisfying salary as a radio executive. You would expect her to be the last woman in Sydney who would need Legacy's help, but she said, "When my husband died I was able to take care of everything but the most important job of all. My daughter Gail felt as if the world had ended. I watched how unhappy and insecure she was becoming. Then I heard of Legacy and I took Gail to see the committee. We've never accepted a penny, of course. But the change in Gail . . . talking with men her father's age, consulting them on little problems that come up . . . It has been the salvation of our family life."

It is little wonder that each year dozens of orphaned girls who get married throughout Australia ask some Legatee to give them away at the altar. Practically no Legacy girls run wild.

I was particularly surprised by the fact that on gymnasium nights dozens of mothers come along too. They form a kind of club where they can talk with other war widows facing similar problems. Inevitably, in recent years quite a few young men who have grown up in Legacy have married girls who did the same.

But throughout Australia, Legacy is best known for the

admirable work it does with boys. Magistrate Murphy says, "When I can turn a troublesome boy over to Legacy, I am happy. It means I have found the best single way to rehabilitate that boy."

This is partly because the men of Legacy actually do look upon the sons of their fallen comrades as their personal responsibilities, and partly because Legacy employs highly trained professional social workers to handle difficult cases. For example, when Legatee George Norton goes to see potential delinquent Tom Ritchie, a trained woman with years of experience in juvenile cases briefs Norton on what to expect. As the permanent secretary of Sydney Legacy said, "The last thing we want is enthusiastic amateurs messing in human lives. What we have found indispensable is enthusiasm based on sound knowledge."

Reports on Legacy from the general community were so laudatory that I felt there must be another side to the picture. Accordingly, throughout Australia I inquired for any criticism that anyone had ever heard regarding this remarkable organization. This is what I found:

Criticism: Legatees are apt to be from the upper class. Only officers are accepted. *Answer:* "Of course our present president is a former general. But one of his predecessors was a private. Many of our best workers have modest incomes."

Criticism: Legacy harms certain children by constantly reminding them that their fathers are dead. *Answer:* "We have studied this problem for many years and have concluded that the absent father is a terrible and inescapable fact. By openly dealing with this problem, by having orphans meet others whose fathers died in battle, we remove the sting."

Criticism: Legacy's help to widows is so generous that these women become unwilling to marry a second time and thus deprive their children of normal homes. *Answer:* "A huge proportion of our widows remarry. It is true that we do step in with help at a highly emotional time when a widow might marry out of desperation. On the other hand, after we have helped her straighten out her affairs, after we have got the children started right, we find that our widows are doubly attractive as marriage risks."

Criticism: Legacy gets so attached to its complete orphans that it is tardy in putting them up for legal adoption. *Answer:* "We get few children who are completely orphaned, but when we do get such infants we endeavor to place them in permanent homes. Most children for whom we accept full responsibility have existing relatives who will not permit adoption. And we have further found that children of eight or nine and older do best if they are not formally adopted."

Criticism: Legacy gives its children too much attention. *Answer:* "Guilty. We think that the best therapy in the world is human love, generously applied. It is possible that occasionally we spoil a child, but it is certain that we rescue thousands . . . with love."

My favorite Legatee is Norman Crosswell, a schoolteacher in a remote corner of the outback. With no widowed families to look after in his community, Crosswell could properly forget his obligation to Legacy, but he says, "I can never forget my mates who didn't get back alive." How does Legatee Crosswell discharge this obligation? Last year he collected about $5,000 through his countryside and sent it off to the nearest city, where Legacy committees could spend the money wisely.

Crosswell says, "The idea of Legacy could operate in any country that was willing to adopt its simple principles. First, a soldier who escapes death has a life-long obligation to his mate who didn't. Second, in the discharge of this duty no money should be accepted from the government. Third, the most valuable contribution, which can be made by any man, is love."

In Australia these principles have accomplished a social miracle. They have minimized one of the worst aspects of war: the tragedy of broken homes.

DOING RESEARCH

The two articles which follow illustrate how I worked in the years when I was traveling to various parts of the world on research trips, writing occasional articles for the *Digest* and vaguely planning the books that I might one day want to write.

The *Digest* editors obviously required much material to fill their magazine each month. They depended primarily on purchasing reprint rights from other magazines, but they also needed original writing. With the requirements of their magazine clearly in mind, the editors developed scores of ideas, and occasionally one would seem appropriate for me. When six or eight such relevant ideas had accumulated in the *Digest* offices, Hobart Lewis would send me a letter summarizing them, with the understanding that I would select the one or two which best fitted in with my private plans.

On my own, during this time I would have been pondering the direction I ought to take next and particularly which areas of the world seemed most pregnant for the type of writing I did. I would often be in a state of indecision, or even confusion, for many months, projecting plans that usually failed to materialize or starting work that quickly fell apart because the basic concept wasn't strong enough. I might have as many as six potential courses open and find myself committed to none. At such moments of impasse, which every writer experiences and I more than most, it was often refreshing to receive the letter from Lewis, for it gave me tangible projects to work upon; what was even better, it made me stop drifting and forced me to select some specific topic upon which to concentrate.

Never, in my extensive geographical-research articles, did I undertake one with the idea of later using it as the basis for a book. Invariably it was the other way around: I went out into the field, did the spadework, wrote up my notes, and not until some years later did I decide that this material might form the basis for a book, or a segment of a book. I was always surprised when the research material came flooding back to me in dramatic form. Without exception, when I did finally attempt to turn what had been nonfiction research into fiction, I returned to the scene and restudied the locale, the people, the spiritual values and the general meaning of the place. Never would I trust my memory.

To be specific. I have lived in Bucks County, Pennsylvania, for sixty-six years, and while living here I have constantly studied the place and its people. But if I were residing in England, and wanted to write about Bucks County, I would have to come back here and restudy everything, because there is a vast gap between knowing a place vaguely and knowing it well enough to write about it. In fact, I have never apprehended Bucks County as a writer would have to know it were he intending to write about it. So my novels have invariably been the result of studied re-visits to old haunts.

When I went originally to a place like Afghanistan or Malaya, or any of the other areas about which I wrote for the *Digest*, I took with me the very best geography I could find, a history of the area's religion, literature and art, and some good maps. Without geography I would have been lost, for I have seen each part of the world as an area with its own characteristics, populated by human beings with unique ideas but limited by the land area they occupied. I have never expected an

162

Eskimo to behave like a Congolese, nor to have the same religion, the same concept of the universe or the same eating habits. When I arrived on the scene I always bought the best local histories, but for me the unrolling of history always came after the geographical and cultural facts had first been defined.

When I reached the country, I traveled everywhere, sometimes to the most extraordinary places and by odd conveyance. And I listened. I had a knack for getting conversations started, probably because I was interested in the basic problems which interested the people I was talking with. This knack, of course, had its built-in weakness: I have always tended to nod my head and agree when something was said, not because I was afraid to argue, but because I wanted the speaker to develop his idea to the fullest. This has sometimes caused my friends dismay, for I can be totally attentive to the reasoning of either an admitted Nazi or a dedicated Communist. Later, when I am off by myself, I sort out my own beliefs.

When I started to write, often under incredibly difficult circumstances, I sought only a large flat space on which to arrange my papers. One of the best working surfaces I ever used was an unfinished door propped up on cement blocks. This provided a big solid expanse on which to spread papers. I have written three of my best novels on such doors. I have written in the tropics, in the arctic, with noise on every side, and in various paradises like Samoa and Ceylon, but the places I remember with most affection were the quiet bare rooms without much view.

I tried valiantly to get everything down on paper, even the trivia, and even now I feel a sense of chagrin at how much work I have given my various editors. I said earlier that for every page that was finally used by the *Digest*, I submitted eight, but in my long research jobs, such as the two that follow, the proportion must have been even greater. I would not change. The job of the writer is to respond in an orderly way to the confusion of impression that engulfs him, and I have found that time and again what the reader has appreciated most has been the odd sidelight, the unexpected relationship that can be caught in no other way.

My writing life has therefore been a constant barrage from my editors and critics that I have written too much, and an unending flood of letters from my readers that I stopped my stories too soon. The truth obviously lies somewhere in the middle, but that happy mean has escaped me.

Afghanistan: Meeting
Place of Nations

NOVEMBER, 1955 ✗

One day last spring I stepped into the shop of Mr. K. A.
Gai, Wholesale Grocer and Wine Merchant, in Peshawar at
the eastern end of the Khyber Pass. There I was handed a
message for the truck driver waiting outside: *Sir: In obedience
to your order I herewith beg to send the following to Afghanistan:* Mr.
Michener. *Please sign and state the number of empties returned.*

Thus I started one of the finest trips of my life, for today
Afghanistan is profoundly exciting.

Here in this high wild land the traveler finds a way of life
at least 5,000 years old. At the same time he finds the only
available close look into modern communist Russia. In this
strange country Russia and the free world collide.

Afghanistan has perpetually been the meeting place of nations. Centuries before the birth of Christ, sophisticated Persia
and savage central Asia met here. Alexander the Great, Genghis Khan and Tamerlane passed through Afghanistan to conquer vast dominions, and in later years fiery Turkish and
Persian kings used this little country as their base for chopping out powerful kingdoms in India.

In fact, a recent scientific expedition to Afghanistan posted
this sign at headquarters: "Everybody who was ever anybody

came this way." Any future conqueror of Asia will surely use Afghanistan as a major base, and if India is ever invaded again, the emeny will, as in the past, drop down through the Khyber Pass.

Today men see that if communism is to expand southward, either from Russia or China, it will move through Afghanistan.

Afghanistan—the *g* is silent and often the *f* too, so that the name resembles Aw-hahn-ee-stahn, with sharp accents on the second and fourth syllables—slopes sharply from the vast Hindu Kush mountains in the northeast to the blazing Desert of Death in the southwest.

It is about the size of Texas but is ninety-two percent barren, receiving almost no rainfall on areas that would normally be cultivated. Only the numerous rivers plunging down from snow-clad peaks make life possible, for wherever water can be led onto the land, the wastes blossom. On one tumbling mountain stream, for example, I counted eleven separate irrigation systems being led away in one mile, and the valley had become a paradise of melon, fruit, nuts, rice, wheat and cattle.

Most extraordinary are the invisible irrigation ditches that probe into the hearts of mountains that seem completely barren but which hide rich stores of water. Sharp-eyed experts will study a slope and conclude, "There must be water running below us somewhere." So they dig a well, sometimes seventy feet deep, and find the water. Then extremely brave excavators descend the well and begin to dig a tunnel along the line of flow. Sometimes they penetrate up to twenty miles, always deep in the earth, always leading water to where it can be used. At thirty- or forty-foot intervals, new wells are dug so that the loosened earth can be thrown out, and in time one can see these wells marching far across the landscape.

Digging such an irrigation system is most dangerous, and men who work at this job are given extra pay, extra clothes, extra food and extra women. When they die from suffocation or falling rock, their clothes and women are passed on to some new digger, and the precious water continues to flow.

Few Americans appreciate the historical role Afghanistan

has played. In religion it was the center from which Zoroastrianism developed, the solid home from which Buddhism traveled to China and Japan, and a major center for Muslim philosophy. Curiously, when Greek art declined in Athens, it flourished in a new birth in Afghanistan, which sent precious samples to inspire the artists of India, Angkor Wat and China. What we call Persian miniatures were done best in Afghanistan, and the foremost Persian poems were written here at the command of Afghan kings. Frequently these kings ruled all of the territory between Persia and central India.

But that is the historical grandeur of Afghanistan. What is it like today?

It is great to be an Afghan man. You are tall, spare, tough. You wear a beard and carry a gun. You don't pay too much attention to what the government says and you are one of the most hospitable men on earth. The minute a stranger crosses your threshold, you order a sheep killed for celebration, and between fights you sing and dance and travel the high mountain passes. It's a rare, free life.

Prior to Afghanistan's informal alliance with Hilter—Germans have always been the preferred Europeans—the nation claimed direct descent from one of the Lost Tribes of Israel, and one does find many Semitic characteristics; but starting about 1935 the Israel business was abruptly dropped and Afghans lodged a formal claim to being the original Aryans, adopting as the original name of their country Aryana. Snaps a French specialist, "Unquestionably the Aryans from the west used Afghanistan as their doorway to India. But that doesn't make the country itself Aryan, because how many people do you know who were born in doorways?"

The Afghan makes a good living from agriculture, karakul skins and the best fruit and nuts in Asia. In the north he also breeds glorious horses and in the south enormous herds of camels which sell for about forty dollars each. In the cities, his bazaars have always been famous, filled with goods from India, Persia, Russia and China. Today many American products are on sale.

An Afghan man, dressed for celebration, is a pretty dazzling object. About a small gold skullcap he wraps a filmy turban, beneath which appears a shirt exquisitely embroidered and worn outside, with tails that reach below the knees. Soft, white, baggy trousers are preferred, topped by a well-tailored coat and vest. Especially popular are U. S. Marine Corps whip-cord aviation jackets, bought in large lots as war surplus. Even more common are U. S. Army blouses bearing flashy division patches.

In spite of the fact that the thermometer often reaches 115 degrees, most Afghan men invariably wear heavy overcoats, the humidity being so amazingly low that one never sweats. Once, with the temperature at 120, I saw a man wearing two overcoats, and I asked him why.

"Gets cold at night," he explained.

Afghan men, reared in a raiding society, must take unusual precautions to protect their property. The first thing a man does when he plants a melon patch is to erect in the middle of the field a tiny house, where he watches. When the fruit ripens, his whole family joins him so that each corner of the field can be patrolled. Otherwise, in a single night every melon would vanish.

As pets Afghans carry about with them handsome little fighting quail. Normally the cocky birds are kept in wicker cages, but several hours a day the owner takes the bird out and massages the leg muscles, pulling them, twisting them, pinching them with his fingers. When the bird seems ready for battle a huge blanket is spread on the ground for the audience. Then two birds are released and a furious fight develops. The gambling is lively, but as soon as a bird has lost three battles, he is popped into the stew.

Afghan men pray constantly, spreading rugs or coats upon the ground and facing west, toward Mecca. Buses stop even scheduled runs to permit prayers. Mosques abound.

The nation's leaders claim from twelve to twenty million population, but a more likely figure would be about eight to ten million, ninety-six percent of whom were illiterate at the last guess. Today, with emphasis being placed on reading, the figure probably has dropped to about eighty percent.

One reason why Afghanistan has never bothered much with statistics is that each measure has a different value in each city. Thus a seer, which weighs about 2.2 pounds throughout the rest of Asia, weighs 18 pounds in one Afghan city, 15 in another, and only 9.5 in the capital. Each city also establishes its own standard time, which may vary throughout the year.

The center of Afghan life is the teahouse, hundreds of them dotting every road. They are clean, open shelters where men can catch a cup of tea and sugar for about a penny. Sometimes a man will drink fifteen pots of tea in an hour. The tea comes by camel train from India, the bright crockery from Japan.

I can still recall the teahouse at Ghorband, high in the mountains. Over a swiftly running brook an arbor had been erected, heavy with grapes. Small platforms of dried mud had been built beside the tumbling stream and covered with handsome Persian rugs. A huge samovar, with a heating stack right up the middle, provided boiling water. The fire was of cow-dung chips, whose burning provided a pungent incense. On another stove, lamb kebabs were crisping and huge flats of whole-wheat bread, exactly the size of snowshoes, were being toasted.

When we arrived at this teahouse, hot and gritty, the regular customers stood aside while we fell to the ground and dipped our heads into the cool stream. Then the community hookah (one never smokes the hubble-bubble pipe alone) was filled with strong tobacco and passed. Strangers grinned at us, and soon we were being invited to their houses for dinner. In some thirty stops at mountain teahouses, we were invited home to dinner at least twenty times. All travelers have remarked upon the warm hospitality of an Afghan teahouse.

There is only one thing wrong. No women are allowed.

If being an Afghan man is fun, being a woman is hell. From the day she is thirteen, the Afghan woman always appears in a shroud which covers her, literally, from head to toe. A pathetic little square is cut away for her to see through, but this is covered by a silken cheesecloth. Since exposure of hands would be especially heinous, even these are folded perpetually in her shroud. I know of many Americans who have been in

169

Afghanistan upwards of eighteen months without seeing the face of an Afghan woman.

Even though they keep hidden in shrouds, they participate in almost no social functions. In the lovely teahouses they are never seen. At the movies, at plays, in public celebrations, at games or riding contests, or at formal dinners no woman is permitted, although sometimes special movies are run off for all-female audiences. Recently a restaurant was closed down because the owner set aside Wednesday noon for women. The police held that a man who would allow women in a restaurant would probably be capable of any crime, so they hauled him away.

One of the most affecting sights in Asia is Afghan school-girls bursting out of their classrooms. Children under thirteen are spectacularly beautiful: handsome features in Persian style, clear complexions, very good teeth and flashing black eyes. But girls thirteen or older appear only in silken shrouds that will cover them the rest of their lives.

A friend of mine stood on a corner as three of these ghostlike figures approached, carrying books. Looking swiftly up and down the street, they saw no policeman, and one softly quoted, " 'The quality of mercy is not strained.' Did you learn that in your school?" Before he could reply the girls gave a frightened yelp, indicated a policeman who had suddenly turned a corner, and silently vanished like ghosts.

I was lucky. I saw an Afghan woman. We threw a party for her husband and he walked openly down the street to our house. Then, after dark, we sent a jeep heavily curtained to his back door. His wife slipped into it, and taking a back-alley route, drove to our back door, where she slipped in unseen by the neighbors, for she was doing an evil thing. But rotten luck was with us, for at that moment our cook, a tall, hungry man with cadaverous eyes, saw this woman boldly visiting strangers. He stared at her with a hatred I have rarely seen and that night hurried off to report her to the authorities. When I left that part of Afghanistan, both she and her daring husband were in serious trouble.

The price Afghanistan pays for this nonsense, not sanctioned by Islam, is bitter. No women work in stores, none serve as waitresses or cooks. Of course, factories use men alone, and no women help in government, or teach boys, or work as librarians. Often men even do the family marketing, and I once traveled for three days through cities in northern Afghanistan without seeing a single woman, while sixty miles away similar women in Russia were helping to run the nation.

The economic cost of this segregation is enormous, the total Afghan economy being about 40 percent less productive than comparable economies where women participate. Some features of the system are regrettable (even in family parties women are often left behind) and some are pathetic (western women frequently see an Afghan woman surreptitiously raise her shroud to disclose Parisian shoes or a New York dress).

But one aspect is unbelievable. In much of Afghanistan a doctor called to visit a woman sits in one room, his patient in another. The husband then moves back and forth between the two rooms, conveying his wife's report of her symptoms. If anything offends either his dignity as a husband or his view of religion, he censors that symptom, and if the doctor's blind guess as to what should be done seems too costly or against local custom, the husband refuses the diagnosis. In some parts of Afghanistan women do not even consult doctors. They die in silence.

European doctors, of course, and some modern Afghans trained in America, will not tolerate such practices, and before visiting a woman, insist upon the right to examine her. But in general, westerners living in Afghanistan rarely comment upon these archaic customs. To do so infuriates traditional Afghan purists and hurts those who are working for change.

A particularly distressing aspect of this system occurs on long trips, where, as I have explained, one needs the refreshing stop in the cool teahouse. Such a rest, of course, is reserved for men only, for women must remain in the truck cabins, windows tightly closed, sun beating down mercilessly on the crowded, shrouded figures. Explain the men, "We respect our women. We don't want loafers in tearooms staring at them."

Today a new problem has arisen beneath the shroud. Com-

171

munism has never had much success in Afghanistan, for the local people say, "We live too close to Russia. We know what goes on up there." But there are rumors that in recent years secret agents have been stirring up hundreds of young Afghan women with the simple statement: "When we take over, the shroud will go . . . as it did across the river in Russia."

There is only one valley in Asia that resembles Shangri-La: the noble Vale of Bamian in the north.

Here a sturdy river plunges down from vast heights and forms a valley so tranquil and delicious that it seems an invention of a happy mind. Tall poplars and cypresses form cool lanes. Quiet irrigation ditches lead onto fields of unusual richness, and an azure sky hangs low upon peaceful villages and farms.

Merely as a display of benevolent nature Bamian would be memorable, but in addition, it is one of the great monuments of human history, for it was from there that Buddhism spread to China and Japan.

To the north of Bamian rises a gigantic, treeless mountain, which in a series of steep slopes drops down to the river. Eons ago the stream cut away the face of the last drop, leaving a perpendicular red cliff. Shortly before the birth of Christ, Buddhists arrived here and carved into the cliff stupendous statues of Buddha, hidden in superb niches, so that the god seems to spring from the living rock. One is 165 feet tall (about the height of thirty men), an overpowering object of devotion.

Into the face of the cliff, on many different levels, these early Buddhists carved thousands of enormous caves, hidden corridors and tiny cubicles. The cliff thus became a living temple, each room of which was ornamented with elegant carving and lovely frescoes. As an art museum alone, it must have been magnificent.

The glory of Bamian is inexhaustible. Once, while friends explored deep caves, I sat in a room as big as a movie theater looking out upon the tender valley. Above the cool trees I counted sixty-one separate mountain peaks, each over 14,000 feet high; each was snow- covered and heavy with valleys and waterfalls. During their peaceful watch over Bamian these mountains witnessed one of history's most anguished tragedies.

To comprehend this event one must retrace his steps down the Vale of Bamian to where a rushing tributary of the main river has cut away another monumental cliff. On its summit, rising tier upon tier like a dream, stands the Red City, shimmering in the sun, a collection of towers and battlements and steep inclines. It is a fairy-tale city, apparently suspended from the heavens.

Here, on one dreadful day in the year 1221, Genghis Khan started his march up the Bamian River. He recognized that the Red City would be difficult to assault and might have passed it by, but the defenders let loose stones and chanced to kill the Mongol warrior's favorite grandson. Swearing inhuman revenge, Genghis Khan roared up the passes to Bamian, where in one fearful orgy he killed every living thing. Even grasses were rooted up and the river was diverted to flow upon the ruins of an ancient civilization.

In later years other conquerors wheeled in huge cannon, which blew away the heads of the monster statues. Earthquakes dislodged the face of the cliff, disclosing cross sections of the interior caves, and Bamian, one of the glories of Asia, became an empty, silent ruin dominating this lovely valley, protected by a giant convocation of snow-capped peaks.

In southern Afghanistan are vast deserts, which have always captivated travelers. Some are sandy and rise in sweeping dunes that are whirled about by endless winds. Others are baked clay beds, but the most famous of all, the Desert of Death (Dasht-i-Margo), is a burning gravel bed, lifted into brutal dunes by parched winds that howl across its wastes.

Twice I had an opportunity to penetrate this sullen, empty hell of wind and rock. Looking back on these trips, they seem even now the most exciting that I have ever taken.

In bouncing jeeps we started with the mournful ruins of Qala Bist, where a thousand years ago an imperial city housing many people flourished. An engineer and I measured merely

173

the walls around one of the the lesser palaces. They were nine miles long, twenty feet high and more than six feet thick. We figured that this wall alone contained over 65,000,000 bricks and that it would have taken one good team of bricklayers more than 352 years to build! Yet it formed only a trivial portion of the ruins, which in themselves were trivial as compared to what we would shortly see on the other edge of the Desert of Death.

There is no road across the desert, so for more than two hundred miles we made our own; and it is an unmatched experience to see tiny jeeps climb and drop and sweep and swerve across limitless dunes, knowing that an hour after their passing, there will be no sign that they had ever touched the desert. Once as we were doing fifty over a rolling dune, my partner said, "What a place for hot-rodders. A highway fifty miles wide!"

At night we sought, for reasons which I'll explain later, some high knoll, and there spread our blankets under the stars. Sometimes a gazelle would pass in the moonlight, and always in the distance we could hear the terrifying shriek of jackals, sounding like tormented humans. When we approached the edge of the desert, foxes and wolves appeared. When sandstorms did not blow, the night-girded Afghan desert was a place of immortal beauty.

When we were lucky enough to camp on some spot where lights could be seen, night on the desert was magical. Once I happened to spot a village that seemed as if it were only a few yards down the row of dunes; it was forty-two miles away, the absence of dust accounting for the deception. Later it was difficult to realize that we were still twelve miles from the lights, for they looked closer than a porch lamp does in city atmosphere when viewed from the front gate. Yet a man who dared to leave his car to walk to such lights would possibly be dead before he could reach them, for he would be overtaken by the rising sun.

I liked the desert best at blazing noon, when for twenty miles in each direction I could see absolutely no living thing: not a mouse, nor a blade of grass, nor a weed, nor even a dried bone to remind me of something that had once lived. This fantastic desert was the emptiest earth I had ever seen, rivaling the heaving ocean or the arctic wastes. And the scarifying wind that blew across it had zero humidity. An incessant whine, it is known as the 120-Day Wind, for it blows constantly. Once I drenched my clothes with water to stave off the heat, and in eighteen minutes I was completely dry. Once a car broke down in this desert wind, and in two days the occupants were dead, literally dried up by the roaring gale.

Ultimately we came to the wonder of the desert, the ruins of Chakhansur. Here at the edge of rocky dunes stood a hundred miles of ruined cities. Fortresses were so common they were not even named, and whole areas as large as Des Moines stood bleak and wind-swept. We found cities that looked as if they could be moved into by hungry families, others whose twenty-foot walls were nearly hidden by shifting sands.

Well over a million persons once lived here, for Chakhansur was old when Alexander the Great passed it in 329 B.C. As late as 1200 it was a flourishing complex of cities reaching well over a hundred miles. What happened?

Scholars blame the catastrophe on salt, goats and Genghis Khan. Remains are common of extraordinary irrigation canals whose prolific waters, over a score of centuries, left such heavy salt deposits that Chakhansur land became useless. Then goats, the curse of Asia, cropped the soil so closely that every tree and shrub was destroyed, leaving the wind free to whip up sand and overrun cities. Finally, we know from historical records that on one hideous day not far from Chakhansur, Genghis Khan ordered 1,200,000 people massacred. It is supposed that his insane policy of total extermination reached the ghost cities we see today, after which they were abandoned to the howling winds.

Paradoxically, on Afghan deserts more people lose their lives by drowning than from heat exhaustion, for at night the temptation is to escape the wind by sleeping in protected gullies; but once or twice a year there will be a cloudburst on the desert's edge and a body of water thiry feet high—called "the earth mover" because it can be heard crushing rocks ahead of it—will come roaring down the gullies. In 325 B.C. Alexander lost almost half his army in such a disaster when rain fell on the desert just south of where we had kept to the high knolls.

Apart from these flash floods, the greatest danger is *gotch*, a pure, flaky gypsum which when mixed with water makes excellent plaster. It lies in beds throughout the desert, but sands drift over it and it cannot be detected, so that a man driving his jeep at fifty on the impeccable roadbed of the desert will suddenly find himself pitched into a trap of *gotch* which stops him absolutely. I have seen several broken noses resulting from such jarring impact, and there have been other instances in which men trying to flee on foot across the desert have fallen into *gotch* beds and died as if in quicksand.

The big surprise of the Desert of Death is that at the southwest corner there is a little kingdom of cool oases, pomegranate groves and lush waters that constitute a miniature paradise in the dusty wastes. Here Sardar Mohammad Alam Khan, a forty-seven-year-old desert chief, rules as if the twentieth century had never happened.

He is universally called Mr. Five-by-Five, for he weighs well over three hundred pounds and has a jovial if determined nature. Owning three separate palaces, he insists upon acting as host, with all expenses paid, for infrequent travelers who come his way. Palace number one is something out of the *Arabian Nights*, a rambling, high-walled fortress lined with stalls for twenty-four stallions and hundreds of camels.

Mr. Five-by-Five is absolute sovereign of his small kingdom, for he is too far removed from governmental authority for anyone to bother him. He has his own army, his own customs guards, his own system of taxation and his own courts. And although his road system extends for only one mile, he has three new American automobiles. When he wishes to leave his domain, he simply informs his men and they build him a road, which lasts for about six months, when the bridges fall in and sand obscures all tracks.

On a recent trip, when a special road had been completed, enabling the chief to go to the capital city, he was completely taken by gold teeth that he saw there for the first time. Having great wealth at his command, he ordered the dentist to install gold teeth all the way around on his eight-year-old son.

The desert monarch gave us his second palace, a caravan-serai dating far back in history, with all rooms littered with rare Persian rugs and silver ornamentation. Twenty-four private guardsmen watched us as we slept, and another sixteen wakened us with a luscious breakfast. As we departed, Mr. Five-by-Five's camel caravans were starting forth for a long journey into Persia, his big herd of prize cattle were off to the grazing fields, his cavalry were mounting their stallions to see us on our way, and his three American cars were being greased in case he might want to ride down his mile of roadway.

He was a true desert monarch, a relic of the centuries.

Rushing through the heart of the Afghan desert is one of the world's most unusual rivers. The Helmand rises in the high mountains of central Afghanistan and quickly becomes a tor-rential stream larger than the Missouri. Twisting and turning, it breaks onto the desert and forms a huge graceful curve, only to lose itself forever upon the parched sands west of Chakhansur.

Five thousand years ago people lived along the river—their villages are only now being excavated—and even then they teased water away from the Helmand to irrigate their fields, for it was this river that kept the lost cities of Chakhansur alive. But each year most of the water escaped onto the track-less desert and evaporated.

Today, thanks to American effort, the Helmand is being tamed and modern Afghans expect new cities to rise along its banks. High in the gorges where the river still carries most of its water, the Morrison-Knudsen Company of Idaho has con-structed one of the largest earthen dams in existence. By jam-ming millions of tons of rock into a tight bend in the river, the Americans have bottled up the water behind a dam 393 feet high. A sprawling lake has been impounded to feed several hundred miles of irrigation ditches already beginning to fan out into what was previously desert.

Model villages have been built, roads thread the area and

177

new crops have been introduced. For example, I saw one large area that used to produce seven bushels of worn-out Asian corn to the acre but which now yields ninety bushels of a new hybrid American corn. The problems faced by such work in Afghanistan are exemplified by the fact that on such an extensive project in America, thirty-six engineers would be required and most of them would be highly skilled men with at least twenty years' experience. Afghanistan has only two engineers available, both just out of college, and one must be used for paper work.

However, Morrison–Knudsen's chunky Otto Oetjen, field boss of the ditches, says, "An Afghan can learn in two months what we require American mechanics to study for three years. Look at that ninty-three-ton dragline. It builds its own platforms as it goes through the swamp. The kid running it took three months to learn."

Oetjen, however, adds one warning: "But no Afghan understands maintenance. Last week that boy burned out his dragline through not giving it any oil. When I chewed him out, he said, 'A machine smart enough to know how to walk through a swamp ought to know when it needs oil.' "

In varied ways Afghanistan is working hard to bring the nation up to date. Hydroelectric plants provide current for spinning mills and big sugar factories. Schools and colleges—some colleges end at the eighth grade—are being improved, and it is not unusual to find in even remote parts of the country hard-working French or German professors who love the upland life.

Everywhere health is a preoccupation, and within a few years the nation will have first-class hospitals and enough native-born doctors to run them. Especially commendable is Afghanistan's tradition of sending bright young men abroad to study, the government footing the entire bill. Any American reading this article can probably find, in the university nearest him, some handsome young Afghan standing near the top of his class. Soon perhaps even women will go abroad for such study.

In each of the major cities—Kabul in the east center, Kandahar in the south, Herat to the west—the leaders of the country dress like Europeans, speak English, drive a hard bargain with American businessmen . . . or Russian.

There is an air of hard work, but because of a hopeless system of communication, Afghanistan's progress is slow. Apart from Tibet and Nepal, Afghanistan is the only substantial country in the world lacking railroads. Moreover, Afghans suffer the worst roads, bar none, that I have ever traveled. Potholes are so deep and so frequent that one broken spring per fifty miles is par. On some roads up to sixty percent of all cars stand wrecked, and since there are no garages, drivers hitchhike into the nearest city and prowl the bazaars, hoping to find a replacement part that someone has stolen from another vehicle.

Once, on the edge of the desert, I came upon a broken-down bus whose twenty passengers were camped beneath it to protect themselves from the blazing sun. When I asked if we could help, they said, "Oh, no. Our driver went to town three days ago and he'll be back any day now."

As a result of this system, Afghan drivers are among the most resourceful known. They make the average American look uninventive. With a piece of string, some nails and a chunk of wood they are able to fix anything.

My own experience with such a driver was memorable. One night, when it was my turn to drive, we were engulfed in a sudden swirling dust storm and I drove our jeep forty miles an hour headlong into a solid stone wall. My Afghan driver, asleep at the time, pitched headfirst right through the windshield, suffering only a minor cut, but the jeep was wrecked. The flywheel was jammed into the motor, all liquid systems were fractured and the wheels were smashed so hard that the flanges were knocked flat.

Sher Ahmad, twenty-six years old, crawled out of the windshield, brushed himself off, grabbed a crowbar and started wrenching the jeep back into shape. To get the flattened rims off, for example, he used brute strength, but to get the flywheel working, he used the crowbar as gently as if it were a jeweler's hammer.

179

Finally it looked as if the jeep would run, except for the broken water, gas and oil systems. For these Sher Ahmad purchased a handful of raisins and some unginned cotton. Mashing them together on a flat rock, he produced a paste of which he said, "When the desert air hits this, it'll dry harder than iron."

Repairing our remaining damage with this raisin-and-cotton glue, Sher Ahmad road-tested the jeep and concluded that it would run, whereupon we set out right across the Desert of Death. Next day an X-ray showed that Sher Ahmad had accomplished all this with a broken collarbone.

I am glad to say that today he is studying in America, to become an irrigation engineer. He says, "When I learn something I'll be able to help my country get ahead."

In spite of its ancient lands and people, Afghanistan as a nation is not much older that the United States. Prior to 1747, when a tribe of Afghan patriots consolidated a kingdom, the high plains and mountain passes had in turn been ruled by Persians, Greeks, Turks, Mongols, Indians and half a dozen other now-forgotten tribes. There was no nation as such, nor did there seem to be the basis for one.

It is most difficult to explain how Afghanistan exists, for it is really five separate countries. North of the Hindu Kush the land along the Oxus is logically Russian. The western section has usually been a part of Persia. The lands below the Helmand are clearly Baluchi. The eastern stretches might just as well be a part of Pakistan. And the important central valley is filled with undigested Mongols.

The reason Afghanistan has triumphed over history and the reason why it is a strong independent nation today is that it was here, in the nineteenth century, that Russia, creeping south through central Asia, finally faced Great Britain creeping north through India and the Khyber Pass. Sensibly these two powers decided that it would be desirable to maintain Afghanistan as a permanent buffer. This accounts for the curious panhandle that stretches far to the east, in some spots less than ten miles wide. It kept Russia and China from bumping into what was then British India.

Today Afghanistan continues to be protected, since all nations which might attack her profit from her neutral existence. In a sense Afghanistan can, and clearly does, trade profitably with both communism and the free world, secure in her knowledge that each will support her.

The tribe of actual Afghans who consolidated the nation in 1747 had the good luck to be led by a prolific and able royal family, whose descendants rule the nation today. King Zahir Shah, handsome and nearing fifty, followed the custom of his family and gave all the best jobs to his brilliant uncles, then later passed them on to his even more brilliant cousins, who now rule the land. Throughout Afghanistan when one meets a high government official it is customary to ask, "What relation is he to the royal family?"

The rulers are supposed to be fabulously wealthy, but lesser officials certainly are not. A clever student who is sent to America for seven years with lots of spending money, "so Afghanistan will look good," comes home with a Ph.D. and a contract to work for the government at $12.50 a month. College professors make $10 and editors $7.50 a month. Regrettably, if a Ph.D. had become an expert in economics, he will surely be put to work in the office of mines, "lest he make the old economics men look stupid."

Yet the nation is not poorly governed. For example, in one northern province dynamic Mohammad Ismail rules with the kind of drive one would expect in nearby India or America. In his mid-forties, he has a big head, a pronounced nose and extremely expressive features. He smiles freely, speaks English well and gets a huge bang out of having become a major governor without having been a member of the royal family. He reminds one very much of Fiorello La Guardia. His accomplishments are enviable, for he has subdued large areas of river-edge jungle and given the land to peasants. He spurred the electrification of his district, developed a better system of taxation and a good police force.

To understand this fiery governor you must see him at *buzkashi* (goat dragging). If there is a rougher game, I don't want to watch it.

181

Two teams of horsemen, about fifty to the side, gather about a small pit into which has been tossed a freshly killed goat. At a signal the players try to grab the goat, ride with it over a distant goal line, then return it to the pit for a score. Anything goes and the violence is so unrestrained that men are often killed.

The game, and utter chaos, lasts up to three hours, for the rules contain one twist that invites mayhem: if a player on your team fights his way clear of the enemy and seems about to score, you are required to gang up on him to prevent his having things too easy. Thus one man really fights off ninety-nine others and it is common for a participant to collapse at the end of a game, his face covered with whip lashes, half administered by the enemy, half by his own teammates.

One recent game, where a small goat was used, ended so quickly that a calf, weighing eighty-eight pounds, was substituted. This game lasted all day and nearly every participant was nicely chopped up by nightfall. Governor Ismail, on the winning team, said it was about the best game he had ever participated in.

All power stems from Kabul, the enchanting capital city. Here the royal family rules with a rigid hand and here the future of Afghanistan is determined.

It is a strange city, built like a capital U with the open end pointing due west, where a massive range of mountains hems in the plain on which Kabul rests. The interior of the U is filled by a lesser mountain along whose base runs the mountain stream which cuts the city in half.

On one side of this intruding mountain clusters the old city, a welter of bazaars and mosques and fascinating alleys. On the other stands the new city, filled with handsome European-style houses, each hidden behind a high mud wall. Here also are spacious gardens, lovely verandas, ancient forts perched high on hilltops—and the traditional cool comfort of Asia.

Kabul is probably the most mispronounced name among the world's cities, for it was spelled by the French Caboul, which completely misled foreigners. Actually, the name sounds like "cobble." In any event, few who get to know the city fail to become enraptured by it.

It is dusty, diarrhea is alarmingly prevalent, you can't get into your own home without banging heavily on the closed gates for the guard who keeps out robbers, and it has no modern stores, no cinemas to which westerners go, no public restaurants or night clubs. And because the ruling family is suspicious of everyone, few Afghans are permitted to visit foreign homes, and almost never with their wives.

Yet the social life is one of the most charming I have ever enjoyed. With so little outside the home, people must entertain themselves, and since there is a big international population (Germans lead the list, for they have always been preferred by Afghans), parties are apt to be scintillating. Because adventurous young people have always been the ones to penetrate Afghanistan, there are more beautiful unmarried young American and European girls in Kabul than in any other city of its size I have ever visited.

But the vision of Afghanistan that persists is not of Kabul, nor the great mountains nor the lonely ruins. It is the Kuchis.

You will first see them as you turn a corner on some dusty road. Ahead of you looms a gigantic caravan in which camels lumber down the rocky steeps, followed by donkeys and horses stolen from some upland meadow, and goats and maybe a tame wolf and hundreds of dogs and fat-tailed sheep, whose ridiculous rear ends have made men laugh ever since they first saw them, for each sheep has a forty- pound tail as big as a pillow, loaded with solid fat that can be used for cooking.

Among the animals walk the proud Kuchis, the last true nomads of central Asia. The men are tall, lean and fiery-looking, and carry rifles. The women are fierce-eyed, extremely handsome and contemptuous of the veil. Hundreds of wiry children, innocent of school and mosque alike, help lead the animals or ride upon the folded black-felt tents.

Each spring the Kuchis enter Afghanistan from Pakistan and India, where they have spent the winter months. Driving their huge herds before them, they climb hundreds of miles—often more than a thousand—into the cool mountain passes. In the autumn this vast caravan, 400,000 strong, comes down from the heights and wanders into warmer areas.

Nothing can stop them. They pay no taxes, respect no

183

boundaries and few laws. Spurning houses and towns alike, they live under the stars, a fascinating, free people. Spirited young Kuchi girls, if anyone can catch them, bring up to $600 each in the marriage marts of Kandahar.

They are at their best, I think, when seen crossing the deserts of the south, for then their powerful camels dominate the landscape, and sometimes I have wakened to see hordes of these gaunt beasts cropping stray grasses at the desert's edge. These endlessly interesting animals can march across the desert heavily loaded without water for twelve days. Recently one kept going for thirty days and brought his master home safely.

If one could see only two things in Afghanistan, they would be the Vale of Bamian and a Kuchi caravan, for these things are unlike what one sees elsewhere.

Occasionally there have been rumors that Russia is about to take over Afghanistan, but a close inspection fails to confirm this fear. For every sign of Russian influence, there are other clear indications of American cooperation. Our agricultural experts can be found in fields throughout the nation. American teachers are active in rebuilding the educational system. The International Cooperation Administration (formerly FOA) has its advisors in most major centers. Americans working for the United Nations are common, and the Helmand Valley Project is by far the biggest operation in the country today. American influence has penetrated the entire nation, and constructively.

If an impartial visitor to Afghanistan saw as many signs of Russian influence as he does of American, he would have to conclude that Russia was about to take over. As it is, literally hundreds of Afghans assured me that one reason they were willing to accept American aid was that it carried no threat of imperialism, whereas Russian aid did. For every Afghan I met who could speak Russian, I met at least three hundred who could speak English. For one who had been to school in Russia, there were ninety-nine who had been to American schools.

Afghans did not decide one bright day that Americans were their new friends; an accident of history injected us into a place left vacant by the British, who had constituted the traditional counterbalance to Russian influence. For two centuries Afghanistan existed because she was able cleverly to play England off against Russia. Now we are being used in the same way, which is all right so long as the nation stays free.

Afghans do not like Russians. They realize that if Russian interests dictate a move southward, communist troops could occupy Kabul in about one week. They know that Russia is the great, permanent threat to their freedom, so although Afghans have never fought Russia, and although they fought Great Britain in three bloody wars—each ending in a kind of draw—whenever the chips have been down, Afghanistan has sided with Great Britain rather than with her enemies. Today the Afghans would probably side with the United States.

The northern sections of Afghanistan are crammed with refugees from the communist revolution. Tadjiks, Uzbeks and Turkomens—most of whom retain their old languages—escaped the terrorism with which Russia tried to put down Islam north of the Oxus, and they would probably resist to the death any attempt to bring them back under Russian control.

Furthermore, when in 1939 Russia endeavored to conscript armies from the lands north of the Oxus, about 650,000 Tadjiks, Uzbeks and Turkomens deserted the communist side and ran over to the Germans. What was more surprising, when they reached German prison camps they insisted upon being allowed to enlist in German armies so they could fight the Russians, even though this meant instant death upon capture.

It is therefore unlikely that Russia wants more of the same kind of people. But working on the communist principle that it is always good to have subversive elements burrowing in any neighboring country, Russia has recently moved into Afghanistan with a series of friendly, conspicuous aid programs. With a touch of brilliance they have allowed the Americans to work in out-of-the-way spots like the Helmand River while they do odd jobs right in the heart of Kabul, where everybody can see how efficient and how kindly they really are.

They pave the streets (with huge Russian machines), build

oil tanks (on the highest hill) and set up stone-crushing works (on the main highway).

The most tragic thing in Afghanistan is not the threat of war, for it can be overcome by common sense. It is the toy train, for it speaks of an opportunity lost which has never been recovered. You can see this train in Kabul, today.

In 1919 the King of Afghanistan was murdered—this has often occurred in Afghan history—and his brilliant, precocious son Amanullah gained the throne after deposing an older brother. Looking at the ancient customs of his people, he decided that he was destined to be the instrument of reform.

Quickly and for little reason, he declared war on Great Britain, united his people in a frenzy of patriotism and engineered a peace treaty that released Afghanistan from all British interference. Then, immensely popular, he made the grand tour of Europe, where royal receptions unbalanced him a bit, and returned home on fire to make his people over.

Assembling his leading chiefs, he launched into a lecture which lasted five full days and left the assembly dazed, whereupon he announced numerous radical reforms: women would discard the veil, Muslim leaders would have to surrender much of their power, and Afghanistan would soon be as modern as Germany.

To signalize the new age, Amanullah started to build, just south of Kabul, a truly magnificent palace with a tree-lined automobile road, nine cars wide, leading to it. The palace was to be the finest in Asia, with flush toilets, steam heat and marble stairways. Acres of earth had to be moved to build the garden terraces alone.

But conservative Afghanistan had had enough. In a surge of reactionary fury, they threw out the reform monarch and destroyed most of his work, and installed in his place an illiterate water carrier, who in 1929 initiated a brutal reign of terror. Soon the father of the present king subdued the water carrier and restored a different branch of the royal family.

Amanullah fled Afghanistan and went to Italy, where he now lives. He left behind a dream of a modern state with real freedoms. He left unfinished his grandiose palace. And he left his toy train.

He had bought it in Germany, a Toonerville midget if there ever was one. The engine had a high smokestack, a screaming whistle and hand brakes. The coaches were rich in plush; the flat cars were businesslike in a toy way. It could carry people and had about half a mile of bumpy track. Amanullah explained that a modern nation ought to have a train and he took his guests for rides in the late afternoon.

When he abdicated, the train remained, but gradually people tore up the tracks for steel, ripped apart the plush carriages. Today this miserable relic of reform huddles in a gloomy shed while the flatcars rot in bright sunlight, mementos of Afghanistan's first brief fling in the modern world.

All histories of Afghanistan contend that it was the mullahs who overthrew King Amanullah. Even today no word commands more attention through the countryside than mullah, which means a kind of rural religious leader. Islam does not recognize a priesthood as such, and one does not have to study or be ordained to be a mullah.

In ninety-five cases out of a hundred, a mullah is simply a man who decides to wear a white turban and instruct his fellow citizens in the good life. In Afghanistan such men are unbelievably powerful, for they interpret the law, patrol the customs and stand united against any reform. Were it not for rural mullahs, many changes would occur tomorrow throughout Afghanistan, making it more like its neighbors.

But the uneducated mullah has three tremendous powers which he uses liberally. If he wishes to condemn an action he merely says, "It is contrary to the Koran." To condemn a king or a government, he pronounces him or it kaffir (infidel). And against a proved enemy of old ways, he declares jihad (holy war).

Amanullah had a chance until mullahs condemned him as kaffir because he sent women abroad to study. Even then he might have withstood the uprisings against him, but the mullahs declared jihad.

There is, however, a small group of mullahs who have gone to college, traveled widely and caught a sensible glimmer of Muhammad's ideal state. In Herat I met the Mir of Gazar Gah, a handsome man in his fifties. Tall, bearded, enclosed in a fine

187

brown cape and flowing white turban, he looked like an Old Testament figure. Remarkably quick in thought and witty in speech, he told us that at fifteen he had decided to become a learned mullah and that he had studied until he was thirty-five. Then he married, had children, traveled to many countries and made the pilgrimage to Mecca seven times. His influence in the nation has grown to be like that of a cardinal of the Catholic Church. He is a fine strong man, international in outlook, conservative in politics. On him the stability of Islam depends when ignorant mountain mullahs run wild.

More striking, perhaps, is the young Kabul mullah, Sibghatullah (Colored by God) Mudjadehi (Renewer of Islam). He comes from one of the most powerful families in Asia and the only one in Afghanistan able to argue with the royal family. No less than sixty of Mudjadehi's immediate relatives are mullahs, eleven in Kabul. All well educated, they are the intellectual and spiritual watchdogs of the kingdom.

Young Mudjadehi, like many of his family, speaks English well, knows seventeen foreign countries, speaks five major languages and has studied the world's principal religions. He is a bearded saint who waits impatiently for the day when his country will catch up to its fellow Muslim states.

"We are determined to build here a strong, just society," he says quietly. "We shall be closer to the Koran than our ignorance permits today. Then we shall become the true Islamic nation."

Whenever he gets the chance, young Mudjadehi gathers Afghan students about him and preaches, "You say you are Muslims, but you have no concept of your religion. Listen to what the good state really is." And he reads in soft tones long passages from the holy book.

"Come back in ten years," he begged me. "See what we have accomplished then."

It is not easy to enter Afghanistan, nor is travel within the country always pleasant, but the total experience is quite unforgettable. The warmth of the citizens outside Kabul is unmatched. The laughter and good times in the upland passes are delightful, and the impact of the desert and the silent ruins is great.

I shall not soon forget what happened in Herat, where numerous refugees from Russia weave what we have come to call Persian rugs, masterpieces of dark red and blue and gold. I had no intention of buying rugs, but an old man grabbed me by the arm and led me to the walled compound where his family worked. Against my will I admired the lovely rugs, so he bundled up about sixty of them and gave them to me for a couple of days.

As he had planned, I found four that were gems but had to report sorrowfully that I had no money with me. He said, "Take them anyway. Send me the money from America." I said I couldn't disappear with nearly four hundred dollars' worth of his family property, so he suggested, "Write me a check." I replied that I had none, so he said, "Give me an I.O.U." We settled with me drawing a check—that is, actually drawing one and writing in the various names. I gave him this and walked off with the rugs. As I left, he said, "We have learned to trust Americans."

Malaya: Crossroads of the World

SEPTEMBER, 1958

Malaya, newest of the world's nations, forms the most southern tip of Asia. Part of a long, narrow peninsula that juts southeastward from the continent, reaching almost to the equator, Malaya looks something like the head of a dragon, its bony crown facing China, its soft underthroat less than fifty miles from Indonesia.

This Malayan dragon rests at one of the supremely important crossroads of the world. It separates China, India and the vast islands of Indonesia from one another, and throughout history what has happened to Malaya has concerned all other nations.

Resembling Florida in size, shape and temperature, with a population of approximately 6,000,000, Malaya is one of the richest nations in the world. It has the best roads in all of Asia, the highest standard of living in Southeast Asia. It has abundant rubber and tin, and per capita it boasts more millionaires than Texas. Yet its wealth is so justly distributed that few people go hungry. Sensible taxation promises to distribute the wealth even more fairly.

Malaya, as you can judge, is quite a country, and it is easy to understand why international communism, at the end of

World War II, decided to capture this golden dragon and rip off its rich scales. The twelve years that have followed have drenched Malaya in blood and terror. Nowhere else in the world has communism shown a more brutal determination to destroy a free government than in Malaya, where thousands of civilians were wantonly murdered, where mines were senselessly destroyed and rubber trees hacked into useless stumps.

Gradually the free people of Malaya were able to fight back. Now they have driven their communist persecutors into a corner. They have saved their land. In recent years there have been few more determined stands against gangster communism than the one made by Malaya.

Malaya, resting as it does between the China Sea and the Indian Ocean, has always been a land of water people. More than ninety percent of the population lives within forty miles of the sea. The rest live near rivers, and in order to understand Malaya, one must journey to some remote coastal settlement at the mouth of a great river, like Kota Bharu at the extreme northeast tip of the dragon's head. Here, not far from one of the loveliest beaches in Asia, the Beach of Passionate Love, live the water people of Malaya.

Even to see them walking through the town is a pleasure. Women, tall, slim and brown, wear three distinctive articles of dress: a sarong, a blouse, a loose-flowing headdress. It is true that other women in Asia wear such clothes, but what makes the Kota Bharu women so vivid is that by tradition the three pieces must be of the most contrasting colors. Shades which western women rarely use together—like red and purple— look fine on these lissome brown figures.

And to see one being pulled along in a bicycle rickshaw, her three flashing colors ablaze in the sun and her head protected by a huge umbrella with its own additional violent hues, is a memorable experience. Many men, intending to visit Kota Bharu only briefly, have caught the eye of some flirtatious local beauty in her rickshaw and have lingered for many weeks.

The time to visit Kota Bharu is during the winter monsoon,

when low, scudding storms sweep in from the China Sea to dump an incredible amount of water on the land. Thirteen inches of rain in a day is not unusual, and rivers rage over their banks, inundating the entire countryside. Transportation halts. A festive air strikes the population, and the people of Malaya revel in the floods.

In the kampongs (villages) outside Kota Bharu, the rivers rise almost to the floorboards of the houses perched on stilts, but the Malays do not grieve. They enjoy seeing the turbulent waters sweeping under their houses, like brooms, carrying away forgotten odds and ends and leaving the earth clean.

But most of all they love the effect of these floods upon unmarried girls, for in the afternoons, when the waters are highest, girls who have not yet caught husbands dress in their finest clothes and wade to the village square, where in great hilarity they play ancient water games.

Soon the girls, reputed to be the fairest in Malaya, are drenched, and their clothes begin to slip awry. This is the moment the men, perched around the square, have been waiting for.

"I didn't know Fatimah was so pretty!" a bachelor observes.

"Look at Rokiah's legs!" another shouts. By nightfall he had worked his way around to Rokiah's home and bargained with her parents for her hand, for it is during the floods that marriages are arranged.

Of course, Malays use their waters for more arduous purposes, too. The land is so mountainous, so smothered in jungle, that for centuries roads were impossible and rivers formed the highways up which boats sailed with produce. And naturally, the waters were used for fishing.

I know of few finer spots in Asia than the village of Bachok, some twenty miles from Kota Bharu. It boasts a beach lined with dipping palms and silky casuarinas. It has small houses on stilts, a handsome village green, and the majesty of the China Sea breaking in thunder on the sand. In gaily colored sarongs its people move in rickshaws under the palms, while the village fishermen pursue their dangerous calling.

In small boats rigged with lateen sails, the men of Bachok

ride out to sea and cast their nets. Their catch, one of the best along the coast, helps feed Malaya, but up until recently they had to sell their fish for little. Now a new kind of Malay lives among them, and he has changed their life considerably.

Salam bin Ibrahim is this new man. His name means Salam the son of Ibrahim, for most Malays use no last names, and he has been to Australia to study cooperative marketing. He has also been to many Asian fishing villages picking up new ideas. Still a young man, with black hair, deep-set eyes, handsome brown skin and white teeth, he has been inoculated somewhere with an energy that few of his people possess.

"Each morning," he says, as the China Sea whips salt spray about him, "I meet the incoming fishermen and help them weigh their catch. Then we get together and figure which market will pay most. And how much of our fish we should sun-dry. How much to salt away for the months when our catch is low. After we cast up our accounts, each man knows what he has earned, and it's more than it ever used to be. After that we sit down and think of new ways to use fish."

The results of Salam's thinking have been spectacular. One day he looked at the huge concrete jars in which fish are salted, and thought, "We always throw the brine away, but that must contain the best juices of the fish, and all the valuable salt." By boiling the brine down, and coloring it with coconut-sugar caramel, he invented a fine fish sauce, "crawling," as he says, "with vitamins and calcium."

Bachok shrimp are tasty and copious, so much so that the season's catch gluts the market. Salam showed his people how to make a nutritious shrimp paste. Baby sharks were once thrown away; now they make delicious dried snacks. Bigger fish are boiled down into a concentrated liquid high in protein and delicious with rice.

All across Malaya dedicated young men like Salam bin Ibrahim are applying their energies to the vitalization of their new nation. They are doing a fine, progressive job, but at the same time they remember the basic structure of their nation. The visitor sometimes forgets, but on Fridays he is reminded, for on that day the fundamental sound of Malaya is heard through the palm trees of Bachok.

It is a high, haunting, wavering sound, the sound of the azan (muezzin) calling the faithful to prayer at the mosque. All Malays are Muslims, for the country was converted in the fifteenth century by Arab and Indian traders who had landed first in nearby Indonesia. Nowhere in Islam have I seen a lovelier mosque than the one at Bachok, not because it is architecturally notable, although its low, strong walls and winding prayer tower are pleasing, but because of its location. It stands beside the China Sea, under palms and casuarinas, surrounded by flowers and looking out upon brilliant sands. Ducks wander across its green lawns, and children in bright garments, or none, play in its shadow. It is more unlike the arid, dry-sand mosques of Arabia or Africa than any I have seen elsewhere, a perfect jewel of a religious edifice.

But the fishermen of Bachok, who lead a very hard life, trust no one religion exclusively, and one of the strangest sights that Malaya provides is the ancient sacrifice of a virile young bull to appease the gods of the China Sea. Surely this strange ceremony, so replete with pagan significance and so based on pagan remembrances, dates infinitely further back in Malayan history than does Islam.

To keep the sea gods satiated, every five years each of the villages near Kota Bharu selects a prize bull and decorates it with flowers and ornaments and facial make-up. It is paraded along the fishing coast and under the palms and finally down to the water's edge. Then, while the entire village congregates, the animal is slain with one vigorous sweep of a kris across the jugular. Men acting as priests quickly rip open the body and tear out the entrails, which are replaced by straw. The head is sewn back on and the bull is taken far out to sea in gaily colored canoes. Chants are sung in favor of the gods, and the people on shore make unusual preparations as the men at sea perform ancient rituals.

Some of the shore-based people are boiling rice. Some are grinding curry. Others are preparing fruit. But the young men are arming themselves with palm-leaf balls, packets of sand and—illegally—rocks. They form a mock army along the shore, entrusted with the job of fighting off the canoes which now bear down upon them with great speed, bringing the sacred bull back to shore.

A violent fight ensues, for the canoes are loaded with Malayan equivalents of rotten eggs and ripe tomatoes. Always the incoming men win—they have to win or nobody eats—and in triumph they drag the bull ashore, where he is chopped up, quickly cooked and made into a delicious curry.

It is baffling to see a thousand Malays eating curry, for they use no knives or spoons or forks. They eat only with the right hand, forming the rice and meat into small balls which they deftly place near their mouth and flick in with a twist of the thumb.

When the feast ends, and the canoes have sailed away, the man acting as priest declares that the beach is again sanctified, the sea gods are again appeased, and the village ensured good fishing for another five years. But for several days that segment of ocean is taboo, and should a fisherman carelessly intrude upon it, he would break the spell of the sacrificial bull and ruin the fishing. Under such circumstances he would be savagely punished.

The social focus of both Kota Bharu and Bachok is a weird and mournful amusement park named by some Malay who had fallen in love with France: the Biarritz. Here one can see the curious *wayang* shadow puppets, cut out of stiff buffalo hide and operated in front of a lantern that throws shadows on a screen. The accompanying music is rich and haunting, the dramatic story coming from India by way of Java. For men visitors there are numerous dance halls and coffee shops, populated with beautiful, saronged young women.

"My name is Zainab binte Abdulla," a striking, dark-eyed girl of twenty says. Like most Malays, she has perfect teeth and fine features, which she piles with make-up. But when you speak to her, even briefly, you come upon one of the bizarre features of Malay life.

"I have already been divorced seven times," she confesses. "I was a kampong girl and believed that a woman ought to

195

bend her will to whatever a man wanted. When I saw the city, I developed a mind of my own, so my husband divorced me by saying 'Get out' and throwing a stone on the ground. I have been thrown out six other times, because I know my own mind. One thing I will not tolerate is for my husband to have two or three additional wives. I suppose no man will want me now. They prefer the old-type girls."

You ask Zainab binte Abdulla, "How many of the people I see here tonight are the children of men who have more than one wife?"

Quickly she surveys the crowd of fifty and says, "So far as I know, about thirty of these people come from plural families." It has always been this way in Malaya, where divorce is extremely simple and where a well-to-do man is expected to support three or four wives. But Zainab adds, "Women like me will put a stop to such plural marriages."

In addition to timeless Kota Bharu, there is a completely up-to-date nation in which men and women dress pretty much as they do in New York, drive British and American cars, enjoy the latest Hollywood movies and worry about the fact that their children seem to like nothing but Elvis Presley, whose rock-'n'-roll rhythms blare from a thousand juke boxes.

The modern cities of Malaya are handsome affairs, often with their principal buildings in Moorish style featuring fine pastels. There are two far-reaching airlines with enviable safety records, a good train system and more than 4,000 miles of excellent hard-topped roads. Hospitals, schools, private libraries and massive modern banks add to the bustling picture.

The ceremonial head of this state is the Tuanku (Prince) Abdul Rahman, a handsome sultan of sixty-three. This dignified leader is unusual in several ways. He has one of the longest titles on record, the Yang Di-Pertuan Agong, but he is called simply Agong. His kingship is not inherited but is elective. He serves for five years and is chosen not by the people of Malaya, but by the nine hereditary rulers whose states make up the federation. These sultans once had absolute power over their individual states; today they have minor duties, flashy uniforms, prime ministers and councils who keep them in line, and responsibility for heading up the Muslim religion in their territories. They also boast the longest-reigning ruler in the world, the famous Sultan of Johore, who has ruled over his rubber-rich state for sixty-three years. His eight brother sultans wanted to elect him Agong, but he said he was too old.

The sultans of Malaya have always been a jolly lot, given to wild spending of money and many wives. Their people support them in their playful follies, and in the past they have served a useful purpose in binding the nation together and in providing a visual head for the state religion. Keen observers of the Malay scene judge that the sultans will be kept on as museum pieces for a good many years to come. Argues one Malay with an Oxford degree: "What harm do they do? And you've got to have somebody to speak when new schools are opened."

The real ruler of the nation, of course, is not the Agong but the prime minister, and the man who enjoys that office is one of the ablest political leaders in Asia. He is the Tunku (sometimes spelled Tengku) Abdul Rahman. The fact that the Agong and his prime minister both bear the same name should not be disturbing. It is a very popular name in Malaya.

Abdul Rahman is a soft-spoken, capable lawyer of fifty-six. The brother of one of the ruling sultans, he had the typical education of a leading Malay: English elementary and secondary schools, Cambridge University and a London law education. As a result, he speaks English better than most Englishmen or Americans. He operates a cabinet form of government patterned after the British system.

He is not an exhibitionistic, dynamic type of ruler. Essentially conservative, he speaks in a low voice and dresses inconspicuously in Malay costume, with a turban and a wide silken sash about his middle. Like much of the business in Malaya, his cabinet meetings are conducted in English. He is a shrewd, hard-working politician who by his stubborn leadership won freedom for Malaya a full ten years before anyone else thought it possible. His great ambition now is to keep his country free.

Abdul Rahman won Malaya's freedom from the British, but

197

how England happened to be in Malaya in the first place is a dramatic story, one that should be understood in these days when imperialism is under fire.

In the mid-nineteenth century England controlled three small footholds in Malaya, but they had either been built on islands off the shore of Malaya or captured not from Malays but from the Dutch. In the process of ruling these three tiny enclaves, the English were naturally drawn into contact with the unruly sultanates of the interior, and in accidental ways, different for each state, the Malays and the English cooperated to their mutual benefit.

Sometimes the English were invited to help organize local governments. Again, they were called in to run some sultan's financial affairs. Never did they conquer a territory or drive a family from its inheritance, although they did sometimes depose obvious incompetents. Strangely enough, the English never even organized Malaya into a single state: four of the sultanates agreed to be joined together in a common federation, but five others refused and went their own way, while the original three enclaves remained a separate unit altogether.

This was Malaya under the British: a confused, rich, happy-go-lucky combination of diverse units. The English never owned Malaya; the local sultans never surrendered their rule; Britain governed by consent, and was specifically forbidden to meddle in local customs or change local religious patterns. Under this system, Malaya was ruled better than any other country in Southeast Asia, and its citizens prospered.

In 1941 Japanese dive bombers swept in from the China Sea, sank the British warships *Repulse* and *Prince of Wales* and showed how unprotected Malaya was. At Kota Bharu, Japanese invasion forces landed practically unopposed, and in seventy tragic days swept General Percival's defending troops completely out of Malaya. In no other part of the world did the British absorb such a humiliating defeat.

The years from 1942 through 1945 were agonizingly difficult. British advisors to the sultans rotted in dreadful jails. Planters who had once run great rubber estates and miners who had dug out shiploads of tin were assigned to the notorious Burma railroad, where many perished. And the Japanese only half-heartedly brought Malays into the governing bodies of the nation.

With Allied victory, all this was changed . . . and more. It became apparent that sooner or later the British advisors to the sultans would no longer be necessary and that one day Malaya would be able to govern itself. A series of extremely wise Englishmen, aided by solid Malays like Abdul Rahman, made freedom possible within a brief twelve years, against some of the most impossible odds a beginning nation ever faced.

Before we look at those odds, it would be appropriate to reflect upon what England accomplished in Malaya. On August 31, 1957, the Duke of Gloucester, uncle to the Queen, handed over to the Agong a thriving nation. The subsequent *merdeka* (freedom celebrations) were brilliant and colorful, and although the new nation enjoyed itself to the hilt in rich pageantry, the honored guests at every occasion were the English who were leaving.

There was no bitterness on either side. Each of the able Malay administrators about to assume control of the nation had been hand-picked and personally trained by English tutors. A fine, liberal constitution had been drafted (in Rome, away from local tensions) by the best legal brains that Malay, England and other commonwealth countries could provide. Malaya's system of justice, her parliament, her way of doing business were all adopted from English precepts. And when the last English official left Malaya, there remained behind the presence of one who, for the time being at least, filled a splendid role. Queen Elizabeth II, as ruler of the commonwealth, continues as head of the organization of nations to which Malaya is happy to belong. As such, she maintains a personal representative in Malaya.

Never was transfer of power achieved with less friction. Malays had to kill no Englishmen to get them out of the country; they went freely and willingly. Malays tore down no English statues, revised no English street names, burned no English books. All this was in striking contrast to the torment

199

that has attended the birth of Malaya's neighbors—the wars, the assassinations, the recriminations.

I have not yet mentioned the most significant fact about Malaya, for if I had discussed this ominous factor before stressing the hopeful side of the situation, the reader might have become depressed, as do some observers who study modern Malaya. To comprehend this omnipresent problem, join me on a stroll through Abdul Rahman's capital city, Kuala Lumpur.

It's a handsome, spacious, modern, clean city that used to serve as the state capital for one of the sultans, and Americans who fail to visit it on their trips around the world are missing a delightful experience. It has broad streets, beguiling Moorish buildings and a scintillating mosque that stands at the confluence of two rivers that cut the town into segments. The name Kuala Lumpur means "the muddy mouth of the river," and reminds one of the fact that up until a few generations ago one came to Kuala Lumpur only by canoe to barter for jungle goods. Now it is a prosperous capital with hotels, inviting restaurants and a fine, dependable police force. What problems can one see in a stroll through such a city?

Look at the signs. This handsome new skyscraper is the Loke Yew Building. That one is the Chan Wing Building. This prosperous biscuit factory is the Thye Hong Company. That modern milk bar is the Hing Kee, and this café is the Lien Fat. So it goes through all of Kuala Lumpur and through all the cities of Malaya. Practically every prosperous business is owned by a Chinese. I could take you for an hour's walk through Abdul Rahman's capital, and you would be a very keen detective if you could spot a single business run by Malays. In fact, you would see precious few Malays. The cities of Malaya are Chinese. Of the 6,000,000 residents of Malaya, nearly half are Chinese. In a few more years they will outnumber the Malays.

They own the stores, run the smaller rubber plantations, mine the tin that is not controlled by Europeans, finance the banks and own the newspapers. They are the economic life-

200

blood of the nation and without them Malaya would collapse.

It is ironic that a new nation, struggling to survive, should be divided equally between Malays and Chinese, for two more incompatible halves could hardly be assembled. Malays play; Chinese work. Malays live along the eastern coast in kampongs; Chinese congregate along the western coast in cities. Malays, being Muslim, abhor pigs and seek to outlaw them; Chinese cannot cook without pork. There are few Malay communists, but many Chinese reds. Malays are not good at learning; Chinese are brilliant. Malays enjoy political intrigue; Chinese tend to avoid official involvement in government. Malays look to Indonesia for cultural leadership; Chinese look to Peking. Malays flock to the army and the police force; Chinese boycott them. An Englishman who has worked with both groups, and who likes each, says, "It boils down to one simple fact. Chinese have money; Malays don't."

Indeed, if the English had not set up procedures ensuring preferential treatment for Malays, and if the present constitution did not require four Malays to be hired before any non-Malay can be given a job in government, Malaya would long ago have become a Chinese nation, and there are many today who fear that such is its inevitable destiny.

In 1948 it looked as if Malaya would be communist within six months, and to follow the terror of that and succeeding years, I want to relate the experiences of one English planter and his wife. They have asked me not to use their real names, since they still reside in Malaya, but what I am about to report was very real indeed.

In 1930 a rubber estate was begun some miles south of Kuala Lumpur. Twenty-five hundred acres of virgin jungle were cleared by hacking down huge trees and burning the rest. Almost the entire area was planted with *hevea braziliensis,* the marvelous rubber tree that had been spirited out of the Brazilian jungles in 1876 and brought to Malaya as an experiment. No one there thought much of it, for none could foresee the invention of the automobile and the subsequent demand for rubber tires.

201

But one small, mustachioed English botanist in waistcoat, high collar and heavy tweed suit kept experimenting with rubber trees until he became known as Mad Ridley, the crazy tree man who bored his friends stiff with talk about making millions from some seeds stolen from Brazil. Then, in the early 1900's, someone discovered that Mad Ridley's trees could be tapped to yield latex, which could be made into rubber for which Americans would pay fantastic prices.

Immediately the planters of Malaya rushed to Mad Ridley and cried, "I say, Ridley, old fellow, d'ya happen to have some of those seeds?" Now he was called affectionately Good Old Ridley, and he went up and down Malaya in an absurd stiff collar showing English overseers how to graft and grow rubber trees, and from his patient work thousands of men became millionaires. He lived to be a hundred and one years old—he died only a few years ago—and to the last he loved to say, "I told 'em there was money in rubber." Of all the people who dealt in this strange tree, he was practically the only one who never made a penny from it, for Mad Ridley had always given his seeds away, in the interests of science.

When Bukit Panjang Estate was planted, Ridley's original type of tree had been so improved by British horticulturists that whereas his trees had produced three hundred pounds of dry rubber per acre each year, the new trees were able to produce eight times as much in the same area. Since a rubber tree requires only five or six years' growth before it yields latex, by 1935 Bukit Panjang was ready to start paying dividends.

In 1937 a twenty-eight-year-old Englishman named John Hunter came to Bukit Panjang to learn the rubber business, but in 1942 he was captured by the Japanese and sent to the Burma railroad, where only his rugged, stubborn courage kept him alive while hundreds of his fellow Malayan prisoners perished. In 1946 he was back on the estate, nerves shattered and hoping for some peace and good food.

In that year he married Sally Cameron, a Scot, whom he had remembered all through his prison years, and they settled down as managers of the Bukit Panjang Estate. The rubber trees, untapped for years, needed much attention, while the estate buildings had been literally ripped apart by the Japanese, who needed all the metal they could find. The Hunters worked hard and in 1948 could consider that they had the estate back in good shape.

They did not know that in February of that year Russia had convened in Calcutta a conference of all the communist leaders of Asia and had there reached a decision that was to terrify the Hunters for the next five years and which continues to plague them today. Russia's decision was simple, and since we have captured some of the documents growing out of that conference, we know what was ordered: "Malaya must be captured through a process of terror."

From Calcutta a group of determined Chinese communists returned to Malaya and set the machinery of their substantial underground party into action. Through village streets, city buildings and jungle hideouts went the simple, easily understood message: "We are about to take over Malaya. To do so we must drive out the English. We will start by destroying the tin and rubber industries, and the easiest way to accomplish this is by murdering the English managers."

John Hunter, his wife and two children were in the estate house on Bukit Panjang when the directive from Calcutta was put into effect. It was ten o'clock in the morning and Hunter had just returned from having checked the day's work, which began at dawn, for rubber flows best in the morning and all work finishes by midday. He was having his late breakfast when a Chinese servant ran screaming into the room, followed by a fusillade of shots.

At first Hunter thought that there had been some family brawling, including an attempt at murder, but a second volley sent bullets ripping through his living room, and he realized that an attempt was being made to murder him and his family. Quickly he grabbed the solitary, and ineffectual, rifle he kept for emergencies and in foolhardy anger rushed to the door. Actually, this saved his life, for as the communists were to prove again and again, they were not willing to fight if their adversaries were armed.

Hunter fired into the trees surrounding his house, and the communists fled. But they had murdered four tappers.

That afternoon a group of grim-lipped British planters met in the Kajang Club some miles from Hunter's estate. They were members of the Incorporated Society of Planters, and they had a grisly tale to tell. In the preceding days three planters had been callously murdered by communists. One planter's wife had been ambushed and killed when the reds thought that by blowing up her car they were getting her husband.

"It's war," the chairman of the planters said. "We must proceed accordingly."

That night John Hunter started to organize the defense of his estate. First, he moved the young assistant manager, a tough-minded unmarried young Englishman, into the main bungalow with him. Together they erected a six-foot barbed-wire fence to protect their headquarters, topping the fence with tall poles from which bright lights flashed outward so that attackers could be spotted.

Hunter, the assistant and Mrs. Hunter went armed with both pistol and rifle. Hunter's truck was covered with sheet metal pierced with small eye-sight slits for driving and shooting. The front lawn was spotted with slit trenches into which Hunter and his assistant could drop at any time and fire upon communist troops who might be attempting to cut through the barbed wire and attack the bungalow. Finally, Hunter, like all his fellow planters, formed a habit of never doing estate chores at the same time on any successive days. If he had to drive his truck to the boundaries to inspect trees, he would do it at dawn one day, dusk the next. He refused to tell even his wife where he was going, lest someone overhear his plans. He never used the phone.

Even so, he barely escaped death six separate times, not counting the first attack. Three of them, according to the planters' code, didn't really count, for these were merely wild midnight forays against the bungalow by chance communist bands. There would be several minutes of furious fire out beyond the floodlit fence. Bullets would spatter through the bungalow, but Mrs. Hunter and the two children would lie on the floor while Hunter and the assistant would head for the slit trenches and fire back into the ominous night. Invariably, as soon as rifle bullets started searching out the communists, the reds would flee. Never did they stand and fight.

Such night forays were not counted as real attacks. "Everybody expects to go through those," Mrs. Hunter now explains. She kept her revolver and rifle handy just in case some communist gunman should break through the wire, but even her children grew accustomed to the night shots.

What planters really feared were the ambushes. John Hunter survived three of them.

The first was typical. Secretly, in his armored truck, he was making his way to the shed where rubber sheets are cured by three-day smoking. As he turned a corner he spotted the fatal sign, a rubber tree felled across the road. His first temptation was to stay in the truck and fight it out. If he had done so, the communists could have fired on him at will until some shots penetrated the plate and killed him. Instead, he grabbed two rifles, flung open the truck door and leaped into a ditch. Now the reds would have to seek him out, and if they did so, he would be able to fire back at them point-blank.

From his muddy ditch John Hunter did not wait for them to charge. He took careful shots at the shadowy figures among the trees, confident that if enough noise was made, troops guarding the estate would arrive in time to save him. They did.

That night Mrs. Hunter asked her husband if he thought they ought to chuck it and go home. He replied, "No. The only thing holding this country together is the determination of the planters. I got through safely this time. Chances are there won't be a next."

Then word of the appalling losses on other estates came piling in. Good men they had known for years were being murdered each night: Leggat, Clarkson, Madder, Alcock, Arnold, Shaw. The remaining planters stayed to carry on the battle. Rarely has there been a group of men more courageous than these stubborn Englishmen. Rarely has an entire nation been saved by the heroism of a few determined civilians.

John Hunter's second ambush was a dreadful affair. Once more he was on a secret mission, this time accompanied by his young assistant. Once more there was the sudden rubber tree blocking the road, but this time instead of desultory rifle fire, there was a fusillade from three separate sten guns which practically tore the truck apart. The second blast killed the assistant, who fell across Hunter's lap. There were fourth and fifth terrible bursts of fire, and when there was no reply from the stricken truck, the communists began to move in.

At this point Hunter shoved the body of his assistant away and started firing from the truck. In this manner he held the reds off for some minutes, until troops could move in to rescue him. They were amazed that he had been able to kill two communists.

When the troops brought Hunter back to the bungalow, it was a long time before Mrs. Hunter could get him to relax. She saw the blood across his front and thought at first that it was his. When she heard that their assistant had been killed, she insisted that they leave Bukit Panjang at once. Her husband sat numb and silent as she talked: "Why do we stay? So that the company back home in Mincing Lane can make a little more money? I'll have no more of this."

It was then that John Hunter showed his wife a paper that had been found on the body of one of his communist assailants. Translated, it read: "We cannot call Selangor ours until that infamous running dog of the imperialists, John Hunter of Bukit Panjang, has been killed. When he is done for, the rest will leave. You are to kill this man. But your previous instructions still hold. Only ambush. Do not stand and fight a pitched battle."

"I'll not be leaving," Hunter said grimly. His wife, studying the document, understood.

Now terror settled over Bukit Panjang. The years passed, and every hour was potential death. The Hunter children always stayed close to their mother, and among the first words they learned were military commands: "Down! Keep away from the fence! Don't show a light!"

The death roll of other planters climbed. Ninety-seven individual Englishmen were murdered in communism's vain attempt to panic the country and terrorize government. Women and children were mercilessly slaughtered, sometimes hideously. More than 2,600 workers were wantonly killed. Trees that could have produced fine rubber were senselessly slashed in anger, buildings were burned, bridges were destroyed.

John Hunter hung on and set a record by surviving his third ambush. It came one dawn, only a few yards from the bungalow. Mrs. Hunter, tending her children, heard the firing . . . the dreadful bursts of the sten guns, the silence, the rifle shots, the blasts of the shotguns, the explosion of the truck as it caught fire from tracer bullets.

After a while her husband staggered back to the bungalow, muttering, "The bastards ran, of course."

It was 1957 when I met John Hunter and his family. His wife, from long habit, still carried a revolver in her handbag, but the barbed wire and the slit trenches were gone. Hunter no longer had to travel in an armored car. A taciturn, yet witty Englishman, he says simply, "We've won the country from the communists." Neither he nor his wife thinks of him as a hero. He says flatly, "If it hadn't been for that captured document ordering my assassination, I certainly would have fled after the second ambush. Why not? But when the enemy specifically states that so long as you last, your side has a chance . . . well, you've got to stick it out, don't you?"

When it seemed that Malaya was doomed—for even brave planters like John Hunter warned that they could not hold out much longer—the British, who were helping govern Malaya on behalf of the local sultans, came up with two sterling men. Lieutenant General Sir Harold Briggs was a quiet, capable soldier who had won honors in jungle fighting in Burma. Tired out from too much war, he had retired at age fifty-five, but accepted an invitation to lead the fight against the Malayan communists. So far as I know, he never defeated any communists in a pitched battle, but he accomplished a much greater victory. He gave the world an idea as to how communist terror could be eroded . . . and he won.

To Briggs it was simple. First, make towns and cities so secure that the inhabitants will be willing to tell what they know about the communists. This Briggs did brilliantly, and in time he had little centers of safety—and information—all across Malaya. Sometimes the reds would reinfect an area he had secured, but by and large when Briggs designated a town as secure, he kept it that way. And its citizens began to talk freely against their former persecutors.

Second, use the information gained in the towns to break the jungle communist armies into smaller and smaller groups. Here again Briggs succeeded brilliantly, for he drove corridors back and forth across Malaya, securing roads and compressing the reds into ever-tightening areas.

Third, keep the communists from getting food. This was almost the central item in the Briggs' plan and the major cause of its success. The jungle provides a man with little food, no oil, no salt. He has got to come out from time to time to replenish his stores, or the implacable jungle will starve him to death. Unlike a northern forest with its store of berries and nuts and shoots, the great jungle provides nothing but hearts of palm, and too much of that causes death. So when Briggs succeeded in preventing villagers from sneaking food into the communist camps, he paved the way for this final step.

Fourth, make the starving communists come out for food in areas where troops will be waiting for them.

With this simple four-point military plan, General Briggs started his systematic assault on the reds. At the beginning he warned that his procedure would be neither dramatic nor quick. But contrary to earlier plans, this one had logic behind it, and as its various parts started to mesh together, the communists began to strangle in the deep jungle. Rarely has an idea been so important or so successful.

The second Briton was better known. General Sir Gerald Templer was a slight, spit-and-polish, extremely brilliant soldier who in early 1952 was appointed supreme commander of Malaya. Dubbed "El Supremo" by the local population, Templer quickly proved that he merited the title. Announcing, "I could win this war within three months if I could get two-thirds of the people in Malaya on my side," he launched into political and social reforms that shocked the nation and won the war.

When ultra-stuffy members of a swanky club refused, even at the height of the emergency, to permit Asian members to enter their portals, Templer said briefly, "Change your rules or I'll close the club in twenty-four hours."

When he discovered that Chinese near Kota Bharu were refusing to cooperate with government solely because prejudiced Muslims would not permit the Chinese to grow pigs, Templer simply said, "I want a farm of pigs in this town within one week. And after it's established, I want half a dozen of the best British boars flown in here to improve the stock."

When new roads were needed, he built them. When new ideas were required, he sponsored them. Few men have ever had the impact on the society of a nation that Templer had on Malaya, but his greatest shocker came one day when he announced casually, "The British government is certainly prepared to give Malaya full self-government the moment you have demonstrated your ability to accept it."

At once the basic contention of the communists—that they were striving to eject the British and thus win freedom—was stolen from them. Word sped through the jungle paths that Malaya could have freedom any time it really wanted it enough to put down the communist terror. Templer's master stroke had won the propaganda war.

I would be unfair to the Chinese of Malaya if I implied that only Briggs and Templer, brilliant as they were, saved the nation. Many brave Chinese, who could expect instant death if a communist caught them, stood forth to lead their people against the terrorists. Big, burly C.C. Too was one of these.

Too is a determined man, in charge of psychological warfare against the communists. He points out: "The rest of the world naturally stresses the gallantry of the lonely British planter defending his estate against the reds. You'll forgive me if I stress the fact that out of 2,600 communist murders, more than 1,700 of the victims were Chinese. Another 600 are missing. Many were brutally tortured. It was my people who really suffered. And when victory came, it was because my people had decided to refuse cooperation of any kind with the communists." Without the help of the Chinese, the salvation of Malaya would have been impossible.

It was Too and his group of specialists who devised two of the simplest tricks in the successful war against the reds. He says of them, "They were so simple they were actually beautiful."

The first was this: all bicycle frames were inspected daily. In a country where almost everyone owns a bicycle on which he rides to work, particularly on rubber plantations, it had long been a clever maneuver for communist sympathizers to bore a hole at the spot where the seat was attached to the tubular frame. The entire body of the bicycle could thus be used for rice storage, and only a few bicycles full of rice grains would enable a communist group to avoid starvation. So Too intercepted all bicycles and plugged up the holes.

"Our second trick was even better," Too confesses. "When we started to police every village in Malaya, and to weigh out rations for every human being in order to be sure that no extra food was escaping to communists, we encountered much resentment. I'd be mad, too, if I had to account for every spoonful of rice. Had we continued this system, we might have lost Malaya.

"So what we did was to establish community kitchens from which anybody who wished could be fed . . . as much as he wanted. All we insisted upon was that every single grain of rice he got was cooked. He could have a handcart full of it, if he wanted it . . . but it had to be cooked.

"Have you ever seen a man trying to smuggle any large amount of cooked rice? It makes a bundle bigger than his head. And the best part of our plan was this. Cooked rice spoils in the tropics within a few hours. So any communist helper not only had to smuggle cooked rice. He had to smuggle it right away."

It was this food-deprivation plan, executed with a severity and a determination that startles the observer, that enabled the formal military forces to go into the jungle and track down isolated communist units. The reds had to eat, and sooner or later this made them disclose their positions.

In late 1957 I had the unique opportunity of being with the jungle army of Malaya when it captured one of the top communist leaders. Ah Chien was a director of the notorious group of murderers who operated along the Malacca–Johore border. His men had been responsible for some of the worst outrages of the emergency, and it was a tribute to his jungle shrewdness that during the ten years from 1948 through 1957 he had never once been sighted by the thousands of commonwealth troops sent in to capture him.

The government maintained heavy pressure on Ah Chien in various striking ways. Low-flying DC-3's, with powerful loudspeaker systems slung under their bellies, sped back and forth across the jungle, announcing: "Ah Chien! Ah Chien! We know where you are. Your companions have left you and have already self-renewed. Come out, Ah Chien! Self-renew before it is too late." (The government never used the word *surrender*.)

Many communists who did self-renew confessed that they had been driven to do so by this demonic voice that haunted them from the heavens, telling them day by day of the success of the government's drive. Early in the emergency General Briggs had laid down fundamental policy: "We will broadcast only the truth. We will confess our own failures, too. Then later, when we tell shocking truths, they will be believed."

In addition to the airborne voice that trailed Ah Chien through the jungle, there were mimeographed letters dropped from airplanes at the rate of 10,000,000 a month, giving Ah Chien the latest news about the breakup of his jungle empire and inviting him to self-renew.

At this point the 22nd Cheshires, from England, were given the job of capturing Ah Chien, and I happened to join Captain Paddy Ford's Company A at the height of their campaign. Ford was a wiry, lantern-jawed young jungle expert who had a monomania about capturing Ah Chien. He kept a picture of the terrorist over his desk.

211

"We're bound to get the monster this time," Paddy Ford swore. "And my men will do it."

Some days before, Paddy's outfit had captured two of Ah Chien's remaining ten terrorists, but in the fight one of the communists had had his left shoulder blown away. "These craven swine!" Ford growled. "Immediately you capture them, they begin to whine and whimper. This man, who might have been dying, insisted that we put him on a stretcher and lug him five miles back into the jungle. He hated the communists so much that he wanted us to kill them all . . . men he had served with for a dozen years."

Thanks to the intelligence provided by the wounded man, who did not die, Paddy at last had a good lead. He then dispatched into the jungle a remarkable young man whom I shall never forget.

Second Lieutenant James, as he was known, was nineteen years old, fresh out of school. He was extremely thin, with a large shock of reddish-brown hair and the angular face of a British schoolboy. His platoon consisted of a sergeant and twenty-four men, accompanied by two incredible Iban jungle scouts from a tribe in Borneo. These flat-nosed, laughing, brown-skinned warriors could look at a track and say confidently, "Five days ago. Two men, one woman, no packs passed here." They were invariably right, and when they got onto a track, they depended upon hunter dogs, who could hold onto it for days. The communists of Malaya were not easily defeated; they were routed out one by one by brave men who endured untold dangers and discomforts.

When James entered the jungle on his last tremendous drive against Ah Chien, his men wore old green uniforms, basketball sneakers and fifty-six pounds of gear. They slogged through marshes and rivers. They slept under jungle trees. They ate cold food out of cans. They fought mosquitoes, and horrible leeches that sucked blood, and snakes, and innumerable jungle insects.

They stayed in the jungle for twenty-five days at a time. They mounted ambushes for the wily Ah Chien, at which men would sit motionless for two days at a time, soaked to the skin, crawling with insects . . . waiting . . . waiting.

212

And always Ah Chien escaped them. His eight remaining supporters began to fall away. In late November two of his most trusted aides walked into the deepest jungle north of Paddy Ford's headquarters near Segamat, and when they felt secure from Ah Chien, made a break for it and surrendered. Later two others did the same.

Second Lieutenant James stayed on their trail as if he himself were an Iban tracker. "He's got to show himself," James insisted. His nineteen-year-old determination infused his patrol, and they forgot the miseries of their position, hanging on like bloodhounds to the red trail.

Then, in early December, James struck a hot lead. His Ibans assured him that three, maybe four men had passed within the week. Later they found irrefutable marks of a camp that Ah Chien had inhabited only a few days earlier.

"I knew then we had him," the wan-faced schoolboy later assured me, his deep-set eyes blazing. He drove his men on, twenty-four hours at a time.

But James was not to make the capture. Headquarters, fearing that Ah Chien might once more elude their trap, decided not to entrust a mere boy with the important job of trapping the most dangerous killer in Southern Malaya. Accordingly, young James was ordered out of the jungle, after thirty-seven days of dogged zeal, and a huge operation was mounted to replace him.

When James left the jungle, so near to victory, he was disconsolate. "My men were ready to revolt," he muttered. "Such an unfair order."

Next morning I rode out with Paddy Ford as he sent his fresh troops into the jungle to resume the job so brilliantly started by young James. It was first light when platoon after platoon plunged neck-deep into the swamp that separated the camp area from the jungle where Ah Chien lay hidden. In the cold light of dawn I thought how much courage men must have to begin a ten-day stint by wading hip-deep into a swamp. They would be continually wet, continually plagued by jungle tormentors. It was such men who fought the communists to the death.

I was back at company headquarters, sitting with Second

213

Lieutenant James, when the word arrived. A colonel bustled in from regimental headquarters and cried, "We took Ah Chien at seven this morning!"

Paddy Ford and I have wild shouts of joy. But young James was tense and silent. Moving to a map, he asked breathlessly, "Where did we take him?"

With his swagger stick, the colonel pointed to the precise spot that James had predicted the night before. The young officer said nothing; he merely looked at me and smiled grimly.

Then the colonel used the young man's full name, and for the first time I appreciated the drama of which I had unwittingly been a part. "This must be good news for you, Lieutenant Percival," the colonel said as he left.

Then I knew who James was. This boy of nineteen, this wiry youth who should have been in school, this scourge of the jungle who would not relinquish his deathly hold upon Ah Chien's throat, was Second Lieutenant James Percival of the British Army. He was the son of General Percival, who in seventy tragic days in 1942 had absorbed in these same jungles one of the most humiliating defeats in British military history. His son had mastered jungle warfare.

More than seventy percent of Malaya is covered by thick jungle, a fact which explains why the nation is actually underpopulated, having only 110 people to the square mile, whereas neighboring Asian areas like Java contain more than 1,100 to the square mile.

The Malayan jungle comes in two sizes. There is a low second-growth mass of weeds, vines and young trees that is practically impassable. Recently a squad of trained jungle experts out to rescue the crew of a crashed plane required two days to traverse 1,800 yards of such jungle, and they were physically exhausted at the end of the short journey. There is no worse jungle in the world than the matted low growth of Malaya.

But there is also the high jungle, in which no undergrowth grows, since the lofty crowns of the trees interlock more than a hundred feet above the forest floor. They are so intertwined

214

with vines and parasitical orchids that no direct ray of sun ever penetrates them, and nothing smaller than a giant tree has any chance of growth.

Walking in such a jungle is a rare, almost holy, experience. A great shadowy silence prevails and almost everyone who has ever moved among the huge trees, treading upon a soft carpet of moss and jungle grass, recalls his visit to some cathedral. Here one moves freely and can traverse easily three miles an hour in relative cool and memorable beauty.

This high jungle, which comprises more than three-fourths of the Malayan jungle, abounds in brilliantly colored birds, rare butterflies, fascinating leaf structures and rare, dazzling flowers. Of course, you never see any of this display, for it exists only in the tree crowns, more than a hundred feet above the earth, where birds dart in and out of the sunlight and flowers bloom profusely. All that you see is the somber green of the shadowy jungle carpet . . . never a flower, rarely a bird.

The Malayan jungle is also crowded with animals. Here prosper the great Malayan tigers, largest and fiercest specimens of what most hunters consider nature's most superb beast. Elephants also abound in the northern jungles, sometimes moving in herds of a hundred. Monkeys, of course, are everywhere in the tall trees, and deer are plentiful, while the wild pig prospers in both the low and the high jungle.

But as with the flowers and birds, you never see these animals, and men have been known to travel in the jungle for months at a time, right through the heart of tiger country, without ever spotting even a wild pig, let alone a majestic tiger. The animals move at night in utter secrecy. Occasionally a man will report that as he stepped from behind a tree he saw threescore of elephants moving upon a salt lick, but when he tried to spy upon them, they vanished among the trees.

There are, however, about 50,000 men and women living in the densest parts of the jungle who do see tigers and who become acquainted with elephants. These are the strange, mysterious aborigines whose antecedents go back thousands of years to southern China, from which they emigrated in the Stone Age. (I once reported that they had come from India, a

215

commonly held belief, but I was wrong.) It was from these extremely ancient people that the Malay nations developed, and probably the Polynesians who went to Tahiti, and some of the forgotten sea adventurers who reached Japan. Today a handful, living according to tribal customs centuries old, hang on in the forgotten jungles.

Let's visit them, for they are some of the most primitive men remaining on earth. On a tableland north of Kuala Lumpur an unusually dense jungle presses down upon the banks of a river which will later empty into the China Sea south of Kota Bharu. A small clearing has been made here for the growing of rude crops, and next to it a long house has been built. It is a remarkable affair, 120 feet long, fifty feet wide, built entirely of bamboo logs, tied securely together with jungle fibers. Its floor stands eight feet off the ground and is reached by numerous ladders, but it's the quality of the floor that is distinctive, for it is built of thin strips of bamboo laid crisscross and suspended in such a way that it can hold the weight of a hundred men, yet give a sharp, metallic click when even a child puts his foot upon it. To walk across this floor is something like flying to the accompaniment of a drummer clicking a wooden block.

Rows of poles sustain a waterproof, matted roof and at the same time cut the outside perimeter of the long house into twenty-four separate cubicles in which the aboriginal families live. Even a whisper from one cubicle can be heard throughout the rest of the long house.

The most important part of the house, of course, is the central area, which is used as a community hall. Men sit along its edges chewing tobacco and ask, "Why would anybody build a floor you couldn't spit through?" Women, sending their children out to play, merely shove them into the central area, and when a young man of twenty sees in the long house of some other tribe a pretty girl of sixteen, he arranges to get one of the twenty-four cubicles for himself, and sets up housekeeping.

But the long house comes into its glory on dance night. Then stones are hauled up the ladders and an altarlike affair is built on the bamboo floor and well covered with wet sand, on which a considerable fire is built. Behind it a big dried-out jungle log is hauled into place, around which clusters an orchestra of twenty women, each with a length of echoing bamboo in both hands. Striking the communal xylophone, the women produce a soft, sweet, mournful music, to which they chant an overpoweringly rhythmical song.

Now the aborigine men, naked except for black loincloths and a necklace of jungle leaves which yield a slightly narcotic effect, begin to dance, and the wonder of the bamboo floor is realized; for with every step of the dozen dancers the floor rises and falls to add its own sensation, and as it moves, its bamboo lathes beat out their own subtle contrapuntal beat. The dried log, the jungle drums, the haunting voices and the bamboo floor thus create a hypnosis upon both the dancers and the observers.

I want to stress this fact because of what happens next. The dance continues its wild gyrations for sixty or seventy minutes, and without the gently yielding quality of the floor and the general hypnosis, no man would be able to continue his really crazy exertions for so long, especially as the fumes of the fire add to the stifling and exhausting effect.

But as the group hypnosis continues, the leader of the dancers, without ever missing a beat, deftly thrusts his hand into the middle of the fire and pulls forth a flaming brand. Then, while you look at him, he brings the flame to his lips, shoves the tip well into his mouth, bites off the flaming portion, chews it up and swallows it, returning the smoldering brand to the fire.

You are so astonished that you are sure you must have imagined what you saw, but to the incessant beat a second dancer plunges his hand into the fire , grabs a brand and shows disappointment when its flame unexpectedly dies out. Whirling it about his head, he revives the flames, then plunges it into his mouth, where he too bites off a sizeable chunk, chews it up and eats it.

Now you are convinced that there must be some trick, that the dancer doesn't actually bite off the tip at all. But a third man, never missing a step on the wild bamboo, thrusts his hand into the fire, grabs a mouth-sized chunk of incandescent charcoal and with no possibility of fraud, resolutely chucks it into his mouth and eats it. All the dancers do this, some six or seven different times.

I sat in the long house not five feet from the fire, my body swaying to the imperious throbbing of the bamboo floor, and I saw these dozen dancers eating the flaming embers. Later I talked with the leader when his face was less than ten inches from mine, and his lips were not even charred. There were no blisters. We had a drink of tonic water between us and then I found him a cigarette. What a pallid substitute that must have been!

These aborigines—a little smaller than an average white man, but with handsome physiques and fine heads—are famous throughout the world for their blowguns, and in the long house I saw one of these strange weapons. They are extremely lethal and effective at distances up to two hundred feet, for their tiny dartlike arrows are tipped with the dried gum of the ipoh tree, one of the most instantaneous jungle poisons known. During the emergency, communists tried to take over one long house as a center for their operations, but the two reds were struck with darts from blowguns. The first dropped dead after two steps. The second ran screaming for a hundred yards and died.

The blowgun I saw was about eight feet long and was made possible only because the jungle north of Kuala Lumpur produces a unique bamboo that has between its nodes a smooth, absolutely straight stretch of eight or nine feet. Such a length, if cleaned out carefully inside, is as true and as strong as a rifle barrel, but for protection it is housed inside a second, and slightly larger, length of bamboo. A mouthpiece is attached, and darts are made of palm fiber, light, true and very sharp. Tipped with ipoh poison, a dart is slipped into the interior bamboo barrel and the blowgun is raised to the lips. With a sudden burst of air from the lungs, the perfectly fitted dart is projected from the gun with considerable force. As we have seen, it can kill a man instantly. Eight or ten darts can kill a tiger, and there are even records of elephants having been brought down.

One of the accomplishments of which Malaya can be most proud is the protection she provides her aborigines. Few nations today are doing a better job than Malaya of preserving a mysterious jungle people who live now as all of our ancestors probably lived thousands of years ago.

So far I have written as if Malaya were divided equally between Malays and Chinese, with 50,000 aborigines thrown in. Actually, the balance of power lies with another group, the Tamil laborers who were brought into Malaya from southern India. Today they number about three-quarters of a million and constitute a powerful force. In physique these very black workmen are perhaps closer to the Malays; in business acumen they are closer to the Chinese; in political ability they stand alone, and it is not impossible that their great role in Malaya will be to act as referees between the two major races.

To appreciate the considerable ability of the Indians, who form twelve percent of the population, you should meet P.P. Narayanan, a handsome, witty, hard-working labor leader who has organized the Tamils, who do most of the work in the rubber plantations. (Chinese, by common agreement, do the heavy work in the tin industry.)

P.P. is known widely as "The Dapper Little Tapper," but he actually started life not as a rubber worker but as a school-teacher. When he was growing up, most labor unions were openly communistic, but P.P. thought it might be possible to organize his Tamils into a non-communist union. The going was very difficult, since communists saw the danger of a union they did not control, and many of P.P.'s men were murdered. Then too, capital, having seen what communist unions were capable of, naturally suspected all labor, especially when led by an agressive, well-educated and able young Indian.

However, P.P. sweated it out. He insisted that all discussion in his union be carried on in Malay, since that, and not Tamil, was the language of the country. He bullied his Indians into building one of the finest new offices in all of Malaya. "When a workman comes into this headquarters," P.P. says, "he has a right to feel proud. Years ago, when I went in to see my first English boss, he wouldn't even let me sit down. Now I invite that same boss here and offer him a fine upholstered chair. All Malaya has to take Indians seriously now."

It is likely that P.P. will one day be an acknowledged leader of the entire Indian community—and not just of the rubber workers. At that time he will probably be invited to sit in the cabinet as the representative of a group that is neither Malay nor Chinese, but which can accomplish much in helping those two larger groups to work together.

It would be gross error to write of Malaya without mentioning Singapore, my favorite city in Southeast Asia. Today and forever, Singapore remains a memorial to Sir Stamford Raffles, the remarkable Englishman who founded this fine seaport. There is the Raffles Hotel, Raffles Square, Raffles College, the vast Raffles design for the city that he alone foresaw and built. Appropriately, his statue surveys his principal accomplishment.

But today Singapore plays a role far different from the one Raffles visualized, for it is cut off from the Malaya of which it is economically and geographically a part. The reason for this divorce—Singapore is a crown colony and is part of nothing; its proud address is simply Singapore—is political. For Singapore is almost exclusively a Chinese city. Out of a population of 1,210,000, nearly 1,000,000 are Chinese, and among the remainder, the Indian minority is large.

Thus, with Malaya already in an uneasy balance between Malays and Chinese, to add mighty Singapore to the federation would result in a clear and strong Chinese majority. "This," say Malay leaders like Tunku Abdul Rahman, "we cannot permit."

"This," retort brilliant Chinese politicians like Lim Yew Hock, the labor-trained head of Singapore's self-government, "is what Malaya will have to accept sooner or later." Thus a complete impasse has been reached.

The outsider cannot hope to understand the various com-
plexities of this difficult problem. If one thinks abstractly of
Malaya trying to continue without its logical greatest city, he
concludes that it can't be done. Malaya without Singapore is
precisely like Austria without Vienna, or England without
London. But if a visitor dares to utter this comparison, the
people of Malay will quickly correct him.

"It is not Malay that needs Singapore," they argue. "It is
rather Singapore that will wither without Malaya. We have
the rubber, the tin and the rice. Singapore lives exclusively on
us, but we can by-pass Singapore. We can ship our products
just as well from Penang or from our new harbor at Port
Swettenham."

In the meantime Singapore is one of the most exciting cities
of Asia, never more so than during the Indian festival of
Deepavali, for then the mystics exhibit their incredible faith,
and the western visitor is reminded that there many things in
Asia which he will never understand.

It was at a Deepavali ceremony that I crowded my way into
the courtyard of a small Indian temple in the heart of Singapore. I found myself pressed into a crowd of several thousand people in what looked very much like an Italian loggia,
with balconies looking down upon a paved square, one end of
which led to the cavernous and shadowy entrance to the temple. The center of the square was filled by a remarkable construction: a pit some twenty-five feet long and twelve feet
wide, at the far end of which, separated slightly from the pit,
was a substantial waterproof ditch into which workmen
poured huge drums of goats' milk, forming there a tiny lake
into which one could easily jump, were he in the pit.

Of course, at this moment it seemed most unlikely that
anyone would be worrying about jumping either into or out
of the pit, since it was brimful of fiery logs which had been
burning for some hours; a deposit of ash a foot deep had been
built up. As current logs crumbled in the flames, new ones
were thrown into the pit, so that by three o'clock in the afternoon the pit was completely filled with ash and ember.

I had a vantage point close to the goats' milk end of the pit,

221

but I had to move, because the heat of the fire was so intense that I could not bear it. If I threw a shred of paper into the pit, it burst into immediate flame, and if the Indians who raked the pit constantly to keep its surface level allowed their rake handles to linger too long in the flames, they caught fire and had to be plunged into the milk for extinguishing.

My attention, however, was diverted from the flames, for at the temple entrance appeared the first of an astonishing parade of figures I was to see that day. He was an Indian mystic, naked except for a brief clout. He was a tall, gaunt man, and through his hollow cheeks, entering on the left side and running through his mouth and out the side of the right cheek, were three steel skewers, but no sign of blood.

Through the muscles of his breast two other skewers had been plunged. From front and back of his torso dangled large fishhooks caught completely through his skin, and from four of these hung heavy weights that pulled his muscles down.

His tongue protruded, and through it passed another skewer. Smaller skewers, like nails, had passed through his legs, and as if this were not enough, from his lower eyelids hung still more fishhooks, each with its own weight to drag the eyelid down.

This holy man, obviously in a trance, for he shivered and shook like a leaf, was lead by four assistants to the edge of the flaming pit, where low flecks of fire played across the evenly raked ashes. It seemed to me impossible that anything—wood or paper or human flesh—could exist in that pit, but as he stood quaking at its edge, the first fire-walker seemed to be vitalized by the extreme heat rising from the ashes, and with a fierce shout, the man with all his skewers and fishhooks plunged into the flames, walked prosaically through them and fell sobbing into the trench of goats' milk. I saw his feet, and they were neither burned nor blistered.

The crowd cheered vigorously at this display of courage, and the man, insensible to everything and shaking like one demented, was dragged out of the milk and off to some other portion of the temple, where the skewers and fishhooks were ripped from his body, which still did not bleed.

The next fire-walking was done by a holy man who appeared with savage slashes across his body and who dragged behind him, by means of rope passed through the sinews of his back, a heavy object. Ecstatically he plunged into the pit, strode through it, contemptuously ignoring the cooling goats' milk. He received an enormous cheer.

But the third man presented quite a different problem. When he reached the edge of the pit he apparently was not yet wholly in the grip of the religious frenzy, for he looked down at the flames with obvious horror and sought to draw away, whereupon the four assistants grabbed whips and slashed at him unmercifully, for it was forbidden to come so far and then turn back. The whips had no effect upon the terrified man, for he could not bring himself to plunge into the flames, whereupon two of the strongest assistants placed their hands in the middle of his skewered back and shoved him bodily into the pit. He stumbled perilously, tried to recover his balance, and pitched face-first into the flames. He then staggered to his feet, a pitiful, burning sight, and tried to find the ditch of saving goats' milk, but he failed to orient himself and pitched again into the flames. Later we were told that he had died.

After him appeared an old woman, who walked serenely into the flames, moved with assurance, and walked with stately demeanor into the milk. The crowds cheered wildly.

Then came a long series of deeply religious individuals, not skewered and not, apparently, in trances. They simply believed that their faith would take them through the coals unscathed. In true mortal trembling they approached the pit, hesitated with understandable fear, felt the sting of the lashes on their backs, and rushed like tormented men through the pit, covering it in five or six giant steps, ending with a gasping dive into the goats' milk. They suffered real burns on their feet; Singapore doctors deplore such fire-walking, because it produces difficult burn cases which are hard to cure.

But interspersed with these lesser performers were occasional men possesed by a St. Vitus dance who would approach the pit in ecstasy, shout to the gods, and walk slowly, even

223

defiantly, through the flames and ignore the milk. They seemed to suffer no ill effects.

I cannot explain what I saw that day in Singapore. I know that only a few minutes before the weird procession started I had found the pit much too hot to stand by. I know that many of the fire-walkers had to be lashed with whips before they would enter the pit. And I know from subsequent doctors' reports that some of the walkers suffered severe burns on the soles of their feet. But I also know that other men appeared before me stuck through with steel skewers, and they did not bleed. They strolled sedately through the fires and were not harmed.

A major reason why Malaya refuses to permit Singapore to join the federation is that Chinese schools in each place are overrun with communists, and it seems very uncertain that either Malay or the city will escape being hauled into the communist camp by its wild Chinese students.

Some years ago I visited one of these schools. It was staffed by weak-kneed faculty members who were afraid to discipline the students, because the schools were paid for and supervised by the students' parents, and if a child failed, the teacher who had given the bad marks might be fired. Since the English wanted to save as much money as possible, they allocated little or no funds for Chinese education and exercised inadequate supervision.

A few of the teachers in the school I visited were industrious and dedicated . . . to communism. For the past dozen years these teachers have been using their classrooms as a means for conscripting young Chinese boys and girls into the party. These schools have idealized Mao Tse-tung. They have branded all Americans as gangsters and murderers. They have preached that communism must ultimately win all of Southeast Asia, and they have taken specific steps to see that this happens.

From these schools many young Chinese have been cajoled into leaving Malaya and Singapore and returning to China for their education and for training in subversion. Parents have been unable to halt this exodus.

During one period when I was in Singapore, communist-led students were setting fire to public buses, killing policemen and making the city hideous with crime intended to break down civilian government.

Later other students kicked to death a friend of mine, Gene Symonds of the United Press, because they didn't want an American newsmen reporting on their subversion. I have a photograph showing high school students hacking a policeman to death with hoes, just to create an incident.

While I was in Malaya recently, Chinese students endeavored to take over one school after another. Last year they succeeded, temporarily, throughout Singapore. The greatest shock came when young Chinese girls in a Catholic convent rioted along strictly communist lines. When Abdul Rahman himself tried to speak before one group of students, they booed and shouted, "Shut up!" And when the Malay minister of education sought to work out some compromise with his Chinese students, they warned him, "Resign or we will murder you." These young people are headstrong, willing to riot and determined to wreck both Malaya and Singapore.

Fortunately, the responsible leaders of the Chinese community support the government's policy. They want the Chinese schools to be made a part of the national school system, to be paid for and supervised by the government.

Unfortunately, even loyal Chinese feel that they have a just complaint in this school business. T.K. Wen, a brilliant young man who has become a spokesman for the rational group, says sadly, "The educated Chinese is truly frustrated. Where can he get a job? Before the government will employ him it must hire four Malays, who are often less well educated than he. And while scores of able Chinese boys sit around doing nothing, the Malay government sends well-paid experts to London and America trying to lure young Malay undergraduates back into government service."

What has aroused both Wen and the students, however, is the government's attempt to develop a Malayan culture, while ignoring Chinese. Says Wen, "Up to now we've had thirteen hundred excellent Chinese schools, all paid for exclusively by our Chinese citizens. Government paid never a penny. Our textbooks taught more about Malaya than English textbooks did in the English schools. But how can we be expected to ignore the great culture of China . . . forget it . . . when there is not yet any real Malayan culture to replace it? What Malay books would you use as substitutes for the great Chinese classics? There are no Malay books."

In view of this great emptiness of Malay culture, the local Chinese are determined to cling to their Chinese education. Yet the results of this are sometimes appalling. A friend of mine interrogated the senior class of a Chinese school.

"Where is Malaya?" "Next to China." But it is actually more than a thousand miles from China. The boys had no idea that Thailand, Burma, Cambodia and Laos intervened.

"Who owns Malaya?" "China used to own it before the British stole it." China never owned the peninsula, although for many centuries there were harmonious diplomatic relations with Peking.

"Who controls the administration?" "The English." When this question was asked, Malaya had been totally free of British influence for three months.

"Where is the district office responsible for running this part of town?" "We don't know." The district office, staffed by Malays and Chinese, was right next to the school.

I was so disturbed by this Chinese ignorance of the land in which they lived that in Malacca I asked a twenty-five-year-old Chinese high school junior, "Where is Sumatra?" (It lies about forty miles across the Straits of Malacca, and throughout history has been a dominant factor in Malaccan life.) He pointed to a tiny island half a mile offshore and said, "That's Sumatra."

I argued, "But Sumatra is a gigantic island, much larger than Malaya."

"Oh, no!" he persisted. "Our teacher told us that was Sumatra." His knowledge of other Malayan facts, imparted by communist teachers, was comparable.

Indeed, it seems possible that this nation, having defended itself from adult communists, may have to surrender its freedom to their schoolboy successors.

But Education Minister Khir Johari, a bright young man of

thirty-five, thinks this will be avoided. He argues, "There are thousands of Chinese students who are fine, dependable children. They love education and they know they have a wonderful future in Malaya. If we can remove the troublemakers from their midst, they will be among the best citizens we have."

And it could happen that way in a land which has already surmounted so many formidable obstacles.

REGRETS

When a writer looks back upon a body of his work, it is inevitable that he will recall certain pieces with pleasure and others with regret. He is surprised that some of them turned out as well as they did and regrets that others missed the mark. It is unusual when the same piece occasions his principal satisfaction and at the same time, his principal regret. Such is the case with the article which follows.

It was ahead of its time, said something that needed to be said and represented a culmination in my thinking. I was proud of it.

For many years prior to 1955 I had been aware that the United States suffered because it did not understand Islam. I had been living in countries like Indonesia, Malaya, Pakistan, Afghanistan and Turkey, where the Muslim religion played a major role in all that was constructive. I had written extensive essays about each of the countries, and in doing so, had found Islam to be a most harmonious religion, one with a notable history and one that inspired men to worthy deeds.

I was fortunate in having as my preceptor one of the world's finest Muslims, Sir Zafrullah Khan, foreign minister of the new state of Pakistan and later president of the United Nations General Assembly and judge of the International Court at the Hague. Sir Zafrullah led me through the intricacies of Islam, taught me its fundamentals and then accompanied me on an extended field trip through Muslim lands. He was a profound philosopher, an enthusiastic exponent of his religion. Under his tutelage I learned as much as an alien could about Islam.

Four times I tried to put my reactions to the religion into words, and four times I failed. Islam was a very manly religion and required strong writing. It was a mystical religion and deserved poetic understanding. It was a religion of the desert, strong in illustrations from nature, and this ought to be recorded. It was also a militaristic religion in that it spoke of men battling for its cause. And it was a religion which preached brotherhood and social change, and the commentator ought to point out that the former principle operated today while the latter did not.

The more I studied Islam the more I liked it, and the more I saw its place in the contemporary world. I was pleased, therefore, when the editors of the *Digest*, after learning from Sir Zafrullah that I had been an apt pupil, asked me to write an essay which would try to reflect some of my thoughts on this misunderstood religion.

I am most proud of this essay, even though I know how far short it falls of what I tried to accomplish. It was reprinted widely in the Muslim world, and when I vistied places like Afghanistan or Jordan, I found that Muslim leaders knew of it and appreciated its intent if not always its execution. It was reprinted in various Islamic nations as an example of the increased understanding the religion was achieving.

It was about then that I developed the concept that I have ever since promulgated when young university students asked me how they should prepare themselves for a writing career outside the world of fiction. I have invariably replied, "If I were a young man with writing talent and wanted to make a major contribution, I would turn my attention to some area of the world about which America knows little, and I would school myself to be an expert in that field. I'd study the language, the religion, the history, the geography and the contemporary politics and literature. After about eight or ten years I'd be in a position to make a positive contribution." And when the students have asked what region of the world, I have replied, "Islam. It's bound to become a major world problem, and will be with us for the next fifty years. Learn Arabic. Learn the religion. And travel in Muslim countries whenever you can." My second choice has been Africa, my third South America. I have used this present essay as an opening wedge to explain what I mean, for the truth of what I began to formulate fifteen years ago is even more pressing today. We need to understand Islam and the Arab nations, more now than ever before.

Why, then, the deep regret? It is twofold. For the better part of a dozen years I had spent much of my life in the Islamic nations I have mentioned, writing about them and getting to know them as well as a traveler could. I did so because in the back of my mind I had plans for writing an important novel about Islam and by 1962 I had pretty well focused on the setting. It would be the city of Constantinople from about the year 50 B.C., when it was an insignificant village, through the age of Constantine and Helena on to the fiery Crusader period when European Christians burned it whenever they got the chance, because it was Eastern Christian, and on to the grandiose days of Suleiman the Magnificent and the miserable days of decline under the last sultans, until the time when Germans took over the city and conducted from it their defense of Gallipoli in the 1914 war.

It would be a vast novel, and might have worked rather well, but just as I was ready to begin writing I happened to go on vacation to Israel to scout out the land from which the enemy had so often attacked Constantinople, and I chanced upon the ruins of a Crusader fortress called Athlit, and in the flash of a second I realized that what I had been preparing myself to do was a book not about Constantinople but about the Holy Land. My first regret is that this diversion from Muslim Constantinople to the Jewish Galilee meant that I could never go

231

back to my first love, for I could not write both books. The long years I had spent studying Islam became the training for a novel on Judaism. It is difficult for a writer to give up even a minor project which has augured well; to abandon a major work that had a chance of turning out superior is painful; the emotional scars never heal.

But it was the second regret that was the more serious and the longer-lasting. I had the bad luck to work in an era when a good word spoken in behalf of Israel was interpreted as two bad words spoken against the Arab states, and although I took every precaution in my novel *The Source* to avoid depicting Muslims as inherent enemies of Jews, which throughout history they have not been, my work was interpreted as being pro-Jewish and therefore anti-Arab.Even now no claim of impartiality will be accepted. I am sorry. It was not intended to be that way. This essay, written ten years before the novel, discloses my true intention, but we are all forced to live in an age when true intentions often go for nought. I take solace in the hope that we shall work out some kind of peace in the Muslim-Jewish areas in my time. I regret that I was not able to write my novel on Islam. It might have helped generate understandings which would speed that day.

Islam: The Misunderstood Religion

MAY, 1955

One of the strangest facts in today's world is that Islam, a religion in many ways almost identical with Christianity and Judaism, should be so poorly understood in America and Europe. Since there are 600,000,000 Muslims in the world, and since they control many strategic areas of the earth, it is essential that we understand them better.

But look what happened recently to a distinguished Muslim who came to the United States. Count the insults we unconsciously heaped upon him.

His hostess showed him a mosaic in a New York church and said, "See! We appreciate your prophet, too." But Moses, Jesus and Buddha were shown seeking men's souls with reason and light. Muhammad was shown with a sword, offering conversion or death.

Later he saw a movie which showed brave and holy Crusaders battling craven Muslims for possession of the Christian city of Jerusalem. The Crusaders appeared as educated, sensitive men, the Muslims illiterate brutes.

A newspaper carried an account of Muhammad's lead coffin, which, according to legend, hovers mysteriously somewhere between heaven and earth. The news story naturally cast ridicule on such a belief.

When he visited in an American home, the visitor found that the children learned their history from a book which reported in lurid detail the horrors of Muslim rule in Spain.

In several discussions he heard his religion characterized as "sumptuous," "voluptuous," "sybaritic" and "pleasure-loving."

Worst of all, wherever he went this man was called a "Mohammedan" and his religion was referred to as "Mohammedanism." These are two of the most unfortunate words one can use to describe this powerful religion.

Let us see why these experiences were so offensive to a believer in Islam.

There are numerous ways of spelling the name of the inspired man who founded Islam. In Turkey he is Mehmet. In Afghanistan, Mahmoud. In Pakistan he is sometimes Mohamad. To the western world he has usually been Mohammad. The preferred spelling is Muhammad.

He was born about A.D. 570 into an Arabian tribe that worshiped idols. Orphaned at birth, he was always particularly solicitous of the poor and the needy, the widow and the orphan, the slave and the downtrodden.

In his twenties Muhammad—the name means the Greatly Praised and was often used before the prophet's day—became a very successful businessman and director of camel caravans for a wealthy widow. At twenty-five his employer, recognizing his merit, proposed marriage, and even though she was fifteen years older than he, he married her and proved a devoted husband. Frequently in later life he attributed to her much of the goodness he had known.

By forty this man of the desert had secured for himself a most satisfying life. He had a fine home, children, wealth and a position of importance. Then, in a series of dramatic and terrifying events, he began to receive from the Archangel Gabriel a revelation of God's word as it was preserved on tablets kept in heaven.

234

Like almost every major prophet before him, Muhammad fought against serving as the transmitter of God's word. But the angel commanded, "Read." And although, so far as we know, Muhammad was hardly able either to read or write, he began to dictate those words which would soon revolutionize a large segment of the earth. His message: "There is but one God."

It soon became obvious that Muhammad's words would infuriate the rich, idol-worshiping Arabs who ran the countryside, and his few followers realized they would become outcasts, persecuted and driven from Mecca, which was his home.

These things happened, and Muhammad, who seems to have been a gentle man, was forced to become a general. Borrowing military tricks from the all-conquering Persians to the east, he became a great military leader, and it is a matter of historical record that he repeatedly went into battle outmanned and outspeared five to one. Sometimes he was soundly beaten. More often he won spectacular victories. But always he kept his band together.

Later he became head of the state, and the testimony even of his enemies is that he administered wisely. The wisdom he displayed in judging intricate cases became the basis for the religious law that governs Islam today.

And because he had been an excellent businessman, he advised his people in their commercial affairs.

Constantly, in the later years of his life, he was invited to become either a dictator or a saint. Firmly he rejected both temptations, insisting that he was merely an average man to whom God had sent another of His periodic messages to the world.

At the height of his power, already encompassing surrounding nations, Muhammad stopped to watch farmers cross-fertilizing their prize dates. "Why don't you do it this way?" he asked. Next year the farmers came to him, complaining bitterly, "We followed your advice, and now our trees bear no dates."

"Foolish men!" Muhammad cried. "You are the expert farmers. I merely asked because of my ignorance."

Through the force of his extraordinary personality, Muhammad revolutionized life in Arabia and throughout the East. He smashed the old idols with his own hands and established a religion dedicated to one God. He lifted women from the bondage in which desert custom held them and preached general social justice. And he organized into meaningful patterns what had previously been a savage, disorganized, nomadic life.

Muslims think it particularly curious that Muhammad is charged by western writers with having established a religion for voluptuaries. Among drunkards he abolished alcohol, so that even today all good Muslims are prohibitionists. Among the lazy he ordained difficult prayers five times each day. Among men who reveled in feasting, he commanded most rigorous daytime fasting covering a full month each year. For a people who had been dirty and unkempt, he made cleanliness and repeated bathing an integral part of their religion. "Wash yourselves, so that you do not offend the nose of the man who prays beside you," he commanded. There can be no question but that Muhammad destroyed a voluptuous idolatry and substituted for it a disciplined, difficult belief in one God.

Western critics have based their charges of voluptuousness mainly on the question of women. But before Muhammad, men were encouraged to take innumerable wives. He limited them to four only and repeatedly said it was better to have only one. After his beloved wife died, he assumed responsibility for several wives, most of them middle-aged widows. He loved the married state and once said to his wife, "I can tell when you are angry with me. When I have pleased you, I hear you pray to the God of Muhammad. But if I have angered you, I catch you praying to the God of Abraham."

The most common misunderstanding arises from Muhammad's promise of paradise. In a land of blistering drought and sandstorms, he predicted that evil men would suffer perpetual fires of hell, whereas good men would be transported to a perpetual paradise of cool breezes, comforting streams and houris.

236

Western imaginations, unfamiliar with this last word, defined it by analogy to one of the ugliest words in English and jumped to the conclusion that Muhammad's paradise would be a sexual debauch. They were wrong. A houri is a fair-skinned, black-eyed woman created from musk and spices, perpetually virgin, incredibly beautiful.

Last summer I stood on the edge of an Asian desert with a devout Muslim, and he said, "Today much effort is being spent to prove that Muhammad's paradise was only symbolic. Wise men are able to explain away everything. But let me tell you this. I have lived my whole life in this baking desert faithful to God. I've avoided one earthly pleasure after another in an effort to gain paradise. If I get there and find no cool rivers, no date trees and no beautiful girls made of musk and spice, I shall feel badly defrauded."

In all things Muhammad was profoundly practical. Upon handing down a decision in a litigation where the facts were unusually obscure, he warned the man who won, "If my judgment is contrary to the real truth in this matter, you are taking home with yourself not wealth but a piece of hell."

When his beloved son Ibrahim died, an eclipse occurred and rumors of God's personal condolence quickly arose. Muhammad, however, announced, "An eclipse is a phenomenon of nature. It is foolish to attribute such things to the birth or death of a human being."

At Muhammad's own death an attempt was made to deify him, but the man who was to become his administrative successor killed the hysteria with one of the noblest speeches in religious history: "If there are any among you who worshiped Muhammad, he is dead. But if it was God you worshiped, He lives forever."

Muhammad, the man, was wrapped in a shroud and buried in an ordinary tomb whose location has always been known. The story of the floating lead coffin arose in Europe in later centuries.

These things explain why people who follow the religion of Muhammad hate to be called Mohammedans. As Sir Zafrullah Khan, Pakistan's foreign minister explains: "A Christian is a man who believes that Christ was a part of God, and the

237

central fact of his religion. A Mohammedan, by analogy, would have to be a man who believed that Muhammad was likewise a part of God, and the central fact of his religion. But Muhammad was a man. He married, had children, earned a living, died and was buried in a grave like the rest of us. No sensible man could worship Muhammad. It is God we worship. Therefore call us only Muslims, those who submit to the will of God."

Because of the nature of Muslim worship, the Koran is probably the most often read book in the world, the most often memorized and possibly the most influential in the daily life of the people who believe in it.

It is an extraordinary book. Not quite so long as the New Testament, it is written in an exalted style. It is neither poetry nor prose, yet it possesses the ability to arouse its hearers to ecstasies of faith. Recent scholars have related its rhythms to the beat of drums, to the echoes of nature and to the chants which were common in all early societies.

The Koran is written in Arabic, and many devout Muslims believe that it should not be translated into another language. One might expect such a rule to limit the spread of Islam, but the result has been quite the contrary. Around the world, men have labored to learn Arabic, not an easy language, in order to read their holy book and pray in the original language.

Englishmen, Germans, Frenchmen, Chinese and the present author have testified to the overpowering effect of the Koran when recited in passionate and flowing Arabic. Five times each day Muslims hear portions of the book, and hundreds of thousands have memorized the entire work. (It requires about six weeks of diligent concentration.) And the faithful, in many diverse nations, try to live their lives in conformity to its teachings.

But to the English reader, the Koran is probably the most difficult and disappointing of the world's major books. Thomas Carlyle, among the first Europeans to inspect the Koran sympathetically, said of it, "It is as toilsome reading as I ever undertook, a wearisome, confused jumble, crude, incondite. Nothing but a sense of duty could carry any European through the Koran." Many have verified this judgment.

The explanation is twofold. Most English translations have been pedestrian, and the Koran itself is most curiously organized.

It was revealed to Muhammad between the years 610 and 632 in the cities of Mecca and Medina. Devoted scribes wrote it down on "scraps of paper, bark, and the white shoulder blades of animals." The early revelations were dazzling assurances that there was only one God, merciful and compassionate. In later years, when Islam had penetrated large areas of Asia and had acquired much power, the revelations naturally dealt with the organization of society, its laws, procedures and problems.

Unfortunately for the non-Muslim who would like to understand the power of this book, it was not arranged in its present form until some years after the prophet's death. Then the simple device was adopted of putting the longest chapter first, the shortest last. This means that the reader who seeks knowledge of Islam must first plow through many very long chapters dealing with law and custom before reaching the overpowering message that there is one God, whose powers and compassion are limitless.

Most western readers of the Koran quit before they reach the central messages of this religion. Yet these were the messages that shook the earth, swept away idols and inspired men to revolutionize their lives and their nations.

The Christian or Jew who stays with the Koran to Chapter 114 finds himself on familiar ground a good deal of the time. If the following verses, chosen from hundreds like them, were suddenly read in a church or cathedral or synagogue, the congregation might have trouble guessing where they came from.

> Cried one of the brothers, "Slay not Joseph, but if ye must do something, throw him down to the bottom of the well; he will be picked up by a caravan of travelers."

> So also was Jonah among those sent by Us. When he ran away to the ship fully laden, he agreed to cast lots and was condemned. Then the big Fish did swallow him.

239

Mary asked: "How shall I have a son, seeing that no man has touched me and I am not unchaste?" The angel replied. "So it will be. Thy Lord saith This is easy for me." So she conceived him, and she retired with him to a remote place.

The revered names of Christianity and Judaism appear constantly in the Koran. The titles of four chapters usually surprise western readers: Jonah, Joseph, Abraham, Mary. Lacking specific chapters of their own, but playing quite important roles in the Koran, are Adam, David, Goliath, Job, Moses, Noah, Lot, Solomon and Jesus.

The three principal early prophets of Islam are Moses, Abraham and Jesus. The Koran does not acknowledge, however, that Jesus was the Son of God and that he was crucified. Obviously, if Jesus were the child of God, it would compromise God's oneness, the belief which is the cornerstone of Islam.

In addition to being a book of religious instruction, the Koran is remarkably down-to-earth in its discussion of the good life. In one memorable passage, which no doubt reflects Muhammad's success in business, the Koran directs:

> When ye deal with each other in transactions involving future obligations, reduce them to writing . . . and let the man who incurs the liability do the dictating to the scribe . . . and get two witnesses, so that if one of them errs the other can remind him. This is juster in the sight of God, more suitable as evidence, and more convenient to prevent doubts among yourselves.

It is this combination of dedication to one God plus practical instruction that makes the Koran unique. Each Islamic nation contains many citizens who are convinced that their land will be governed well only if its laws conform to the Koran.

In addition to the Koran, Islam relies upon traditions as to what Muhammad said and did. Vast collections of anecdotes appeared during his lifetime, and each Muslim who needed to prove a point was tempted to create a new tradition. Before long Muhammad, a profound revolutionary in both theology and government, was being cited in defense of the most reactionary behavior.

About two hundred years after his death, more than 600,000 separate stories were current, and several great scholars undertook the job of checking them for historic validity. More than 597,000 were rejected.

The remaining 3,000 traditions, called the Hadith, are fascinating. When accepted, such a tradition became binding upon the Muslim community and remains so to this day.

These traditions portray Muhammad the man. In colloquial and often jovial prose, they deal with everyday life.

> One dark night Muhammad had to escort his wife home from the mosque. On the way he saw two men giggling in the shadows, so he called them to him, lifted his wife's veil and said, "See, it is my wife with whom I walk." When the strangers protested that they trusted him, he said, "I was not worried about your trust of me. I did not want your religion to be affected by your suspicions."

All critics have remarked that the tone of the traditions is entirely different from that of the Koran. The latter has universally been held to be in the nature of the world's leading revelations. The traditions are affectionate campfire gossip, the odds and ends that would be remembered after a great man had died. Much of the common-sense nature of Islam springs from the traditions.

> Once a Jew came to the prophet and protested that Muhammad's chief assistant had outraged Jews by claiming that Muhammad was more exalted than Moses. The prophet said to his assistant, "You should not have said this, as the feelings of other people must be respected. There is no need to exalt me above Moses."

Also, some of the profoundest elements of Muslim faith derive from the traditions: the whole ritual of congregational prayer is taken from the traditions, including the well-known call to worship.

Then, too, some traditions influenced western behavior.

> One occasion Muhammad saw a donkey being branded on the face. When asked why this was being done, the herdsmen said, "The Romans taught us to do this to prevent theft." Muhammad studied a moment and said, "A donkey's face must be the most sensitive part of his body. Let him be branded on the flanks, where the flesh is thicker." And the custom spread.

As a successful general, Muhammad left many traditions regarding the decent conduct of war.

As a businessman, he stressed honesty: one day he dug his arm into a basket of fine-appearing corn and found the hidden portions musty, whereupon he ordered that in displaying goods, the worst should be placed on top to safeguard the purchaser. He established several principles widely respected today: "No person should enter upon a transaction if negotiations are already under way with another possible customer." "Commodities must not be hoarded on the chance that the market can thus be forced to rise."

Such a practical man understandably denied the necessity of miracles and rebuked those who sought them. There are no traditions regarding miracles. The famous story of Muhammad and the mountain relates to a clownish fakir of that name who lived in Turkey centuries after the prophet. In a bit of horseplay he announced that on the morrow he would make the nearby mountain come to him. When the mountain declined, he shrugged his shoulders and said, "Well, I'll go to the mountain."

Throughout the traditions, Muhammad appears as a saintly man, one whom his Jewish or Christian cousins would immediately have recognized as a man deeply concerned about the nature of God. He preached that slaves should be set free, that fathers should not kill unwanted baby girls, that those oppressed by society should inherit the earth, that peace is better than war, that justice prevails, and that there is one God.

It is particularly well documented that on one occasion when a deputation of Christians from the desert visited him, he said, when time for prayers arrived, "Conduct your services here in the mosque. It is a place consecrated to God."

True, there were times when the early Muslims battled both Jews and Christians—sometimes because the older religions insisted upon battle—but there is much proof that Muhammad hoped for the day when all who shared a common belief in God would exist together in peace: "On entering Jerusalem as conqueror, he refused to say his prayers in the Christian temple lest his Muslim followers take that as a precedent for turning the temple into a mosque."

Especially prized are those traditions which prove that Muhammad was an ordinary man: "Once when a child started wailing at public prayers Muhammad rose and said quickly, 'This service has lasted too long. Listen! The children protest.' And he ended the prayer."

"One day he came upon a woman who wailed pitifully beside the grave of her dead. Admonishing her, he said, 'Be patient and accept God's will.' The woman, not recognizing him in her grief, complained, 'If you had lost a child you would not speak so.' The prophet replied, 'I have suffered the loss of seven children,' and passed quietly on, leaving the woman to grieve as she wished."

Islam differs from most other religions in one respect: it is not only a religion, it is also a body of law.

This law, known as the Shariat, has developed from the Koran and the traditions. But since these sources covered only a small portion of the problems met in law, wise men were forced to hand down decisions based upon their deduction of what the prophet would have advised had he studied the problem.

The resulting law is binding upon Muslims and is indeed part of their faith. Authority for this springs from a tradition which says that a newly appointed judge was about to depart for his post when the prophet questioned him.

"How will you judge?"

"According to the Koran."

"If it is not in the Koran?"

"I will try to recall what you have said."

"But if I was silent?"

"Then I will have to use my own intelligence."

"Good. You will be a fine judge."

As years passed, four great scholars developed four different interpretations of Koranic law, and today in a Muslim nation each citizen must announce which of these four systems he and his family elect to live under. Naturally, adherence to a given system becomes traditional for entire territories, but each individual retains the right to select another system if he feels that it is closer to God's intention.

The differences between the systems are juridical and not theological. Mainly they concern the laws of inheritance.

Of course, each Islamic nation also enacts criminal and business law which binds all members of the community, but in family and social matters it is as if in America there were special laws for Jews, for Catholics, for Baptists and for Episcopalians. One of the first questions that would have to be settled when a man went to court would be, "Under which law do you live?"

This system makes a Muslim's religion somewhat more important to him than it would be in a western community. For there is no Christian nation, no Jewish land whose basic law so clearly stems from one holy book. Shariat law helps bind the nations of Islam together.

To be a Muslim one must submit to five disciplines.

1. The Muslim must confess that "there is no god but God, and Muhammad is his prophet." Like the God of the Christians, Muhammad's God developed from the Jewish Jahveh (Jehovah), and critics agree that this great central concept is identical in the three religions.

The confession does not mean that Muhammad was God's *only* prophet. The Jewish prophets are included and the Christian prophet, Jesus, is given special reverence. What Muslims do contend is that Muhammad was "the seal of the prophets," who brought God's final message.

244

This confession has an importance unequaled in other religions. There are numerous instances in which defeated enemies were about to be slain when they gasped merely the first words of this confession, and they were instantly received into full Muslim citizenship.

Even within this century rough characters escaping into Muslim territories have blurted out this confession, whereupon they have promptly been given a Muslim name, a Muslim wife and a good job.

2. The Muslim must pray five times daily. At dawn, at noon, twice in the afternoon and at night the muezzin calls in a powerful, entreating voice, "God is most great. There is no god but God, and Muhammad is his prophet. Come to prayer, come to security. God is most great." Movements to accompany prayer have been retained since the time of Muhammad, and all visitors to Islam have testified that one of the most extraordinary sights in world religion occurs in a dimly lit mosque when hundreds of men stand shoulder to shoulder, bowing, kneeling, reciting in unison as they face Mecca. It is in such prayer that the brotherhood of Islam is born.

3. The Muslim must contribute two and a half percent of his gross yearly income to charity. This was one of Muhammad's first laws, but it soon became transmuted into a formal tax. Today, however, like the Christian tithe, it has become a matter of individual conscience. The principle, however, is of great importance to Muslim nations, for it justifies modern taxes for social welfare.

4. The Muslim must fast for one lunar month each year, and it is amazing how many devout people do so. Just before dawn a man takes his last food, drinks his last cup of water. Throughout that entire day, no matter how exhausting the heat, the true Muslim refuses food or water. Then, at dusk, he breaks fast. Since the lunar month is slightly shorter than the calendar month, the time for fasting rotates slowly throughout the year, coming sometimes in winter, when the fast is not rigorous, and sometimes in midsummer, when it is fearfully harsh.

5. The Muslim, if physically and financially able, must dur-

ing his lifetime make at least one pilgrimage to Mecca, after which he is entitled to call himself hajji. This custom arose when most Muslims lived within a few miles of the holy city. It is preserved today when men must travel across continents.

Last year I flew with a group of Turkish peasants headed for Jeddah, the gateway to Mecca. At Beirut we picked up four Senussi tribesmen from Africa, six feet six and thin as wands. At Jeddah other planes arrived from Egypt, from Pakistan and from Indonesia. Later a Russian plane brought bearded Muslims from the steppes of Central Asia, and a Pan American clipper delivered a group from Brooklyn.

Long before the advent of Muhammad, Mecca was a holy city, crowded with idols. Before human memory it contained a sacred black rock, and some historians have contended that Muhammad merely perpetuated a pagan rite. This is not so.

Mecca was not the original holy city of Islam. Jerusalem was. It was toward Jerusalem, home of Moses, Abraham and Jesus, that Muslims first faced in their daily prayers, for it also contained one of Islam's most cherished relics, a fragment of the temple of Solomon. Jerusalem has always remained a major Muslim shrine.

But it was soon dropped as the focus of prayer in favor of Mecca, for it was in this city, Muslims believe, that Abraham volunteered to sacrifice his oldest son Ishmael. (The Koran says it was Ishmael, ancestor of the Arabs, and not Isaac, ancestor of the Jews.) The black stone of Mecca, so revered today, is held to be the one which Abraham intended to use.

No other religion in world history spread so rapidly as Islam. By the time of Muhammad's death (A.D. 632) Islam controlled a great part of Arabia, and much of the Near East. Soon it triumphed in Syria, Persia, Egypt, the lower borders of present Russia and across North Africa to the gates of Spain. In the next century its progress was even more spectacular.

The West has widely believed that this surge of religion was made possible by the sword. But no modern scholar accepts that idea, and the Koran is explicit in support of freedom of conscience. The evidence is strong that Islam welcomed the peoples of many diverse religions, so long as they behaved

246

themselves and paid extra taxes. Muhammad constantly taught that Muslims should cooperate with "people of the Book" (Jews and Christians). He specifically advised his followers, "You will find your most affectionate friends will be those who say, 'We are Christians.' "

True, there were often wars between Muslims and either Christians or Jews, and the Koran contains passages of primitive violence relating to these wars, but testimony is overwhelming that most "followers of the Book" were given decent treatment, sanctuary and freedom to worship as they wished. Cynics point out, wittily, that Muslims would have been fools to force Christians and Jews to accept their faith and thus lose the higher taxes! Of course, pagans were forced to accept Islam, and that is probably where the legend of the sword developed.

To Americans, accustomed by their history books to believe that Muslims were barbarous infidels, it is difficult to comprehend how profoundly our intellectual life has been modified by Muslim scholars. They laid the foundation stones of much science, medicine, mathematics and philosophy. They were of extraordinary importance in geography. Crusaders who invaded the Holy Land to fight Muslims returned to Europe with new ideas of love, poetry, chivalry, warfare and government. Our concept of what a university should be was deeply modified by Muslim scholars, who perfected the writing of history and who brought to Europe much Greek learning.

Islam, although it originated with the Arabs, soon became an international religion. Today only seven percent of the world's Muslims are Arabians. And only twenty percent speak Arabic as their native language. To consider all Muslims to be Arabs because the religion started in Arabia would be like calling all Catholics Italians because that religion thrived in Italy.

More than most religions, Islam preaches the brotherhood of all races. Muhammad himself probably had exactly the same skin coloring as Jesus—a very suntanned white—but today his

247

followers embrace all colors: black men from Africa, yellow men from China, brown men from Malaya, white men from Turkey. The religion is especially attractive to Africans, and some students of that troubled continent have thought that if any religion is destined to unite Africa, it could be Islam.

For long periods in history Muslim nations strayed far from the spirit of Muhammad, and gloomy darkness settled upon much of Islam. If one focuses only upon the worst Persian and Turkish caliphs, one can easily condemn Islam as a religion that failed. Unfortunately, one can do the same with Christianity. But if one looks at the enormous good Islam has achieved, and particularly if one considers the promise of this religion in new nations like republican Egypt, Pakistan and Indonesia, one sees the permanent greatness of Islam.

Like Christianity, Islam has broken into many sects, which in this case differ mainly on matters of law and hereditary succession, rather than upon theology. The Sunnis comprise the major sect and dominate most modern Islamic nations. The Shias are the principal minority sect and rule Iran. The Aga Khan is spiritual ruler of one of the principal Shia sub-sects. But the difference between Sunni and Shia is more like the difference between a Presbyterian and a Lutheran than between a Catholic and a Protestant.

I have been studying Islam for many years, and I cannot see any valid reason why this religion and Christianity cannot cooperate. I know that some crazy men in Islam preach jihad (holy war) against unbelievers and sometimes try to assassinate their own leaders to foment such war. But no sensible Muslim listens to them. They are today's equivalent of hot-headed Christian knights who in the Middle Ages vowed to exterminate Muslims. Age cures such rashness.

Nor can I find any permanent reason why Islam and Judaism should continue their temporary enmity. In the long sweep of history Muslims and Jews cooperated in areas of mutual interest. True, there were repeated troubles. (Muslims claimed that a Jewish girl tried to poison Muhammad. Jews can point to isolated massacres.) But even under the worst caliphs, Jews held positions of influence and in general prospered under Muslim rule. Today the State of Israel is an exasperation to Muslims and a temptation to rash action, but once the attendant problems have been amicably settled, Muslims and Jews should be expected to exist in harmony as they did for more than thirteen hundred years.

Of great importance to America is the fact that Islam, as a religion, is unalterably opposed to communism. Sometimes, when living in Islam, I feel that God is a much greater reality to Muslims than He is to Christians. It is difficult to believe that Muslims would willingly surrender their faith for a communism which denied the existence of God.

On the other hand, Islam as a society is much closer to communal life than it is to capitalism, and if the United States, by unwise economic or political moves, were to alienate the Muslim world or were to permit economic ruin there, I would expect much of Islam to embrace communism while attempting to hold on to God secretly.

I am convinced that the United States will in the future meet many problems in the Muslim world, and I am therefore reassured when I see how logical it is for us to cooperate with the people who trust in this great, practical religion.

SPORT

My second regret is that I did not find an opportunity to write as much about sports as I would have liked.

I have played games all my life, and even today at an age when many of my friends are immersed in retirement, I love to get onto a tennis court to play a rowdy game of doubles with opponents who enjoy trying to see if they can ram the ball down my throat. I have been an energetic competitor and believe that much of my ability to keep intellectually concerned has stemmed from my participation in such sports as I could handle.

I have also loved to watch games, find an excitement and a nonsense in them that never stales. In Fiji I used to watch giant blacks playing rugby barefooted with a zest that transmitted itself to everyone who saw them. In Australia it was great fun to watch the mayhem committed in their unique game of football called Rules. In Spain it was fascinating to see how soccer had captured the affection of fans who previously had devoted themselves to bullfighting. And in the savage New Hebrides Islands, perhaps the most backward area on earth, it was unbelievably thrilling to watch Stone Age natives climb to the tops of tall trees, their ankles fastened to vines of a nicely calculated length. Tying the loose ends of the vines to the tops of the trees, these daring men would dive headfirst a hundred and fifty feet, trusting that the vines would haul them up short just as they were about to dash their brains out on the ground.

The line-up of the great Philadelphia baseball team I watched in my youth rattles glibly off my tongue today. What a marvelous crowd of Yankee-killers Connie Mack had put together for the Athletics in those years: Cochrane catching, Foxx on first, Bishop at second, Boley at short, Dykes at third, Bucketfoot Al Simmons in left, Mule Haas in center, Bing Miller in right and that incomparable pitching sequence of Lefty Grove, George Earnshaw, Rube Walberg, Ed Rommel, Harold Ehmke and John Picus Quinn. You could move the whole lot into the Hall of Fame tomorrow and occasion no protest.

I enjoyed the tennis championships, followed the boxers, watched what was happening in football and kept up to date on most of the other sports, but my abiding love was always basketball. For a game with the beauty it commands and the intricacies of its maneuvers, it has not been well written about. Of all the athletes I have watched, the one superlative performance I've seen, outdistancing all others, was Wilt Chamberlain playing in a run-of-the-mill game at Madison Square Garden one night. It had to be one of his greatest nights. He shot from all angles and netted some seventy points. He swept the boards on defense and dominated the game like a master magician.

I used to play basketball, kept it up till I was past forty, and that night I realized with a certain sadness that no man I either played with or played against in all my years could even make one of the good teams today. When I hear old-timers argue that "baseball was better in the days of Ty Cobb," or that "football was rougher in the days of Jim Thorpe," I smile. Very few basketball players of fifty years ago could make the squad today. It's reassuring, I think, to know a game which has grown infinitely better in one's lifetime.

252

I wish I had written more about sport. I see an enormous amount of good and bad in athletics. I think some real nonsense is talked on this subject. I would suppose that in general our sports reporting has been more misleading than the reporting of any other national enterprise. Football coaches who were tyrants have been lionized, and individual atheletes who were monsters have been protected.

And yet, if I were asked with whom among my contemporaries I would most like to be compared, I would say unhesitatingly Robin Roberts, the big, outgoing, voluntary right-handed pitcher who toiled for the Philadelphia Phillies during the middle years of my life. Roberts was a distinguished gentleman, a tremendous competitor. When his fast ball was working he could breeze it in like a stick of dynamite and explode it under the batter's nose. He had courage, and he had the quality of sticking in there when the going got rough. Because he played on a weak-hitting team he lost a lot of games each year by one run, and if his teammates gave him two runs a game, that was big news. He never complained, just kept blazing them in.

But what I admired especially about Roberts was that when his arm lost its zing, when the old fireball exploded no longer, he kept plugging away. Four innings, good. Six innings, still okay. Then in the eighth and ninth the opposition hitters would start to clout their home runs. Few pitchers ever threw more home-run balls than Robin Roberts. Zinggg! out of the park they went, day after day.

He didn't bellyache. He didn't cry over his lost speed. He simply stayed in there and kept throwing. He was a man whom thousands of Philadelphians would always remember with affection. He was the professional. His job was to pitch, in good years and bad. He was a man I admired.

I did only two sports articles for the *Digest*, the one included here and one on Calesero, the Mexican bullfighter who was much like Robin Roberts. He fought till he was in his fifties, an unheard-of thing. He had been hit by the bulls so often he looked like a pincushion. I did an affectionate study of him some years ago, and I believe he liked it because it spoke of him as he thought of himself, the old professional.

Then, three years later, Calesero decided to retire. He went to each of the bullrings in Mexico and gave a farewell performance, with the ritual cutting of the pigtail which signified that he was through forever. Crowds turned out in each city and he made a lot of money. There was some talk of his making the circuit again and really cleaning up. But the day came in Mexico City when he really had to cut his pigtail. This was the end, no fooling.

A fantastic crowd turned out to see the brave old man fight his last bull. He was sensational. When the fight was over, he marched to the center of the ring. His family came out of the stands, a beautiful wife and seven children. The band played "La Golondrina." Someone released four hundred white pigeons. Old-timers who had fought with him came to the center of the ring, and with a pair of silver scissors, one of them cut the pigtail.

Calesero wept. His wife wept. His seven children wept. The President of Mexico wept. The pigeons kept flying and the band kept playing and I wept. It was some afternoon, believe me. Sport can sometimes be like that.

Soccer: The World Cup

It was a typical midsummer day in 1966, and Madrid was throbbing with activity. Streets were crowded. Men were ogling pretty girls. And traffic was impossible.

Then suddenly this city of more than two million fell silent. Cars pulled to the side of the road. Pedestrians left the streets and a tension developed so real that you could feel it. Madrid became a ghost town.

For the next ninety minutes the city remained silent, listening to radio and television reports of a soccer game being played in Birmingham, England, between Spain and West Germany.

"Why the anxiety?"

"Good God! Don't you realize what's happening? If we lose, we're out of the World Cup."

At half-time the score was 1–1 and Madrid began to pray. For many years Spain had been the top soccer power in the world, but now? In the second half excitement increased. Spain had three different chances to score, but missed. Then, in the eighty-fourth minute of the game, West Germany booted home a goal.

I shall never forget what happened next. Spanish men

around me began to weep. One knelt in the street and began to pray. Others stood in shadows, crossing themselves. One man stood on tiptoe for the remaining six minutes, as if by doing so he would help Spain score an equalizer.

In vain. The whistle blew and Spain was eliminated from the World Cup. In Madrid men cursed, kicked at dogs, snarled at their wives and proclaimed, "This nation is finished."

What I saw that day in Madrid was tame when compared to what happened in Italy and Brazil when their two great teams—most powerful in the world, the experts had said as the competition began—were ignominiously defeated in early rounds. The Italian team, beaten by unknowns from North Korea, was afraid to go back to Italy. Their plane sneaked into an unscheduled field at one o'clock in the morning, but bitter partisans had anticipated the ruse and were on hand to revile the players and pelt them with tomatoes as they crept into waiting buses.

"You have shamed Italy!" the crowd roared.

In Brazil, where the collapse of their champions was a shock of incredible magnitude, fans tried to commit suicide or dropped dead from excitement. The government intervened to find out what had gone wrong.

This was my introduction to the madness that sweeps the world every four years: the World Cup.

This year (1970) Americans will have a good opportunity to see what happens when sixteen championship teams from various parts of the world meet to fight for what many consider the world's most avidly sought trophy, the Jules Rimet Cup. On May 31, in massive Aztec Stadium in Mexico City, play will begin with Mexico facing Russia. The teams will be divided into four groups, with each conducting a round robin. The two top teams from each group then move to a quarter-finals, where knockout competition begins. On Sunday, June 21, the championship will be determined in a game between the two finalists. Around the world some 500,000,000 fans will be watching on television, delivered by satellite, with other millions listening on radio. The winner gets the Cup, a small golden goblet which can be held in one hand—named for the

French official who dreamed up the international championship.

This tournament is without question the most important sporting event in the world. It dwarfs a baseball World Series or a football Super Bowl, and makes even the Olympics seem trivial.

Clive Toye, the affable English sportswriter who serves as administrator of the North American Soccer League, explains: "In the Olympics a national team is no more than a congregation of skilled individuals who you hope will do well. If they don't, who cares? Because it really isn't a team in the competitive sense. But the World Cup! When Italy sends a team onto the field, the heart and soul of all Italy runs with it. If Italy loses, every Italian feels diminished. If she wins! That night Italy sings!"

Throughout the world, 140 nations from Argentina to Zambia play soccer—most of them call it football—and of these, 71 participated in the World Cup elimination rounds which started two years ago.

In 1966 the games provided a confrontation between two theories: the rugged run-and-rush style of England and Germany, as opposed to the dancing-master control and beauty of the Latin countries. For a generation the latter style had dominated, as the list of the eight World Cup winners indicates: Uruguay, Brazil, Italy, twice each; Germany, England, once each. Sometimes an Argentine player or an Italian could juggle the ball so deftly that he would drive northern opponents crazy, but in 1966 the stolid type of play won. Italy, Brazil and Argentina were knocked out early; England and Germany made it to the finals. England had the game tucked away, 2–1, but in the very last seconds Germany scored an unbelievable goal to send the game into overtime. England scored a questionable goal to put them ahead, then drove home a clean-cut beauty to clinch it at 4–2.

It will be a strange World Cup this year, because four of the most notable soccer countries in history have failed to qualify: Portugal, Spain, France, Argentina. The grief in those lands is difficult to describe.

The competition should be wild and woolly. Italy and Brazil are out to avenge the disasters which humiliated them last time. Uruguay and Peru are hungry to reestablish the supremacy of South American soccer. Russia is about ripe to pick off the world title, while rugged Germany and England are hopeful of proving that their good showing last time was no fluke. (The United States was eliminated early by Haiti.)

This year the games will be influenced by an unknown factor, altitude. In soccer men run back and forth at breakneck speed for two halves of forty-five minutes each, with no time outs and no substitutions except for disabling injury. Can the English and Germans, who depend upon tireless running, survive at high altitude? Or will the Latins, who rely more upon ball control and minimum exertion, have an advantage? Finally, in the past the host team has won four times and been runner-up twice, which proves that playing at home before a partisan crowd is worth a couple of goals. Will Mexico, accustomed to the 7,415-foot altitude, have a sharp advantage over teams which on paper look stronger?

Most competing nations are training their teams at high altitudes. Russia, for example, is training in the Caucasus, and all nations will bring their players to Mexico well in advance of Cup play. If the play-offs were held at sea level, I'd pick Germany and England to be near the top, but when I think of players rushing back and forth for ninety minutes at a mile and a half up—add an extra half-hour in case of tie—I realize that anything can happen.

Interest in soccer is so great because it is the one truly international team sport. Legend says the game started when two Cro-Magnon men started kicking around the skull of an adversary. A game much like soccer was known in China before the birth of Christ, but it was the English in the early decades of the last century who regularized the game. Subsequently, British ships traveling the world carried the game with them, and I have often been in remote spots where signs like this were posted on trees: "Saturday afternoon. A team from the H.M.S. *Valiant* will play a local side."

There is some question as to whether international soccer should be classified as a game or as open warfare. When Liverpool traveled to Italy to play Inter of Milan, the English team sought out a quiet resort on Lago de Maggiore, but partisans of the Milan team found them and circled their hotel all night on five hundred coughing motorcycles. Said one cyclist, "The least we could do for our team. Keep the enemy from their sleep."

When the Rangers of Glasgow, one of the most passionate soccer cities on earth, traveled to Newcastle, England, and lost, 2–0, their enraged fans destroyed so much of the center city that a special parliamentary commission, already studying the growth of rowdyism, visited Newcastle to see for themselves what a berserk crowd could do.

In the 1966 World Cup, Argentina and Uruguay were so determined to prove that South American soccer was supreme, they practically kicked their European rivals out of the stadium. Players were dismissed from the game, officials had to suspend the matches for long intervals, and in one wild game the nine Argentinian players left on the field almost defeated the eleven English.

Early in the Brazil-Portuguese game Pele, the great Brazilian star, was brought down by wild kicking and forced to quit the game for five minutes, limping futilely through the second half. John Rafferty, writing in *The Scotsman*, described the Cup as "marred by chauvinistic dissension, nastiness and ill-feeling."

This year the Cup faces a unique problem. Both Israel and Morocco have qualified for the play-offs, but the latter has announced that out of respect for her Arab allies, she will not step on the field if her opponent is Israel. The officials handled this one rather neatly, rigging the draw so that Israel will have to subdue powerhouse Italy and Uruguay before she could get to Morocco, while the latter will have to pull a miracle and defeat Germany and Bulgaria to stay alive. "That's one problem we've taken care of," the officials say. They also arranged that Russia and Czechoslovakia would not meet in the early rounds.

In 1967 the violent partisanship of soccer produced a real tragedy in Turkey, when supporters of the Kayseri team launched a full-scale battle with pistols, knives and broken bottles against fans from neighboring Sivas. The fight continued for two days, at the end of which forty-two were dead and more than six hundred seriously wounded.

The ultimate in soccer rivalry, however, occurred only a year ago in the elimination trials for the 1970 World Cup. Honduras and El Salvador were competing to see who would play the winner of the Haiti-United States match, with the trip to Mexico City as the reward. In such eliminations, two games are played, one in each country, total goals to decide. In case of tie, a third game is played in a neutral country.

After two games the two Central American countries were tied, but before the play-off could take place, the wild behavior of the fans in each country led to actual border clashes and finally to open warfare with tanks, airplanes and invasion. More than 2,000 people were killed, with whole villages laid desolate and peace throughout Central America imperiled. Of course the soccer games came on top of other seething irritations, but it was football which provided the spark, and the war has gone into the history books as "the Soccer War."

It is difficult for an American to understand soccer. I learned the hard way. As a student in Scotland, I had to choose which of the two mighty Glasgow teams I would support—Celtic in green, Rangers in blue. Because as a boy I had cheered for the New York Celtics basketball team, I cast my lot with their namesakes. This surprised my Scottish friends, because you weren't supposed to be for them unless you were Catholic.

Year after year these two teams battled. They played two games, home and home, and it was open warfare: athletic, geographical, spiritual and religious. One wintry afternoon when Celtic had won a brutal game at Ibrox, the Rangers' park, I was walking home wearing my green ribbon when a Ranger fan leaped out of the shadows, grabbed me by the throat, and without saying a word, punched me in the mouth so hard I fell backward.

Other Rangers fans picked me up and apologized. "Jock don't mean nothin' personal. He just hates Celtic."

Last year a Rangers fan locked himself in his sixth-floor room and watched the Celtic game on TV. When Rangers fell behind he yelled to his family, "If they lose this game I'll throw myself out the window." They lost and he jumped. He broke most of his bones but survived.*

Identification of the fan with his team is absolute and lasts a lifetime. Harold Wilson, Prime Minister of Britain, still carries in his wallet a dog-eared photograph of the great Huddersfield Town team of 1922, champion of its day. Industrial psychologists in several football countries have noticed that factory production goes up or down, depending upon whether the home team won or lost. Say the experts, "The drop in production comes because the men are sick . . . really sick . . . when their team loses." After England's victory in 1966, Billy Snedden, Australia's Immigration Minister, noticed that emigration to Australia dropped by twenty-eight percent. "It made Englishmen feel that Britain still has a future," he explained.

When Brazil was ignominiously knocked out of the last Cup, the nation went into mourning. Fights erupted across the nation and many people were hospitalized. One woman tried to drown herself, crying, "I hate Pele."

Interest in the game in Italy is so great that there are four *daily* newspapers which report nothing but football. Lamar Hunt, whose Kansas City Chiefs won the Super Bowl this

---

*Shortly after publication of this article the ultimate happened in Celtic-Rangers rivalry. On Saturday, June 2, 1971, the two teams, meeting at Ibrox, the Rangers' park, played eighty-nine scoreless minutes. Then, at the last gasp, Celtic scored a dramatic goal, and thousands of Rangers fans left the park in disgust. But then an incredible thing happened. In the final seconds of play, Rangers miraculously kicked a goal, converting what had been certain defeat into a moral victory. A mighty yell rose from the stadium, so that those disconsolate fans who had left early turned around and started running back to see what had happened. They were met head-on by wildly screaming Rangers fans cascading down the stairs, and in the crush sixty-six were killed.

year, took time out to study soccer as played in Europe, and reported: "I found that the crowd enthusiasm and participation far exceeded any which I have ever seen at American pro football, baseball World Series or college football games."

In Corsica last April an ardent Ajaccio fan named François Ramacciotto became so despondent when his team lost to Gazelec 2–0 that he whipped out his pistol and shot a Gazelec fan twice—once for each goal. And in Amsterdam a very close game between Delft and Utrecht caused such a riot that police whisked the two teams away to another field and had them play the remaining two minutes in secrecy.*

Liverpool, the home city of the Beatles, has two major teams, Liverpool, which wears red, and Everton, which prefers blue. All Liverpudlians are supposed to choose between the two, and in local pubs they tell the story of a girl who asked her Everton father for permission to marry a boy who rooted for Liverpool. He refused: "It's been my experience that no good ever comes from these mixed marriages."

Soccer inspires such loyalty for several good reasons. It is simpler than any other game, for it requires nothing more than a ball twenty-seven inches around and weighing fourteen ounces. Surprisingly, the field can be of almost any available size: from 100 to 130 yards long, 50 to 100 yards wide. For international games, the limits are 110 to 120 yards and 70 to 80 yards.

Soccer is a game that men of any size can play. Unlike football and basketball, which have become restricted to giants, the finest soccer stars are apt to look like the rest of us. On England's championship team, four players are five feet eight or under, and Nobby Stiles, the toughest one-man gang in the business, was only five feet six. The great Brazilian star Pele stands only five feet nine and weighs 160 pounds, and Luigi Riva, whom Italian fans acclaim as today's finest player, is half an inch shorter.

*On June 18, 1971, an elimination game between Tunis and Sfax ended with such a great riot and with so many people in the hospital, the Tunisian government wisely decreed that all remaining games in the tourney be played on vacant fields without spectators.

One of the crucial facts about soccer is that scores are kept low, with 2–1 being typical. This means two things: on any Saturday afternoon (Sunday in Catholic countries) some weak team will unexpectedly clobber a very strong team; and a champion who should have won will be held to an unexpected tie. This makes soccer a marvelous game on which to bet, because each team has a chance of winning, losing or tying. Thus any game can have three possible outcomes, a possibility no other sport provides with such regularity.

So in most soccer countries bookmakers draw up a list of fourteen games, including all the toughies, and all you have to do is indicate how each home team will do: win-lose-draw. Since there are 4,782,969 different combinations in which the fourteen games can end, once or twice each year only one lucky bettor will have the right outcome on his card. He then wins a fortune, as much as $100,000 for a penny.

Even more tempting is the task of spotting fourteen tie games. On August 27, 1966, Percy Harrison, a laborer in the little town of East Stockwith in England, did so, and on the bet of one cent had hauled down $927,352.

Interest throughout Great Britain is so intense—one company alone, Littlewoods, pays out nearly $2,000,000 a week in prizes—that on weekends when unexpected blizzards force the postponement of games so that betting cannot proceed, a panel of experts is locked up in a hotel room and they determine what *might* have happened had the canceled games been played. Bets are paid off on these hypothetical results and everyone is happy. It's the bet that matters, not whether the game was actually played.

In Spain the mania is so rabid that on weekends when Spanish teams are not scheduled, the betting list is based on games being played in the Italian league. The Spanish bettor cannot possibly know much about the Italian games, but he goes ahead and bets anyway and sometimes wins $100,000 on teams whose names he does not even know.

When I was in Angola, thousands of miles from homeland Portugal, betting shops stayed open late on Saturday night to accept bets on teams that would be playing in far-off Portugal the next day. Late on Sunday people throughout Angola stayed by their radios, waiting for the flash that would tell them whether their favorite teams had won or lost.

Excitement is maintained by a clever device peculiar to soccer. In each nation numerous leagues operate on the basis of merit. League A comprises the best twenty or twenty-two teams, several League Bs include the second best, a group of League Cs the third, and so on. At the end of each season, in a League B for example, the two top teams are promoted to League A (whose two worst teams are dropped back to League B) while League B's two tail-end teams are demoted to League C. Consequently, in the final weeks of a season there is intense excitement to see which teams will go up, which down. A game between two teams near the bottom of a league can become a mortal affair.

For example, on May 18, 1969, the citizens of Caserta, a town of 70,000 northeast of Naples, were overjoyed when their League C team beat Trapani, because this meant that next season Caserta would be promoted to League B. The celebration, which lasted for several days, was dampened by ugly rumors that Caserta had won only because it had bought off one of the key Trapani players.

Belatedly, on Monday, September 8, Italian radio carried the chilling announcement: "Players involved in the scandal are barred for life. Caserta forfeits the game and is refused promotion to League B."

When the news flashed through Caserta, all shops closed and people started massing in the street. By afternoon the news was officially confirmed, but no damage was done. That night the citizens of Caserta found that the game scheduled for Sunday, when they were to play their first game in League B, had been canceled. On Tuesday a sullen, embittered mob began ripping iron shutters off store windows and setting fire to municipal buildings.

When water pipes supplying the town were torn up, fires could not be checked, and barricades were erected in the streets. Football fans in nearby Naples, hearing that a first-class riot was under way, came to Caserta by bus, just to be in on the fun. By the time peace was restored, eighty people were in the hospital, ninety-nine in jail, and damage estimated at two billion lire had been done. Caserta is still in League C.

The weakness of soccer is something which adds to its wild excitement. With scoring so infrequent—in the last World Cup three of the matches were 0–0 and nine were 2–1—the referee's decision becomes vital. If in the waning minutes of a game he spots what could have been a foul by the defending team inside the penalty zone, he has a most difficult decision to make. If he calls the foul, the attacking team gets a free kick at the goal at point-blank range, with only the defending goalkeeper to stop the shot. It's practically an automatic goal, a gift from the referee, and all hell is sure to break loose. Referees do not have happy lives.

In Naples not long ago the fans became so enraged at a bad call that they chased the referee all the way to Rome. In a small town near Khartoum, the referee was so inadequate that toward the end of the game the losing team kicked him to death, and their supporters said, "Why did they wait till the second half?"

Things got so bad in South American soccer that the teams agreed to import impartial referees from Europe. They were given three promises: "Good pay, good lodging, and a decent burial."*

Team rivalries are so furious in Brazil that deep moats have had to be dug entirely around the playing field so that spectators cannot invade the area to mob the referee. When I went to my first game in Haifa, Israel, I was astonished to find myself sitting behind a barbed-wire fence which kept the Jews who had grown up in Europe from mobbing the referee, as they had done in their youth.

---

*Several years ago the rumor circulated that fans in one African jungle town had become so enraged at a referee's bad call, they had eaten him. This was never corroborated, but on February 11, 1972, eleven players from Sportivo Rural, of Córdoba, Argentina, had to be jailed on a charge of murder. Objecting to a referee's decision, they started roughing him up. When Linesman Augustin Basso, forty-two and the father of four children, ran to help the referee, the angry Sportivo players kicked him to death.

One referee who learned how perilous his trade can be is Angel Eduardo Pazos, of Uruguay, who flew to Lima, Peru, on Sunday, May 24, 1964, to officiate at a crucial game between Argentina and Peru to decide which team would go to the Olympics in Japan. The first half ended in a scoreless tie, but midway through the second Argentina scored. In the eightieth minute a clever Peruvian forward booted home the equalizer, but Referee Pazos disallowed it because of a Peruvian foul, a decision which gave the game to Argentina.

The field at Lima was protected from spectators by a steel-link wire fence nine feet high, but among the Lima fans was a giant called Bomba (The Bomb) who had become famous for his ability to scale the fence, run down errant referees and beat them to pulp. Just as the game ended, Bomba scrambled over the fence and bore down on Referee Pazos, screaming, "I'm going to kill him!"

Police intervened to save Pazos, but the crowd was so vengeful, so completely irrational, that it began storming the fence and by concerted, rhythmic pushing tore holes in it. It was obvious that some kind of calamity must ensue, so the police started lobbing tear-gas grenades to protect themselves from the infuriated crowd. Then, for a reason which has never been explained, they began tossing their grenades into the stands, where panic followed.

Escape doors had been left locked by careless attendants and a massive crush developed as spectators tried to escape the tear gas. Enraged, the crowd proceeded to murder three policemen, pitching them headfirst onto concrete runways, stamping them to death. In all, somewhere between 287 and 328 people perished that day, and authorities around the world began to wonder what they could do to control football crowds.

Soccer players, eleven to a side, give an exhibition of skill and endurance hard to match. For ninety minutes they race back and forth at breakneck speed with no substitutions allowed (except for dire injury) and no time-outs. With all parts of their body except their hands, they control the ball with a

266

kind of magic, one of the spectacular exhibitions coming when a player in a corner lofts the ball in a high arc toward the goal, where one of his teammates leaps into the air and with his head deflects the ball into the net.

Eddie Stanky, the baseball coach, has said, "If I were drowning in a lake and there were a bunch of athletes on shore, I'd want the soccer player to rescue me, because I'd know that he had the endurance."

For their grueling performances, star soccer players draw down salaries that are somewhat higher than those paid American baseball and football luminaries—$125,000 a season is good pay. With an individual star meaning so much, it has become the custom to buy and sell players from one country to another. Italy and Spain are the great importers, Brazil and Hungary the largest exporters.

The great Brazilian star Pele—born Edson Arantes do Nascimento—used to dominate soccer so completely that three Italian teams formed a consortium to buy him . . . for something like $2,000,000, but Brazil's then President recognized a national crisis when he saw one. Acting swiftly, he declared Pele a national treasure, not to be exported. "If they had sold Pele," one soccer fan said, "there would have been a revolution."

Naples paid $533,000 for the Brazilian star Jose Altafini, and Turin laid out $280,000 for the great Scottish player, Denis Law, peddling him later to an English team for $322,000. These prices are bargains, for when Inter of Milan paid $500,000 for the great Luis Suarez, they got back an estimated ten times as much in ticket sales.

Such international trading has been profitable in league play but harmful in the World Cup, which has a rule that a player can play only for the nation in which he was born or to which he has been legally naturalized. Spain and Italy have suffered from this practice, since they did the most importing. Their club teams were practically unbeatable, Madrid having won the European championship six years in a row. But the team contained so many foreigners from Hungary, Argentina and France that when Spain had to depend upon native-born players, they accomplished little.

To combat this, Italy now limits the number of aliens who can play on any team, and to ensure a reliable supply of new Italian players, has gone back to ancient Rome for guidance. In those days there was such a need for gladiators that schools were established where slaves could learn how to use the trident, net and small sword. Today, in various spots throughout Italy, there are soccer schools to which boys are sent at the age of ten. In Milanello, for example, the school outside Milan, the youngsters are fed a controlled diet and drilled for endurance and soccer skills. Old professionals keep an eagle eye on the kids and weed out those who are not learning fast enough. Those who progress become professionals while still in their teens—to fill the positions once occupied by players imported from abroad, and Italian football is experiencing a resurgence.

If more countries should follow Italy's lead in training their own soccer players, the international contests would become once again a more faithful test of true native-team skills.*

---

*The 1970 World Cup produced no startling surprises. Russia played well. Germany gained revenge by defeating England in a crucial game. Mexico performed ably at the high altitude. But it was Italy and Brazil, the two teams who had disgraced themselves in 1966, who won through to the finals, which Brazil won in a superbly played game, 4–1. Since this was Brazil's third victory, she gained permanent possession of the Jules Rimet Cup. Pele played well, then announced his retirement.

268

THE WORLD OF ART

The constant avocation of my life has been the study of art. Indeed, I might be described as the archetypal culture-vulture. I have haunted all the world's major museums except the Pinakothek in Dresden. From high school days I have collected postcards of the best paintings, arranging them and rearranging them into what might be called the "ideal museum." I have filled filing cabinets with handsome colored reproductions of art, then given them to museum libraries so that others could have as much fun from them as I did.

And I have written about art. When DeWitt Wallace learned of my persistent hobby, he encouraged it by sending me to various notable museums in Europe and Asia. I have written five books about Oriental art and am as excited today as I was fifty years ago when I find myself before a new painting or entering some small new museum.

For me, the world of art has grown constantly larger, constantly more rewarding. If you add music to painting, they represent together the two subjects which have engaged most of my leisure time. Rarely a day goes by, no matter where

I am, that I do not in some way enjoy art or listen to music.

There might have been some wiser way for me to have spent my spare time, but I cannot at this moment think of any.

The Magic Hand of Hokusai

In 1804 an impoverished Japanese artist already in his mid-forties concluded that some dramatic gesture was needed to attract attention to his work. Accordingly, he lined off an area before a temple in the city of Edo (now Tokyo) and set about painting the largest picture so far seen in Japan.

With rocks he weighted down his pasted-up sheet of heavy paper covering 2,250 square feet. One end he lashed to an oak beam, so that when completed, the picture could be hauled aloft. Then, with big vats of ink and tubs of color, with brooms and swabs of cloth tied to sticks, he went to work. Tucking his kimono up about his waist and kicking off his sandals, he ran back and forth across the huge paper, outlining a portrait of Japan's best-loved saint, Daruma, who once sat so long contemplating the nature of world and man that his arms withered away.

Soon the temple court was filled with people marveling as the artist sped about slapping color down in tremendous and apparently unplanned strokes. At dusk, when men at the ropes hauled the oaken beam into position, the vast expanse of paper disclosed a portrait of Daruma nearly sixty feet high. It is recorded that a horse could have walked into the mouth of the gigantic saint.

The artist, Katsushika Hokusai, had accomplished his purpose. He was talked about. Not content, he next painted, with an ordinary brush, the picture of two sparrows so small they could be seen only with a magnifying glass. These exploits were reported at court and Hokusai was summoned to exhibit his unusual powers. This he did by ripping down a paper door and smearing it with indigo ink. Then he caught a rooster, whose feet he proceeded to dip in red ink. Shooing the bird onto the flat door, where its tracks produced an impression of red maple leaves, Hokusai cried, "Leaves in autumn on the blue Tatsuta River!"

Actually, Hokusai was a most careful and painstaking artist who worked out meticulous experimental studies before putting his designs on paper. He became one of the most famous and popular artists in Japan and was among the last and most gifted practitioners of the art called *ukiyo-e*, which in common usage means paintings or woodblock prints depicting scenes of everyday life. What Hokusai did was to perfect conventions already thousands of years old and to specialize in new woodblock techniques—colors, dominance of scenery over human figures, perspective—which produced prints whose total effect was revolutionary.

The marvel is that he accomplished this at an age when most men are either dead or retired. Many of the color prints which the world today treasures were designed when he was in his eighties. He was doing some of his strongest work when he died at eighty-nine.

Hokusai was a prodigious worker, with more than 30,000 drawings to his credit. He lived in ninety-three different houses, abandoning them in turn when they became either too dirty to clean or too burdened by back rent. He spent his entire life in poverty because he held money in contempt: he paid his bills by tossing packets of uncounted yen at tradesmen. He used more than fifty aliases, abandoning them, too, whenever he discovered some new artistic principle meriting a new name. But it is his late, authentic Hokusai style that is prized: that rugged, powerful, handsomely organized world with the touch of awkwardness that is a touchstone of his art.

In his youth he was a precocious, poverty-stricken boy in Tokyo. By the time he was nineteen, he was a wood-carver. He was by turn a bookseller, a hawker of calendars, a merchant of red peppers and an itinerant painter of banners. He married twice and had several children, who were a tribulation, plus a grandson whose financial operations finally threw Hokusai into bankruptcy.

His only solace was his gifted daughter Oei, who was one of the few Japanese women to become skilled in *ukiyo-e* and who left creditable prints of her own. She watched over her father, reporting that one day when he was past eighty she found him at his drawing bench weeping because "even at that age, and in spite of all his study and effort, he had not yet truly learned to draw things as they were." It was to Oei that Hokusai cried in anguish from his deathbed, "If heaven could only grant me ten more years! Only five more, and I would have become a real painter."

His interests were as vast as the world. He wrote excellent poetry, was a good novelist and published many humorous works. At sixty-eight he suffered a stroke which should have killed him; but he doctored himself back to health, wrote and illustrated a medical report on his self-cure.

Had he died at sixty, Hokusai would be known chiefly for his extraordinary volumes called *Manga,* which should properly be translated *Drawing Things Just as They Come,* but which has come to mean something like *Sketches from Life.* In these fifteen paper-bound books of prints, thousands of human beings in all postures and conditions of life swarm the pages, crabs crawl from the sea, ghosts and flowers appear. Men dive under the sea in bells which hold air captive for them to breathe, while horses swim to show how their legs operate. Architecture, history, wildlife, wrestlers, warriors and mythological fantasies mingle in a catchall that is a joy to study.

Fortunately, Hokusai went on to fulfillment in his later years. Among his major accomplishments in this period is *Hokusai Gafu,* a collection of sketches which contains Hokusai's finest drawing, a group of blind men leading one another through a stream. The *Thirty-Six Views of Fuji,* his most famous series, contains two massive views of the mountain, one in storm and the other in clear weather, which are popular favorites and worthily so, for they demonstrate what tremendous control Hokusai finally attained. "The Breaking Wave Off Kanagawa," an almost perfect piece of art, has also been enjoyed by people of all lands; it is typical of the series in that it is mainly done in Prussian-blue, a color that Hokusai began to use in old age.

At the age of seventy-five Hokusai wrote, in a postlude to a book of sketches, what has been held to be an epitome of his life:

> From the age of six I had a mania for drawing the forms of things. By the time I was fifty I had published an infinity of designs; but all I produced before the age of seventy is not worth taking into account. At seventy-three I learned a little about the real structure of nature —of animals, plants, trees, birds, fishes and insects. Thus, when I am eighty I shall have made still more progress. At ninety I shall penetrate the mystery of things. And when I am a hundred and ten everything I do, be it a dot or a line, will be alive. I beg those who live as long as I to see if I do not keep my word.

He signed these words with his last, and most appropriate, name: Old Man Mad About Drawing.

The Hermitage:
Russia's Art Palace

MARCH, 1965

For two centuries people interested in art have been tantalizing themselves with legends about a fabulous treasure hidden in the Hermitage, that sprawling collection of buildings standing along the left bank of the Neva River in Leningrad, formerly Petrograd, and before that, St. Petersburg.

I remember being told, "The Hermitage has a cellar full of Rembrandts better than any you've ever seen. Whole rooms full of Picasso and Matisse." But whenever I tried to pinpoint what the mysterious museum actually owned, I received only evasive answers. "It's just the richest museum in the world."

The mystery about the Hermitage grew up naturally. In 1762 Catherine the Great, originally a minor German princess, found her stupid husband, the Czar of Russia, conveniently murdered. Gossips whispered, "Catherine arranged this murder," but no one could prove anything. But all could see what happened. Catherine refused to punish the known murderers. Instead she promoted them.

After her husband's death, Catherine finished building a vast royal dwelling to be known in history as the Winter Palace. In order to decorate its 1,051 rooms, she looked about for a few paintings, but she soon found that there were none in Russia. France seemed to own them all, so she fell into correspondence with the most brilliant Frenchman of his age, Denis Diderot, the guiding spirit of the French encyclopedia.

Providing Diderot with almost unlimited means, she gave him a simple commission: "Buy all the great collections that come on the market." In 1763 she got her first prize, the Gotz-kowski collection, and soon thereafter the entire gallery of the Comte de Bruhl, confidential minister of the King of Saxony. In 1781 Catherine's French advisors snapped up the 119 choice canvases owned by the Count Baudoin, but the two purchases that made Catherine the greatest collector of her age occurred in the years between.

In 1771 Diderot got wind of the fact that the top collection in France was up for grabs, the four-hundred odd master-pieces which had been put together by "Poor" Crozat. Some decades before, there had been two Crozat multimillionaires, but since the younger had a few francs less than his brother, he was known as "Poor" Crozat, with a palace filled with masterworks by Raphael, Veronese, Rubens, Rembrandt and Van Dyck. Catherine gobbled up all of them.

In 1779 she made an equal haul, the magnificent collection assembled by Lord Walpole, first minister of England's George I and II. It contained 188 beautiful works, including fourteen by Van Dyck, thirteen by Rubens, four by Murillo, three by Rembrandt and two masterpieces by Franz Hals. For this treasure Catherine paid only $175,000.

Her agents, led by Diderot, continued the looting of Europe. Single works of choice merit were picked up from any likely source, and in the records one finds startling entries: "A Madonna by Correggio purchased by the Empress Catherine from Casanova." What was he doing with a Madonna?

Diderot, who had started it all, wrote: "I am basking in the public's most fervent hate. And do you know why? Because I send you pictures." He stripped France of its glories more ruthlessly than any conqueror, and the process continued after both he and Catherine were dead.

Czar Alexander I, for example, bought the entire contents of Malmaison, Empress Josephine's former palace, while Czar

Nicholas I acquired the noted Barbarigo holdings. When an expert pointed out that the Russian collection of Dutch art was a little weak, the czars bought entire collections. Gerrit Braamkamp's beautiful group of Dutch masterworks sailed to St. Petersburg on a ship which unfortunately sank off Finland, with all cargo lost. The czars merely ordered the purchase of larger collections to be dispatched on safer ships.

As a result of these stupendous accumulations, the Winter Palace, large as it was, could not provide a home for the masterpieces, so in 1764 Catherine authorized the building of an adjacent art gallery topped by a hanging garden complete with trees, flower beds and marble fountains. "My small Hermitage," Catherine called this marvelous building. It was always a museum. The Winter Palace never was.

Still the paintings rolled in, so in 1775 Catherine had to add a second gallery, which she called the Old Hermitage, and in 1839 yet another was required, the mammoth New Hermitage. A theater completed the complex which today, along with the Winter Palace, comprises what we know as the Hermitage.

It is like no other art museum. It contains about 2,500 rooms, two and a half million art objects including fourteen thousand paintings. Merely to walk through each of the rooms requires a hike of twenty-five miles. If one wished to spend only a minute inspecting each room, he would need a full week to do so, working from nine to five. When I had finished my study of the Hermitage, I wanted to recheck a few of the outstanding rooms to be sure in which building each stood. At a stiff pace, led by a top guide, the trip took me three hours.

In 1774 Catherine issued in French the first catalogue of her collection. It contained 2,080 paintings, and here the mystery of the Hermitage begins, for in a letter to Diderot she gloated: "Only the mice and me can admire it all." She refused permission to see her collection, and her successors did the same.

For the Hermitage was always a private gallery, belonging solely to the czar or czarina, as the case might be. In 1852, submitting to great pressure from persons who wanted to see what lay behind the mysterious walls, Czar Nicholas I finally allowed a handful of nobility to view the fabled rooms. Engraved invitations were circulated to a few of the nobility, who had to wear full-dress uniforms and gowns and present themselves formally at the entrance to the New Hermitage, where ten granite giants, each eighteen feet high, guarded the museum.

Stiffly these lucky few entered the Hermitage, and what they saw continues to amaze visitors. Here were some of the most magnificent rooms in the history of the world, rooms covered with rare marble from Italy or the Caucasus, rooms with whole façades of green malachite and gold, rooms whose ceilings were festooned with flying stucco cupids, and rooms whose floors were inlaid with precious woods. The noblemen in their formal jackets also saw one of the most extraordinary stairways ever conceived, heavy with marble and porphyry and gold. They were also allowed into one massive room containing forty-eight shimmering marble columns and enough rich ornament for the average city. They found colonnaded hallways, parquet flooring and an amazing loggia in which the entire series of paintings which Raphael had done for the Vatican in Rome had been repeated stroke by stroke. And finally there were reception halls filled with not one or two graceful marble statues by Canova but dozens.

In 1852 the Hermitage was an architectural marvel, and today it is even more so. I can only report that normally I don't care much for stucco cupids and green malachite edged with gold and gigantic porphyry vases, but in the Hermitage I surrendered. The czars may have had flamboyant tastes, but in the Winter Palace and its four Hermitage buildings they created a symphony marked by balance, judgment and a sense of humor. These huge buildings represent, in precious stone, choice wood and flawless marble a memory of an epoch we shall never know again.

As for the art, there is one room of Scythian gold-work dating from the time of Christ that can be matched nowhere else. It is breathtakingly lovely. Another room contains Sassanian silver from Persia, and it too is unique. There are great bronze cauldrons, true works of art, one of which was made to the order of Tamerlane, and small cameos made in the time of Hadrian.

And of course there are the paintings, of which I shall speak later, but perhaps I should mention here that in a group of special rooms on the third floor of the Winter Palace there is something that the fortunate nobles of 1852 could not have foreseen. Today these rooms constitute one of the chief treasures of the Hermitage and their existence was an accident.

In the early years of this century two modest, soft-spoken Moscow merchants did most of their importing from Paris, and on their visits to that city fell unaccountably in love with a group of painters then relatively unknown. Sergei Shchukin and Ivan Morosov began to outrage their neighbors back in Moscow by carting home van loads of work by men with names like Van Gogh, Gauguin, Matisse and Picasso. To the amusement of their friends, these two quiet Russians bought not one Matisse but forty or fifty! Without knowing it, Shchukin and Morosov had acquired the world's greatest collection of the earliest work of the painters who were to be the foremost art figures of this century.

And then in 1914 it all ended. World War I made it impossible for the two strange Russians to buy any more French art. And in 1917 the communist revolution overwhelmed them, and in one sad afternoon the two men saw all their paintings confiscated. Shchukin, the leader, managed to flee Russia, making his way to Paris, where friends saw him wandering the boulevards, unable ever again to look at paintings.

Today the Hermitage catalogue lists many dozen Matisses, including the finest painting that master ever did, a large diptych showing five nude musicians playing for five nude dancers. Of this tremendous work in red and green and blue, Shchukin had written pathetically to Matisse, asking him if he couldn't "do something about the flute player" since young girls came into the Shchukin home. Matisse refused, so Shchukin found a local artist to paint a little fig leaf on one of the top works of this century.

The Hermitage also lists thirty-one of the best Picassos,

fourteen fine Gauguins and ten Cézannes, to mention only three artists among many. The wealth of the collection is difficult to describe, but it has one curious gap. It contains no work by the four finest artists that Russia herself has produced in this century: Kandinsky, Chagall, Soutine and De Stael. For Russian work, one must look elsewhere.

The fact that the Hermitage exists today, and in almost exactly the form it knew when the czars inhabited the Winter Palace, is a threefold miracle. No other museum in the world has survived so many disasters.

On a windy night in 1837 an inconsequential fire broke out on the second floor of the Winter Palace. Since in those days some two thousand servants lived in the palace, there were enough people to fight the flames. But it wasn't quite that simple. For the servants had the habit of keeping pigs and ducks in some of the ground-floor rooms plus piles of hay for the animals' bedding. Therefore, as soon as the fire fighters brought one section of the fire under control, sparks leaped into one or another of the hay-filled rooms. For five hopeless days the fire raged on, until it burned down almost the entire Winter Palace. Only heroic efforts by soldiers kept the blaze from the four Hermitage buildings.

As soon as the fire ended, Czar Nicholas I ordered an immediate rebuilding, so that what we see today dates only from the 1840's. When the new palace was ready for occupancy, Nicholas moved back with his two thousand servants and a new rule: "No more ducks and hay."

In the revolution of 1917 the entire Hermitage structure could have been lost, for the Winter Palace then served as headquarters for the moderate Kerensky Government. In October of that year hard-core communists decided to assume power, and revolutionary troops burst into the Winter Palace with guns ready. For some hours no one knew what might happen, for this was the supreme test of power, but in the end the troops gained control without destroying the palace. Lenin was in control and ready to build the Soviet Republic. Whole generations of Russian painters have commemorated this event in large canvases invariably titled "Storming the Winter Palace."

In those frantic days there were many who expected the communists to dismantle the Hermitage, for it more than any other building summarized the old regime. Instead, the communists accepted the buildings along the Neva as a major cultural monument and maintained each room as it had been in the days of the Czars. Prior to 1917 the Winter Palace had served only as royal living quarters and never as part of the museum complex, but now residence in the palace ceased and its thousand rooms and 117 staircases became part of the Hermitage as we know it today.

Communists are proud that their revolution respected these buildings, and four different times I was told, "During the storming only fourteen minor items disappeared, so strict was our discipline." The same statement appears in histories and guidebooks, but one old communist told me sardonically, "Technically, that's right. But you must remember that when our men stormed in there in 1917, everything worth stealing had long since been crated up and shipped east of the Urals. For protection in World War I."

The Hermitage's mortal danger was faced during World War II when Leningrad was besieged for nine hundred days. German armies wheeled huge guns to positions only eight miles away and began to lay down smothering barrages. The Hermitage absorbed thirty-two major artillery shells plus two devastating hits by oversized airplane bombs. Six hundred rooms were destroyed, while numerous fires were set by incendiaries. Almost no windows remained. I have seen photographs of one sculpture gallery which sustained a direct hit. Greek and Roman torsos lay everywhere, with heads rolling dizzily across the inlaid floors.

Of course, the museum lost no major treasures. These were once more well behind the Urals. The shattered statues could be reassembled, windows could be replaced and floors relaid.

But the really surprising fact is that when peace came, Russia was able to find workmen who knew how to repair the ornate gingerbread decorations of the eighteenth century, to

281

carve cupids in stucco and gild the wings of angels. Resolutely, this extraordinary team of workmen set out to restore every one of the six hundred rooms until it looked as it had a century before.

Last month I saw Room 216 on the northeastern corner of the Old Hermitage. It was a small room, originally decorated most lavishly with plaster cupids from floor to ceiling. A German bomb had destroyed it, yet now on the day of its reopening it stood almost exactly as it had in 1784 when Catherine the Great opened this section of her gallery. The inlaid floor was back in place. The chubby plaster cupids had been recarved. And the whole effect was one of eighteenth-century splendor.

I asked a communist why the government took such pains to restore this echo of the czars, and he explained, "They were part of Russian history and we love everything Russian."

So many legends have been circulated about the Hermitage paintings that the serious visitor is obligated to report some kind of critical appraisal. In what follows I shall restrict myself, for reasons which will become apparent later, to the Hermitage as it exists in 1964.

In providing the viewer with an orderly survey of western painting, the Hermitage does not begin to equal the National Gallery of London. Whole schools, such as the Sienese, are largely missing. The great primitive work of all nations is largely absent. After all, the massive collections which Catherine the Great acquired had been formed before experts had discovered that a Giotto was at least as good as a Raphael and that a Duccio might even be preferred to a twenty-fifth Rembrandt.

Nor does the Hermitage offer the public a carefully chosen sequence of masterpieces like those presented in the National Gallery of Washington, where the paintings now to be seen represent the end product of severe winnowing by collectors like Mellon, Widener, Kress and Dale. Of the 14,000 canvases in the Hermitage, a good many are either repetitious or second-rate and most are poorly hung and lighted.

Certainly the Hermitage does not offer that multitude of

masterpieces one finds in either the Louvre in Paris or the Uffizi in Florence. Yet it is a great museum. It can best be compared, I think, with the Prado in Madrid, for each of these two museums has an unbalanced collection of dazzling richness. If one wants to study Spanish or Flemish painting, he must go to the Prado; if he wants to study French or Dutch art he must go to Leningrad. Several experts who heard me compare the two museums were offended that I should link them. Said one group, "There's nothing in the Hermitage to compare with Madrid's hall of two dozen Velázquezas. Or those downstairs rooms crammed with Goyas." But others argued, "What has the Prado got to equal the Hermitage's Impressionists?"

In spite of such objections the comparison is apt, and the traveler who knows one of these great museums will find himself at home in the other. But in a sense of fairness, it is improper to make any comparisons involving the Hermitage, for what we see today in Leningrad is a collection from which the eighty greatest paintings have vanished!

In recent decades the rulers of Russia have removed from Leningrad whole truckloads of masterpieces for the enrichment of Moscow and lesser centers. An elderly Russian told me, "If you think the French Impressionists in today's Hermitage are good, you should have seen them in the old days. For every fine Picasso or Gauguin you see now, there used to be four."

When I checked the Pushkin Museum in Moscow, I found that he was right, for there I saw the Hermitage's finest Cézannes, Picassos, Gauguins and some of the best Matisses. Take the case of Van Gogh. Today the Hermitage shows four paintings by this great master. Two seemed rather ordinary to me, but one marvelous landscape with blue houses and reddish roofs was excellent, and a strange, foreboding picture of red grape vines at harvest captivated me. Later I discovered that this was the only painting Van Gogh had ever sold in his lifetime . . . and it was bought by another artist.

But Moscow shows five top Van Goghs, each superior to the

best at the Hermitage. There is the blue and red portrait of Dr. Rey and what may be the last painting Van Gogh ever did: an exquisite little train chugging across a lemon-yellow landscape of Arles. There is also a most haunting work. When Van Gogh was nearing insanity in 1890, he was committed to the asylum at San Remy, where he found an old book by Gustave Doré showing scenes of London. In this Van Gogh discovered an etching showing prisoners marching in a circle while hemmed in by remorseless walls, and this work by Doré he copied in his unique style. It is a work that would make any museum noteworthy.

The loss suffered by the Hermitage in the removal of its best Impressionists could be corrected any time the authorities wished to reassemble the treasures. As a matter of fact, Leningrad is so rich in pictures that it is not illogical to move some to Moscow and the various other cities.

But the Hermitage has also suffered a more profound damage, one that can never be repaired. In Russia no one speaks openly of what they call in private "a savage cultural crime." It is a crime unreported in Russian books, unmentioned by Russian guides, for it is now recognized as one of the foremost errors made by the communists.

In 1927 the leaders of the revolution needed money. They decided that the country must have "machines, not masterpieces." So they decided to sell off several dozen of the very best Hermitage masterworks. Trusted emissaries fanned out over Europe in a sardonic reversal of the days when Catherine the Great's agents were gobbling up everything in sight. Many of the world's finest paintings were offered for sale.

Finally the Soviet emissaries reached the art dealers M. Knoedler & Co., Inc., in New York. One of their clients, Andrew Mellon, the Pittsburgh millionaire and one-time Secretary of the Treasury, was quietly assembling choice masterworks with a view to establishing a National Gallery in Washington, D.C. Working closely with Knoedler, Mellon finally bought many of the Hermitage masterpieces.

Details of the purchase were not made public, but the National Gallery reports that by 1931 Mellon had acquired

284

twenty-one major works for about seven million dollars. They included five by Rembrandt, four by Van Dyck, two by Hals, two lovely Raphaels, and stunning masterpieces by Botticelli, Titian, Rubens, Perugino, Van Dyck and Velázquez. Today these paintings would bring several times the amount Mr. Mellon paid for them.

Today if one wants a glimmer of how magnificent the Hermitage once was—and still is in many ways—he need only go to the National Gallery in Washington.

Most Russians who know about this extraordinary page of recent history resent it, especially the unfeeling judgment of "machines, not masterpieces." That is one of the reasons why the communist government, in its recent devotion to art, as demonstrated by the loving rebuilding of the Hermitage, has sought to prove that it cherishes its masterpieces. The only Russian who was willing to speak openly to me about this episode said, "Don't judge us too harshly. In 1927 we needed machines desperately. And Mellon could spare the millions. So in that sense the sale was defensible. But even so, we wish our leaders hadn't done it."

In any event, the treasures that Catherine and her successors hid from the public can now be seen by all, some in Washington, but the bulk of the vast collection still in Russia. Some two and a half million people now stream through the five buildings of the Hermitage each year.

The National Gallery:
Washington, D.C.

NOVEMBER, 1966 ✕

This year, in the city of Washington, a very beautiful young lady is celebrating her twenty-fifth birthday, and all America is invited to join the festivities.

A quarter of a century ago, on a bitterly cold St. Patrick's Day in 1941, the President of the United States officially opened the National Gallery of Art, a massive marble building recently erected on Constitution Avenue between the Washington Monument and the Capitol Building. When that first group of distinguished visitors finished touring the vast halls of the new museum, what they had seen convinced them that within a remarkably brief period our nation, starting with not a single picture, had put together one of the fine collections of the world.

This sudden creation of a major museum was a miracle, or rather, a chain of miracles, and America can be both proud and astonished that it happened.

The first miracle was this, that both the building and the nucleus of its contents were given to the nation by a man who was being hounded as a near-criminal by that nation. Andrew Mellon, a taciturn, conservative financial wizard from Pittsburgh, had served as Secretary of Treasury under three Presidents, Harding, Coolidge, Hoover, and also as Ambassador to England under Hoover. During his governmental experience he had a chance to see how very little in the way of art Washington had to offer its visitors, especially when compared to cities like London, Paris, Madrid and Rome. It was in 1927 that he began to visualize the establishment of a major museum in Washington, and to this end he started seriously to accumulate a batch of outstanding canvases.

While he was so engaged, his party lost control of the government and incoming Democrats saw in him a chance to embarrass their opponents. Forthwith they slapped him with a criminal charge of having evaded paying his taxes, and a full-blown scandal was under way.

I have always been grateful to Andrew Mellon for his sense of balance. On the one hand, he must have been outraged by the attack his government was making upon him after his years of service, and the newspaper headlines must have been cruel punishment. On the other hand, he still wanted America to have a top-notch art collection, and he remained not only willing to spend millions upon millions to buy the necessary paintings but also to give the money required for a building to house them. An ordinary man, caught in these conflicting emotions, might well have growled, "To hell with it all." Mellon did not.

At the height of the investigation, when he was being daily traduced as a thief, he sent President Roosevelt this letter:

> My dear Mr. President: Over a period of many years I have been acquiring important and rare paintings and sculpture with the idea that ultimately they would become the property of the people of the United States and be made available to them in a national art gallery to be maintained in the city of Washington.

And he offered both his paintings and a vast new building to the nation.

In more ways than one, the resulting museum represents a triumph of the human spirit. It required a big man to get this museum launched under the conditions that Andrew Mellon faced, but it must be remembered that once the offer was made, President Roosevelt put all the resources of the nation behind the project, and at the dedication he said, "The giver of this building has matched the richness of his gift with the modesty of his spirit, stipulating that the Gallery shall be known not by his name but by the nation's." Mellon, unfortunately, could not hear these generous words. He had died before the museum opened, content with the fact that the jury had failed to indict him for criminal wrong; what he could not know was that long after his death he was also acquitted in the civil courts.

It was this "modesty of spirit" that constituted the second miracle. An ordinary man, having plowed so much wealth and energy into a project, might justifiably want the result named after him, and in the 1930's there was talk that the museum under construction ought to be called the Andrew Mellon Gallery. But if this totally wrong thing had been done, our National Gallery would have been dead before it was born. A friend who knew Mellon in those days explains his thinking: "Andrew had seen at firsthand in Pittsburgh the result when Andrew Carnegie allowed the art museum there to be named after himself. Nobody I knew would give paintings or money to a museum glorifying one man."

What also guided Mellon was the fact that in America in those days there existed four or five dazzling private collections whose owners were older men. Only if the new museum could attract these collections would it have any chance of becoming a major institution. An expert had calculated that if only Mellon's paintings were available to hang on the walls, there would be twenty-four works of art to the acre and a man might have to walk four city blocks before coming to the next picture. Other collections simply had to be attracted.

It is to the credit of Andrew Mellon that he refused even to consider having the museum named after him, for now the curators could logically go to other collectors and say with honesty, "You will be giving your treasures to the nation."

While the building was still under construction, two dramatic events proved the wisdom of his decision. For some fifty years the multimillionaire Widener family of Philadelphia had been quietly assembling a stunning collection of masterpieces. There were Vermeers from Holland, world-famous panels from Italy, a series of portraits in the heroic style of England and the Low Countries and, of course, the much-publicized Rembrandts which had once been the subject of a lawsuit with Prince Youssoupoff, their former owner in Leningrad. If these Widener paintings could be added to those of the Mellon collection, the new museum would be off on the right foot.

Other museums were fighting to get these masterpieces, for no similar collection was still in private hands, but a clever plan by David Finley, formerly Mr. Mellon's assistant in the Treasury Department and now head of the new museum, finally decided the matter. He directed the architects to build a series of small models of the gallery rooms, with the Widener pictures reproduced in scale so that the family could see how their paintings would look in Washington. The persuasion worked! The paintings would go to the National Gallery if . . .

The Wideners said, "We'll give you the collection if the government will see to it that our estate is charged no taxes on it!" This was a reasonable request, and other cities fighting for the pictures were willing to reimburse the Wideners for any tax losses, but no legal way could be found for the federal government to do so. Then President Roosevelt himself sent Congress a message asking the nation to pay whatever taxes might be due, no matter how great. Congress gagged at issuing what amounted to a blank check, but when experts demonstrated that for this the nation would receive the finest collection of masterpieces still in private hands, the bill was passed, one of the few times when Congress wrote out a check for an unspecified sum. This might be called the second miracle, and with the arrival of the great Widener paintings, the new museum was assured that its collection would not be a provincial thing but rather a massive assembly of masterworks.

My special admiration is reserved for what happened next, for in my opinion it was this lucky break that converted our National Gallery from essentially a nineteenth-century museum (by which I mean one emphasizing big standard paintings which collectors have always wanted, like Rembrandt, Van Dyck, Botticelli, Raphael) to a twentieth-century museum (by which I mean one that exhibits the whole perspective of western painting and in which a splendid example by a so-called minor painter might prove to be as significant as one by an established name). Today we insist that our big public museums illustrate the growth of man's genius, and no gallery consisting only of the Mellon and Widener paintings could do this. Those canvases illustrated the mountain peaks of art; it was the valleys where people lived that needed filling in.

For some years the five-and-ten genius, Samuel H. Kress, reared on a small Pennsylvania farm not far from where I live, had been buying European art in truckload lots. Reasoning that his predecessors like the Wideners had skimmed the cream from the top of the market, he explored in unexpected places and came up with some of the most wonderful minor paintings to be uncovered in this century. True, he acquired much that was not of top museum quality, but as he progressed he began also to ferret out some major masterpieces, and museum curators began to whisper, "Sam Kress has himself an unbelievable collection."

Time was ripe for a third miracle. Kress was on the verge of deciding to build a private museum for the preservation of his riches and had even chosen the land along Fifth Avenue in New York and the architect when two Washington friends, not connected with the National Gallery, sent him a letter suggesting that before he gave his builders the go-ahead he look into the possibility of giving his paintings to the nation. Following this hint, Kress invited David Finley to New York, and there the latter saw what Sir Kenneth Clark of the National Gallery in London was to describe as "one of the most remarkable collections of fourteenth- and fifteenth-century Italian art ever formed." Another critic said simply, "The most complete and systematic collection of Italian art ever brought together."

Finley and Kress talked for seven hours, at the end of which Kress tore up his plans for the private museum. His paintings would go to Washington. Later Finley learned that if his lucky visit to New York had been delayed by even a week, the nation would have lost this splendid collection.

Equally exciting was the fact that the Kress Foundation continued to purchase additional great works, nearly all of which went to the National Gallery. It is estimated that between 1945 and 1956 the Foundation spent $25,000,000 on works of art, possibly the largest capital expenditure dispersed in so short a time in the history of museums. Working together, the museum curators and Kress representatives acquired a series of works which are today among the most satisfying in the entire Washington collection.

At the same time, the Kress paintings that were not quite up to Washington standard, or which were similar to works already in that collection, were used to set up handsome Renaissance rooms in eighteen different smaller museums across the nation, from Allentown, Pennsylvania, to Honolulu, Hawaii.

I cannot emphasize enough how fortunate our National Gallery was to acquire, in so brief a time, these sharply different yet complementary collections, the Mellon, Widener and Kress. Any one alone would have been incomplete; taken together, they created a major museum. No man starting today, not even with half a billion dollars to spend, could possibly duplicate these collections. The pictures are simply not available. If we had missed these wonderful gifts, or any one of them, we could of course still have had a National Gallery, but it would have been second-rate.

Then came the fourth miracle, and in some ways the most necessary of the lot. "Today," says John Walker, since 1956 the learned and delightful director of the gallery, "the average person who visits our museum comes in the front door, stands for a moment in the rotunda, then turns left."

"Why left?" I asked.

"To see the modern French." For without a fine selection of Impressionist and Post-Impressionist canvases, no museum can claim to be up to date. How the gallery obtained its famous French wing constitutes this fourth miracle.

Chester Dale was a tough-minded, quick-acting, red-haired

financial genius whose skill provided him with substantial wealth, and with it he ventured into what has been called "the hobby of kings," that is, the purchasing of fine works of art. Just as Samuel Kress had seen that his millionaire predecessors had preempted the collection of masterpieces, so Dale realized that Kress had snatched the available great works by lesser figures. He therefore directed himself to the works of men like Manet and Renoir, Cézanne and Van Gogh. In a relatively short time he had one of the world's top collections, and paintings like ones for which he had paid $3,000 were being sold for $600,000. No other major collector ever saw his holdings appreciate in value so astronomically as did Chester Dale.

When I first saw the collection it was hanging in the Chicago Art Institute, and I assumed, as did everyone else, that it would remain there. But Dale, impressed by what was happening in Washington, decided to give his paintings plus a large cash fund to the new gallery.

With the acquisition of these French masterpieces, the gallery rounded out its collections, and today in its rooms one can follow the development of western painting from the lovely wooden panel on which Cimabue, the father of Italian painting, painted Christ between two saints, through all the major schools to that stunning canvas which I consider the best thing Picasso ever did, "Family of Saltimbanques." It is a study of a family of acrobats at rest. The lucky miracles that combined Mellon, Widener, Kress and Dale have produced a result of which Americans can be proud.

If you visit the gallery during its twenty-fifth birthday party, what will you see?

First of all, one of the finest buildings in America. Chief Justice Earl Warren has recently described it as "one of the most beautiful modern buildings in the world." To build it, whole new quarries had to be opened in the mountains of Tennessee to provide a special kind of matched pinkish-white marble, but even so, when the first blocks reached Washington from different quarries, the variation in pinkness was so marked that someone pointed out, "When the building's finished, it'll look like it had the measles." The architects avoided this by deciding to keep all the darker pink near the bottom and save the lighter hues for the top.

"But bringing so much stone here at one time will cost a million dollars extra," the builders pointed out.

"To avoid a building that would look as if pink postage stamps had been pasted on, we'll spend the million," the architects said. Actually, twenty-five years later the marble has weathered so evenly that one can scarcely detect the pinkness, top or bottom—so that the extreme caution of the builders proved unnecessary.

The massive building, the largest marble structure in existence, has suffered from only one serious criticism: "It's too beautiful. It detracts from the paintings." It's also big. When it was under construction, signs read: "Trucks driving inside the building must not go over ten miles an hour." In the early days, when there were not enough paintings to fill the rooms, one was blocked off to make a dandy· basketball court for the guards. Exhibition rooms alone cover five and a half acres.

I find the building magnificent and well suited for a museum. I love the long sweep of marble and the dignified circle of green-black columns; the inviting manner in which one handsome roomful of paintings leads to the next and then to an intimate courtyard graced with statuary. I especially like the way in which one can look up from his study of an Italian painting and see, far away, a Rembrandt or a Hals which he will be visiting an hour later.

In that first moment, twenty-five years ago, when I entered this building, I sensed that it had been designed and built with great affection, but not until recently did I understand why. One who knew John Russell Pope, the architect in charge, said, "Just as the big decisions about the gallery were to be made, Pope was told by his doctors that he had terminal cancer. 'How much longer can I live?' Pope asked. 'If you quit work and allow us to operate now, you could have three years. If you continue working, maybe six months.' Pope went home to consider what to do with his life, and he quickly decided that his true responsibility was to design this great building. So he refused medical aid, completed the design and died

exactly when the doctors had predicted he would . . . before
a single stone was in place."

That same day Andrew Mellon died. The two men who had
put their hearts into this project never saw it completed!

Like millions of other servicemen in World War II, I knew
the gallery when it served as a glorified U.S.O. center, a cherished relief from the drudgery of war. I recall especially the
reception book in which soldiers were invited to share their
opinions of the place, and in this book an enlisted man from
Vermont who was training in Georgia wrote with feeling: "I
got two pieces of advice for any buddy in uniform. If you're
in Washington, don't miss these beautiful paintings. If you're
in Georgia, don't never order hominy grits."

In the years since then I have visited the museum well over
a hundred times, and each time it seems lovelier. To me it is
neither massive nor overpowering. It is my museum, and in
it I feel at home.

But no building alone ever made a museum. It's what's
inside that counts, and the contents of our National Gallery
are exceptionally good. About a thousand paintings are on
regular display, and of these, some fifty are acknowledged to
be among the very top examples of western art. Of these fifty
I shall select nine to indicate the range and richness of the
collection. Another writer, of course, would choose a different
nine, but we would both agree that the collection offers at least
half a hundred works that are not surpassed elsewhere.

The lovely circular painting by Fra Angelico and Fra
Filippo Lippi, "The Adoration of the Magi," almost didn't get
into the collection. For years Bernard Berenson, dean of critics
of Italian art, had considered this one of the high-water marks
of western cultural history and one of the greatest Italian
paintings extant. He pointed out that it was not only a fine
devotional painting which showed Mary and the Child holding their rude court, but an equally find landscape filled with
delicate flowers and a handsome peacock. It was also a trave-
logue; the interior of the barn provided one of the first genre
paintings, and the naked youths on the ruins foreshadowed the
anatomical studies of the later Renaissance. It was a remarka-

ble painting, a gracious summary of Italian art. It was offered to Samuel Kress, who refused it because he did not understand that Fra Angelico had worked on it. When one of the museum curators, while pointing out that Berenson considered it a masterwork of major dimension, mentioned the name of Fra Angelico, Kress reconsidered and thus acquired one of the paintings for which his collection is most famous.

Raphael's "Saint George and the Dragon" is a little marvel, one of the most nearly perfect things this great artist ever accomplished. It has a fascinating history in that its ownership can be traced from the day it was commissioned by the Duke of Montefeltro, ruler of Urbino, and sent as a flattering gift to King Henry VII of England. King Charles I, who inherited it, traded it off for the renowned series of Holbein drawings still in the Royal Collection at Windsor Castle, and after passing through a series of French hands, it reached Catherine the Great of Russia. For the next hundred and fifty years its home was the Hermitage Museum in St. Petersburg, until that day when a mysterious courier advised Andrew Mellon that the Soviet government would consider selling twenty-one of its chief masterpieces for hard cash. Luckily, Mellon was in a position to put up the money, whereupon this Raphael plus twenty other magnificent works traveled to Washington.

Dürer's "Madonna and Child" is a work which the powerful German master adapted from the ideas of Giovanni Bellini, of whom Dürer reported to his friends back in Germany: "Bellini came himself and asked me to do something for him, saying that he would pay me well for it. He is very old, but yet he is the greatest painter of them all." This painting is thus doubly valuable, in that one sees the classic charm of Italy tempered by the rude strength of Germany.

"The Small Crucifixion," by Mathias Grünewald, is a profoundly moving statement by the religious painter whose huge altarpiece at Colmar in Alsace is counted among the half-dozen masterworks of the world. No other museum west of Colmar owns a Grünewald, so this panel must be considered one of the rarest treasures in Washington. It has been termed "from the point of view of both rarity and emotional intensity the outstanding German painting in America."

Jan Van Eyck's "The Annunciation" is valued not only because of its deeply religious feeling, but also because tradition attributes to Van Eyck the discovery that linseed oil was a better medium in which to mix colors than egg whites, which had been used previously. This fine painting, originally done on wood but in modern times transferred to a canvas backing, demonstrates the enchanting delicacy Van Eyck was able to achieve with his new oil paints.

El Greco's "The Virgin with St. Ines and St. Tecla" hung in a small Spanish chapel in the painter's home city of Toledo until it was taken down for sale to a collector. It is a fine example of the artist's experiments in color and design and shows the elongated figures that were his trademark.

One of the chief glories of the National Gallery is the room where the Vermeers hang. This enchanting Dutch artist painted only some forty canvases, but they are unequaled evocations of sunlight and the serenity of mankind. Vermeers are so rare that most museums must do without, but the National Gallery has six, none better than "Woman Weighing Gold," a simple portrayal of a woman using a delicate pair of balances while light filters through the window to illuminate her face.

When today's visitors enter the museum and turn left to see the French paintings, it is frequently Manet's "Gare St. Lazare" that they seek. Here a young mother and her daughter wait at the iron fence of the St. Lazare railway station in Paris, and the tableau they present is one of the finest specimens of modern French painting. When I stand before it I am in the railway station. I can smell the escaping steam and hear it too. The iron fence is cold to my touch, the bench is sooty. I can hear the rustle of the little girl's starched dress. The mother is about to speak and I can hear her breathing, while throughout the painting echoes the sound of a busy railway terminal. It is this remarkable capacity to draw the viewer into the world of the painting that characterized the Impressionists, and Manet's railway station is one of the best examples of this skill in America.

It is difficult for me to speak of Picasso's large canvas "Family of Saltimbanques" because it has had such a profound effect upon me personally. When I first became acquainted with it, it hung in the Art Institute of Chicago, and whenever I had work to do in that city I used to study what I then believed to be one of the top paintings of this century. During the opening years of the National Gallery's existence, I often thought, "What this place needs is that big Picasso in Chicago." I was therefore delighted upon returning from a period of work in Asia to find that Washington had acquired this noble work. The picture shows a family of *saltimbanques* at rest somewhere on the dry plains of northern Spain, and the grandeur of the forms is unforgettable. Much of the style of writing I have developed through the years has stemmed from my wanting to achieve in words what Picasso has here done with paints.

I have never met anyone else who loved this work as I did, nor have I read much about it, so I supposed that my personal enthusiasm had tricked me into believing that the painting was rather better than it really was. How delighted I was, therefore, to come upon the correspondence recently conducted between the French government and the National Gallery. It began: "Mr. André Malraux, Minister of Cultural Affairs, has decided to organize a big retrospective exhibition to celebrate the eighty-fifth birthday of Pablo Picasso. It is a tribute of the French nation to the most illustrious creative artist living on its soil. The objective is to present an impeccable selection, and each period should be represented by Picasso's masterpieces. For the success of this special event we beg you to lend us 'Les Saltimbanques' of 1905."

The National Gallery, which had only just returned the "Mona Lisa," which France had generously loaned us, had to report with embarrassment, "The Terms of the Chester Dale bequest forbid us to lend any of his paintings." The French curator replied, "I am terribly sorry about your negative answer but I do understand. However, I must insist upon 'Les Saltimbanques,' for the artist himself has just told us that this is the picture he would most like to see on his eighty-fifth birthday." I am relieved to know that Picasso liked the painting as much as I did. To me it seems a towering masterpiece.

In addition to its paintings, the gallery owns a fine collection of prints donated by Lessing Rosenwald of Philadelphia and the best collection of Italian sculpture outside of Italy. The most popular piece is also one of the best, Verrocchio's "Lorenzo de' Medici." This terra-cotta bust shows the Medici ruler of Florence as he appeared shortly after political assassins had slain his brother Giuliano and tried to kill him. The stern harshness of the man, his scowl, the firmness of his lips bespeak not only the ruler of Florence but the other condottieres who ruled Italy in that violent age.

A greater work, artistically speaking, is Donatello's "David," which has been called "the finest piece of Italian carving outside Italy." There is a mystery relating to this depiction of victorious David, slingshot in hand, head of Goliath under his foot, for Donatello originally carved it in sturdier dimensions. Later he chipped it down to the size that we see today. Some think that he did so in order to bring the statue into balance with his own "St. John the Baptist," a thin, starved figure near which the "David" stood in the Florentine courtyard.

Of the eleven works just mentioned—two sculptures and nine paintings—two came from the Mellon collection, three from the Widener, four from the Kress, one from the Dale, while the lovely Manet, like many other outstanding examples, came from a private donor. This kind of balance would probably be maintained regardless of which eleven masterworks one might choose to discuss. It illustrates how harmoniously the principal parts of the National Gallery fit together.

As befits a national museum, the gallery engages in many activities beyond the mere exhibition of pictures. For example, it maintains in Pittsburgh the Arts Research Project, whose duty it is to investigate any scientific problem relating to the preservation of paintings. One of the first things the Project did was to come up with 27-H, an almost perfect varnish for paintings. Almost, but not quite.

Traditional varnish has three weaknesses. It cracks, it discolors, and at regular intervals it must be removed so that fresh varnish can be applied.

After extended experiment, the Pittsburgh scientists—they keep their headquarters there so as to have access to millions of dollars' worth of scientific equipment in the laboratories maintained by the steel, coal and glass industries—discovered a "perfect" varnish. It was clear yet it filtered out damaging light rays. It was invisible but tough. It could be easily applied yet just as easily dissolved if it had to be removed—or so the early tests showed. It was labeled 27-H, and museums around the world were eager to adopt it.

Just before it was released for general use, one of the Pittsburgh experts happened to read in an obscure journal an article, not on 27-H, but about one of the ingredients which went into it. The writer wondered whether this ingredient might not, after fifty or sixty years, combine with other ingredients in a new way so to form an indissoluble bond which could never be removed. "Cross-linking," the process was called, and once cross-linking occurred, you would have on your picture not varnish but a kind of glass, forever bonded to your painting!

Accelerated aging tests were run. What they proved was that 27-H was too good. It did everything the experts said it would. But after half a century it became so hard that no solvent could remove it.

It had to be discarded, and in its place a less perfect varnish was developed. It's not quite so clear, not quite so tough. But after fifty years you could still remove it easily, and this is the varnish that all museums are now using.

The second big discovery at the Project was that daylight does fade oil paints. I always believed what I had been taught when I first studied pictures: "Bright light is good for oil paintings. It vitalizes them." But apparently this notion was dead wrong. Project scientists are demonstrating that if light has access to paint surfaces, damage must result, and it doesn't have to be direct sunlight. Tradition-minded curators ask, "But what about the old masterpieces that have survived so well?" The answer is simple. Very quickly in their lives these paintings were smothered in old-style varnish, which attracted soot and dust, the whole forming a screen through which damaging light-rays were unable to penetrate. The fact was that because the old paintings were preserved so poorly, they were preserved well. The damaging rays of light, the Project experts have proved, should be kept off paintings by use of filters built into windows.

It is the third discovery made by the Pittsburgh team that may in the long run prove to be the most important. Suppose that a conscientious museum director, plagued by conspirators who try to sell him recent forgeries as old masters, had a sure-fire test which would tell him the approximate age of the paint that had been used in a suspected work. How helpful it would be if he could remove, with a tiny scalpel, a fragment of that paint and subject it to tests which would proclaim its age. (No use to test the wood or canvas. Forgers keep on hand antique supplies of each.)

Well, the Project has determined that the white paint used by artists contains two elements, radium-226 and lead-210, whose relative strengths vary according to the amount of time the paint has been in existence. When the paint is fresh, the radium predominates; as the paint ages, the two achieve a balance. Theoretically, then, the suspicious curator need only test the white paint in a suspected work to obtain, perhaps not a final answer as to authenticity, but at least a good hint.

Like all museums, the National Gallery owns several canvases of considerable importance whose authenticity has been questioned by neutral experts. This is no reflection on either the museum or the donors but merely one of the problems faced by all curators, and the men in Washington have been meticulous in weeding out suspected fakes. You can imagine that some of the first samples of white paint sent to the Project were flecks lifted from these challenged masterpieces. Results so far? Nothing conclusive, but what evidence there is to date looks hopeful. The Washington people are keeping their fingers crossed.

Curiously, the most significant scientific advance in picture care came not from the Project but from a decision made early in the life of the museum. John Walker says, "When we decided to air-condition this whole building we did the best possible thing for our paintings. Soot and grime have been kept out, so pictures never need cleaning. Temperatures and humidity have been kept constant, so the wood on which most early paintings were done neither expands nor contracts. Blisters and flaking are eliminated."

The gallery also set the pace in developing a separate, hidden radio transmitter for each room. The visitor can rent a lightweight earphone which he carries with him from one room to another. In each, the unseen broadcasting system sends him a helpful description of all the paintings in that room. Then, as he moves from the Rembrandts to the Van Dycks, the voice from the first room slowly dies away while the voice from the new room rises in volume. It's a cheap, practical way to provide tours.

I remember with affection two radically different services of the museum. On Sunday evenings an orchestra of high professional quality gives free concerts in the East Garden Court; and every day the cafeteria on the floor below provides some of the best meals in Washington. And at attractive prices. In fact, the food is so good that government employees from miles around slip in at mealtimes. I've been eating there for twenty-five years and have never had a bad serving, but when I warned Mr. Walker that I was going to praise his cafeteria, he shuddered. "We already have too much patronage," he said.

Twenty-five years in the life of a museum is like twenty-five days in the life of a man. How good is our young gallery?

I put this question to several dozen experts, and their answers were reassuring. Harry Kurnitz is a brilliant playwright who has made a hobby of "museum crawling," as the sport is called. His Broadway play, *Reclining Figure*, dealt with the international art market, and his current motion picture, *How to Steal a Million*, exposes art forgeries. Kurnitz says flatly, "Best museum in the world. Not only are the paintings superb, but the building they're in is the most enjoyable place I know to see art." Many experts share his opinion. Brinton

Sherwood, on the staff of the National Fund, whose purpose it is to save historic sites, said, "About the building I have some reservations. Too cold. But the pictures are as fine as any in the world."

My own judgment, reached after having inspected practically every major museum, is this: The building? Best I've seen. To view pictures on its walls, so handsomely spaced, is a privilege. The pictures? Second-best collection I've seen. But if American donors continue to be generous, after the passage of another fifty years it could be the best.

What collection is in first place now? For all-around excellence, the National Gallery in London, and it is appropriate that this should be so, because it was while exploring this museum as Ambassador to the Court of St. James's that Andrew Mellon formed his judgment as to what a national museum should be. In a very real sense our National in Washington is an offspring of the National in London.

As to top masterpieces by top artists, the two galleries are equal. London has its great Leonardo Da Vinci, a fine Michelangelo, an unsurpassed Piero della Francesca. Washington has its Grünewald, its Botticellis, its Vermeers. In what have been called "the staggering masterpieces" it's a draw.

It is in superb works by secondary artists that London is so superior, and only the patient picking up of excellent canvases will enable us to catch up. Three paintings of the type we need already rest in Washington and will explain what I mean.

Piero di Cosimo cannot be classed as a major artist, but his tough, well-studied compositions are important in the history of Italian art, and in his "The Visitation and Two Saints" we have one of the best things he ever did. I can think of eighteen or twenty similar Italian painters who ought to be represented by major canvases, and some of these will come on the market in the next fifty years.

Pietro Perugino can no longer be considered a foremost artist of the rank of Botticelli or Velázquez, but he is one of the most engaging painters of history, and his magnificent "Crucifixion" from the Mellon Collection is precisely the kind of painting we must uncover in the next half-century.

Finally there is the little panel by Domenico Veneziano, "St. John in the Desert," showing St. John throwing aside his fashionable clothes preparatory to putting on the hair shirt of repentance. It is one of the finest Italian paintings of its period, and while no one could sensibly argue that Veneziano was a major artist, this work is important in the history of art and has no equal in other museums.

There is room in the National Gallery right now to hang about two hundred additional paintings, and we must all hope that the right ones are found to fill these spaces. Our Flemish, Spanish and early French schools need bolstering. We show none of the great Mexicans. We are building a choice American collection, but there are quite a few missing Italians.

There is a limit, of course, as to what can be done. We can never display a room filled with Velázquezes like that incredible hall in Madrid's Prado, nor a roomful of Breughels like Vienna's. We can't match that first room in the Uffizi in Florence, where top works by Cimabue, Duccio and Giotto greet the viewer. But we can aspire to having the best-rounded collection of them all, and I believe that with the passage of time we shall have just that.

I have stressed this lack of second-echelon masterpieces because I believe that if a museum is to be great, it must contain so many different kinds of paintings that the casual visitor will always have the chance of falling in love with some work he did not expect to find there.

For a quarter of a century I have been trudging the long corridors of our national museum, and always with a sense of elation and agitation. The elation I've explained. The agitation comes when I consider what might have happened.

When I lived near the gallery during World War II, I was so impressed with its quality that I decided to work there when the war ended. To that end I sought an interview, during which I hoped to place my name on the waiting list for a job. But the man who interviewed me said: "You have enthusiasm but no credentials. To qualify for a job here you ought to have done graduate work in either the Fogg Museum at Harvard or the Jarves Collection at Yale. You should speak both French and German, but you have only Spanish." He winced. "Finally, since our pay for beginners is rather low, you should have substantial savings to see you through the first dozen years. I'm afraid you just don't qualify."

I remember still the sorrow with which I left his office and walked again past those exquisite pictures of which I could not now be a part. They were as precious to me as personal friends, and it was to them that I said goodbye when I started for the South Pacific, where I became a writer instead.

The Prado: Madrid

JUNE, 1969

Around the world, wise travelers plan their trips to ensure at least one day in Madrid, for they know that this can
be the highlight of their journey.

They do not come primarily to see the city, for it is typically
modern and therefore less interesting than Seville or Toledo.
Nor do they come just to see flamenco, that delightful combination of wild dance and haunting song. They do not come
even to renew their acquaintance with gazpacho, that cold
garlic soup which Spaniards claim was invented one hot day
by two thirsty angels.

These experienced travelers revisit Madrid to see the Prado
Museum, one of the most extraordinary collections of paintings in existence. The Prado is unique. No other museum can
provide a comparable experience.

In order to understand the Prado one should begin, not in
Madrid with the museum itself, but on a bleak mountainside
some thirty miles to the northwest where a massive, gloomy
monastery, the Escorial, looks exactly as it did three centuries
ago.

This enormous building holds the secret not only of the
Prado but of all Spain. It was begun in 1563 when Philip II was

king and quickly became the center of Spain's spiritual life. In its mausoleum the monarchs of Spain were buried. In its splendid chapel leading churchmen officiated. And what was most important to us, in its granite lofty-ceilinged rooms the royal family lived part of each year.

Because the Escorial was a dark and heavy place, the kings decorated it with the finest paintings obtainable in their realm, and since Spain controlled parts of Italy, where Titian and Veronese were working, the Low Countries, where Rubens and Van Dyck were painting, and of course Spain, where Velázquez and El Greco were busy, the Spanish kings had much to choose from.

The Escorial, in its heyday, overflowed with the best paintings the world produced, and the collection existed, not in any impersonal way, but because the kings of Spain loved art. What seems especially fortunate was the fact that when one art-loving king died, his successor inherited his good taste. Even the pathetic and feeble-minded king, Charles II, who reigned from 1665 to 1700, added new masterpieces to the treasure without surrendering any of the old.

In addition to the Escorial, the royal family stuffed other castles, hunting lodges and churches with great paintings, so that when the time finally came in 1814 to draw all this treasure together in the Prado, the curator had no trouble in gathering more than 2,000 first-rate paintings from which the 311 best items were hung. Before long the collection numbered over 4,000 pictures.

Of them a Spaniard said to me with pride, "Our Prado contains not one painting brought here by theft, expropriation or war. Our kings could have taken what they wanted by force, but they refrained from doing so. Every royal picture you see on these walls is here because some Spanish king loved art and paid for it out of his own purse."

Therefore, to appreciate the Prado you must spend at least a few hours in the Escorial. Stand in the granite courtyard at dusk and imagine that you are back in the year 1558. In the royal chambers beside the chapel King Philip II is in residence, struggling with reports from all parts of his empire. He is a man of moderate size, bearded, slightly stooped but with penetrating eyes, the most powerful ruler on earth. He looks up as a courtier reports, "Sire, the wagons are coming." He hurries, almost at a run, to the bronze-studded gates near which we stand. Creakingly they are thrown open so that the tired horses can haul their burden directly into the court, and there Philip moves from one driver to the other.

"What news?" he asks, for he is apprehensive about the Armada which he has dispatched to attack England. The carters know nothing of the distant battle.

"We have brought more paintings," they reply.

"From where?" the king asks.

"Brussels. Venice."

Eagerly the king directs his men to rip open the boxes, and in the dusk he inspects the latest treasures to be added to his collection. It is precisely these paintings that we see in the Prado today.

The Prado, as we see it now, is peculiarly a family museum. Most of the pictures reached Spain as the specific purchase of a king or queen who loved art. Here there was no buying of ready-made collections formed in Paris or London by other people of other tastes. There was no spoliation of museums in nations defeated in war. Nor was there expropriation as an accidental aftermath of revolution. The Prado is a collection formed for the most part by the people of one continuous family, at first Spanish, later Hapsburg and finally Bourbon. From 1492, when Queen Isabella I of Castile was making her first cautious purchases, to 1868, when Isabella II of Bourbon ended her reign, the pictures were assembled, and what we see today are the family heirlooms of this extraordinary sequence of individuals.

Of course, when the Prado was opened as a museum, other Spaniards added pictures to the treasure, and some of these are among the choice paintings of the collection. But essentially the museum reflects the taste of Hapsburg and Bourbon.

Among the royal donors, three kings stand out. Charles V of Austria was the grandson of the Isabella who started the collection and sent Columbus to discover America. He inherited the throne through his mother, a half-mad queen, who lived locked up in a castle during practically his entire reign. Charles was a canny ruler who fended off adversaries like Henry VIII of England, Francis I of France and Suleiman the Magnificent of Turkey, all the while extending his holdings in Europe and America. It was he who recognized Titian as the finest painter of Europe, and the Prado contains several portraits of Charles by the great Venetian. In the best, the emperor appears in full armor astride a black horse caparisoned in purple. In a stormy landscape the setting sun illuminates the small, bearded king as he appeared during a notable victory of Spanish forces over German.

The second of the great collectors was Charles's son, Philip II, a ruler almost impossible to assess fairly. The portrait by Titian shows him as a young, intense and capable man. In addition to Mary of England, he was to marry three other wives, each of whom helped him strengthen his position. A devout Catholic, he nevertheless battled the Pope, allowing only such papal decrees as he wished to be enforced in Spain. He brought into Spain the full riches of Mexico and Peru, yet he left his country weakened and impoverished. It was he who dispatched the Armada against England, sought to subdue the Low Countries and wasted national energies in Italy. Yet he was also a brilliant governor, a fine administrator and the defender of both Europe and Christianity against all enemies.

Philip has always been known as an ascetic, yet if one studies the paintings he brought into Spain, one finds that he was responsible for the marvelous nudes of Titian and Rubens; he added the wonderful sex-filled Boschs to the Escorial collection and other lush canvases from Venice and Brussels.

The third of the master collectors is as familiar to us as one of our own family, for Philip IV, grandson of Philip II, was painted numerous times by Velázquez—on horseback, standing in lace ruffles, half-length in austere black, and even as seen in a mirror while having his portrait painted. The king stares back at us with heavy-lidded eyes, huge curling mustache and that enormous chin which characterized the Hapsburgs. In addition, we are familiar with the many Velázquez portraits of Philip's family: his two wives, his handsome son and above all his adorable little daughter.

The relationship between Philip and Velázquez was one of the most rewarding in history, for not only did the royal family provide the artist with some of his finest subjects; Philip also commissioned Velázquez to travel in Europe and buy great paintings on his behalf. Twice the master painter toured the Continent, and many of the choice works in the Prado are there because Velázquez, riding back and forth between Italian cities, came upon canvases which he thought the king of Spain might like.

Today the royal collections are housed in a long, dark and handsome building located in the center of Madrid. The Prado was orignally built in 1787 as a natural history museum, but in 1814 was converted to its present use. Its outward appearance has been little changed in its nearly two hundred years of use, but internally great alterations have taken place. Wings have been added, empty courtyards have been filled in, space for pictures has been trebled.

The highly personal way in which the collection was assembled means that the end result had to be uneven. The kings of Spain did not care for English art, so practically none existed in the Prado until a few years ago when a wealthy New Yorker who had grown to love the museum gave it a Gainsborough and a Lawrence. Spanish kings failed to appreciate Dutch painting, so today the Prado has few works of the down-to-earth school. French painting is represented unevenly, and several major Italian schools are poorly portrayed, if at all.

But where the Prado is strong, it is unbelievably good. Thanks to Charles V and his son Philip, it has the world's top collection of Titians. One room alone contains sixteen prime works by the Venetian, a staggeringly beautiful collection of portraits, religious subjects and nudes. As if that were not enough, in the next room hang eleven others, each good enough to be a major item in an ordinary museum, and the storeroom hides a dozen more!

Equally rich is the vast collection of Rubens. In room after room the visitor finds those huge masterpieces crowded with nudes—paintings with which he has been familiar for years without realizing that they were in Madrid.

It is a miracle that we can still enjoy these great nudes of Titian and Rubens, for although they were among the favorites of the early kings, they were judged scandalous by later monarchs and toward the end of the eighteenth century were condemned to be burned. Plans were made to destroy every nude in the collection, but in 1792 a group of men, at considerable risk to themselves, hid the offending pictures in a back room of a lesser museum, where they stayed unseen for more than thirty years until it was safe to bring them forth again. Now they form one of the principal treasures of the Prado.

The museum contains many Italian masterpieces. Raphael's "Cardinal" is here, staring at us coldly from beneath his red hat, and also Paolo Veronese's radiant little jewel, "The Finding of Moses," probably the best painting this gracious artist ever did.

Stuck away in another corner of the Italian wing is one of my favorite paintings, Correggio's exquisite "Do Not Touch Me." I have always felt that this is about as fine a work as the late Italian school could produce, for the figure of Christ, with his arms extended, has the quality of supreme religious painting, while the figure of the Magdalene in her rich brocade represents humanity at its most enchanting. The landscape, showing as it does the hour of dawn, is faultlessly done and the parts are combined to make a most gratifying work of art.

The stunning surprise of the Prado is the series of small rooms on the second floor, so inconspicuous that many visitors miss them. Here are displayed the Flemish and German paintings collected by Philip II and his contemporaries, and to understand the work of these schools one simply must visit the Prado. Two works easiest to grasp are the powerful self-portrait by Albert Dürer and the exquisite little blue painting by Gerard David showing the Holy Family resting on its way to Egypt. It is one of the purest of paintings, a jewel perfect in all parts.

The picture that no one should miss in the Flemish rooms is, of course, Jerome Bosch's "Garden of Delights," in which the half-mad precursor of surrealism presents a huge teeming canvas flanked by two wings in which the delights of sensuality are portrayed with heavy but not unpleasant emphasis on sex. The central panel is divided into three parts: at the top a lake on which fantastic pleasure boats appear and over whose rivers nightmare bridges rise; in the middle a pool in which lovers swim and around which ecstatic couples parade on all kinds of beasts, including pigs and camels; in the foreground a bewildering maze of persons engaged in various delights including lovers entrapped in a giant clamshell, dancers whose heads unite to form an owl, and a pair surrounded by an evanescent soap bubble.

Visitors from many different countries stand for hours before this intricate painting, for it is a lovely summation of medieval life, a kind of earthy sermon in paint; yet at the end each viewer will discover some new witticism tucked away which he had not studied before. I know this work as well as I do any major painting in Europe, yet I am sure that on my next visit I'll see something new to startle or amuse me.

The curious thing about the "Garden of Delights" is that it was a favorite picture of Philip II, and we know that it occupied a place of honor in the Escorial. Therefore, the painting has an additional value in that it throws fresh light upon Spain's mysterious king. This particular Bosch is only one of several in the Prado, for the more the men of Philip's time brooded over religious matters, the more they appreciated these lusty pictures from the north.

Early in his life Philip II heard that in a small chapel in Louvain, dedicated to the Confraternity of Crossbowmen, there stood an altarpiece by Rogier van der Weyden depicting the dead body of Christ being lowered from the Cross. Visitors familiar with the marvelous painting reported to Philip, "It is the greatest painting of the north." In vain Philip tried to buy it, and when this proved impossible he sent a court painter to copy it, and with the copy he was content for several decades. Later his aunt, the Queen of Hungary, succeeded in acquiring the painting for her collection, and remembering how much her nephew desired it, gave it to him as a present.

311

In the depiction of the ten differentiated figures, in their placement, in the use of color, design and space, and above all in the symbolization of religious emotion, this marvelous stark painting is one of the major accomplishments of western culture. The best painting in the world? That may be too strong. One of the half-dozen best? Surely.

I could continue for many pages, picking here and there from the various national schools and identifying excellent paintings of Italian or German or Flemish origin well known to art students, but the true glory of the Prado lies not in these arrivals from foreign lands but in the paintings from Spain. In this rich field the Prado has no equal nor even any close competitor.

Come to the second floor of the museum, walk down the long and lovely corridor housing the works of the Spanish school, and see for yourself the incredible richness of this collection. To take only one example, near the rotunda you will find not one elegant Murillo "Immaculate Conception," with Mary standing on a new moon surrounded by angels, but three separate versions.

The third and finest has a strange history: when Napoleon conquered Spain in 1808 and placed his brother Joseph on the throne, his general in command of the Spanish invasion, Marshal Soult, packed up this Murillo and hauled it back to Paris with him, where it found a home in the Louvre. More than a hundred years later, in 1941, the French and Spanish governments arranged a deal whereby the Soult Murillo was returned to Spain in exchange for a Velázquez, which went to the Louvre, whereupon certain Spanish art critics said, "To trade a Velázquez for a third copy of a Murillo! We Spaniards must indeed be crazy!" A kinder judgment would be that the Soult Madonna is much superior to the other two versions, and to have three such Murillos together in one spot, whereas other museums have none, is itself a measure of how lucky the Prado is where Spanish painting is concerned.

Leading off from the rotunda is a long, specially lighted hall which is without equal in the other museums of the world. Known simply as Room XII, it is the magnet which attracts many of the visitors who make special trips to Madrid.

It contains twenty-six of the greatest paintings of Velázquez, works so varied and magnificent that of themselves they constitute a museum. One Spanish guidebook says bluntly, "In this room and those nearby hang all the best Velázquezes in existence." Certainly, if one wants to understand this superb master, he must come to Room XII.

I have spent so many hours in this room that they must add up to days or even weeks, and even yet I don't know how to view it properly. First, of course, one looks at the huge and stunning "Lancers" on the end wall, a painting, like Rembrandt's "Night Watch" in Amsterdam, so excellent that one either perceives its majesty or does not. Words cannot help. There it is, a mammoth canvas overflowing with vitality and perfection, and some people sit quietly before it, ignoring the other paintings.

There is, however, another series which I prefer, those powerful portrayals of contemporary Spanish life: the weavers, the blacksmiths and the wine bibbers. Any one of these paintings, given a room to itself in some museum in London or New York, would be the gem of the collection, but in Room XII they are merely three of twenty-six masterpieces.

Most visitors to the Velázquez room stand a long time before the two portraits of Baltasar Carlos, for these are two of the most engaging and tragic child portraits ever painted. In one we see Carlos at the age of four or five, dressed as a knight astride a pudgy brown horse set in an idealized landscape. In the other we see him at the age of six—the canvas tells us that was his age—posing as a hunter, cap awry, attended by two brilliantly painted dogs. It is as fine a portrait of childhood as has ever been accomplished.

The pictures are tragic because Baltasar Carlos was the son of Philip IV. He was a handsome child, quite intelligent apparently, and Spain was relieved to know that the throne one day would pass into good hands. As the boy matured, he became even more attractive, and Velázquez painted him at various ages, showing him finally as a young fellow of sober bearing with a conspicuous "Hapsburg chin." But from fifteen on, the young heir fell into extreme debauchery, from which at seventeen he died. The throne passed into the hands of his near-idiot brother Charles the Bewitched, and Spain was doomed.

Women visitors to Room XII linger before the graceful portrait of a little princess. The child is Velázquez's personal favorite, the Princess Margarita, who would grow up to marry the emperor of Austria. Velázquez painted this little girl many times—several European museums contain portraits of the child standing regally in extremely wide dresses made of lace and satin—and in a moment we shall see that his masterwork focused on her. By all accounts the little princess was a charming child and later a responsible empress, but like her brother Baltasar Carlos, she died prematurely at the age of twenty-two. That Velázquez loved her strange mixture of imperial dignity and childish charm, there can be no doubt.

In a separate room not far from XII, there hangs in solitary majesty a painting which has attracted attention since the day it was finished. On a special plaque set into the wall nearby, the curators of the Prado state simply, "The culminating work of universal painting." It is "Las Meninas," the Maids of Honor, and it unfolds in six principal planes, one behind the other: first, an amazingly lifelike dog; second, little Princess Margarita attended by her maids of honor and a well-known dwarf; third, Velázquez working at an easel on which he is painting a picture which we cannot see; fourth, a man and woman observing the scene; fifth, a wall containing a mirror in which we see that Velázquez is painting the portrait of Margarita's father and mother, Philip IV and Queen Marina; sixth, a flight of stairs up which is walking a chamberlain.

The picture is unbelievably complex, a kind of exercise in dexterity that only an established painter would attempt "just to show that he could do it." The various planes are indicated solely by perspective, the interplay of light and dark, and a clever use of colors. The figures are well done and breathe vitality, but the essential mystery of this work lies outside such considerations. It is a moment of family life caught in suspension, and the groups represented are as real today as when Velázquez painted them.

For visitors interested in modern painting, that is to say the work of artists like Cézanne, Manet and Van Gogh, two small pictures in one of the lesser Velázquez rooms attract most attention. These two unimportant landscapes show the gardens of the Villa de Medici in Rome and were done on one of Velázquez's scouting expeditions to Italy. The first landscape appears finished and shows simply the façade of a supporting wall of some kind, tall cypresses, a hedge and two male figures.

The second, and more important, painting shows a comparable scene, except that the wall is replaced by an archway beyond which rocks and landscape can be seen. Three male figures populate this picture, which might seem unfinished, except that this was the way Velázquez intended it. It is an extraordinary work. It could have been done by any of the modern artists mentioned above, or by Renoir or Pizarro. The subtle brushwork, the spare use of color, the impressionistic drawing and the manner in which space and planes are indicated combine to make this small canvas one of the gems of the collection. It speaks directly from the age of Velázquez to the present, reminding us that all artists face similar problems.

As one might expect, the Prado contains the best works by a host of other important Spanish painters like Ribera and Zurbarán, but the real test of the museum comes with the question: "How good are the El Grecos and the Goyas?" The masterpiece of the former, a mysterious Greek who spent his productive life in Spain, stands not in Madrid but in a Toledo church some forty miles to the south; however, the Prado does boast three magnificent rooms filled with works of this master, and the tall "Adoration of the Shepherds" is one of the best— awkward, violent, compelling—and well fitted to serve as our introduction to El Greco. In this painting one sees the characteristics which identify the master: strange shadows, clashing colors, swirling movement and off-center composition, elongated figures and almost demoniac faces.

Others prefer the quieter "Holy Family," in which El Greco's distinctive blue and purple dominate. It is a beautiful picture, but its taut faces remind one of a fascinating experiment which Spanish medical authorities have conducted in the field of art. Disturbed by strange faces shown in El Greco's work, these doctors have visited the insane asylums of central Spain, the same ones that El Greco might have known, and have demonstrated in photographs that each contorted face painted by El Greco can be found today in the local madhouses. This is an intriguing theory, that the great Greek painter used the insane of his community as models, but I doubt that we require this explanation of the psychological penetration he displayed in both his religious paintings and his portraits.

So rich is the Prado in Goyas that a major room on the second floor is given over to them and a large section of the first floor. In the former is found that intriguing pair of portraits, "Woman Nude" and "Woman Dressed." Legend whispers that the portraits represent the Duchess of Alba, with whom Goya was in love and whom he painted with no clothes on. Then to cover his guilt and to mislead the Duke, who wanted to see the portrait, Goya quickly painted a clothed version and thus escaped with his life. No support can be found for this enticing fable; modern critics doubt that the portraits have anything to do with the famed Duchess of Alba, with whom Goya was never in love.

It is the downstairs section of Goya's work that is most impressive, for only here can one see this virile, tough artist at his best: the etchings on the horrors of war, the bullfight series, the dark and powerful paintings. Here also are those exquisite scenes of picnics and parties in the outskirts of Madrid, and the little landscapes that seem to be from another artist, so delicate and poetic are they.

The most famous of the Goyas are those showing the brutality of life, and none excels "The Third of May," in which soldiers are shooting down unarmed citizens against a leaden sky which shows the spires of a nearby town. This powerful work might almost be termed a summary of Goya's social philosophy, but it is also a masterful work of art.

Goya also did pictures exhibiting a wild imagination, and of these the Prado contains the top example. It shows a brooding landscape with turbulent sky, a low mountain range flecked by purple clouds, and a valley down which cattle and covered

wagons and people are fleeing in obvious panic, driven on-
ward by some terrifying apparition. At the head of the valley,
his legs hidden behind the mountains, rises a colossal nude
figure, bearded and with enormous arms which he brandishes
like a boxer. He is thousands of feet high and is obviously
infuriated by some unseen thing that has attacked him. With
one hand he could crush all the fleeing people. The total scene
is so bizarre and the flight so headlong that the picture remains
a masterpiece of terror, as psychologically bewildering as it is
artistically exciting.

There are many such Goyas in the Prado, some so revolting
in their horror as to repel the average viewer, but when one
is surfeited with them he finds a small painting, perhaps the
last that Goya did—a beautiful work in grays and blues depicting the young French woman who used to deliver milk to his
home when he was living at Bordeaux. It was painted, the
signature states, when Goya was eighty-one, and like the
"Medici Gardens" of Velázquez, seems as modern as any work
done by Cézanne or Renoir. It is a marvelous thing, an evocation of all women everywhere, a true portrait of one real
milkmaid yet a summary of all the women that Goya had loved
throughout his life. To see "The Milkmaid of Bordeaux" is
worth a trip to the Prado.

Whenever I see the Prado Goyas, that incredible blizzard of
beauty, I am tormented by the fact that in 1870, during a period
of trouble, some dozen top-quality Goyas disappeared from
the museum. They were never recovered, but Spanish experts
believe they are in existence somewhere. So at any time some
lucky seeker, rummaging through old stacks of paintings, may
discover one of the missing Goyas and find himself half a
million dollars richer.

I rarely leave the long rambling Prado without stopping to
pay my respects to two small items tucked away in corners, for
to me they typify this royal collection. Unnoticed by many,
Van Dyck's "Equestrian Portrait of Charles I of England" is
a much smaller canvas than those customarily painted by this
regal Fleming, but it is a little beauty, showing Charles in
black armor astride a spirited white horse. Not long after Van

317

Dyck finished this work, Charles was beheaded and his pictures dispersed. A Spanish knight, happening to be in England at the time of the sale, picked up this fine work and shipped it back to Spain, where it became part of the royal collection.

And in one of the farthest rooms of the Prado stands a little-known work which year by year attracts experts from all parts of Europe. It is a statue of a woman found near the village of Elche in eastern Spain. It dates back to the most ancient times and relates to the original Iberic peoples who inhabited the peninsula. For many years it rested in the Louvre, a beautiful and mysterious work, but it returned to Spain as part of the deal which brought back the Soult Murillo, so that today critics of that trade are saying, "On the other hand, to trade just another Velázquez for 'The Woman of Elche' isn't so stupid."

The mystery of this strange sculpture continues. Who was the woman? When did she live? What does her headdress signify? When did Iberians wear necklaces like that? There are no answers. All we know is that this is one of the finest pieces of carving ever to have been done. And the strangest part is that today critics are beginning to believe that the famous "Woman of Elche" probably isn't a woman at all. Most likely she's a young male warrior in ritual battle dress! When you visit the Prado, look and see what you think.

Why I Collect Art

Of all the decisions I have made in my life, one of the best came when I was riding a gondola along the canals of Venice.

I had gone to that city for a vacation after months at war in Asia, and after an initial tour of the museums, I was casting about for something to do when I saw by accident that on an island at the edge of the city a group of nations had combined to hold a large art exhibition. I grabbed a water taxi and went out to the island and saw there a score of large pavilions in which the best contemporary art of the world was being shown. France, Russia, Italy, Germany and England had stunning exhibitions, as did two dozen smaller nations, but wherever I went I found that critics, artists and all persons interested in painting were agreed that it was the Americans who were showing the way.

A British critic told me, "It's astonishing how you chaps have caught up with the parade. From a position at the rear, you've moved forward to lead the procession."

A group of Italians drooled over the large American canvases, and one said, "Miraculous how your painters have broken out of the old patterns. All the world looks to New York for leadership now."

I remember especially the French experts. One wrote: "It is not easy for us to confess how brilliant this new American painting is." The French did not admit it then, but the knowing ones sensed that the leadership which Paris had so long provided the world of art no longer resided in Paris.

In a group session at a café near the pavilions, it was a German art processor who predicted, "The next cycle will be known as the American one."

When I was alone I wandered back to the American pavilion and saw again how tremendous this new art was, how exciting. The old idea that American painting was nothing but a pale imitation of Europe was dead. It had been killed by an army of inspired paintbrushes wielded by a batch of daring young Americans.

On the way back from that island, I could think of little but the gratifying idea that at last American painters were doing work which the world had to acknowledge, and as I was phrasing this thought, a clear, sharp decision loomed up from the waters of the canal.

"You make your living in the arts," a voice seemed to be saying. "Why not devote any savings you have left at the end of each year to the painting that was done in America during your lifetime?"

When the idea first came to me, I shied away from it. And when I saw the prices—$4,000 for a single painting—I dropped the matter. I had not grown up in a family accustomed to wasting that kind of money on squares of canvas daubed with globs of paint.

But the concept must have been a good one, for it came back to haunt me whenever I thought about the future. And so one day, when I had spare time in New York, I dropped by an art gallery run by a friend of mine and told him of my plans. He happened to know where some good buys were available, and that day I started a journey which one never abandons, once he has been bitten with the collector's bug.

The first American work I bought was one of the best. It was a water color by John Marin, who had loved Maine and who had died a few years before. It was bold, stunning in effect, and a perfect evocation of sea and shore, with a trim boat heading toward the sunset. Like most of the paintings I bought in the first rush of enthusiasm, this great Marin has grown better year by year. Today the whole art world recognizes him as one of the true artists of this century. On my first try I had picked a winner.

It was the next purchase, however, which meant most to me in those early days. It consisted of two matched paintings, each showing the heads of two girls. They were the work of a man who has not yet been discovered by the world at large, Alfred H. Maurer, a brooding genius who died relatively unknown in 1932. One painting showed the two girls in more or less normal guise, except that their heads were sharply elongated in the fine style of El Greco and Modigliani. I loved it at first sight and always thought of it when I wanted to recall some one painting which best symbolized my growing collection.

However, as the years passed, it was the second version of this subject that became my favorite, a highly stylized semi-abstract cubist treatment. It seems to me that if someone who knew little about art wanted to gain the quickest possible understanding of what recent painting is all about, he should do as I did, and live with these two splendid canvases. Before long, I believe, he would find that he preferred the cubist portraits, as I now do, because they are a distinction of art.

A remarkable feature of the collection was the fact that almost everything I liked, my wife liked also, for although we were quite different in backgrounds, our tastes coincided. I understand that this is not always the case with collecting families. The first painting she chose by herself turned out to be one of our most delightful acquisitions, and her second, one of the most significant.

She came home one morning excited about a canvas she had seen in New York. "It's exactly what we've always wanted!" That afternoon she took me to see it. There it was, an enchanting fairy-tale painting of two waitresses at a summer inn. The girls minced along on funny legs and pointed feet. They had curious half-Japanese faces, and the landscape was sort of unworldly. It was the work of a Japanese-American painter named Yasuo Kuniyoshi, a dapper little fellow who painted like an angel and made self-portraits of himself in dashing golf outfits. He was one of the best painters our country has produced in this century, and his two saucy little waitresses have danced their way into our hearts, for this was one of the happiest paintings we have acquired.

My wife's other selection was quite a different matter. She bought it without knowing what it signified. All she knew at the time was, "It's by Ben Shahn, and he's one of the best painters we have. And it literally sings with beauty and emotion." It was a tall blue portrait of a man in sandals and some kind of skirt, holding a little boy. That was all, but it carried a sense of mystery that was immediately detectable. And then we found out what the painting was.

It was one of a series of six or seven large canvases titled "The Fortunate Dragon" and it showed one of the doomed Japanese fishermen from the boat of that name which had accidentally sailed into an area of the ocean where an atomic bomb was about to be exploded. The man in the picture was saying farewell to his son before dying of radiation. Suddenly Shahn's painting became more than a picture. It was an evocation of the tragedy of our day, and it remains doubly strange to my wife and me, for without knowing why she had chosen this particular painting, she had chosen one which represented a facet of American-Japanese relations. And she is an American-Japanese.

Part of the job of collecting is getting to know those artists of one's own time who are doing the good work, and in my case the most rewarding acquaintance has been a cantankerous, rough-spoken, beer-guzzling Irishman who lives down the Delaware River from me. His name is Lee Gatch, a rocklike man who has been one of America's finest painters during the last forty years, a recluse fearful of the city, a born naturalist who can talk to squirrels and deer.

His canvases have been small poems to the beauty of nature and living things, and one memorable day when I climbed his hill to have a few beers with him, he showed me something no one else had yet seen, a painting on canvas in which the central area consisted of a piece of rock ground down to the thinness of cardboard. Somehow, the canvas, the paint and the rock were transfused into a hymn to nature.

"You like it?" Gatch growled.

"It sings."

"Should I go ahead?"

"Anyone who loves art has got to love this," I assured him, and this has proved to be true. Patrons around the world have snapped up Gatch's great stone paintings as soon as they leave his easel. The other day I was down to see him and he was just completing one of the best he's ever done, a stone bull grazing in a meadow of the mind. When some lucky collector gets that one, he will get an instant masterpiece.

The first Gatch I bought is one of the quietest, loveliest paintings we have, the picture of a Viking ship sailing out from a Norwegian fiord. Of itself it is a thing of rare beauty, but in the lower right-hand corner appears an addition, slapped on late one night by candlelight. For some it might mar the painting. For me it adds a touch of grace: "For Jim and Mari Michener." And it's signed by Lee Gatch, my gifted neighbor.

Collectors ought always to ride their hobbies, for when one searches for something he has always liked, the chances are he will wind up with a work which will please him through the years. I have always loved politics and found pleasure in being with politicians. I therefore always wanted one of William Gropper's famous series of paintings depicting our American politicians in action, and one day I found just what I wanted. The man speaking could be a Pennsylvania politician I know. The man seated in the foreground is a friend from Colorado. I once served on a committee with the man in back, who looks like a bullfrog. And in certain ways each of the five burlesqued figures reminds me of myself.

In my collecting I have tried to find examples done by those Americans who created the great paintings of our century. Some gained fame in their lifetime. Others died in obscurity. But two who struck a middle ground were Morris Graves, who grew up on our western coast with a wild sense of nature's mysterious quality, and Marsden Hartley, who painted some of the finest landscapes ever produced in America. Graves' "Golden Goat" is a marvelous creation, a work of lyric beauty, while Hartley's brutal "New Mexico Recollection" simply shouts of the west and the passing of cattle and the dark and lonely days spent on the range. So far as art is concerned, these are two of the best paintings in the collection.

Since I grew up in the depression, the social content of art has always been my special interest, and even though paintings which stress this are now looked down upon, I cherish a handful of great works which depict that social turmoil. None is more dramatic than Philip Evergood's tumultous "Dance Marathon," in which, on the forty-ninth day of a non-stop dance, the couples like ghouls stumble through the murky haze at one o'clock in the morning, while a skeleton hand holds the prize money in its bony fingers. I am deeply indebted to this painting, for it never lets me forget a crucial segment of American history.

But the choice painting of this school is Thomas Hart Benton's noble panel "Romance," in which a Negro couple walk homeward through a powerful southern landscape. I acquired this picture in a manner as romantic as the subject matter. I was driving across the United States and saw that Kansas City lay only a short distance south of my route, so I dropped down to discuss with Benton the old days in American art. He was a peppery man in his late seventies, recalling with gusto the days when he used to teach the men who are now famous, his epic fights with museum directors, his long-drawn feuds with critics. Finally he said, "You know, there's another old codger around here I'd like you to meet," and he took me across the river to Independence, where we met with Harry Truman. "A couple of tough old geezers," Benton said, describing himself and the former President, and as I looked at the two old fighters I had to agree. I am glad to say that I have lived to see Benton's work come roaring back into fashion. The painting "Romance," bought at a reasonable price on my visit to Kansas City, is now one of the more valuable in my collection, which makes me happy.

In collecting, one is always prepared for surprises. In Barcelona, Spain, friends told me, "There's an American painter living here, a very difficult chap named Norman Narotzky, and he's done some works which have the city on its ear." It seems that Narotzky had depicted Queen Isabella of Spain and her husband, King Ferdinand, not only as great Spanish rulers but also as tyrants, with modern accouterments like swastikas and gallows. Barcelona was in an uproar over the portraits, so I went to see them, liked them and wanted to buy them, but Narotzky proved a tough nut and we could not reach an understanding.

What is remarkable about this story is that a month later a friend of mine, traveling in Italy, sent me an excited letter. "I was walking through this gallery in Rome when I saw a truly marvelous portarit of Picasso by an American painter I'd not heard of before, Norman Narotzky. I put up a deposit for you, because I know you'd want it if you saw it." In this roundabout way I got one of the fine American portraits of this generation, a painting which is sure to become famous because of its powerful presentation of Picasso with symbols from his works scattered through the imagery. Ironically, the "Picasso" acquired by accident in Rome is a better work than the Ferdinand and Isabella which I had tried to get in Barcelona.

In collecting, one often stumbles into experiences that prove more rewarding, in odd little ways, than others which at the moment seem more weighty. For example, last year we were surprised to find that the United Nations Children's Fund had selected one of our religious paintings to be its featured Christmas card. It was by Margo Hoff, a joyous work in red and yellow and blue depicting three angels in stylized form. Millions of these charming cards circulated throughout the world to earn money for children, a dividend we had not anticipated.

So far I have mentioned only those paintings which show recognizable subject matter, whereas the collection is strongest in abstract paintings of the kind that have made America famous in recent years.

Let me explain how I became interested in abstract painting. Some years ago the name Jackson Pollock burst on the

325

American scene. Press agents described him as a wild man from the west. (Actually, he was a well-trained art student who had studied with Thomas Hart Benton; he could draw and design with the best of them.) He had devised a new style in which ordinary house paint and radiator enamel were splashed and dripped across violent canvases to create works of incredible complexity and force.

Everything I read made fun of Pollock and his wild new paintings. "He ought to have his knuckles rapped," wrote one famous critic in words he must often wish he could retract. Others discovered that Pollock had left imbedded in his paintings bits of rubbish from the floor of his studio, and still others condemned him for being a nihilist.

Then I saw one of his works, by accident, in an out-of-the way place—a loft-studio occupied by another artist who had traded with Pollock for a small drip painting. And in that first encounter my eyes literally popped! This was powerful, revolutionary, and strange to say, intensely pleasing.

I was not then collecting art, so I did not buy a Pollock, but I followed his career with keen interest and watched his prices rise from $100 a canvas to $100,000, if you were lucky enough to find one. When I say that American painting startled the world in the late 1950's, I refer primarily to these turbulent paintings of Jackson Pollock. How often, in the years when I did collect, I yearned to go back to those early days when I could have acquired a stunning Pollock for $100.

Much later, in a small gallery which I frequent, I came upon a Pollock of exactly the size and style I wanted, one of the best drip paintings done with house paint and shiny Duco. It carried with it a letter purporting to be from Pollock's widow, Lee Krasner, who is an excellent painter herself, stating: "I have inspected the painting '29–52,' signed on the back Jackson Pollock, and I am satisfied that it is an original painted by my husband." I congratulated myself upon having acquired a major Pollock, for he had exploded the art world of my time. Alas, two weeks later I discovered that the work was a clever fake.

Two of our abstracts are among the most popular paintings in the collection. The first is a little gem by Stuart Davis,

"Lawn and Sky," and I cannot imagine how anyone could see this delightful work without loving it. It is bright, humorous, fresh and filled with surprises. Davis died only recently, a man covered with honors because of the sturdy series of noble canvases he produced in the abstract vein. He is one of the easiest of the difficult painters to enjoy, but alas, his paintings have now become so extremely valuable—$28,000 for one of average size and average quality—that the typical collector can no longer hope to own one.

The other popular favorite is George Ortman's "The Good Life, or Living by the Rules." Some might not call this a painting at all, for it is really a heavy wooden construction onto which is pasted strips of canvas and into which is inserted that handsome series of geometrical symbols. It's the left-hand side of the picture which really gags some people, because hiding inside half of those twenty-eight circles are ping-pong balls, painted blue.

"What in the world are ping-pong balls doing in a painting?" my neighbors ask. I have to reply that I don't know, but they are very effective and help to create a lively image.

This question of whether the modern artist who uses ping-pong balls could paint like the classical artists if he wanted to comes up all the time. Ben Shahn told me once that he had finally developed a satisfactory answer when some disgusted man growls, "Hell, I have a ten-year-old son at home who can paint better than this." Shahn says he used to argue with such people, trying to explain that almost any of the good modern artists can draw and design as well as the average Renaissance master. "Now I don't argue. I tell the man, 'If your son can paint as well as this, feed him well. Because in another five years you can retire and live off what he earns.' "

Max Ernst, the notable German painter, has an even better reply. He stalks through a gallery of modern painting and complains in a loud voice, "I have a forty-year-old son at home who can paint better than this." He is referring to his son Jimmy, an American citizen, who painted one of the most enchanting works in our collection, a spider web of lines and Christmas trees and shimmering imagination. We have kept

327

this painting on our walls for years at a time without tiring of it, for it is the imagination and inventiveness of the artist that infuses his work with life. Old Max Ernst could honestly claim, "I have a forty-year-old son who can paint better than this."

Which, among the 275 American paintings in the collection, do I prefer above all others? I suppose it would be judicious to say, "I like a good many, for a good many different reasons," but that would be evading the question, because there is one work which captivates me. It is by an artist little known to the public but of great reputation among fellow artists. He is known as a painter's painter, and the work I am speaking of is a painter's painting. It is by George McNeil, who teaches at an art school in Brooklyn, and is called "Schwanda, the Bagpipe Player." It is an abstract work, marked by slashes of color and vast areas of luminous paint. It has movement and depth and stark vitality. I suppose the artist did not intend for me to see real figures in his glowing canvas, but I do.

I see Schwanda, the legendary bagpipe player of central Europe swinging mysteriously out of the hills. I see the valleys this demented musician wandered down, and I hear the growling lament of his pipes. I paid a modest sum for this compelling work; if one considers the inspiration and sense of beauty it has given me, it has been worth ten or twenty times what it would sell for, because for me it has been a true, a majestic work of art. It has fired my imagination and reminded me of past historic movements of which I was for a while a part. I consider the money I spent on "Schwanda" the best I ever spent on my education. Sometimes art can do this for a man.

The point I want to make is this: I doubt if a representational painting of a real bagpipe player could have done for me what "Schwanda" has done, even though in McNeil's painting he does not appear. Furthermore, I would expect that few other viewers would find in this strange painting what I found in it. One of the beauties of modern art is that it invites the imagination to participate in a profound adventure. If your particular imagination finds less in "Schwanda" than I found, don't worry. There will be something else that will affect you

328

if you look with an open mind and a discerning eye, and I might not like it at all.

What about the recent developments in American art? Friends ask me, "Do you really like this new pop and op?" Others refer to it as "Pop, op and slop."

I like it. I find that I like whatever the brightest young minds of this generation are doing. I like rock and roll. I like the soaring new architecture. I like new forms of writing, like Truman Capote's *In Cold Blood*. And I like what our younger artists are doing. I don't think they're Rembrandts, but they are dealing with a new vision of our old world, and that's always to the good.

I remember one wintry night when I climbed the long stairs to the studio of Edward Wesley. My guide whispered, "He's one of the new pop artists who's been getting favorable comment. You must be prepared for something unusual." I looked at the pictures Wesley had stacked about his studio, and although in general I liked what I saw, I failed to find that one canvas which shouts, "I'm the good one! Buy me!"

Then off in a corner I saw a series of rough sketches which Wesley had been making, and they quite charmed me. On the spot, I said, "Would you paint me a picture based on those sketches?" Wesley said, "I'll give it a try." The result? One of our best pop-art pictures, "Annunciations," in which, in bold poster-like outline, six young wives stand in a formal row, the first with a baby in her arms, the next five obviously pregnant. Everyone who has seen the painting loves it, because the artist has caught a modern, youthful vision of motherhood.

Let me explain how I became interested in optical painting, known as op. One day I was walking along Madison Avenue in New York and saw in the window of one of the galleries that line this street a dazzling big painting more than six feet high composed of clashing red and green addition signs arranged in subtle ways so that the signs turned alternately red and green. It was a dizzying composition, an optical illusion quite unlike anything I had been interested in before, but in that moment I was satisfied that I had come upon a bright new artist who had something to say. I asked who had painted the picture, and was told, "Richard Anuszkiewicz. We think he's going to be heard from." I bought the painting and thus became the first general collector to support the work of a man who was destined to become one of the brightest lights of recent years. It is this constant opportunity for discovery which excites the collector, for to watch the progress of an artist one has discovered when others did not know him, and to see him take first rank among his contemporaries, is a true intellectual delight.

Of the collection, some three dozen paintings were done on specific commission. I would meet a talented young painter, like his work and ask him to do a special canvas for me. Some of these adventures with the artists—beginning before the artistic idea was even born, and continuing through the long hours of invention and imagination and hard application in a drafty studio—are the most cherished rewards of a collecting experience. The artistic process is always complicated, and to be able to watch it in operation, with a stunning picture as the end product, is most exciting.

For example, I first met Bill Ronald at a party in New York and found him to be an intense, brooding young man with a striking wife. He kept apart, as if the crowd bored him, yet he obviously wanted to talk—as if he had much to say. We struck up a friendship, and once when I was visiting with him in Princeton, I suggested that he do a large painting for me on a set of themes he had been developing. Because I sometimes like to write my books in episodic form, I asked him if he had ever thought of constructing a painting in episodic fragments, and he said, "That might be good," and he went ahead. The result was totally pleasing, a beautiful mural-type painting that dances with color and movement and gratifies the eye in many unexpected ways. Few commissions have worked out so well. Museumgoers who have seen this striking panel on its travels across America and in Canada have applauded its freshness.

If I had to identify one man of the new school who meant most to me personally, it would be an old, gnomelike figure from Germany, a man who murdered the English language but who at eighty had a youthful vitality that astonished us all. He was Hans Hofmann, and anyone who dislikes modern art could well blame him for everything, because he was one of the most profound teachers ever to operate in the United States. Many of the artists in our collection have studied with Hofmann, and all pay tribute to the vital old man.

He died recently, mourned by the art world. At eighty he was painting with greater vigor than at any other period of his life. I last talked with him down on Eighth Street, in Greenwich Village, where he had been conducting an informal class for young people. I told him that I already had two of his best canvases but wanted a third. "Do you have any special favorite in the shop?" I asked.

The eighty-year-old face broke into a wreath of smiles. "Ach! There's one you ought to see. I call it 'Elysium.' It's where old artists go when they die. It's very clean and simple —only a nest of squares, but they tell everything."

I went to see "Elysium" and found it to be exactly as he had said, a nest of heavenly squares of color, very simple, very clean, a revered place in which the spirit of an artist could well reside. I believe that in the years to come, Hans Hofmann will attain a notable place in American art history, not so great as Jackson Pollock's, not so world-respected as John Marin's, but a secure place as the man who turned upside down our old understandings. I can hear him now. "It's push and it's pull. And this way the color flows and that way." I never understood what precisely he was saying, nor did many of his pupils, but he showed us all new pathways to old beauties, a giant of a man cast in the whimsical form of a Grimms' fairy-tale gnome.

There is a final joy in collecting art. It is one that none of us is aware of on that fateful day when we buy our first painting. It is the joy of turning one's personal collection over to a museum or a university which can put it to better use than one can do alone. Not long ago my wife and I began looking around the larger American universities to identify one doing an outstanding job in art education. This country should be

331

proud that we found no less than nine, any one of which would be a logical repository.

In the end we chose the University of Texas, at Austin. From now on anyone who wishes to share in the fun we've had with these paintings will find them residing there permanently—to be used by scholars and to be enjoyed by the public.

Most Americans are not aware that over the last twenty years American art has, according to world opinion, excelled American poetry, drama, archicture, music and fiction. Consequently, the collection we have put together has an added importance. It represents the best our nation has been doing.

I have never thought of the collection as a great one. In fact, anyone could duplicate it, but it does represent greatness in that it contains the work of some of our best artists. Well, you can judge for yourself if you ever get to Austin.

THE APPLICATION OF ART

My concern about art has not been limited to museums, and I early discovered that one of the finest uses to which it can be put is as an application to things in daily use. I have therefore always been interested in architecture, the manner in which man builds attractive places in which to live and work and hold public assemblies. I enjoy seeing a well-thought-out store rather than a hodgepodge jumble. The things we use, like stoves and shovels, ought to be beautiful of themselves, as they were in the days when skilled craftsmen made them. I love a good fabric, a well-made piece of clothing, solid shoes that fit, a chair that feels good to sit in.

Many years ago I spent the better part of a week searching for just the right office chair. I wanted it to have some leather so that I could get up and down easily, some wood because I respond to this substance, a back that reclined, because I am nervous when I work, and casters that really moved without binding, because I shift around my desk a good deal. Well, finally I found the chair I wanted. It cost nearly fifty dollars more than I expected, but since that time I have spent many hours in it, and it has helped me write a dozen books. It's as good today as when I bought it, for not even the leather is cracked. The casters still work, and when I want to watch the deer in the field beyond my window, I can lean back comfortably and do so. That chair was a bargain because it had been in every part designed by an artist and built by a craftsman.

In my travels I have often discovered objects as functional and as beautiful as my chair, and for them I have considerable respect. I suppose the most beautiful artifact I have seen on earth—a handcraft, that is, as contrasted to nature—was a pale lemon-yellow celadon ceramic made in Korea some five hundred years ago. As fragile as the petal of a flower, it had been used as a deep saucer by some ancient family and had survived innumerable washings and careful handlings. It glowed with an inner light of its own, a simple country dish, a lantern illuminating the way for all of us who want art to be a functional part of life.

No article that I have written for the *Reader's Digest* was more pleasurable in its research than the one which follows on Italian industrial design. Maybe I was in a good mood; maybe I enjoyed the companionship of Dennis McEvoy, one of the world's great cicerones and storytellers; and maybe it was because the Italian designers were such a raffish lot, men and women who obviously enjoyed their work.

Highlight of the trip was a hilarious event which I still remember with wry delight. Accompanied by the attractive daughter of Jack Radcliffe, a senior editor of the *Digest*, I reported to the atelier of Valentino, Italy's leading dress designer. It is true that I was wearing a sloppy overcoat, while the young lady with me had a trench coat; we looked like journalists, which we were.

The haughty woman in charge of the atelier took one look at us and apparently thought, "That couple wouldn't spend ten lire," and she proceeded to elbow us around from one waiting room to the other, warning us that we mustn't touch anything and must in no way interfere with the real customers. Finally she could stand us no more. Placing herself imperiously before me, she said, "I wish you would go now. We have some important people coming into the shop." And with that she bounced us right out onto the Roman sidewalk.

Naturally, I was curious as to who the important incoming people were, so Radcliffe's daughter and I lingered on to catch a glimpse of them. I didn't recognize their faces but they did look important, and they certainly looked as if they were going to spend a lot more than ten lire.

Korean Culture

In December, 1950 the half-destroyed city of Seoul in war-ripped Korea was about to be captured by the communists for a second time. Only a few hours remained to salvage precious national treasures from the wreckage, and a government ship stood by for one last-minute cargo.

What should be evacuated that would do the nation the most good? Gold, machinery, engraved plates for printing money? Finally the government chose something that every Korean would applaud. They rescued the Seoul Symphony Orchestra, for without music there could be no Korea.

Americans on the scene were astonished, for we have never had an ally about whom we knew less than we know about Korea. In fact, we have always known more about our enemies than we know about this tough-minded little friend.

The reasons for Korea's bad publicity are many. The war there has been unpopular and Korea has shared that unpopularity. Because many Koreans were starving, they stole from our Army and became branded a nation of thieves. In the frozen wastes of North Korea our soldiers suffered humiliating defeat when the Chinese crossed the Yalu. Our men remember the country bitterly. Furthermore, the Korean is one of the most stubborn human beings on earth and is called by some pigheaded. And because President Syngman Rhee tried several times to wreck an armistice he could not trust, the entire nation was charged with duplicty and ungratefulness.

But let's look at the facts. Koreans have to be tough. Theirs is the most destroyed nation on earth. You would have to go back to the Middle Ages to find another nation so completely wiped out. Yet today's destruction is merely one more in the long series of devastations which have ruined the land. First came the ancient Chinese marauders, who ravaged the nation. They were followed by the Mongols of Genghis Khan. In 1592 the Japanese destroyed almost every city in Korea, and in 1636 the new Manchu rulers of China roared down from the north and repeated the job. In 1910 the Japanese took over completely, and when liberation finally came in 1945, the Russians occupied North Korea and the United Nations assumed responsibility for South Korea. Then, in 1950, war again shattered the land.

It is doubtful if any other nation on earth except possibly Poland has maintained its integrity under such conditions, and it is a historical miracle that Korea exists today. Four explanations have been suggested.

First, Korea serves as a bridge between the mainland of Asia and Japan. From the most ancient days cultured Chinese and savage tribes from Siberia and Manchuria have gathered at the northern end of the bridge, while at the southern have stood the capable Japanese. The history of Korea must properly be viewed as the passage of these great nations back and forth across the peninsular bridge. These vast movements have brought not only the destruction of war but also the benefits of peace. To a strong, capable Korean people their bridge has brought the best of China, the finest of Japan and the most vital forces of Siberia.

Second, Korea is tremendously mountainous. It is claimed that if its peaks were flattened out, Korea would cover the entire earth. Such chopped-up terrain encourages tight little groups to hide away in remote valleys and continue their immemorial customs regardless of who occupies the cities.

Such isolated living engenders conservatism and rugged individualism.

Third, Koreans as a national group are well suited to absorb the shocks of history. Unbelievably resilient, they bend with the winds of war and even today in ruined cities it is difficult to find a Korean whose mind has cracked up. The Chinese have always called them "the gentlemen and scholars of the east." A Japanese governor said it was difficult to make them work because "they are always drinking and talking and laughing and telling stories." An American colonel, who watched Korean men patiently rebuilding a village which would have to be destroyed in the next big push, said, "They work slowly, but nobody can stop them." I remember asking a three-star admiral in command of forces trying to destroy a Korean railroad bridge what he would do when he retired. Quickly he replied, "I'm going to cash in my insurance, pawn my wife's jewels and invest every cent I have in any railroad in the world that will hire Koreans for maintenance men."

Fourth, as a people and as a nation Koreans possess a stunning integrity. Occupied, defeated, mutilated and outraged by war, they still exhibit this positive integrity. They have always kept themselves proudly intact through generations of invasion. A Korean sociologist says, "I think it's because of our women. They treasure this sense of personal purity. Japanese occupied us for thirty-five years, but our women ignored them. One enemy after another has swept our land, but none were able to seduce our women. Your American troops, coming as allies, have had a little better luck, but we must remember that the troops of Genghis Khan didn't have Sears Roebuck catalogues to help them do their wooing."

What major ideas from Asia moved down this Korean bridge to enrich the world? Practically an entire civilization was exported to Japan. Almost every facet of Japanese culture was first polished in Korea, the way Europe polished its culture before exporting it to England and America.

Three religions came down the bridge, Confucianism from China, Buddhism from India, and Shamanism. or spirit worship, from Siberia. Each took hold in Japan, where the latter two prospered, Buddhism under its own name and Shaman-ism under the much improved form of Shinto.

In architecture the pagoda and its accompanying temples with upswept roof poles were passed along by Korea. In art the secrets of Chinese pottery and woodblock printing were transmitted. In sculpture some of the finest work in Asia was done either in Korea or in Japan by Korean artists working there.

And many American gardens have been enriched by the glorious flowers which reached us through Korea. Some, like the forsythia, azalea and plum, came from China, but the Japa-nese cherry originated in Korea, where the world's finest groves of this spectacular tree still stand. Korea has always had fine gardens, the most notable being the one in which the playboy king, Yun San Kun, used to cavort in the year 1500. On warm spring days Yun would round up cartloads of pretty young girls, force them to undress, then chase them merrily through the woods. Fortunately for Korea, this sybarite died early, of complete exhaustion.

There were other lovely things that developed in Korea, sometimes with an initial hint from China or Siberia, but always with a strong Korean color.

Korean dance is a wild, passionate, sweet thing. It is quite unlike the Chinese or Japanese dance, and many have thought they saw in it a glint of dark Siberian campfires, although it has now become far more sophisticated than any dances of Siberia we know. At times the Korean dance tells some his-toric story in the manner of western ballet. More often one gets a sly commentary on the pompousness of human life, the ridiculous upsets of love or the folly of old men. The dances I like best are crazy little ones that tell no story other than that of a man or woman having a rousing good time. It is safe to say that every Korean can dance, not mystically as in India, nor with iron skill as in Japan, nor with religious dedication as in Java; Korean dancers are just a bunch of country people in billowy costumes leaping and twisting with the joy of life.

Probably the most treasured Korean gift was ceramics. As early as the year 900 Korean potters were making exquisite bowls and dishes with lustrous glazed finishes. These ancient things are now prized around the world, the finest being those with soft blue or yellow or cream surfaces. Neither the design nor the finish of these rare pieces came from China, but they did move on to Japan, for in the great invasion of 1592 the principal loot taken away by the conquerors was a colony of potters, who settled in Japan, where they built the Japanese ceramics industry which later sent its superb products across the earth.

Unfortunately, the Japanese refused to borrow Korea's great invention, the floor-heated home. The germ of this idea probably originated in Manchuria, but the Koreans perfected the simple trick of piping hot air and smoke through floor ducts, over which were placed large slabs of laminated paper lacquered with bean oil, so that the Korean floor is beautifully polished and permanently warm. As long ago as the time of Christ, Koreans enjoyed radiant heating.

It is music, however, for which Korea is most famous today. It is unique and wonderful, the only Asian music which compares in richness and emotional complexity with the best of Europe. Founded upon a three- or six-beat system, its best songs sound like spirited waltzes, whereas the music of surrounding Asian lands is in two- or four-beat patterns and sounds like a march. If a dozen Koreans gather, three or four will have powerful voices and it won't be long before singing starts. Recently, I heard such an impromptu songfest when no one knew I was listening, and in the course of half an hour these village singers tried half a dozen folk songs, part of a Korean opera, Brahms' Lullaby, "My Old Kentucky Home" and the "Habañera" from *Carmen*. Four Koreans and a bottle of wine will provide music for an entire night. Some trained choruses sing principally Handel and Haydn. Schoolgirl groups love the wild old folk songs. Boys' choirs sing western music and street singers chant "How Much Is That Doggie in the Window?" Only the strikingly similar nation of Wales provides as much music as Korea, so that the evacuation of the Seoul Symphony Orchestra made sense. Here was a real national treasure, for music is the currency of Korea.

There were lesser Korean inventions which were sent down the bridge. Most curious is the *kisang* house, where professional entertainers sing and dance and serve food to customers who pay a lot of money. In Japan this system became the highly formalized geisha house. In food Korea made a notable contribution in kimchi, that fiery pickle whose vitamins have helped account for the rugged health of this mountain people. Of kimchi it is said, "Like molten lead, it burns going in, going through and going out."

In science Korea has made several distinguished advances: one of the first astronomical observatories, the first controlled system of measuring rainfall, cast-metal type for printing books at least fifty years before Gutenberg, and one of the first comprehensive encyclopedias. But two inventions have been outstanding.

In 1592 Admiral Yi Sun-sin, a stocky sailor with drooping mustaches, got the job of halting the Japanese invasion, but his inadequate wooden ships were knocked out by a secret weapon imported by Japan from Europe: cannon. When the Japanese had landed, Yi quietly assembled his remaining ships in hidden estuaries and encased them in metal so that they looked like turtles.

In 1593, 270 years before the *Monitor* and the *Merrimac* fought in our Civil War, Yi's ironclads sped out and destroyed the Japanese fleet.

When peace came, jealous courtiers caused Admiral Yi's demotion, so in 1597 the Japanese again swarmed ashore. Belatedly, tough little Yi was restored to duty and with his iron turtles crashed through the Japanese supply ships and transports, chopping them to pieces. He saved Korea, but in the culminating battles he died, a profound tactician and a brilliant inventor.

However, it is the Korean alphabet that is the major intellectual accomplishment of Korean science. For the first fifteen hundred years of Korean history, all writing was done in borrowed Chinese characters. This caused many difficulties and kept Koreans largely illiterate, for spoken Korean is as different from Chinese as Finnish is from English.

341

So in 1445, after the Chinese system had been firmly established, a brilliant Korean king announced, "Everything is good in its own place but when forcibly moved it becomes useless. It is true that many of our customs and ideas are borrowed from China, but our language is separate and distinct. It is exceedingly difficult to express our ideas by the use of Chinese." Forthwith he handed his people a scientifically accurate alphabet which anyone can memorize in an afternoon. Illiteracy in Korea has practically disappeared.

In considering the cultural traffic along the Korean bridge, two facts must be kept in mind. First, it is wrong to imagine that all the ideas which obviously came from China originated there. Some came from India, others from Persia, and a substantial few from Greece and Italy. Marco Polo was by no means the first European to travel through Asia. He was merely the best known. Throughout history there was a rich interchange of ideas between East and West, and one lonely Korean cave contains extraordinary carvings whose graceful drapery copied Greek statues which were well known as early as A.D. 300.

The second important fact is that even though Korea borrowed heavily from China, and Japan took many of its ideas from Korea, each nation adapted its borrowings to its own culture. It is unfair to brand Japanese as copycats, for they did exactly what England did when she borrowed from Greece or Rome, or what America did when she borrowed from England. Ideas were taken but they were improved upon. Only a nation which borrows an idea and allows it to deteriorate deserves censure. That didn't happen in Japan or Korea.

Furthermore, movement along this crucial Korean bridge has often been from the western world to Asia. Koreans say, "The Germans brought us breweries and public architecture. The English taught us how to collect customs and work out a financial system. The French brought civil law and museums, while the Americans gave us schools and hospitals."

Rarely do Americans appreciate the significant part our nation has played in Korea. Dr. Choi Jung-woo, who translated Shakespeare into Korean, says, "Take an average hundred men in government today. About forty of them were educated in American missionary schools. About eighty speak English." With Dr. Karl, Director of Information, I ran down several recent cabinets and found that an average of seven out of sixteen top posts were held by men educated in American schools. Some, like Dr. Rhee, held degrees from universities in America.

American religious influence has also been profound. Korea is unique among the major nations of the world in that it has no generally accepted national religion. At one time Buddhism predominated but never really captured the country. Ultimately it was outlawed. In its absence Korean men were usually Confucianists, while women, who are practically excluded from that religion, clung to Shamanism and its warm world of spirits. Today the leading religion is actually Christianity, fostered by Americans, but its numbers are not great.

The permanent religion is love of the land. I know of no national patriotism equal to Korea's. Against the flood tides of disaster the people cling to their land. A Korean village today, with its grass-roofed houses built around tiny central patios, looks pretty much as it did a thousand years ago.

This means that the people are stubborn, hard to get along with at first, conservative and sometimes even smug in their assurance that they know what's best for Korea. A scholar told me, "Until we see some other nation that has survived the way we have, we must be suspicious of good advice from the outside." This attitude has prevented Korea from developing a modern democratic government. The tough old ways are good enough.

At the same time the Korean is a delightful friend, trustworthy, diligent and usualy good-natured. No people in Asia have honored beauty and learning more than the Koreans. No men at close of day get more hilariously potted at the local wineshop. No people sing more.

But in spite of its wonderful people, Korea as a nation seems destined for tragedy. Geographically it must always be a bridge nation, and it is the function of such nations to be invaded periodically by those superior forces which hang around the bridgeheads. Belgium and Holland know this role well. And today, in addition to the historic pressure from China, Siberia and Japan, the new forces of Russia and the western world meet on the Korean bridge. It therefore seems that for the present Korea must remain invaded as she has so often been in the past.

That she will stay invaded permanently is unlikely. In the cold December of 1953, I saw vivid proof of Korea's determination. At night there was no electricity for most homes in Seoul, no running water, no heat. There was insufficient food, and of every five buildings, three were bombed out. Shops were empty and streets were deep in mud. Seoul was a destroyed and miserable city, but its artists decided to hold an exhibition.

In a beat-up hall whose rooms were cold and dreary a collection of pictures was hung whose beauty was overwhelming. These canvases would have graced any major capital in the world, not even excepting Paris. They were bright, modern, brilliant. Foreign experts wrote excited reviews praising the show as unbelievably good. Here was no doleful emphasis on war. Here was the vigor of Korean dancing, the joy of Korean song. And not one of the artists who painted these pictures had known security or comfort or warmth or enough to eat. But they didn't complain. They worked with what they had.

That is the spirit of Korea.

Italian Designers

It was the last week of a crucial Italian electoral campaign. The leading candidates were to debate on television, and the studio had set up what it hoped would be a typical Italian living room for them to use.

When the program ended, switchboards across the country lighted up with a deluge of phone calls. Nobody complained about the debate. Everyone wanted to know, "Where can I buy a table lamp just like the one shown on the program?"

A style hurricane has hit Italy. Bright new lamps, colorful chairs, dashing automobiles and heavenly clothes are seen everywhere, and knowing stores in other countries are laying in stocks for their customers. *La linea Italiana* (the Italian line) is all the rage, and if you haven't met up with it yet, you will soon. Look at what's happening.

. . . In Tokyo young people going to college are carrying handsome new Italian typewriters made by Olivetti. Shocking scarlet, these trim machines are housed in a radical new type of portable cover, also scarlet. Called the Valentine, these attractive typewriters will soon be seen in all countries.

. . . In better New York stores customers can buy brilliantly colored armchairs made of transparent plastic which shimmers when light strikes it. When you buy this huge chair it comes in a small package plus a foot pump, which you use to inflate it. The designer who created the chair says, "You are then sitting on beautiful air. You want to move the chair to another room? Let the air out and pump it up again."

. . . Maria Callas is about to start another tour of operatic performances and naturally needs a few dresses. So she flies not to Paris but to Milan, where a sharp-eyed Italian couturier whips up twenty dresses for her, at about $1,200 a dress.

. . . If you like enticing new products, chances are your next telephone will be an amazing one designed by an artist in Milan. It's called Cricket and folds in the middle so that the whole phone is almost as small as a fist. the good part is that when the phone rings, the sound doesn't grate on your ears. Says designer Marco Zanuso, "The telephone is always summoning us, so it should sound pleasant. On Cricket you have this little knob which makes him sing anything from high soprano to low bass, according to your mood."

. . . When King Faisal of Saudi Arabia visited an automobile show in Europe, he saw a radical new kind of car so dazzling that he had to have one for himself . . . right away. The Bertone people from Turin explained, "It's not a car, really. It's a one-of-a-kind prototype. If we sold that car it would cost you about a hundred thousand dollars." The king said, "I'll take it," and for three days he toured London streets in the world's most sensational car. "On the fourth day," say the Bertone people, "he gave it back to us. Shifting gears in heavy traffic was too tiring."

. . . In Spain no matter where you go you will find that nine-tenths of all electrodomesticos (ranges, refrigerators, washing machines) are of Italian make. "Their design and workmanship are the best in Europe," explains a Spanish dealer. "They seem to know what women want."

. . . At the *Newsweek* office in New York the bright young research girls tell each other what they are going to do with their pay checks. Reports one girl, "When I said I was going to buy this or that, nobody listened. But when I announced one week that I was going out to buy a pair of Ferragamo shoes, direct from Florence, all the kids wanted to come along. Because Italian shoes were news."

... When the decorators who were finishing the new palace for the Shah of Iran wanted something really splashing to set off the whole scene, they came to Milan and bought eighteen Arco lamps, dreamed up by Achille Castiglioni, and when they lined these about the main hall they had something that came right out of the *Arabian Nights*. The lamps, which you can now buy in New York, were not only conversation pieces but also true works of sculpture. They cost about $750 apiece and each is rooted in a huge block of polished marble from which an enormous stainless-steel arch reaches high and away.

"Let's face it," says Joe Colombo, the mustachioed young leader of the movement, "Italian design is the new thing. You must know what we're doing with the new materials, the new forms and especially the new colors, or you miss what's happening. You'll also miss some very beautiful designs."

No one with a sensitive eye can visit Italy today and remain unaware of the revolution in color and line that has struck the country. Department stores burst with handsome new products geared to modern living. Boutiques are ablaze with daring new colors. Specialty shops are loaded with exquisite leatherwork styled in new ways. And ships heading for foreign ports carry cargo of bright new things for London, Sydney, Cape Town and Dallas.

The Italians even have been called to Russia to help put some flash and dash into Soviet auto production. Italy has one sovereign thing to export—good taste.

How did this good taste develop so spectacularly in Italy? What does it mean in Italian life? Why is it so alluring to others? And why did the explosion happen at this particular time? Recently I wandered up and down Italy looking for answers to these questions.

Forty years ago, when I first set foot in Europe at the almost unknown seaport of Civitavecchia—used by Rome for more than two thousand years as its main outlet to the sea—I learned that Italians took this matter of good taste seriously. From my ship I saw what one sees in any historic seaport, a huge warehouse protected by a fortress castle. But this was not just any castle, nor was the warehouse merely a building. Each was a work of art.

When I landed an Italian told me proudly, "Our castle? It was built by Michelangelo. Our warehouse? Designed by Bernini."

And there was the secret of Italy. "If you are going to have a fortress, why not appoint Michelangelo, the best artist of his age, to build it?" (I later learned that it had been designed originally by an even greater architect than Michelangelo, Bramante, who laid out the seaside masterpiece, then died, leaving his young friend Michelangelo the task of completing the job.) "And if you must have a warehouse cluttering up the shore of a beautiful harbor, why not commission the finest sculptor of the time, Bernini?"

The genius of Italian design, of course, was Leonardo da Vinci, whose immortal notebooks contain his experiments— many extremely silly, others of incredible prescience—in the design of practically everything then used in Italy or to be used in the centuries ahead. Airplanes, automobiles, sky-scrapers . . . he tried his hand at designing them all. Today his gifted descendants in Milan and Florence and Turin also try everything. The fantastic automobile which King Faisal bought for three days' use was not meant to run on public highways . . . yet. But when the time comes, Italian designers will have this prototype in the back of their minds, reminding them of what can be done.

It was in this questing tradition of Leonardo that Pininfarina, the dean of automobile designers, began some years ago to study how to make cars safer. This was long before Ralph Nader and United States Senate investigations. In fact, Pininfarina built a whole new car—one copy only, at huge expense —to demonstrate possibilities. The Sigma, after having been shown around the world, now rests in the transportation museum in Lucerne, a monument to Italian ingenuity. Says a Pininfarina expert, "The Sigma anticipated everything that safety engineers have since come up with. Engine footing slanted downward, so that in a crash the heavy motor will pass underneath the driver. Steering wheel broadened so as to provide a less compact area to strike the driver, post shortened and made collapsible. Front and rear ends made like accordions to absorb shock. All surfaces inside and out free of protuberances which might cut or kill. All important windows ejectable outward. And most important, doors which slide forward and backward rather than swinging open. In a crash you cannot be thrown out of the car." Leonardo would have been proud of this new car. Had he been alive today, he would probably have doodled something pretty much like it himself.

The third great Italian who serves as spiritual ancestor is Benvenuto Cellini, the master craftsman whose exquisite work in gold still tantalizes the mind. It has been said that every Italian man fancies himself to be part Benvenuto Cellini. "After all, he did dress well, he was much interested in sex, he had splendid taste and he knew how to make beautiful things."

This heritage of craftsmanship is the backbone of Italian industry. Says Micol Fontana, one of Rome's famed Fontana sisters of high fashion, "From the beginning of Italian history the artisan has been the strength of our nation. Italian women are the best seamstresses in the world. . . . and their brothers the best shoemakers."

Roberto Gucci, whose family make handbags and accessories famous in all countries, says it this way, "The Italian artisan has hands of gold. It is he who has always created the wealth of our nation. We have no mines, no big herds of cattle, only a few raw materials, not even much wood. So what we must do is allow our workmen to make things of rare beauty which the rest of the world will want to buy. And they do."

But workmanship, no matter how skilled, needs to be guided, and that is where the current crop of designers comes in. These are men highly trained in architecture, but with side interests in art and engineering. They are adventurous, witty, clever with hand and eye and good businessmen. Paolo Lomazzi, an extremely bright young man who looks like an instructor in freshman art appreciation, explains, "The thing to remember about the current explosion is this. In the early 1960's Italy wobbled into a severe economic recession. The

349

sector to feel it most was building, so here were all these fine architects with nothing to do. Common sense drove them into designing smaller things than palaces. And suddenly big business found that ideas paid off... handsomely. Good design was something the world wanted . . . not only Italy but Germany and Australia and the United States.

"Pretty soon we were designing everything . . . chairs, lights, bedrooms, radios, clothing. And when it was all gathered together, somebody shouted, 'It's the new Italian line!' And now everybody wants to climb aboard. But only because we started with very solid ideas developed by solid men who knew what they were doing."

This solid training of the Italian designer begins early. Pierluigi Spadolini, the young, bearded professor of architecture in Florence, who could be called the philosopher of the movement, says, "Consider a boy who grows up in Siena. The landscape around him is his university, his graduate course in style. He cannot escape the olive trees, the tower in the distance, the balance between hills and valleys, the cypresses lending their grave accents, the unparalleled clarity of the light. And when he looks within the city walls, he sees that majestic cathedral with its alternating layers of black and white, the noble monuments, the beautiful gates, and that marvelous dipping line of the central square. Each summer he sees the ancient pageantry of Siena with its medieval banners twirling in air, and from all this he catches a sense of color. Such a boy, whether he knows it or not, is absorbing the principles of art. He learns to respond automatically to fundamental artistic problems. Said another way, he is a born designer."

As a man, his education continues. If he puts his hand in a pocket to draw out some money, what does he find? On the 1,000-lire note, a portrait of Verdi the musician, Michelangelo the artist. On the next, Leonardo da Vinci the designer. And on the 100,000-lire note (about $160), Manzoni the novelist. According to one Italian, "I haven't read a thing Manzoni wrote, but I love him. Whenever I see his face I am very happy."

350

If this man goes to the post office to buy stamps, he finds a splendid series of small stamps, each showing a different figure from Michelangelo's Sistine Chapel. And if he enters a dress shop he sees the colors used by Botticelli and Raphael. The golden heritage of Italy is constantly around him, so that the Italian designer has a built-in advantage.

Achille Castiglioni, who designed the arching lamp and many other good things, has a unique theory: "The thing that saves Italy is that we have no school of design. If you want to be a designer, you must first be an architect, or a painter or a sculptor. In other words, you learn art first, business second."

Italy is thus a fusion of skilled handicrafters working under the guidance of artistically gifted architects. The designers, with their flashing ideas, would get nowhere without the artisans to rely on, and the workmen, no matter how skilled, would very likely turn out well-made junk if left to themselves.

Italy proves how a nation with few resources other than brain and a capacity for careful work can secure a place for itself in a competitive world if it does well those things it does best.

Contemporary Italian design stems from a remarkable man from the Turin area named Battista Farina, who died in 1966 after a lifetime of designing the most beautiful automobiles in the world. Ferrari in Italy, Peugeot in France, Porsche in Germany, Leyland in England and General Motors in America all sought the talents of this gifted man, whose nickname "Pinin" was finally incorporated as a legal part of his name. Today the Pininfarina people design cars for many firms but also build three or four super-luxurious Ferraris each day.

"And occasionally we do special jobs for long-time friends, but they have to be patient. A gentleman in England asked us to touch up his Bentley with some Pininfarina styling, and we agreed, but it is taking three and a half years. Of course, he can afford to wait because when we do something it stays in style for thirty years."

Pininfarina was the first Italian name to burst upon the firmament of international design. Its reputation was main-

351

tained by hard-headed attention to business, but even so, when the firm's present leaders are asked what one ingredient has accounted for Pininfarina success, they say unhesitatingly, "A sense of fantasy. Ordinary men can care for the mechanics and make a good car. To build a great one requires first a sense of fantasy."

Today one of the best-known names is Gucci, the fabled Florentine family that specializes in one thing only, leather goods. Old Guccio Gucci, an artisan in the noble tradition, had a bright idea: "Make women's handbags so beautiful that they are works of art." He did, and saw his business grow until he had stores in distant places like Palm Beach, Beverly Hills and London. Today three of his sons and three of his grandsons run the business with a blend of art, canny judgment, theatricality and super good taste. The last two ingredients are supplied by an extraordinary gentleman, Rodolfo Gucci, who at an early stage decided to chuck the family business and become a movie star. He succeeded and was a leading matinee idol prior to the war. (He looked much like Rudolph Valentino.)

After the war he rejoined the firm and assumed responsibility for design, in which he exhibits a real flair. He also takes care of public relations, at which he is a genius.

When talking with strangers about his famly he assumes all roles in turn.Now he is the old father, now the mother, now a baby grandson, now a German infantry officer, now an elderly priest, now his dead wife, who was a most beautiful actress. He enacts whole scenes, jumping around the room to be now one character, now another. He has a good half-dozen distinctive accents—German, Rumanian, American gangster, English lord—and a limitless range of facial expressions.

I reported to the Gucci office in Milan with sixteen questions in my notebook, but I never got beyond the first: "Is your father still living?" This precipitated such a violent monologue that I was alternately guffawing with laughter or silent out of respect for tragedy. Any trip to Italy that included even ten minutes with Rodolfo Gucci would be worth the effort, but to have two hours of unbroken theater was a joy, and I put aside my serious questions.

352

The important thing about the Gucci family is that they have blended the classic line laid down by their father with the most modern trends of today. Roberto Gucci, who runs the Florence office, explains, "My uncle, who does the designing, has a unique capacity for reeducating his eye every year. When he walks the streets of Florence he sees not only classic Italy but the bright young faces of German and English and Australian tourists. He knows the world is young and that it wants young ideas."

At one point in his dramatic recitation, Uncle Rodolfo said, "At Christmas each year I let my imagination go absolutely wild. I make up a handbag that nobody in the world could afford and that no woman in her right mind would want. I put it in the window as a kind of Christmas present to all women. Cost? Maybe eight thousand dollars. By nightfall it is always sold. We must remember that the world requires both the classic and the positively nutty."

The third historic name in Italian style would have to be Ferragamo. In the beginning years of this century a six-year-old boy in southern Italy contrived the idea of becoming a master shoemaker. Since this was one of the lowliest occupations available to men, his middle-class family forbade him to pursue such nonsense, but with a monomania that was startling he clung to his idea and at the age of eleven he opened his own shop, volunteering the information to his astonished community that he was now ready to make superior shoes.

After a reassuring success as southern Italy's youngest bootmaker, he emigrated to the United States, where he had the good sense to settle near the film industry in California. In quick time he was making shoes for Mary Pickford, Clara Bow and Douglas Fairbanks. Then his customers began to include people like the Queen of Rumania, the Duchess of Windsor and Claire Booth Luce.

At the height of his American success, he decided to come back to Italy and build a large factory which could produce many shoes according to the excellent precedents he had established. He did so, and promptly went broke. Starting a second time from scratch, he then rebuilt his empire until he became the most highly regarded shoemaker in the world. In 1960 he died, leaving behind him an ancient Florentine palace, country estates and a business worth millions, all accumulated because he held fast to one principle: "In a shoe, the fit is everything." Of course, when they did so they got a shoe which was in its own way a work of art, cunningly designed so that even a large size looked smaller.

Today the design end of the Ferragamo empire rests in the hands of a beautiful, soft-spoken young woman not yet thirty. Fiamma Ferragamo looks as if she ought to be in college, a swinging, stylish young lady who has inherited from her father his devotion to shoes.

Perched on the edge of a chair in the Feroni-Spini palace, from which she conducts her business, and surrounded by several hundred mocked-up shoes, fully designed but not all in production, Fiamma repeats her father's credo: "With us it's comfort." Fortified by his belief, she sends her shoes to Lord & Taylor, Nieman Marcus, Harrods and the large emporiums in Paris. She also keeps in her storeroom the personal lasts of more than 6,000 famous women throughout the world, who pay thirty-four dollars at the beginning to have a personalized last made, then sixty for each pair of shoes made from that last.

"One of our most intriguing customers was the Maharani of Baroda. When her last was made she saw a style she liked and ordered one hundred pairs in all known colors. One pair would be gray and red, the next red and gray. Our workshop looked like a butterfly convention."

A friend who has watched Fiamma for some years says, "She could be considered our typical Italian designer. She knows raw materials, from the tanning of leather to the weaving of canvas. She has personally worked at each process. She has a wonderful sense of colors and a keen feeling for line. And she has that fantastic family to back her up." Mother Ferragamo handles the finances. Brother Ferruccio manages the inventory, and Cousin Jerry the factory. Sister Giovanna, one year younger than Fiamma, designs the high-fashion clothes that accompany the shoes, but it is pert young Fiamma who is mainly responsible for seeing that the family name remains high in the world of Italian design.

354

"I design every shoe," she says simply. "And we still aim for comfort."

Outstanding as are these glittering names—Pininfarina, Gucci, Ferragamo—I, like many persons throughout the world, first became aware of Italian design through the practical work done by two industrial firms. I can remember the shock I experienced some years ago when I saw my first Olivetti typewriter. The simplicity of the design astonished me, but when I used the machine and felt how sensibly all parts worked together, I appreciated the taste and the planning which had gone into this remarkable product.

From magazines I learned that this typewriter was no accident, that the Olivetti firm in northern Italy had carefully studied the tastes in various nations and had concluded that the time was ripe for a machine that looked beautiful. Later I saw this keen sense for design reflected in other Olivetti products. This year the company offers a desk-top computer which again is at the head of its class in beauty and utility.

The world-wide success of Olivetti stemmed in large part from the compelling freshness of the design that characterized all its products.

At the time I was admiring the typewriter so much, my wife was discovering the Necchi sewing machine, another instance in which the radical new approach to design produced instruments which delighted the artistic sense of women while encouraging them to sew well. Again, design was largely responsible for the success of a commercial product.

The story behind Olivetti and Necchi is significant. In each case, the canny manufacturer took his design problem to an artist, with this commission: "Restudy the whole problem of this machine, then determine how it ought to look in a modern world, ignoring all previous concepts." The man to whom these industrialists went was a super-gifted architect, Marcello Nizzoli, born in 1887 and now retired. In all he did he had a mysterious feeling for balance and line. He worked with Olivetti for fourteen years before he produced the typewriter that startled the world, but he used that time to learn the problems of mechanics and industrial design. It was from this long prag-

355

matic experience that he finally built his great machines, which in pure art were equal to most painting or sculpture done in Italy during these years.

Nizzoli was the first of a new breed. A free-lancer, he could be employed by any manufacturer with a problem. Skilled in both art and architecture, he would tackle any assignment from designing a whole new city to devising a screw to hold two pieces of wood together. Most of all, he was a man who applied his superb taste to practical problems. Let us see what some of his pupils and successors are up to.

Italy today has about forty clever, hard-working, artistic designers who are remaking the look of their country. One of the most important is an amazing fellow in that he is not an architect, is not trained as a designer, is not an artist, and does not work at designing. He runs a department store.

Domenico Longo Dente is about forty-five, tall, lean, handsome, suntanned from his athletic life and with the prematurely graying hair that makes so many Italian men look distinguished. Much of his year he travels to places like Japan, Thailand, Brazil, but when he is at home in Milan he supervises the artistic efforts of the powerful Rinascente chain stores. (Branches in eight major cities plus a large chain of cheaper stores and a fleet of supermarkets.)

Longo Dente says, "About fifteen years ago our store decided to develop a strictly Italian look. We wanted everything we sold to tend toward one image . . . color . . . design . . . workmanship . . . flair."

One of the first things Dente did was to create a yearly award for the best Italian design, the Compasso d'Oro (the Golden Compass), and it was this prize, now supervised by a board of experts not connected with the store, which started the general public talking about local design.

"We try everything," Dente says, speeding through his commodious warehouse-office to discuss the most recent items he has helped develop. "When we make a mistake we pay the bill and throw the stuff away. More often we succeed."

The dean of the designers with whom Dente and the other industrialists work is Marco Zanuso, a youngish-looking architect in his early fifties. His interests have been enormously wide—large buildings, typewriters, television sets, a sofa-by-the-mile of which you buy as long a length as you need, and one of the handsomest leather chairs I have ever seen. "Only one copy made," he says ruefully. "It ought to sell for about twenty dollars, but we couln't make it for less than a hundred and fifty."

Zanuso is most famous for Cricket, the singing telephone, but what captivated me was an extraordinary ceramic tile. Of uneven shape, longer than it was wide, this tile consisted of six roughly defined sides, each of which was either a concave or a convex part of a circle, so arranged that when you had a group of the tiles they would fit together in a wild variety of ways, the jutting-out parts of one tile fitting into the receding parts of another. With this one tile, made in various colors, one could make almost any design he wanted: straight lines, circles, waves, half moons, mountains, setting suns and gorgeous flowers. It was a silly thing of itself, a strangely shaped chunk of ceramic, but only an artist could have devised it. Incidentally, it has been a big commercial success.

The introspective patrician of the group is Roberto Sambonet. A man of medium height, quiet in speech, he is a successful artist with a steady sale for his easel paintings. In order to find out what was happening in Italy, Sambonet worked for five years at the big Rinascente store in all sorts of jobs. "I arranged window designs, visited manufacturers, sold to customers, worked with artists. In the end I knew what a store was . . . what people wanted in their lives."

Sambonet has had spectacular luck with some of his designs for kitchenware. His trays have been best-sellers in Germany and America, and a long, slim container for serving fish was a sensation when photographed for *Life*. He says, "Right now the world is in a period of pause. We are all looking cautiously ahead. But a very modern era is about to explode all around us."

The wild man of the school is Giuseppe Cesare Colombo, a delightful young fellow with a beatnik beard, expressive hands, close-cropped hair and boundless vigor. Known throughout Europe as Joe, he has produced many of the items which have startled Italian and world markets: huge chairs, small spidery chairs, large blocks of furniture on wheels, machines for living. He growls, "The big concept I brought to Italian design was a belief in anti-design.By this I mean that the artist must not add gimmicks to his article in order to make it sell better or to please his own sense of art. The ideal is to design a product which is perfectly functional, of excellent proportions, and so neutral that it will take on the personality of its owner."

The old pro of the group is a delightful, spritelike little man of impeccable taste, fine clothes, large cuff links and bubbling wit. To talk with Achille Castiglioni is to chuckle.

"In 1959 I designed what was probably the best thing I ever did . . . this vacuum cleaner. Instant success! Nineteen major art journals in all parts of the world carried stories about it. Industrial magazines hailed it as the new way to the future. The Museum of Modern Art in New York bought it as the best machine of its kind ever made. Prizes everywhere. Achille, you are a genius. But one fault. When the salesmen saw it they cried, 'It doesn't look like a vacuum cleaner.' So the manufacturer got scared and the machine was never made. Only one copy, the best thing I ever did, and it landed in a museum."

With his equally radical machine for making espresso coffee he had better luck. "What a simple, beautiful machine this is . . . designed to fit inconspicuously on any counter in a crowded store." Lovingly Castiglioni points out the exquisite lines he built into this machine. "So what happens? From all over southern Italy storekeepers protest, 'It doesn't look like an espresso machine. What we need are colored lights, mirrors, large brassy handles and, if possible, a few angels.' Another flop, except that storekeepers in the cities began to see that the new machine took up little space, could fit in anywhere and made better espresso. I was saved, but in America it doesn't sell very well. You still like brassy handles and, if possible, a few angels."

It was one of Castilgioni's lamps that stole the television

show away from the politicians. Artistically, his success has been the lovely Arco lamp with its enormous sweep across the room. Commercially, he has done well with a new machine for dispensing beer, a child's camera that is a joy and a weirdly shaped spoon for digging mayonnaise out of a jar.

The quiet genius of the group is a hard-working young fellow, who resembles a college senior, with tousled hair, expensive sport shirt and disarming manner. Paolo Lomazzi believes that above all else a design must serve its proper functional need. "One of the first designs in all industry was the Coca-Cola bottle. It fitted the hand, enhanced the quality of the contents, felt good when cool and was less breakable than an ordinary bottle. I wish I could do as well with some of my ideas."

Lomazzi's inflatable chair comes close. In brilliant coloring, it is a big, amiable thing into which a tired man can comfortably flop after a long day. It speaks of home, and of a youthful modern life. "People are always asking me, 'Will the transparent plastic hold up?' I tell them that the army has used it for thirty years and it hasn't sprung a leak yet."

Like many other young men, he confesses that one of the big influences in his life was Pininfarina. "His automobiles were not only the most functional being made at the time but also the most handsome. That's a good target for us to shoot at."

While these things were happening in the world of machines and shoes and lamps, an even greater success was being enjoyed by a much different branch of Italian life. It started hesitantly in a private home in Florence in 1951. Let Jean Spadea, one of America's top fashion writers, explain what happened. "Word reached us that a group of Italian designers had screwed up their courage and were going to offer a challenge to Paris and New York in the world of high fashion. Sophisticates predicted the trial show would be a flop. Who had ever heard of Italian designers? But we went. And we saw a miracle!

"Fabiani of Rome, Veneziani of Milan, the Fontana sisters originally from Parma, plus three other designers! They showed us not a bunch of interesting dresses but a complete

359

coordinated line with a definite something . . . an Italian flair. One journalist from Paris whispered, 'This is not a good day for France.'

"We writers went wild with enthusiasm. We stated precisely what had happened. Buyers went wild, too, and before the year was out, women in Texas and California were wearing Italian clothes and loving them.

"The secret? Italian women are good seamstresses. Italian fabrics are among the best in the world. Italian colors are good, too. But the hidden ingredient is always taste, a feeling for art which the Italian acquires as a child and never betrays."

The Italian splash into the world of high fashion was not only spectacular; it was also permanent. Yearly shows at the Pitti Palace kept the world informed, and soon notable women from all countries were coming to Rome for their dresses. Margaret Truman wore an Italian dress at her wedding. Audrey Hepburn flew down from London for her outfits.

Typical of the men who now mastermind this multimillion-dollar industry is Roberto Cappucci, born in Rome thirty-eight years ago. Slim, he wears original fabrics which he helped develop, whereby a single piece of heavy cloth will start at the top with a light orange color, then deepen by imperceptible degrees until at the bottom it is the deep color one sees in a sunset on a stormy day.

"I will have nothing to do with a folklore approach," Cappucci says. "For me no happy Italian peasants dancing at the wine-making. I seek the fine, classical look. After all, it's just as Italian."

Cappucci shows are international events, with reporters and buyers from all nations. "We allow reporters in free, of course, because we want the fashion press to know what we're up to. But before a buyer can get in he must plunk down a deposit of a thousand dollars . . . to prove he's serious. Of course, if he buys anything he gets the thousand dollars back . . . so they all buy." When the wife of a head of state visits Rome for a new wardrobe, appointments with Cappucci are arranged by the appropriate embassy, but any woman, if she wishes, can walk in off the street and pick up a few dresses at three or four thousand dollars apiece.

The most interesting house, in some ways, is the old, established one run by the three Fontana sisters—Micol, Zoe and Giovanna—now of Rome, for they have combined the highest fashion, in which they make thousand-dollar dresses to order for a select clientele, with a large factory in suburban Rome where they turn out ready-made dresses of fine quality for their countrywomen who cannot afford top prices. In between, they run a series of boutiques where a man can buy his wife a lovely outfit for seven or eight hundred dollars.

Micol says, "Each season, we sisters design three complete collections—one for our salon, one for our boutiques, one for our factory. That makes 210 dresses every season, and since we have three seasons, that's 630 dresses in all. And we are responsible for every button on every dress."

She adds, "It's not such a big task. After all, our family has been making dresses for the last two hundred years . . . and it's always been the women in the family who run the business."

Micol feels that the other branches of design owe the fashion people a debt. "During the last decade the Italian line has been well received throughout the world, but it was the visiting card of fashion that got us through the front door." It still commands most of the attention.

Wherever I went in Italy, I asked one question, "Why did it happen here and not in Yugoslavia or Greece or Austria?" The answers were varied.

The last general style explosion came at the end of World War II and was provided by the Scandinavians. Then the world was weary of holocausts and sought the cool, orderly clean lines of the north. Scandinavian design was a psychological fulfillment of a deep-felt need. Today the world seems to be weary of cool government, orderly socialism and unemotional answers to continuing problems. The costume changes that started in England in the 1960's are having repercussions in other fields. Color, vigorous line, wild invention and zany new devices are wanted, and the Italian approach is the one that best fills this demand.

Scandinavian design featured wood, some of the handsomest ever used in furniture, because wood was what the northern countries had. Italy, lacking both wood and metal, turned naturally to plastic and other invented materials and found the world market eager to try them.

Scandinavia, naturally a dark land, inclined toward restrained colors which the rest of the world found soothing. Italy, accustomed to the violent moods of the south, splashed color about freely. Zanuso points out: "Italian color? It comes straight to us from medieval times when each Italian city had its dazzling procession, every palace its brilliant wall hangings. Have you ever seen the pageant of the banners held at Arezzo each summer when the flags are tossed high in the air?"

Joe Colombo has a simpler answer: "We were lucky. Foreign buyers were looking for something new and stumbled on us. We had the sharp ideas, the superb workmen, the daring approach to color."

Roberto Sambonet, the artist in stainless steel, has a fascinating explanation: "World taste changes every five years, and we just happened to catch it at the end of a cycle when it was hungry to begin a new one. And where has good design come from since the Scandinavians? Germany, Japan, Italy. Three countries that lost their wars. Three ruined nations that had to rebuild. Small industries were launched with small capital. New ideas were essential. Our good design wasn't an accident. We had to have it or perish. It stays alive for the same reason."

It is difficult for a non-Italian to appreciate the role played by the automobile in Italian life. Men truly worship their Fiats —no dark colors here; most popular today, a jazzy mustard-yellow—and as for a new Lamborghini! The other night I walked home from the opera through the dark streets of Rome, and at one hotel a guest had parked his Miura, probably the handsomest car made today, and not less than a hundred men stood there, drooling. In Florence I saw a new sports car after what had apparently been a dusty trip. With his forefinger an envious young man wrote in the dust that covered the cowling, "*Lavami per l'amor di Dio.*" (Wash me, for the love of God.)

One of the reasons for Italy's success in design has been its willingness to give young men and women freedom to draw exciting things. The people at Bertone, where the Lamborghinis are made, say, "Our head designer, Marcello Gandini, got the job when he was twenty-seven years old. In this business a man at thirty-five is an elder statesman, fit only for a desk in the front office. It's young men who have the fantasy, the love of sheer movement."

Italy also profits from the fact that almost every industry I have been speaking of is a family operation, run by a tightly knit group of relatives. It is the Ferragamos who make shoes; the six Gucci men who make bags; the Bertone family and the Pininfarinas who run the large factories connected with auto design. The Fontana sisters make dresses, and even a rebel like Joe Colombo learned his trade in his family factory. Roberto Sambonet designs primarily for his family business, and everyone remembers that when the original Ferragamo shoemaker allowed outside capital into his business, everyone went broke. "Never again," swear the present Ferragamos, and the others agree.

This family control means that decisions can be quickly reached, radical new ideas can be adopted if the family agrees, and quality is maintained because each partner has been trained in the fundamentals. "We want no bankers telling us how to design a dress," Micol Fontana says.

But the basic secret has got to be the Italian flair for handicrafting. "The Italian shoemaker simply makes a better shoe," says pert Fiamma Ferragamo. Almost every designer I talked with said the same thing. The men who make the great automobiles have a flair for their work. The plastic men love to experiment with bold new ideas. The seamstresses sew handsome stitches. And the leatherworkers accomplish stunning results.

That Italy is undergoing a style revolution no one could deny, but it would be an error to think that it has affected large numbers of Italians living within the country itself. The big stores of the Rinascente chain may be filled with bright new things, but many others are still filled with what one expert called "the most god-awful junk on earth."

The current rage throughout the countryside is a ceramic statue of Dr. Christian Barnard, a notable hero in Italy, performing a heart operation. About eighteen inches high, in gleaming white doctor's smock, he holds upraised in his left hand a terrifying scalpel dripping ceramic blood, in his right a valentine-shaped human heart also bleeding copiously. I tried to buy a copy for my tourist's chamber of horrors, but was told in four different shops, "We sell Dr. Barnard as fast as we can get him in."

A walk through any city will convince the visitor that Italy still prefers its espresso machines with flashy mirrors and curleycues. When I told Giovanni Giovannini, the news editor of *La Stampa*, that I was interested in examples of Italy's good design, he laughed and said, "I hope you find some."

Joe Colombo said flatly, "Ninety-five percent of my countrymen fail to understand the new Italian line and would permit none of it in their own homes. Our products are made strictly for export, and that's a pity."

But when one probes a little deeper he finds that Italy's automatic sense of good taste still operates. Achille Castiglioni confirms this faith: "In every Italian city, no matter how small —Asti, Vercelli, Siracusa—we find groups of people who respond to our new design and who are willing to pay for it." As if in proof, he sells about five hundred of his Arco lamps a month, even though they cost $185 in Italy. Cappucci told me, "Of my really beautiful dresses, I sell ninety-nine percent to Italian women. They know." I judged that Italy's finest new products were being accepted at home . . . in modest numbers.

The one product that impressed me most was designed for Italian children. On a visit to Rome's Rinascente store in search of a notebook, I saw many of the ordinary type. Then the salesgirl said, "Or maybe you could use this beautiful new kind we just got in." She showed me three notebooks for beginners, each with a cover in brilliant colors and superb design. I was so struck by this approach to education that I made inquiries and found that the books had been developed by Rinascente as part of its continuing education process. Domenica Longo Dente told me, "We instructed our designers that the first thing a child ought to see in school is an example of really fine design, and these books were the result. Kids love them."

The most spectacular tribute to Italian design was reported by the Bertone people in Turin. "There was this New York banker . . . very rich . . . loved automobiles . . . came to our factory and said he wanted the most beautiful Miura we could build. Took it to New York, hired a helicopter and lifted the car right up to the garden of his penthouse overlooking Park Avenue. There he keeps it for his guests to see. Once a week he revs up the motor and his neighbors think that enemy rockets are landing. We asked him why he did this, and he said, 'A car like this is too beautiful for the streets. It's a work of art.' "

MY FIRST ARTICLE

A writer recalls with special affection that first article of his to appear in a magazine. This was the traditional entrance to the world of writing. Today, as the number of magazines published in America diminishes, it is difficult for the beginner to publish; and when the magazines that have survived cut back on the amount of text used in each issue, the problem becomes acute. I wish we had fifty additional magazines in this country publishing fiction and articles, because they provide the best-known apprenticeship.

The first story I sold to a recognized magazine was a lucky shot . . . in two ways. In late 1946 the *Saturday Evening Post* bought a story from my first book, *Tales of the South Pacific*, and since they could not find space for it until one of their early issues in 1947, publication of the book had to be delayed from 1946 to 1947. It is traditional that if a magazine purchases an excerpt from a book, magazine publication must come first. This forced postponement had a fortuitous result: the Pulitzer Prize is awarded each year to books published during the preceding calendar year, and had my inconspicuous little volume appeared in 1946, as planned, it would have been in competition with Robert Penn Warren's success, *All The King's*

Men, and would not have been heard of. Instead, it was moved into 1947, not a rich year for novels, and it copped the prize. This lucky accident made it possible for me to devote my entire efforts to free-lancing, and for it I must thank the now defunct *Saturday Evening Post.*

The second unexpected by-product of the *Post's* publication was that it allowed my mother to die in peace. A solid citizen living in a solid Pennsylvania Dutch community, she knew the value of a secure job and was appalled to find that I was considering shifting to a career as fickle as writing. She predicted, not once but many times, that no good would come of it, and not even my winning of the Pulitzer Prize appeased her, for that was an evanescent one-time thing which had happened by accident. But when she saw a story of mine actually in print in the most permanent of all journals, Ben Franklin's *Post,* which our family had subscribed to for decades, she felt that I might one day make it. I heard her telling a neighbor, "Well, he did sell a story to the *Saturday Evening Post,* and they don't fool around." She maintained her suspicions that no grown man could build a decent life on writing, but that issue of the *Post,* which she kept close at hand for reassurance, did give some comfort.

The first article I sold to the *Reader's Digest* was the one which follows. It was also a chapter from *Tales of the South Pacific.* I remember its appearance with affection. I wish I could say that on that day I had a vision that it was the beginning of a long association with this magazine. I didn't. I remember thinking, "Boy, I sure needed that money." And I was grateful to the *Digest* for having searched out the article and published it. I did not know then that publishers are so keen to find gifted young writers, they watch with hawk eyes everything that is being printed.

Every respectable publisher in New York keeps a file on young writers who appear in the little magazines, and by the time a beginner has three or four really good stories in these publications—sometimes at no pay—a dozen scouts are aware of it and are sending memoranda to their bosses: "We'd better keep a close eye on this girl Cynthia Cook. I'd suggest sending her an advance right now on whatever she's doing, because she's proved she can write." I have watched this happen a score of times; out of the blue an envelope arrives inviting the young man or woman to submit a novel.

The rules seem to be these: If you have written a successful novel, everyone invites you to write short stories. If you have written some good short stories, everyone wants you to write a novel. But nobody wants anything until you have already proved yourself by being published somewhere else. Cutting this Gordian knot is as difficult now as it was in 1750, and as essential. You cut it by writing and writing and writing and doing everything possible to find any publisher anywhere.

When I first met DeWitt Wallace he had before him a slip of paper listing all the writing I had done; his scouts had been at work. Today they are even more careful; since the number of magazines in which first work can appear has diminished, a scout must look farther to find his leads.

The reader may find it profitable to compare this story, which deals with the adventures of Bus Adams, a Navy pilot, with the comparable scene in the play *South Pacific*. Oscar Hammerstein and Josh Logan, in preparing their book for the musical, found that they needed more comedy than I had provided. They therefore took my story about Bus Adams and changed the focus from him to his outrageous passenger, Luther Billis. Instead of having Adams crash in the waters off New Georgia, they had Billis fall out of the plane, with hilarious consequences. For their needs, they improved considerably upon my version.

The Milk Run

It must make somebody feel good. I guess that's why they do it—The speaker was Lieutenant Bus Adams, SBD pilot. He was nursing a bottle of whiskey in the Hotel De Gink on Guadal. He was sitting on an improvised chair and had his feet cocked up on a coconut stump. He was handsome, blond, cocky; just another hot pilot shooting off between missions.

But why they do it—Bus went on—I don't rightfully know. I once figured it out this way: Say tomorrow we start to work over a new island, well, like Kuralei. On the first mission long-range bombers go over. Sixty-seven Japs come up to meet you. You lose four, maybe five bombers. Everybody is damn gloomy. But you also knock down some Nips.

Four days later you send over your next bombers. Again you take a pasting. "The suicide run," the pilots call it. It's sure death! But you keep on knocking down Nips. Down they go, burning like the Fourth of July. And all this time you're pocking up their strips, plenty.

Finally the day comes when you send over twenty-seven bombers, and they shoot down the only four Zekes to come up and they all come back. The next eight missions are without incident. You just plow in, drop your stuff and sail on home.

Right then somebody names that mission "the milk run." They even tell you about your assignments in an offhand manner: "Eighteen or twenty of you go over tomorrow and pepper Kuralei." They don't even brief you on it, and before long there's a gang around takeoff time wanting to know if they can sort of hitchhike a ride. So first thing you know, it's a real milk run, and you're in the tourist business!

Now get this right, I'm not crabbing. I'm damned glad to be the guy that draws the milk runs. But if you get bumped off on one of them, why, you're just as dead as if you were over Tokyo in a kite. It wasn't no milk run for you. Not that day.

You take my trip up to Munda two days ago. Now there was a real milk run. Our boys had worked that strip over until it looked like a guy with chicken pox, beriberi and the galloping jumps. Sixteen SBDs went up to hammer it again. We flew low across New Georgia, about fifty feet off the trees, and we rose and fell with the contours of the land. Soon we were over Munda. The milk run was half over.

I guess you heard what happened next. I was the unlucky guy. One lousy Jap made a hit all day, on that whole strike, and it had to be me. It ripped through the rear-gunner's seat and killed Louis on the spot. I had only eighty feet elevation at the time, but kept her nose straight on. Glided into the water between Wanawana and Munda. The plane sank in about fifteen seconds. All shot to hell. Never even got a life raft out.

So there I was, at seven-thirty in the morning, with nothing but a life belt, down in the middle of a Japanese channel with shore installations all around me. A couple of guys later on figured that 8,000 Japs must have been within ten miles of me, and I guess that not less than 3,000 of them could see me. I was sure a dead duck.

My buddies saw me go in, and they set up a traffic circle around me. One Jap tried to come out for me, but you know Eddie Callstrom? My God! He shot that barge up so it busted into pieces. My gang was over me for an hour and a half. By this time a radio message had gone back and about twenty New Zealanders in P-40s took over. I could see them coming

371

a long way off. At first I thought they might be Jap planes. I never was too good at recognition.

Well, these New Zealanders are wild men. Holy hell! What they did! One group of Japs managed to swing a shore battery around to where they could pepper me. On the first shot the New Zealanders went crazy. You would have thought I was a $90,000,000 battleship they were out to protect. They peeled off and dove that installation until even the trees around it fell down. They must have made the coral hot. No more Jap shore batteries opened up on me that morning.

Even so, I was having a pretty tough time. Currents kept shoving me on toward Munda. Japs hidden there with rifles kept popping at me. I did my damndest, but slowly I kept getting closer. I don't know, but I guess I swam twenty miles that day, all in the same place. Jap rifles are a damned fine spur to a man's ambition.

When the New Zealanders saw my plight they dove for that shoreline like the hounds of hell. After that there were fewer Jap shots.

I understand that it was about this time that the New Zealanders' radio message reached Admiral Kester. He is supposed to have studied the map a minute and then said, "Get that pilot out there. Use anything you need. We'll send a destroyer in if necessary. But get him out. Our pilots are not expendable."

Of course, I didn't know about it then, but that was mighty fine doctrine so far as I was concerned. And you know? When I watched those Marine F4Us coming in to take over the circle, I kind of thought maybe something like that was in the wind at headquarters. The New Zealanders pulled out. Before they went, each one in turn buzzed me. Scared me half to death!

The first thing the F4Us did was drop me a life raft. But my troubles were only starting. The wind and currents shoved that raft toward the shore, but fast. I did everything I could to hold it back, and paddled until I could hardly raise my right arm. Then some F4U pilot with an IQ of about 420—boy, how I would like to meet that guy—dropped me his parachute. It was his only parachute, and from then on he was upstairs on his own. But it made me a swell sea anchor. Drifting far behind in the water, it slowed me down.

It was about noon, and even though I was plenty scared I was hungry, so I broke out some emergency rations from the raft and had a pretty fine meal. I judge it was about 1400 when thirty new F4Us took over. I wondered why they sent so many. Then I saw why. A huge PBY came gracefully up The Slot. He was low and big and a sure target. But he kept coming in.

The PBY landed beautifully. The F4Us probed the shoreline. The pilot taxied his huge plane toward my small raft. While the F4Us zoomed overhead at impossibly low altitudes, I climbed aboard.

The next moment hell broke loose! From the shore a Jap let go with the gun he had been saving all day. There was a ripping sound, and the port wing of the PBY was gone. The Jap had time to fire three more shells before the F4Us got him. The last shell blew off the tail assembly. We were sinking.

The PBY was manned by New Zealanders. We threw out the rafts and as much gear as we could, and soon nine of us were in Munda harbor looking mighty damned glum. Now a circle of Navy F6Fs took over. I thought they were more conservative than the New Zealanders and the last Marine gang. That was until a Jap battery threw a couple of close ones. I had never seen an F6F in action before. Five of them hit that battery like Dempsey hitting Willard. The New Zealanders, who had not seen the F6Fs either, were amazed.

"They sure don't let the barstards get many shots in, do they?" an officer said.

We were glad of that. Unless the Jap hit us on his first shot, he was done. We were therefore dismayed when half of the F6Fs pulled away toward Rendova. An hour later, however, we saw thirty new F4Us lollygagging through the sky Rendova way. We wondered what was up.

And then we saw! From some secret nest in Rendova, the F4Us were bringing out two PT boats! They were going to come right into Munda harbor, and to hell with the Japs!

373

Above them the lazy Marines darted and bobbed, like dolphins in an aerial ocean.

You know the rest. It was Lieutenant Commander Charlesworth and his PTs. Used to be on Tulagi. Something big was on, and they had sneaked up to Rendova, specially for an attack somewhere. But Admiral Kester said, "To hell with the attack. We've gone this far. Get that pilot out of there." He said they'd have to figure out some other move for the big attack they had cooking. Maybe use destroyers instead of PTs.

I can't tell you much more. A couple of savvy Japs were waiting with field pieces, just like the earlier one. But they didn't get hits. The Marines in their F4Us crucified them. That was the last thing I saw before the PTs pulled me aboard. Twelve F4Us diving at one hillside.

Pass me that bottle, Tony. Well, we figured it all out last night. We lost a P-40 and a PBY. We broke up Admiral Kester's plan for the PT boats. We wasted the flying time of P-40s, F4Us, and F6Fs like it was dirt. We figured the entire mission cost not less than six hundred thousand dollars. Just to save one guy in the water off Munda. I wonder what the Japs thought of that? Six hundred thousand dollars for one pilot— Bus Adams took a healthy swig of whiskey. He lolled back in the tail-killing chair of the Hotel De Gink— But it's sure worth every cent of money. If you happen to be that pilot.

374

ON ASSIGNMENT

I n the autumn of 1956 I flew to Rome after a spell of
difficult work in Asia. My intention was twofold: to
enjoy a vacation in the world's best tourist city, and to do some
last-minute editorial work with Albert Erskine of Random
House, who had flown from New York to meet me. I had been
in the city only a few hours when the streets and avenues
became thronged with young people engaged in a massive
demonstration.

It took me some time to decipher what the trouble was
about. The fact that one large detachment of students was
headed for the American embassy made me suspect that my
country had again done something which enraged the Italians,
but that was not the case. The throng swept right past our
embassy, and as they went, I saw their signs. Hungary seemed
to be involved, but in what regard I could not determine.

In the days that followed, I caught rumors of a major
upheaval in Budapest, and such newspapers as I could get
spoke of a revolution. The editors of the *Digest*, knowing that
I was already on the periphery of the revolution, had the
sensible idea of proposing that I move immediately to Hungary to report on what was happening, and so cabled me. I had

no interest in a revolution which was sure to prove abortive, and declined the invitation.

I left Rome for Madrid by way of Tunis and Algeria, where we heard details of the French-British-Israeli invasion of Egypt. In Madrid, which I always visited whenever chance permitted, I heard the first substantial news of the Hungarian revolution. For two days I brooded about what must be happening along the Danube, and received two more cables from the *Digest* editors. I replied that they must have in their string other writers who could do this job better than I.

I went to Paris: more news, more agitation, more cables. And I went to Amsterdam, where I met a Dutch newsman who had fled Budapest. It seemed strange to me that having been on the scene already, a writer would voluntarily leave what was obviously a great story. But then it dawned on me that for the past days I myself had been on the perimeter of a notable revolution, and I too had rejected my opportunity.

On the spur of the moment I went to Schiphol airport, bought a ticket to Vienna and caught the first available plane. I was in the Hotel Bristol—the best I've ever worked in—only a few hours when I met that wonderful and tragic girl, Dickey Chapelle, free-lance photographer, with whom I left immediately for the Hungarian border.

Miss Chapelle and I were to spend many nights across that border, behind the Russian lines. She was more daring than I; indeed, she did not know what fear was, as she later proved in Algeria and Vietnam, where she worked with commandos and parachutists. We formed a good team, for she would lead us into places that would have terrified me had I been alone, and I would get us back safely, when she might have stumbled impetuously into serious trouble. One night she went alone, against my advice, and did not get back. She spent half a year in a Russian prison, from which she was released largely because of my wife's persistence in pleading her case. Later, in Vietnam, she was killed because she insisted on walking through a minefield. I remember her as the bravest person I have ever known.

As a result of these forays into Russian-held areas, and because of the wrenching stories told by the Hungarian refugees, I launched upon a book-length reportage. It was a burst of work I have never since been able to equal: twelve midnight till four in the morning in Hungary with Dickey Chapelle; brief sleep, all day talking with refugees, typing till midnight, back to the border. I did this for six weeks, and remember it as the most professional of my experiences.

What gratifies me most, when I look back on that frenetic job, was that I met with a couple of wonderful Catholic priests and a wild-eyed Brooklyn rabbi, whom in some small measure I was able to assist in their rescue work.

The United States had grudgingly announced that it would accept a certain number of refugees, but left their selection to religious groups in proportion to the religious affiliations of Hungary as stated in the most recent census. This meant that the Catholics could choose the greatest number, the Protestants some, and the Jews not many. However, a disproportionate number of Jews fled, and we were faced with the problem of what to do with them. I well remember going from place to place one day and asking, "Can anybody find a slot for a rabbi with a beard?" Had he been beardless and not so completely Jewish-looking, the cooperative American priests would have found a place for him in their quota, as they did for many, swearing that refugees with names like Rabinowitz were long-time Catholics. But with a beard he had to be a Jew, and that quota was oversubscribed.

We taught Hungarian Jews how to be Baptists and Methodists, whose quotas were never filled. I explained that it was pretty easy to be a Baptist if you kept your mouth shut, and even easier to be a Methodist, because then you didn't have to worry if the examiner asked, "Where were you baptized?" I told the bearded rabbi, "Shave and we'll make you a Baptist." He did and we did.

I taught a lot of rough-and-ready theology in those days and helped save a lot of Hungarians. The priests were invaluable, while the rabbi who sifted the refugees for us, assuring us that this Jew or that was worth our effort, was as resolute a man as I have ever known.

It was this kind of life-and-death passion that I tried to compress into the material I was writing. Ultimately the book would be translated into fifty-three different languages and read throughout the world.

A footnote on writing on assignment may be interesting. My relations with the *Digest* editors have obviously been most harmonious, and they have often been eager to get manuscripts from me, yet it is a fact that only once have I ever proposed an idea which found acceptance. On my own initiative I have written a good deal for the *Digest* which has never seen print, and I believe the reason is this: If an editor conceives the idea for an article, and if he assigns it to a specific writer whom he trusts, when the manuscript comes in, the editor is already predisposed to like it, for it reflects his judgment. He tells his associates, "Good old Andy! He's done it again." But if a writer submits an idea which he has originated in the dark as it were, there is no one in the home office to sponsor it, and when it arrives, the editor is apt to say, "Here's something by Andy. It's not bad. You might want to look at it." And that cool indifference is the kiss of death.

In the publishing of books, too, it has surprised me to find how many first-rate nonfiction books are initially conceived by some clever editor, who brings the concept to the attention of one of his tested writers. Even some very good novels have been initiated in this way. Fortunately, I have had more ideas of my own for books than I have had the time to write.

The Prison at Recsk

Seventy miles northeast of Budapest, outside the Hungarian village of Recsk, there is a place of infamy and horror which can stand as the ultimate end product of the communist system in any country. This is the most notorious of the AVO (Secret Police) prisons.

From what I have seen of communist regimes, I am convinced that Recsk (pronounced Retch-ka) is not unique, that every communist country has its Recsks, with the same kind of sadistic guards, the same bestial methods of torture and abuse. But before we see why the road to communism leads inevitably to such nightmare places, let us first look at the hideous prison itself—through the eyes of those who were there.

Recsk forms roughly a square, a thousand yards on a side, surrounded by three concentric fences of intertwined barbed wire, each nine feet high, the two inner fences charged with electricity. In the thirty yards between these, the ground has been carefully plowed so that footprints will show, and beneath the fresh soil are powerful mines. The middle fence is studded every fifty yards with tall watchtowers equipped with machine guns and searchlights. Recsk is known as escape-proof.

But it was not the fences that made this prison intolerable. It was the life inside. Only the most hardened AVO men were assigned here as guards, and since duty at Recsk was a form of punishment even for them, they made the prisoners' lives hellish.

When I met Ferenc Gabor in Vienna, after he escaped to Austria last November while revolution rocked his country, he was a broken man of thirty-five. He had spent three years as a prisoner in Recsk.

"Our quarters," he told me, "consisted of two compounds containing small rooms into each of which eighty men were jammed. We were allowed no books, no radio news, no newspaper. We could have no visitors, no mail, no parcels of food, and our families did not know where we were. We did not know for how long we were there, nor for what reason. We lived a life of blank terror.

"Toward one end of our compound was a granite outcrop about 280 feet high. I was among the prisoners given the job of reducing this hill to gravel which would pass through a small sieve. Each prisoner was required to produce two hand trucks of gravel each day. We worked from four-thirty in the morning until nightfall.

"If I did not make my day's quota of gravel, I was forced to stand in a clammy cell for the entire night with cold water up to my knees. Then, if the guards wanted to play with me next morning, they would make me carry a hundred pound rock up and down a ladder fifteen times. If I fainted, they resumed the game when I recovered. The only break in our schedule came when the AVO summoned us at night for interrogation. Then we were brutally beaten, abused and humiliated. They screamed at us to talk, but they never said what about.

"One night a guard shouted, 'Let's make him the white mare!' They inserted a broomstick under my knees, then doubled me up into a tight ball, lashing my wrists to my ankles. This punishment placed such stress upon the stomach and heart that no man could bear it longer than two hours. If the

AVO were particularly playful, they made a man into the white mare and forgot him. Then he died without anyone's caring.

"But even normally, this treatment was almost unbearable, for after a man had crouched on his knees for some time, while his taut muscles were beaten with rubber hoses, he would fall over, and then new portions of his body would be exposed to the hoses.

"On this night they had another man and me for the white mares, and after they had beaten him until he was numb, he rolled against the hot stove. His left hand had become so insensitive that he was not aware that it was against the fire, so that two fingers and half his palm were burned off. He became aware of what was happening only when he smelled his charred flesh. The AVO men knew, but they were laughing.

"Only one group ever escaped from Recsk. A tailor manufactured out of his prison suit one that looked like an AVO uniform. Then from scraps he painstakingly built up a cap and ornaments. When he was properly fitted out, he assembled a group of daring fellow prisoners and with a make-believe Tommy gun in his arms, boldly marched the whole contingent out the main gate. 'We're bringing in dynamite,' he told the guards, and off his crew went into the woods and freedom.

The AVO response was diabolical. They rounded up 250 prisoners, anyone who had been seen talking or loitering at meals or laughing, and those who had fallen below their quota at any time during the last two weeks. The prisoners knew that something terrible was about to happen, and everyone seemed eager to spy upon his neighbor in hope of escaping punishment.

"The 250 victims were herded into a special prison within the prison. After a week of constantly increasing pressures—beatings, wormy food, unusual and hateful punishments centering on the sexual organs—it became apparent that the AVO had decided to reduce these men to the level of screaming animals.

"They succeeded. The experience of that prison within a prison was so unimaginably horrible that within two months

381

there was not a sane man left. And each day when the guards threw the animals their meat, laughing as the crazed men fought and tore at one another for the inadequate chunks, a voice would announce over the loudspeaker, 'You are in here because your friends escaped.'

"The hatred thus built up against the tailor and his brave crew was terrifying. Perhaps not even the guards knew how inhuman it had become. For some three months later one of the escapees caught trying to flee Hungary was brought back to Recsk and led into the prison within a prison. The voice in the loudspeaker cried, 'Here is one of the men whose escape caused your misfortunes.' Within two minutes his former mates tore the recaptured prisoner to pieces."

Studying the AVO dictatorship in Hungary, my senses were often numbed by the magnitude of the terror. Like the world at large, I found it hard to accept the full horror of the truth, and I would mutter, "Probably the prison at Recsk was bad, but it couldn't be that bad." Then some casual question of mine, in talking to refugees, would uncover a story of such intensity that it would illuminate the entire subject, and I could perceive what communism in Hungary was like. When the mind refuses to engorge a horror of national magnitude, it can still accept the limited story of one man.

There was the revolting story I thus stumbled upon in interviewing a man whose name would be widely recognized, since for some years he was a world champion in an exacting sport. I found this man among a group of escaped Hungarians at the border. He was quick and lean and had laughing eyes which let you know immediately that he knew why you were asking so many questions.

Describing an earlier attempt to escape from his homeland, he told me that after several trips to England and France, he had said to himself, "Hungary is a hell of a place to live. I'm leaving." But at the border they shot him down. He proceeded to recite the familiar story of beatings, indignities and years of slave labor in a filthy, deadly coal mine. By this time I was so deadened to what I knew was coming that I took only desultory notes. But as we were about to part, he said almost gaily, now that he had gained freedom and left the evil behind, "But I'm not a crybaby, remember that. When things were worst I always told myself, 'Well, anyway, you missed Major Meat Ball.' "

"Who was he?"

"It was a she. Her name was Piroshka—Russian for meat ball. I met her in the AVO torture cellars at 60 Stalin Street, in Budapest. She was a redhead, plump, about thirty-five years old. She was about five feet two and not bad-looking except that she was pockmarked. Everyone knew she was a horrible sadist.

"I say I missed her; that means I missed the worst part. But I had enough. One time she went into the cell next to mine with a bottle and told the man, 'Urinate in it.' Then she brought it in to me while it was still warm and said, 'Drink it.'

"With women prisoners she was especially sadistic. She did things to them that even now I can't describe. But I was forever grateful that I missed her. The man in the next cell didn't. She came in to see him one day wearing only a dress. 'You must get hungry for a woman,' she said, nuzzling against him. 'Well, I get hungry for a man, too. Tonight I'm going to take you up to my quarters.' So that night she took him to her quarters and got undressed. But just than an AVO burst into the room, shouting, 'You rapist! Messing around with my wife!' This AVO called others and they beat my friend almost to death. They ended by ramming a thin, hollow glass tube up his penis. Then they beat him till it broke into a million pieces. That was how Major Meat Ball operated."

Weakly I asked, "How do you know?"

The world champion said simply, "I had to hold him when he went to the toilet."

I talked with over a hundred Hungarian refugees and was always careful never to be the first one to bring up the AVO, yet in almost every conversation the dreaded name was mentioned. Stories of AVO bestiality grew out of any normal discussion of life under communism.

This led me to think about the foundations upon which the

AVO was built. Hungary, a long-troubled country, has had other major terrors, most recently under the Horthy regime, Hitler's Nazi occupation, the Szalasi dictatorship. The typical AVO man, I came to realize, had been a bully boy for these fascist governments, which were supposed to be the worst enemy of communism. When the Soviets assumed control, they simply took into their "security" system the worst elements of the police forces from earlier regimes and called them good communists. Many of the AVO didn't even know what communism was. Some were illiterates, homosexuals, petty criminals.

The officers, however, were dedicated party members and many of them were educated. Those who progressed most rapidly in the system were apt to be graduates of the Moscow schools of terrorism. Their loyalty to Soviet Russia was unquestioned.

The Hungarian Secret Police are no worse—and no better—than such organizations in other communist countries. They are merely typical. Similar forces operate in Russia, Bulgaria, Latvia, North Korea, China, wherever communism is in power. Testimony from people who have fled these countries is unanimous in support of this contention.

Why must communism depend on such dregs of society? The answer, I believe, is that communism, because of its inherent fallacies, sooner or later runs into such tough economic and social problems that some strong-arm force becomes necessary to keep the population under control.

What happens is this: When communism first woos the workers, exaggerated promises are made to awaken men's aspirations and their cupidity. These promises are couched in such effective symbols that they become immediate goals of the revolution. Review briefly, for instance, what communist agitators promised the Hungarians: consumer goods such as they had never known before, increased wages, increased social benefits, shorter hours of work, improved education for everyone, greater social freedom, and a government directly responsible to the working classes.

But in Hungary there never was a chance of attaining these

vast and unrealistic goals, and within two years the people realized that the hopes which had seduced them would never materialize. Instead of freedom, they had gotten a tyranny worse than any they had ever known before.

When an awakening of such magnitude begins to spread across a nation, the communist leaders must take steps to silence the protests that naturally arise. At first they simply sentence to jail those intellectuals who see through the empty promises. But soon they must begin to arrest workingmen who ask when their pay increases will begin, and housewives who want more bread and cheaper shoes for their children, and clergymen who protest the earlier rounds of arrests. The ordinary police begin to balk at such senseless arrests, so a special police must be organized. And it is a dismal characteristic of humanity that in any society there are men and women who enjoy sadistic work and would accept it if the opportunity arose.

I do not believe—although some Hungarians say I am naïve —that when an AVO is first instituted in a communist country, its regime intends it to become an instrument of torture. I rather think that frightened bureaucrats call it into being with the intention of keeping it a simple force to protect their position. Later, like Dr. Frankenstein, they find that they have created an uncontrollable monster, which ultimately entangles them in its evil grasp.

I am sure that if Japan were to go communist tomorrow, as some of its citizens desire, within a year it would have one of the world's most terrible secret police forces. If Indonesia goes communist, it will know the same sullen fury as Budapest knew. If communists in India succeed in taking control over that vast land, a secret police would terrorize Amritsar and Delhi as those cities have not been terrorized since the day of Tamerlane. Everywhere communism must have an AVO to silence the protests of the people it has defrauded.

A PERSONAL CONCERN

I have already stated that only once did I originate an idea which caught the fancy of the *Digest* editors. In November, 1968, following the presidential election, I was so shaken by the narrow escape our nation had suffered because of our outmoded system of choosing a President, that I implored the editors to publish an article which would bring this folly to the attention of their readers. I was gratified when they encouraged me to go ahead. The result was an example of how journalism can be used in the national interest. I worked so hard on the article and compiled so much material, that what I had started as an article grew into a book, one which I hoped would lead to an amendment to our Constitution.

The problem was fourfold. We elect our President not by popular vote of all citizens, but by an electoral vote among the states. This means that a state with a small population like Alaska has a much greater proportional strength (its two senators provide two electoral votes) than a populous state like California. The electoral vote of a state is not transmitted automatically; instead, a group of electors meets to transmit the vote, and they are bound neither by law nor by honor to vote the way their state voted. If the electors do not give one candidate a majority, the election is thrown into the House of Representatives (into the Senate for Vice-President), where turmoil and chicanery could result.

I felt a sense of urgency in this matter because I had been an elector in the 1968 election and had served as president of the Pennsylvania college, with consequences which alarmed me. I have never written on a public matter with more driving force than I did this time. I wanted Congress to produce a simpler system of electing the President, a system which would avoid the dreadful dangers inherent in the one we now use. I tried to muster support for a constitutional amendment. I failed.

Presidential Lottery

On Election Day, 1968, the United States once again played a foolhardy game with its destiny. We conducted one more Presidential election in accordance with rules that are outmoded and inane. This time we were lucky. Next time we might not be.

We preserve a system of electing a President which contains so many built-in pitfalls that sooner or later it is bound to destroy our country. It places the legal responsibility in the hands of an Electoral College, whose members are "faceless men." (Almost no one can name the state party's electors for whom he votes during a Presidential election.) Further, for all practical purposes electors are not bound to follow their state's vote. If they do not produce a majority vote for some candidate, the election is thrown into the House of Representatives, where abominable things can happen.

In 1823 Thomas Jefferson described this incredible system as "the most dangerous blot on our Constitution, and one which some unlucky chance will some day hit." Today the danger is even more grave.

One day late last August, my phone rang and a voice I knew well asked, "Michener, you want to be a Presidential elector?"

It was Milton Berkes, Democratic chairman for my home county. At the moment I was sick in spirit over the debacle of the party convention at Chicago, and wanted no involvement with politics. But as a historian and as one who had worked hard in the practical politics of Pennsylvania, I sensed that the 1968 election was going to be of special significance. I therefore agreed to serve.

All across America similar phone calls were being made. "Hey, Joe. You wanna be an elector?" "Sure." It was as simple as that.

The Constitution says that each state shall appoint "in such manner as the legislature thereof may direct" electors equal in number to its U.S. senators and representatives. In many states, party conventions nominate electors. In other states, they are picked by the state committee, the governor or by state primary. What it comes down to is that men and women are chosen for the responsibility—potentially one of the most complex in our political life—simply because they contributed money to the party, or are known as reliable party hacks.

Only sixteen of the fifty states have laws requiring their electors to vote the way their state voted—but such laws are probably unconstitutional. And even if an elector were punishable after the fact, no one can compel him to vote right in the first place; nor could the wrong vote, once cast, be corrected. States may cajole (Massachusetts), exhort (Nevada) or threaten (New Mexico), but the qualified elector is in effect free to vote precisely as he wishes.

In general, electors have acted as they were pledged to act —but this does not mean that they always will. The fact is that this system is open to violent abuse.

In August it seemed that the Democrats had no chance. But as the campaign progressed, the situation changed dramatically. By late October it became obvious that Humphrey would carry Pennsylvania, maybe even New York—and probable that Nixon would not get the necessary majority of electoral votes (270 out of the total 538) required to win.

The significance of a deadlocked election was unavoidably clear. If George Wallace carried several states, their electoral votes could give him the balance of power. Then when the Electoral College met, he could throw those votes (on which he had a strong hold) to one of the two major candidates—whichever one might promise him most. One man—a clever, quick-thinking judge from Alabama—could determine the destiny of this nation. It was not an attractive prospect.

Wallace had outlined his strategy: "We may decide the question in the Electoral College, because one party may have to make a concession to the people of our country, a solemn covenant to them." He used the phrase "solemn covenant," he explained, because "the word 'deal' doesn't sound too good."

Both Nixon and Humphrey volunteered that they would not accept a deal with Wallace. However, in the forty days between the popular vote on November 5 and the electoral vote on December 16, pressures would become so tremendous and the stakes so compelling—the Presidency of the most powerful democracy on earth, with all the prerogatives that position entails—that any man or party might be tempted beyond the breaking point. I expected a deal.

I found repugnant the idea of permitting one man to dictate who our next President should be. It could lead to turmoil, if not actual disaster, dictatorship or rebellion. Therefore I determined to beat Governor Wallace to the punch.

If Nixon failed to win his 270 electoral votes but led by a clear margin, and also won the popular vote, I would recommend to my party leaders that they arrange an honorable compromise with the Republicans—by which I mean certain consideration as to Cabinet positions—and direct enough Democratic electors to swing their votes to Nixon to ensure his election. I would volunteer to be a member of that group and to absorb whatever opprobrium fell upon us. Or if Humphrey clearly led in both popular and electoral votes, I would propose a similar compromise to elect him. I was convinced that across the nation other potential electors, weighing the alternative, were coming to the same conclusions.

On one factual point I must insist: Governor Wallace was entitled to play his dangerous game, because our election laws encouraged him to do so. The members of the Electoral College were also entitled to try to forestall him, because our election law is so damnably inexact.

On election night I followed the returns with apprehension. It was quickly apparent that the popular vote was going to be extremely close. Fairly early in the evening Pennsylvania went Democratic—so I was sure to be an elector.

But then the long hell of the night commenced. At two in the morning most experts were predicting that the election would wind up in the House of Representatives. I went to bed suspecting that the election would be deadlocked, and that the electors would waken to find themselves at the center of a hurricane. I could not sleep, appalled that our democracy had allowed itself to fall into such a calamity.

I swore then that whatever result the new day brought, I would do what I could to abolish this ridiculous and unnecessary anachronism, the Electoral College. For it serves no possible purpose except to invite the very kind of insecurity which then threatened us.

If an inconclusive election is not resolved—honorably or otherwise—by the Electoral College, it is thrown into the House of Representatives. The risk to the nation is no less; invitation to corruption is greater. To have these two monstrous systems back to back is an insanity.

The House chooses among the three leading candidates. Each of the fifty states is given one vote, with twenty-six being required for election. In case a delegation happens to be evenly balanced—or in case some member is ill or absent, producing a tie—that state is totally disfranchised. Obviously, enough votes might be immobilized to prevent an election.

All kinds of injustices and imbalances are produced by this system. Imagine a close election, where the vote of each state is crucial. Alaska (population 277,000) then has one vote—and so does California (population 19,221,000). So, in comparison, Alaskans have maybe sixty-nine times the leverage of Californians. These enormous discrepancies are duplicated when comparing Nevada with New York, or Vermont with Pennsylvania. This is minority power with a vengeance.

Presidential elections have only twice wound up in the House, and the performance each time was frightening. In 1800 the winning party backed Jefferson for President and Aaron Burr for Vice-President, and this was so clearly understood that the electors did not specify which man was to hold which position. The result was that each got seventy-three electoral votes and the election went to the House. Burr, a man without principle, saw a chance to grab the Presidency for himself and worked behind the scenes for it.

The balloting started on Wednesday, February 11, 1801, in a snowstorm. There were sixteen states, so nine votes were required for election. The first ballot showed Jefferson, 8; Burr, 6; deadlocked, 2. Jefferson had lost by one vote. The two ties were of interest in that Vermont's was due to the personal disgust her two representatives felt for each other, while Maryland was prevented from voting for Burr only by the courageous presence of a man who was so near death that he was kept on a cot off the voting chamber. A crucial question before each ballot was, "Is Joseph Nicholson still alive?"

A second vote was taken, and the results stood the same. All that night the House balloted—twenty-five times—without a change in the stubborn lineups. The two Vermont men refused even to speak to each other, and Joseph Nicholson continued to rise from what all judged to be his deathbed to vote.

In the cold dawn of Thursday, February 12, the House recessed until eleven A.M. At that hour, and again on Saturday, the same results were forthcoming: Jefferson, 8; Burr, 6; deadlocked, 2. No President.

A great deal of politicking took place over the weekend. Deals were proposed; there was talk of rebellion, fear of anarchy. And on Monday the voting resumed—to reveal the same obdurate 8—6—2. But there was a rumor that the Maryland delegation might be prepared to break its tie.

The House reconvened on Tuesday morning, to wild rumors. But on the thirty-fifth ballot Maryland continued her deadlock. When the thirty-sixth ballot was called for, however, members saw with amazement that one of the two chairs in the Vermont delegation was empty—and it was the Burr supporter who was abstaining! His state could now vote for Jefferson. A President had been elected.

As a result of this disturbing performance, the 12th Amendment to the Constitution was passed, altering some of the electoral rules. But the confusions that grow out of allotting each state one vote in the House remain the same, and to that extent what happened in the 1800 election is exactly what we could expect today.

The second House election came in February, 1825. Andrew Jackson had nearly won the Presidency outright. He led by a large margin in both the popular and electoral votes, but since three candidates had opposed him, he failed to gain a majority. This time the House took only one ballot, but it was a beauty. Second-place John Quincy Adams seems to have made a deal with fourth-place Henry Clay, whereby Clay threw his votes to Adams in return for the post of Secretary of State. That was how it worked out, and Jackson, robbed of an election, fulminated, "Was there ever witnessed such a bare-faced corruption in any country before?"

We came very close to having the 1968 election thrown into the House. For example, with a swing of only 67,481 votes (out of 4,618,424) in Illinois and 10,245 (out of 1,809,502) in Missouri, Nixon could have lost those states and had just 264 electoral votes—insufficient to be elected. And efforts to settle the issue in the Electoral College might have failed.

On the day it became clear that the election was headed to the House, a band of the most expert character analysts in the nation—the henchmen of the major parties—would have been studying each House member with a microscope—his family, his college deportment, his bank loans, the possibility of his business interests—in order to find the weak spots in that man's armor. And when those spots were found, a dozen prying fingers would be thrust in to tear that man apart. It would require supermen to withstand such pressures.

James Madison, who had helped draft the Constitution, said in 1823: "The rule of voting for President by the House of Representatives is so great a departure from the principle of numerical equality, and so pregnant with a mischievous tendency, that an amendment to the Constitution is justly called for."

If an amendment was needed then—before the Jackson-Adams deadlock—how much more is one needed today.

In the gloomy hour before sunrise on December 15, I headed westward through a blizzard to Harrisburg, to play my role as a member of the state Electoral College. The old parliamentarian who would supervise the proceedings had explained over the telephone that the other Democratic electors had been consulted, and they wanted me to serve as their president. So when we met next day in the senate chamber of the capitol, I would lead the College in the routine performance of its constitutional duties.

I found that of the twenty-nine electors, six had already phoned in to report that they were not going to make it to Harrisburg. That meant we had to round up substitutes—ten of them, before it was over—choosing anyone who came to mind. In some states, criers go up and down the capitol halls asking if anyone wants to be an elector, and those who respond are sworn on the spot, and by this accident, attain a critical power.

In the hour before the opening of the College, Monday morning, I had a revealing conversation with delegate Matthew Gouger. He, too, had been reluctant to serve, but had finally accepted, with the same thought I had had: that if the election turned out to be inconclusive, he was going to do everything in his power to have the two major parties settle it between themselves in the Electoral College. We felt like conspirators until Tom Minehart, our state chairman and as tough a Democrat as I have known, volunteered that we wouldn't believe it, but this day might wind up with him asking Democrats like ourselves, for the welfare of the nation, to vote Republican.

Apparently there would have been many like us, so concerned that we would have done whatever was legal to ensure the safety of our nation. The knowledge dissipated any apprehension I felt about the propriety of my serving as president of my state's Electoral College.

When we opened with a prayer, one substitute was still absent. He made it, late and breathless, just in time to be sworn in as our twenty-ninth duly authorized elector. This same farce was being repeated in all the other forty-nine state capitols. These capriciously assembled men and women were free to determine history. Why had they agreed to serve? It wasn't the pay: three dollars, plus three cents a mile, one way.

We moved through the forty-nine separate steps of archaic ritual with respect and decorum. There unfolded the pageantry of recording the vote six times, in most meticulous detail. When the scratching of the pens had ended, and our work had been legally sealed into bundles for transmittal to the proper authorities, a powerful voice boomed, "When do we eat?" I banged the gavel and announced that Pennsylvania's Electoral College was adjourned. As I left the rostrum, I uttered a quiet prayer of thanks that this day had passed so uneventfully when it could have been so destructive.

We had not left the capitol before a newsman advised us that in North Carolina a Republican elector had voted for Wallace instead of Nixon, and in Michigan an elector had refused to cast his pledged vote for Humphrey, resigning from the College instead. Such arbitrary action left me more convinced than ever that this dangerous College, this time bomb lodged near the heart of the nation, must be abolished.

When the Constitutional Convention assembled in 1787, scant support was found for the election of the President by popular vote. Opponents said that the suggestion was viciously radical. They argued, "The people are uninformed and would be misled by a few designing men." When the plan was finally voted on, the count was two in favor, nine against.

At first, a proposal calling for Congress to elect the President seemed logical and practical, but after protracted debate laid bare every weakness, all saw that a President chosen by the Congress would perforce become subservient to Congress. In the end, a committee was appointed, which worked four days without interruption, then reported to the floor the plan under which we operate today.

It was a brilliant compromise. With its specific protections for small states (the two electoral votes corresponding to the two senators) and for large (one elector for each representative in Congress), it aided conspicuously in obtaining the ratification votes necessary to put the Constitution into operation. Philosophically, the plan was impeccable; technically, it had many faults.

The principal reason it began producing unexpected results was that political parties emerged with an importance that no one had foreseen. The splendid original concept of men of high principle convening to select a President of their own choice swiftly degenerated into the practical maneuver of party hacks meeting to confirm the choice that their party had already made. By 1804 it was an ironbound custom.

Also, it did not take long to see that if a state's electors voted as a bloc, their leverage would be consolidated and magnified. Once one state acted upon this discovery, all had to follow. By 1800 this winner-take-all principle was widely recognized, and by 1836 it was a nationwide ritual, with few exceptions. Since then, no changes have occurred in these principal features of our system.

Let's keep two points in mind. The United States functions under an electoral system, which has many good features; this system operates through an Electoral College, which has none. The electoral system is a compromise plan worked out by our founding fathers to protect the rights of large and small states alike. Electoral College is a phrase which appears nowhere in the Constitution or in any enabling legislation; it is merely a convenient mode of describing the electors, considered as a group.

Because the American people have got to face up to the gamble they are taking, it is necessary to explore a proposal which was made only semi-seriously during the 1968 campaign, but which was practical and in the future might tempt desperate men who want to grab the Presidency.

Suppose the electoral votes had divided in this inconclusive fashion: Nixon, 248; Humphrey, 248; Wallace, 42. Suppose, too, that the election had produced a fairly balanced House, so that neither Nixon nor Humphrey could count upon a victory there either. In this impasse, a beautiful stratagem lay open to other forces: simply persuade the forty-three members of the New York electoral delegation to cast their votes for Governor

397

Nelson Rockefeller. He would then wind up in third place in the electoral voting, one vote ahead of Wallace, and would be one of the three names sent to the House. Then, in the House, a deal might be struck between the deadlocked Republicans and Democrats whereby Rockefeller, who might prove acceptable to both, would be given the Presidency upon his pledge to conduct a bipartisan administration.

What if the vote had been Nixon, 234; Humphrey, 234; Wallace, 70? All that is required is for Pennsylvania's electors to join the compact with New York's electors. With Pennsylvania's twenty-nine votes, Rockefeller again winds up in third position and is put before the House as a compromise candidate.

This is not preposterous. New York and Pennsylvania laws do not attempt to punish electors for voting as they wish. They could have voted for Rockefeller; there may be some who would have preferred him to either of the two major candidates. But no man should be elevated to the Presidency by a trick of this nature.

The only way to protect ourselves from such possibilities as I have mentioned is to revise our election laws.

On two points there appears to be widespread agreement: that we ought to take steps immediately to abolish the Electoral College in its present form and the choosing of Presidents by the House of Representatives. But as to what further reforms we should make, there is considerable difference of honest opinion. Following are three basic principles which have governed my own attitude in the matter:

The need for legitimacy. The more I see of the manner in which nations govern themselves, the more convinced I become that a prime requirement of any good government is that it be legitimate, its sources of power clear-cut and aboveboard. Its citizens must see for themselves that laws are honestly passed, that court decisions are untainted, that leaders are fairly chosen. One damning weakness of our present system is that conniving in the Electoral College or the House could cast doubts upon the legitimacy of the succession. That is the best single reason for reform.

The validity of our two-party system. The two-party system is infinitely better than any three-party system—or twenty-party system. It would be senseless for us to flee the known dangers of the Electoral College only to create the greater dangers of a multi-party system. In order for American government to function, we require two strong parties to assume responsibility for the organizing of our political life—and we must introduce no reforms which would weaken them.

The validity of federalism. The fact that I am appalled by the Electoral College does not mean that I am also opposed to the electoral-vote system. Much of our national vitality has derived from the compromises worked out in 1787. I have lived in states with few electoral votes, like Hawaii and Colorado, and in states with many, like New York and Ohio, and I know at firsthand the inequalities. But I cannot imagine a federal balance more adroitly assembled than ours, to give due consideration to each of the states and regions and minorities. The delicate arrangements so painfully worked out to bind them together should not be upset.

I therefore look with suspicion at any proposal which would submerge the fifty individual states into a conglomerate mass. When one considers the crises that have grown out of the problem of finding a just system of federalism—in nations as disparate as India, Belgium, Nigeria, Indonesia, Spain—one is inclined to advise any nation which has developed a workable system to cling to it and not to modify it capriciously. As historian and educator Clinton Rossiter warns, "We should hesitate a long time before replacing a Humpty Dumpty system that works with a neat one that will blow up in our faces."

With these principles in mind, let us look briefly at the four following major suggestions for reform:

The Automatic Plan. This plan is a limited reform, purging only the most glaring weaknesses of our traditional system. Under it, each state would continue to have as many electoral votes as it is entitled to. These would continue to go to the leading candidate in that state, on a winner-take-all basis. And a majority of the nationwide total of electoral votes would still be required for election. The crucial improvement: each state's vote would be recorded automatically, without any Electoral College.

If no candidate received a majority, the three top contenders would be presented to a joint session of the House and Senate. There each of the 535 members would be free to vote for the candidate of his choice; this vote would be publicly recorded; and a majority would be necessary for election. (Alternatively, under the latest refinement of this plan, a candidate could win if he led the field with as much as forty percent of the electoral vote; and if no one did, a national run-off election would be held between the two top contenders to produce a quick, final and easily accepted solution.)

The District Plan. Under this plan, in California, for example, the thirty-eight electoral votes corresponding to that state's membership in the U.S. House of Representatives would be awarded separately in accordance with the voting results in each of thirty-eight districts. (The two other votes, corresponding to California's two U.S. senators, would be decided by the vote of the entire state.)

Note what a significant change this would introduce. Last fall, the popular vote was close in California—3,467,644 to 3,244,318—but Nixon garnered all forty electoral votes. Had the state voted by districts, the count would have been Nixon, 23; Humphrey, 17.

The Electoral College would be retained under this plan, but each prospective elector would take a pledge to vote the way his district voted. Inconclusive elections would be decided by a joint session of the Senate and House, with all members voting individually, and an absolute majority necessary for a choice. Should a three-candidate deadlock develop on the first ballot, only the top two candidates would be voted on in the second, to produce a winner.

In the early years of our nation a number of states selected their electors on the district plan. It was proposed often as a nationwide alternative, and narrowly failed to win Congressional approval.

Proponents cite a long list of advantages. In effect, the nation would be composed of 436 small states of comparable population and more or less comparable influence. The plan

400

would diminish the influence of minorities centered in cities, since their swing votes would influence only the electoral vote of their district, not the total vote of their state. For this reason the plan has usually been considered advantageous to rural areas as opposed to urban, to small states as opposed to large, to conservative elements as opposed to radical.

The Proportional Plan. This plan, too, gets rid of the winner-take-all principle. A state's electoral votes would not all be awarded to the candidate winning the most votes there; instead, they would be divided among the candidates according to the proportion of the total state vote that each got. The results, in figures carried to three decimal places, would be automatically recorded, without any Electoral College. If this plan had been in operation last fall, the California vote would have read: Nixon, 19.127; Humphrey, 17.895; Wallace, 2.687; others, 0.288.

The drawback is that this plan would encourage third parties—even nineteenth and twentieth parties. To avoid the problem of fragmentation, which has stricken so many other democracies, proponents suggest, first, that the leading candidate be declared the winner if he gets as much as forty percent of the electoral vote. Then, if no one wins forty percent, the top two candidates would be presented to a joint session of the House and Senate, where, voting as individuals, all members of Congress would elect the next President.

Proportionalism is an alluring concept, for it provides the nearest practical approach to direct popular voting while retaining the historic principle of state electoral votes. It was formally proposed to Congress as early as 1848. In 1950 the Senate passed the proposal, but the House rejected it.

Direct Popular Vote. Under this plan, the only factor involved in electing a President would be the actual number of votes cast throughout the nation. A candidate would be permitted to win with as little as forty percent of the total popular vote, and if no one gained that percentage, an immediate run-off election between the two leading candidates would be held.

With one sweep of the broom, the conglomeration of past accidents and errors would be swept away: electors, weighted voting, the power of minority blocs, the disparity between states, inconclusive elections and the dread confusion of

401

House elections would be abolished once and for all. But the essential historical values, such as a free vote and an independent President, would be preserved. Above all, our citizens would then vote according to a system whose working parts they could all understand—a system which yielded clear-cut results, and which enhanced the visible legitimacy of the succession to the Presidency.

Critics of our present system point out that on three occasions the man with the highest vote has been declared the loser. In 1824 Andrew Jackson won a plurality, but John Quincy Adams was named President. In 1876 Samuel J. Tilden won by a quarter of a million votes—a substantial margin in those days—but lost the Presidency when four states' electoral votes were contested and a Republican-oriented electoral commission awarded them all to Rutherford B. Hayes. And in 1888 Grover Cleveland won by 95,096 votes, but lost to Benjamin Harrison. In each instance, the loser—who might have shouted "Foul!" and rallied his supporters to dispute the results—put patriotism first, and so the stability of the nation was preserved.

"In the past we have been lucky," the advocates of a direct vote argue. "We should not depend upon such luck indefinitely."

In 1966, when more than 8,000 state legislators were polled, 59 percent of those replying favored a direct popular vote. The American Bar Association, the Federal Bar Association and many American leaders have recommended the direct vote. The general public is strongly in favor of it. Polls have produced these striking results: 1966—63 percent; 1967—65 percent; 1968, before the election—79 percent; after the election— 81 percent.

With the nation agitated by its narrow escape from chaos in the election of 1968, we must take remedial steps now and not wait until some horrendous foul-up has occurred. We as citizens must keep unrelenting pressure upon Congress until at least the most grievous errors of our present system are corrected.

We must abolish the Electoral College.

This curious institution serves no creative purpose, but is

calculated to produce chicanery, fraud and uncertainty. As long as it exists, it will be a potential menace. I can think of more than a few figures in our national history who would not have hesitated to browbeat, corrupt, imprison or otherwise manipulate the electors in order to attain the Presidency.

I know of no serious student who proposes that we retain the Electoral College in its present form. Congress must put the necessary machinery into motion immediately to abolish it by Constitutional amendment. If we work hard, we can achieve it in time for the 1972 election.

We must terminate the process whereby inconclusive elections are thrown into the House of Representatives.

Not even among the small states who would profit from it do I find any serious defense of this totally unfair, unmanageable, dangerous procedure as it now operates. Fortunately, we have two excellent escapes.

I can see nothing wrong with the system of throwing inconclusive elections into the House and Senate meeting jointly with members voting as individuals.

True, it would produce a situation where tremendous personal pressures might be brought to bear on the members of Congress. But they are duly elected public officials, in the public eye and vulnerable to public discipline; they must go back to their constituencies for further support. Today these same pressures can be applied to members of the Electoral College, who are not known to the public or responsible to it in any way.

The other alternative is a run-off election between the two top contenders. True, this delays decision, but it produces a clear-cut one. It has worked in many foreign nations and in various of our states.

Congressional hearings on the four proposed plans should continue until it is possible to offer the people one amendment which would abolish the old Presidential election system and initiate a new one.

Whether such a far-reaching amendment could be activated in time to govern the 1972 election is debatable. But if we want the change even by 1976 or 1980, we must start now. Committees should be formed across the nation, and Congress should be reminded at every session that action is obligatory.

We must all start studying the four proposed plans and decide which one to support. Inform your Congressmen and state legislators of your recommendation.

As one who has been long and deeply concerned with the workings of government, I find myself supporting the automatic plan, with a run-off election if no candidate wins forty percent of the electoral vote. Its unchanged features have been historically proven. It is about as close to a true democracy as we ought to get, and it is just.

I have never believed in a raw democracy of merely adding up total votes. I fear that a direct popular vote for President would be vulnerable to demagoguery, to wild fluctuations of public reaction. Yet I see much merit in the direct-popular-vote plan—it holds far more promise than danger. This is my second choice, and I would be willing to work very hard to attain such an amendment.

The district plan has much to commend it. I would work for it if my first two preferences proved impractical of attainment —and if its sponsors jettisoned the Electoral College and also opted for the direct run-off election.

Proportionalism does not seem to work in a complex democracy like ours. The benefits are more than offset by the disadvantages. Most serious is the growth of numerous minority parties, and to this I am strongly opposed, due to my long experience in foreign nations which suffer from such proliferation.

When the Jefferson-Burr House election resulted in chaos in 1801, the very men who twelve years earlier had launched the election system did not hesitate to alter it, to offer the nation an amendment and to ram the change through in time for the next election. If those founding fathers were alive today, if they could see the idiotic mess into which their invention of electors and House elections has led us, they would abolish both before the 1972 election. They would whip up an amendment and campaign for it across the nation, because to do otherwise would be illogical, and they were not illogical men.

If we persist in the present reckless lottery, we deserve the anguish it will ultimately bring upon us.